D0851516

The
Complete
Roadside
Guide to Nebraska

and comprehensive description of items of interest to one and
all travelers of the state, whether native or transplant,
sedentary or transient,

including:

a mile by mile tour of all major roads and side roads, lanes, avenues, highways,
and interstates, destinguishing for the traveler all sights both ordinary and unusual,

profusely illustrated by James Exten

and compiled and written for the edification and
pleasure of the reading public in its second edition by

Alan Boye

Second Edition

Prefaces by Ron Hansen and Wright Morris

"They camped one night on the banks of the Platte
Where Ike found a place that was muddy, but flat
When Ike in his robes, 'neath the snow did lie
Said Betsy, 'Dear Ike we'll move on by and by.'"

UNIVERSITY OF NEBRASKA PRESS
LINCOLN AND LONDON

For Benjamin and Andrew

First Nebraska paperback printing: 2007

Library of Congress Cataloging-in-Publication Data
Boye, Alan, 1950–
The complete roadside guide to Nebraska: and comprehensive description of items
of interest to one and all travelers of the state, whether native or transplant, sedentary or transient, including: a mile by mile tour of all major roads and side roads,
lanes, avenues, highways and interstates, distinguishing for the traveler all sights
both ordinary and unusual / profusely illustrated by James Exten; and compiled
and written for the edification and pleasure of the reading public in its second edition by Alan Boye.—2nd ed.
    p. cm.
Originally published: St. Johnsbury, VT: Saltillo Press, c1989.
Includes bibliographical referencs and index.
ISBN-13: 978-0-8032-5968-3 (pbk.: alk. paper)
ISBN-10: 0-8032-5968-9 (pbk.: alk. paper)
    1. Automobile travel—Nebraska—Guidebooks.   2. Nebraska—Guidebooks.
I. Title.
GV1024.B74   2007
796.709782—dc22   2006031824

Contents

Roads Heading **East and West** That Are:
South of the Platte

North of the Platte

Acknowledgments

The Second Edition of the Complete Roadside Guide to Nebraska represents a major enlargement and revision of the first edition. Over 5,000 new entries have been added and the original information has been revised and updated to provide the roadside traveler an expansive view of the folklore and history of the state.

Just as nothing in history happens in isolation, so too does this book owe its existence to an entire community of people. One part of that community deserves to be mentioned first. Many fascinating details of what lies beyond the striped lines of the highway were provided by hundreds of stalwart local historical society volunteers. More than the immense help they gave to this book's evolution, their selfless work has preserved much of Nebraska's fascinating past that would otherwise have been lost forever.

Likewise across the state were hundreds of librarians, mayors, Chamber of Commerce participants, museum directors, newspaperwomen and men, ranchers, farmers and others who took time out of their busy schedules to provide information and sources for the book. Without their gracious participation this work would not have been possible.

A particular mention needs to be made of the staff of the Nebraska State Historical Society Library, the University of Nebraska Library Special Collections, Center for Great Plains Studies, the Lincoln Public Library, the Omaha Public Library and the library staff at Vermont's Lyndon State College. A specific incident will illustrate the kind of help these fine people were able to provide. One muggy July afternoon a classic Nebraska thunderstorm bulldozed its way across the state. By the time it reached Lincoln the force of its winds had snapped so many power poles that the bright lights in the Historical Society Library flickered once and then left the building permanently. As I fumbled for my notebook and pen, cursing the rolling thunder, a librarian appeared over my shoulder, holding a flashlight. "Could you use this to finish copying the information you need?" she asked.

I would like to especially thank the staff of the Nebraska Heritage Room at Lincoln's Bennet Martin Library who for the past 15 years have been unfaltering in their support and encouragement of my creative efforts.

This book was researched in part under an advanced study grant generously provided by Lyndon State College.

And to these, I am indebted:

Jim Exten for his skills with pen and ink and imagination as well as his long and fine friendship; Ron Hansen for his kindness and considerable talents; Wright Morris, Anne Burkholder, Keith Chamberlin, and Audur Winnan.

Any praise for the prose in this book is owed to my editor, Eddie Elfers, while any omissions and commissions are entirely the fault of the author.

And my greatest thanks is extended to my family:

For research assistant David Boye, who spent hours seeking out the most elusive facts with cheerfulness and good humor;

For my assistant John Boye whose constant and enduring support has taken so many valuable forms;

For my brothers and parents who shared and inspired my love for the mysteries of the land around us;

And for my wife Linda Wacholder and my children Benjamin and Andrew who lovingly have tolerated enumerable "shortcuts" over thousands of miles of Nebraska roads to see another one of Dad's "hysterical sites."

PREFACE

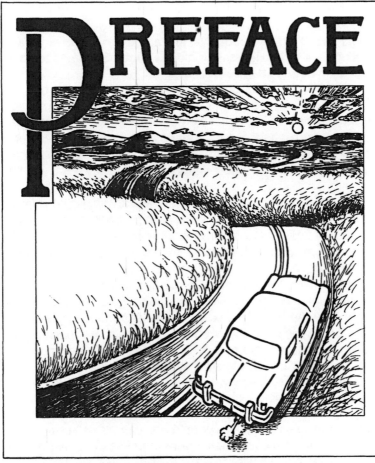

We're talking about highways here — hilly, slow, two-lane blacktops with fall leaves flowing across them, home to roadside attractions and tractors with hoisted plows and hidden old drivers with both hands on the wheel of a car that will soon be on blocks — not Interstate 80 and that flat, hard-driving stretch of the Great Plains between Kearney and Ogallala where the few radio stations peter out, the weather is either too hot or too cold, and even people who ought to know better find themselves thinking, *Why would anyone choose to live here?* You tell friends in the East you're from Nebraska and you get these looks, like you'd used a spoon to chip your way out through the floor of a prison in China. But then it turns out that the only Nebraska those friends have seen is from behind a parade of semis in the hell of July, as a green blur of cottonwoods hiding the Platte and heat waves shimmying the farmhouses and silos in the distance as the travelers floorboarded it to get to Omaha or Denver. Whereas those of us who love Nebraska probably first learned about it on highways on hunting trips or family visits or old-fashioned Sunday afternoon outings to no place in particular.

The fifties were full of such jaunts for me. We'd go to church, and my brother, Rob, and I would lie on the floor to look at the comics in the Omaha *World-Herald* that weren't too hard for us while Mom cooked a full noon dinner of red potatoes and gravy and green peas and soft-as-butter roast beef. And then we'd watch television for an hour or so until we all got bored with it and Dad asked, "You want to go for a ride?"

My father drove, of course, my mother sat with him in the front, and Rob and I stared out our own windows in the back of a black, four-door, 1950 Plymouth that is still my favorite car. We'd head west from Omaha on Highway 6, but Dad would turn north or south according to fancy, halting for a yard sale in Wahoo that seemed interesting or for a truck gardener's market basket of corn outside Blair. We'd visit shirttail relatives in Pender who were two old bachelors and their sister and hear how the harvest was as we ate a fresh cherry pie that seemed to be heating in the oven on the off chance that city folk happened by. I have a memory of us shamelessly heading up to a farmhouse near West Point in order to get four glasses of water and of the farmer being so happy to have our company that it was tough politics to get away before nightfall.

We mostly just stared out the Plymouth's windows with the faint puzzlement and irritation of people who can't read, seeing bleak cemeteries of tilted gravestones, sudden creeks unnamed on our map, and grand old buildings that hid their histories like pearl necklaces under a handmedown coat. We depended upon serendipity for the success of those weekend trips, and often our discoveries were so few that Rob and I fell asleep to the hum of the tires.

If the Hansen family had owned Alan Boye's *Complete Roadside Guide to Nebraska* in the fities we would have found more wonders and surprises than we did, for if Alan Boye has proved anything it's that the Cornhusker State is full of marvels far greater than its football team — formerly called, he tells us, the Rattlesnake Boys and the Bugeaters — and that there's more to Nebraska than first hits the eye.

You find out here that the town of Weeping Water gets its poetic name from the French *L'Eau qui Pleure*, which in turn was a mistranslation of the Otoe for water running over a falls; that the Republican River near Alma was once known by a scatological name because of the huge buffalo herds that filled it with their manure; and that Loup City, the Polish Capital of Nebraska, gets its name from a fur trapper's French term for a famous wolf that roamed the river banks.

Without this guide, the highway traveler would be hard put to guess that the True Value Hardware store in Falls City was once the Gehling Opera House, that Plattsmouth was home to cigar factories, that Glurs Tavern in Columbus is the oldest saloon west of the Missouri River, that Lincoln was the origin of the Frisbee, Lawrence Welk's champagne music, and my college friend, *Cliff Notes*, or that it was in DeWitt in 1929 that the Vise-Grip wrench was invented — "a tool so useful, some say, that the object it is used on will often lose its usefulness."

Even the names of places conjure up the irony, misery and violence of our nineteenth century past — Devil's Nest, Dismal River, Dogtown, Dumbbell Ranch, Massacre Canyon, Rawhide Creek, Robbers' Cave, Whiskey Run — but Alan Boye here provides the history that few of the residents know. (When will the locals finally forget that their town of Herman was named for a railway conductor? Are there people now in Cody who think it was named for Buffalo Bill?) And Alan Boye gives us thumbnail biographies and tales of the famous — Willa Cather, Black Elk, Wild Bill Hickok, Mari Sandoz — as well as those who ought to be — Antonine Barada, Doc "Evil Spirit of the Plains" Carver, Iron Eyes, J. Sterling Morton, Madam Anna Wilson.

Unidentified flying objects seem to have a fascination with Nebraska, for there have been sightings of foreign machinery in the sky as long ago as 1884 in Max — my favorite account — and 1897 in Omaha and Invale; and no less than ten towns, from Sidney to Bellevue, seem to have been inspected by "elliptical," "hovering," "glowing" objects "as large as a hangar" in the twentieth century.

Children's highway games could be made of the questions asked throughout these pages, or invented from information inside: Taylor, on US Highway 183, has seen its population increase by just two between the years 1930 and 1980. At that rate, it will be 7490 before Taylor's population achieves five hundred. What, therefore, is Taylor's present population? And how many know the titles of our eight roadside sculptures? ("Arrival," "Crossing the Plains," "Erma's Desire," "Nebraska Gateway," "Nebraska Wind Sculpture," "Over/ Under," "Praxis," "Roadway Confluence.")

This is irresistible reading, a book browser's delight, full of affections, oddments, trivia, well-informed opinions — Nebraska's prettiest small town is Peru, its most underrated novelist Wright Morris, its greatest philosopher John G. Neihardt, its meanest reputation the town of Arnold — and full, too, of the kinds of funny and frightening things that my mother might have read aloud in the car as we waited at a railroad crossing for the Burlington freight train to clank past. *The Complete Roadside Guide to Nebraska* would have been a book impossible to write were it not, for Alan Boye, so obviously a labor of love. Readers of this wonderful second edition may well find that his passion has become theirs.

Ron Hansen
December, 1992

Preface to the first edition

In a note to me, Alan Boye described his *Complete Roadside Guide to Nebraska* as one the traveler might carry in the glove compartment of a car. Would that it had once been in *my* glove compartment in those days, in the 1940s, when it would have been a welcome companion. Nebraska was hardly a tourist mecca at that time, nor is it now, but today even native sons and daughters take the time to look freshly about them. Since *my* time, for example, there has been a bit of history and visible change. More than change, there is now new interest in what was once taken for granted.

The town of Schuyler, for example, once known to me as the location (if I could find it) of the empty piano box where I — for most of one long 4th of July morning — concealed myself while I smoked *punk* in neatly rolled sheets of toilet paper. This may well still be frowned on. I was not in the condition the rest of the day to speak publicly about my experience. Places of concealment have always been special to me, and in these Nebraska is still not lacking where there are front porches with a fence of cross slats at the bottom. The culverts that once ornamented street crossings might well now be gone, signifying progress. Mr. Boye's comment, in his guide, sites Schuyler as having once been a rip-snorting cowboy town. That would have been of keen interest to me in 1917, but it comes a little late for me to act on it.

A fine example of touring literature at its best will be found on page 330, where he cites Duncan as a small village between here and there. How can you beat that? Precisely what a good guide should do, if given the chance.

Wright Morris
April, 1989

How To Use This Book

This book is designed so that a person may start using it from any point on nearly any highway in all of the state's 93 counties.

To locate a particular highway:
Look for the name of the higway listed in the contents.

To use the Guide as you travel:
The chapters always read from east to west, or from south to north. If you are traveling in either of these directions, simply read **down** the page.

If you are traveling south, or east, read from entry to entry going **up** the page.

Distances given are between entries. If you are reading **up** the page, follow the distiacnes in the **parentheses**. The distance between entireis are in **bold**.

Sites which are off the main road or highway a fair distance are given in *italics*. The distances to these sites are in **bold**.

Please see below for a sample page description.

While a great many of these sites have been visited by the author in order to test the distances, the wise traveler will not explore without a map of the state close at hand, or travel too far afield without stopping to ask for directions locally.
 Because of the variety in maps and automobile audometers there may be slight differences from the distances indicated in the book, so always hunt around a bit if a site is not immediately visible.

Because the landscape is a changing and living being, time, progress, erosion and the elements may make some of the sites in the book less than immediately discernable. Get out of the car and look around. Use your imagination. Get down on your hands and knees and search among the prairie grasses. If you still can't find the site get up and brush the dust off your knees and take a deep breath of the clear Nebraska air, as it does its part at replenishing the earth.

Boldface ——————— *West of Tryon 22 miles on State Highway 92 to turn off to the*
indicates *south for Diamond Bar Lake vicintly. Good fishing and hunting. Inquire*
distance *locally. Ten miles southeast of here, accessible on backroads only,*
 was the small town of Forks, located at the forks of the East and West
Italics ——————— *Birdwood Creeks. It had a post office until the early 1920s.*
indicate
sites off the   *West of Tryon 28 miles to Flats, another near ghost town.*
main road. *Because of an early pioneer named Lombard the area was called*
 Lombard Flats. The US Post Office, in its infinite wisdom cut off the
 Lombard part because it was too long and simply left Flats.

Distance from –Twenty nine miles (5 miles.)
previous entry,   Take the narrow paved road leading off to the west. Down
while traveling this road 15 miles to the banks of the North Fork of the Dismal River,
north cross the river and continue another eight miles to the banks of the
 South Fork and the site of the North and Cody Ranch.
(distance from   This grassy expanse of hills was once the range of thousands
previous entry of buffalo, antelope and deer. In 1877 William F. Cody, who would
traveling south 126
In parentheses.)

later become world renowned as Buffalo Bill, along with Major Frank North, purchased a herd of cattle at Ogallala and spent a good part of their summer driving them to this range land. Here the men started a ranch that would become known as the North and Cody Ranch. Not much is known about the success of this ranch, or Buffalo Bill's part in it, but for years the ranch was made welcome to any traveler who happened this way. In later years many dignitaries were entertained here. Today the quiet and peaceful river flows through beautiful country of grasslands and thickets along the banks.

Distance from previous entry, while traveling north (distance from previous entry traveling south in parentheses.)

Five miles (0 miles.)
Mullen.
Junction with State Highway 2 and the end of State Highway 97.

For information about Mullen, see entry for State Highway 2.

Italics indicate sites off main roads.

North of Mullen the road continues as county roads into the vast Cherry County. Under most weather conditions the road is passable, although it might be a bit washboardy in spots. In forty miles is the Samuel McKelvie National Forest, the hideout spots for the state's most famous outlaw, Doc Middleton, and other interesting sites.

For a full discussion of the area North of Mullen see the entry for Valentine and US Highway 20.

Reference to intersecting roads. See index or contents for those chapters.

Chapter Heading for US Highways

Chapter Heading for State Highways

Zero miles (5 miles.)

Kansas Border. For five miles Route 73 is joined by US Highway 159. For information about the strange and interesting southeast tip of Nebraska, please see the entry for US Highway 159.

Five miles (9 miles.)

Falls City.

If you are the type of person who wants to know exactly where the falls is when a town has a name like Falls City, it is nearby on the Nemaha. Prichard Museum is open midafternoons weekdays, and by appointment.

The special collections at the Falls City Library include art collections by artists John Falter, Alice Cleaver and others. Included in the collection is the *Saturday Evening Post* cover collection.

The True Value Hardware store in downtown Falls City is in the Gehling Opera House, built in 1892. The capacity was 700 to 800 and, as was the case with most local opera houses, the upstairs was used for productions and stage shows, and the downstairs for restaurants and saloons. A grand spiral staircase once went from the center of the main floor to the second floor. Some of the frescoes can still be seen on the second-floor walls, and some of the old-time equipment used to run shows is still in storage. William Jennings Bryan spoke here, and many vaudeville shows stopped at this grand hall in Falls City.

The city became the county seat after a battle with Salem, in 1860.

Nine miles (2 miles.)
The intersection of 73 and state 67.

North on State 67, six miles, then east five miles to Barada. On the way you will pass old red brick church at about 2 miles.

Barada was named for Antonine Barada, and his story is one of the most interesting and strange tales of the state's history. Barada's father was a French nobleman, well-trained in the arts and culture, and destined for a high rank in the finest circles of French society.

During the reign of Louis XVI, Barada was strolling about Paris one day when a rose fell at his feet. He picked it up, looked about, and determined that the rose had been flung there by the most beautiful woman he had ever seen. She stood above the street in a window and smiled down at him. She had the blackest hair he had ever seen, and a dark, brown skin the color of wild and free nature itself.

He went about his business and returned to the same place the next day. The window was boarded up. He inquired at the house and learned that the woman whom he had seen was gone, and he would never see her again. "Why not?" he demanded.

The man in the house laughed. "That woman was called Taeglena. She was an Indian from Louisiana, in America. She has left to return to her buffalo and campfires."

Barada sold what possessions he could, gathered his money, and within days was on a boat for America. He knew nothing about the woman, except for her name and that she lived somewhere in the vast expanse of French territory in the New World.

Eventually Barada worked himself into the far north Canadian woods, working as a trapper and hunter, and traveling among the Sioux. He became rather well known as a good shot, and as the strange Frenchman who searched relentlessly for an Indian woman.

Barada roamed the vast territory of Louisiana for ten years, learning a bit of the language of the Sioux and about the wild country,

2

so different from his long-lost, distant France.

He searched every village of Indians. Once, in an Omaha village in Iowa, he passed by a teepee. An old woman sat in front of it, working on some hides and talking. "Taeglena," she said just as he passed. "What was that?" He glared at the woman.

The doorway of the teepee flipped back and there, after ten years of searching, stood the woman who had thrown him the rose. They were married and lived in various locations along the Nebraska side of the Missouri River.

One of their sons was Antoine. At age seven he was kidnapped by the Sioux and held ransom for six months until his father paid two ponies for his return.

At nine Antoine worked with a fur trading company and made excursions up the Missouri River.

Antoine was renowned for his extraordinary strength. Legends abound to this day about his powers. He was known to be able to snap a canoe paddle in his hands. Even his toes were so strong that he once pinched a man with them until the man pleaded for mercy.

Some say they saw him pick up a derrick that was being used to drive piles into the Missouri. In St. Louis there remains today a stone doorsill that he lifted from the ground. On the side of the stone is carved the words: "Antoine Barada lifted this stone, 1,700 pounds, 1832."

Antoine worked for a while in California, trying, along with thousands of others, to strike it rich in the gold fields. Shortly after that he settled here, in the small town that still bears his name, on his parents' land. He and his French wife lived here until his death in 1887. He is buried next to his wife in the Barada cemetery, but his legend lives on and on in the tales and folklore of the people for miles around.

On October 21, 1990, a farmer just east of Barada was cutting alfalfa in his field when he discovered three mysterious rings burned into the earth. "I'm convinced something flew over the ground," he said. "It didn't land, but it burned that field with perfect circles." Two of the rings were 18 feet in diameter, and the third was 12 feet. Although tests of plant samples at the University of Nebraska suggested the damaged was done by a rare but earthly fungus, sightseers and local citizens were convinced that the marks were left by a space craft. What gave their idea some credence was that a few nights earlier two hunters reported seeing something with bright lights and legs on it and another farmer had reported seeing four red discs flying around.

Northeast from Barada, three miles: southern edge of Indian Caves State Park. See entry for US 136 for information about this wonderful state park.

Two miles (7 miles.)
Verdon. Just west of here is Verdon State Recreation Area. A small, natural lake that makes a nice getaway.

Seven miles (1 mile.)
Intersection with US 75.

For a continuation of sites to the north, please see the entry for US Highway 75.

US Highway 75

Zero miles (4 miles.)
Kansas border.

Four miles (5 miles.)
Junction with State Highway 8.

East on State Highway 8 seven miles to Salem. From the Bible, meaning "peaceful." The name was given to suggest to the local Indians what the pioneers hoped they might be.

West on State Highway 8 seven miles, then three miles south on State 105. A large Boy Scouts of America Reservation. These 370 acres are temporary home to those who promise to obey, honor, etc.

West on State Highway 8 nine miles, two miles west of the Boy Scout Reservation to Kinters Ford State Wildlife Management Area. Just four miles southwest of here, at DuBois in Pawnee County, is the Iron Horse Trail Wildlife Area.

Five miles (1 mile.)
Junction with US Highway 73.

These two highways are joined together from here to the northern edge of Omaha. This is a busy road, but with plenty to see along its path. For information about sites along US Highway 73, south, please see the entry for US Highway 73.

One mile (4 miles.)

Just west of here is an ancient stone house, believed to be one of the oldest in the area. Ask locally for directions.

West on county road seven miles to Kirkman's Cove Recreation Area.

Four miles (11 miles.)

Junction with State Highway 62. East to Indian Caves State Park and Barada, named for one of the most interesting characters in American history. Please see entry for US Highway 73 for further information.

Eleven miles (5 miles.)

Auburn.

There is something wonderful about coming into this town from the north along US 73/75, passing the city park and slowing down for the center business district. Something about the place that reminds one of a day from youth, long ago when the future was endless and unimportant, and the present was a five dollar bill in your pocket and the chance to meet up with a new friend, a chance to find that someone of your dreams.

It may be that kind of reckless and priceless freedom of being able to stick out your thumb on that highway and catch a ride for just about any place you wanted to go, or it may be the way the sun gleams off the store fronts and the courthouse, but Auburn still glistens with a bit of that sense, that exhilarating feeling of being young.

Auburn is the county seat of Nemaha County, and its original limestone courthouse still serves as the center of county politics. Auburn was originally two towns, Sheridan and Calvert. Sheridan was the older of the two, founded in 1868, and Calvert was settled sometime later. A lumber company was formed in 1881 and is still in existence as the oldest business in Auburn. In 1882 the two towns agreed to merge into a single entity. The courthouse was built on the land equidistant between the two town centers. The current courthouse, built in 1900, is at that same location. Auburn's city center is a bustling area yet and has the charm of a bygone era.

The Nemaha Valley Museum, south of the county courthouse, features two three-story buildings and a number of outstanding displays. It is open most Sundays, or by appointment.

Junction with US 136 — please see that entry for information

US Highways 73 & 75

about sites along this route.

Five miles (1 mile.)

Junction with State Highway 67 east. East here to the most beautiful town in the state, Peru. Please see the entry for US Highway 136 for information about this area.

One mile (14 miles.)

Junction with State Highway 67 west.

Six miles west on 67 to Brock.

Brock is located in a belt of timber, which originally attracted the town's founders to the area. The name of the town has changed seven times since it was formed in 1855. At one time Brock was called Podunk. Podunk, Nebraska.

Three miles south of Brock on county roads is privately owned but free Coryell Park. Coryell Park supporters claim that for the first-time visitor the Park is nothing short of amazing. The park is an unusual one as it was formed when the original homesteaders, the Richard Coryell family, decided to donate their land as a park for all the people.

The old homestead house was reproduced out of lumber that grew on the land, and the house in which several of the children were born was moved to the site. Picnic grounds and swings were added, as well as a tower, a reproduction of a prairie schooner, and a chapel. The chapel was built so that it would last for ages. The front wall of the stone building is 28 inches thick, the side walls, 24 inches. The inner walls are made of the same limestone as the state capitol building. The foundation is six feet deep and the walls are reinforced with steel and concrete. The floor is seven inches thick and the pews made from oak.

It was the intent of the builders that the chapel be made free and for the sacred non-denominational worship of God. It is available for weddings and special events. The park boasts an auditorium, a museum and a bell purchased in the memory of one of the Coryell children.

Four miles (10 miles.)

Take the county road to the east from this intersection and soon it will swing north close to the river. It is a breathtaking and beautiful drive. There are camping areas along these roads. Inquire locally. The route is a pleasant way to get to the lovely town of Peru (see entry for US Highway 136) or you may continue north 12 miles

6

to Nebraska City.

Ten miles (1 mile.)
Nebraska City.

Do not take the bypass around the city because no tour of the state of Nebraska can be complete without a stop and a look at Nebraska City, one of the oldest and most important cities in the state. Nebraska City was founded by William Nuckolls in the early 1850s as a trading post and river boat stop. Soon the town began to grow. Its convenient docks and natural land access to the Platte, Nemaha and other ways west made it quickly bloom into a full-fledged, snorting, cursing river town. The trails that led west out of Nebraska City made it the jumping-off place for trail drivers, bushwhackers, mule skinners, pioneers, gold rushers, and an entire host of con men.

In 1860, a Nebraska City gentleman tried to combine two important current items: the covered wagon and the steam engine. He was a few decades too early, and made several mistakes in design, so his steam-powered wagon was a dismal failure. The machine had four engines, front wheels six feet in diameter and rear wheels 12 feet in diameter. It was supposed to run for eight hours on a cord of wood. It was designed to run between Nebraska City and Denver, and made its maiden voyage on July 22, 1862. Ten miles west of here a drive shaft broke, and since New York was the closest place to replace the shaft, and since the inventor soon learned his wife and family had been captured during a raid by Indians, the project was put on hold. By the time he was able to resume his steam wagon, the railroad had started up in earnest and the project was abandoned.

But transportation is what made Nebraska City. Two important trails led out of Nebraska City. The Nebraska City Cutoff of the Oregon Trail started in Nebraska City and zig-zagged in a more or less straight line due west until it joined the more frequently traveled branch of the Trail near present-day Kearney.

The Oxbow Trail, which connected Nebraska City with the Oregon Trail but swung north toward Columbus, also started here.

Before the pioneers arrived, this area was visited by the Lewis and Clark Expedition on July 18 and 19, 1804. Clark noted in his journal that the area was treeless and that a hillside had slid into the river. The National Park Service's decision to build a 49-acre historical center to commemorate the Expedition on the south side of State Highway 2 was controversial, because historians claimed the area north of Omaha was far more significant to the voyage.

The site of the old Fort Kearny Blockhouse is marked on the

7

corner of Central Avenue and 5th Street. The original Fort Kearny was built in 1847 at this site but abandoned in 1848 when the government decided that a better location for the fort would be some 200 miles west. The government then abandoned this fort and moved everyone west, a mere year after building and stocking this place. Nice to know that some things, like competency of governments, don't change.

Nebraska City was the location of the first high school in the state, and possibly the first one west of the Missouri. It was built in 1864.

North of the cemetery on South 19th Street is the site of John Brown's Cave, which is where Brown hid runaway slaves from Kansas and Missouri for the Underground Railroad. The "cave" was essentially a small cellar under a house, which until the 1930s had no windows or doors to the outside. A 30-foot tunnel went from there to Table Creek. If there was danger, someone on the floor above would tap out a prearranged signal on the floor and the slaves would escape down the tunnel to the creek and eventually to the river. From here the slaves were taken into Iowa, where they were given the final preparations for flight into Canada. It is good to remember that there were those who sought to help the mistreated in our nation, but it is also good to remember that only a few decades ago there was a kind of life that made it necessary for men and women to stay hidden and in fear of their lives just to gain their freedom in Canada.

The Wildwood Center on Steinhardt Park Road, open daily from spring until autumn, features a ten-room historic brick house and a barn in which the exhibits are changed to present a varied display for the return visitors.

Also in town is the Old Freighter's Museum, featuring exhibits from the long-ago days of freighters.

The old Farmer's Bank and former post office was built in 1889 and is beautifully restored.

Nebraska City is the center of Nebraska's finest apple growing area. Without mentioning specific names, the country roads in Otoe County are filled with fruit and juice stands and it is an unfortunate traveler who zips past these roadside meccas without stopping for a taste of utter ambrosia.

Of all the communities hit by the Halloween blizzard of 1991, Nebraska City suffered the most. Thousands of trees came down from the ice and homes had to be evacuated because of falling limbs and trees. Power outages were widespread and damage from the storm was substantial.

Nebraska City is the county seat of Otoe County, which

almost seems secondary to the distinct historic river town feel of the place. There are many fine smaller restaurants here, as well as many fine parks. Do not leave Nebraska City without going down to the river and sitting for a spell to watch the water flow.

Just north of the city is one of Nebraska's shrines: Arbor Lodge. Follow 2nd Avenue, a quaint brick street, to the Lodge.

The Lodge was the home of one of the state's wealthiest and best known early-day citizens, J. Sterling Morton. Morton moved to the area in 1855 and became a squatter on this strip of land near the young Nebraska City. After a bit he built a four-room house with a view of the river and the Iowa hills. He added an unusual feature for that time and place: a shingled roof. The land he claimed did not have the rich timber that the river bottom land, just a few miles distant had, so Morton began to transplant a few trees. Soon he brought more trees, then more, then more. He added an orchard, shade trees, vines, shrubs, flowers, evergreens and hedges.

In 1874, Morton had become quite the well-rounded citizen, so much so that he was appointed president of the State Board of Agriculture. While in that position he persuaded Governor Furnas to proclaim a day of tree-planting. It became a regular feature of the state, and in1885 the state Legislature declared it a state holiday and moved the date to April 22, Morton's birthday. Morton later became Secretary of Agriculture during the second term of Grover Cleveland.

Arbor Day is now observed in Nebraska on the last Friday of April. Celebrations for Earth Day usually coincide with Arbor Day and often overshadow it; however Morton's contributions to the planet are observed in every state as well as in several other countries.

Morton's legacy is carried on through the efforts of the Arbor Day Foundation, a non-profit educational organization which sponsors tree planting and other environmental activities nationwide.

It may be difficult for us to understand just how big a celebration Arbor Day was at the turn of the century, but across the country, and especially in the west, the holiday caught on like wildfire. In San Francisco, for example, such notables as author Jack London and naturalist John Muir encouraged the city to declare the day a holiday of great importance.

Across the bay in Oakland, a poet little known today but of international celebrity status back then — Joaquin Miller — organized his own celebration of the day by getting the city's school children to have a day away from classes and out in the parks, streets and yards planting trees. Oakland owes most of its greenery to Arbor Day.

In Lincoln and other communities, school children are often given free trees to plant at home, and although the prohibitive costs of such a program have eliminated it from Lincoln schools, Lincolnites can direct you to pine trees, beautiful blooming red buds, crab apples and cherry trees in yards all across the city that date from the program.

A committee from the Nebraska Association of Resource Districts estimated that member districts have planted over 50 million trees in the state in the past 20 years. If those trees were planted in a straight line it would create a forest of trees 113 rows deep from the Missouri River to the Panhandle.

The Arbor Day Foundation sponsors a three-day fair and festival in Nebraska City starting each Arbor Day. The events include a fine Old Time Fiddlers contest. Such toe-tapping, foot-stomping music is a tradition in southeastern Nebraska.

Morton's mansion is open to the public and tours are given often. It is quite a house, with hand-hewn timbers, a beautiful staircase or two and semicircular porches. It took Morton and his heirs 50 years to bring the original three-room house (which is still a part of the structure) to the 52 room monster that was donated to the state in 1923.

Morton's son Joy was the founder of Morton Salt, and became something quite less than poverty-stricken himself.

The land around the house is either nicely manicured, or left to retain a native and wild atmosphere. There are over 200 varieties of trees on the grounds, as well as an equal number of shrubs and, at last count, a million or two flowers. Other gardens, buildings and monuments are scattered about the park, which is run by the State.

One mile (10 miles.)

One half mile north of Arbor Lodge is the site where the Table Creek Treaty with the Pawnee was signed in 1857. This treaty, which was signed by Hawk Chief, Grey Eagle and others, ceded all Pawnee claims to land except for a small parcel along the Loup River. In essence, this meant the three or four chiefs were giving up about a third of the state for an area a little larger than Otoe County. In exchange the government gave the Pawnee $40,000 a year for five years. What happened to the money is not clear, but the land became the State of Nebraska.

Ten miles (2 miles.)

Cass County line.

The earliest documented exploration of Nebraska mentions

a location in Cass County. Pierre and Paul Mallet reached the mouth of the Platte on June 2, 1739. They went up the river for 70 miles.

Later, Long's expedition reported that Nebraska was "uninhabitable for people depending on agriculture for subsistence," a line similar in style to Custer's "what Indians?"

In 1854 the Government made a treaty with the Omaha and Otoe Indians in which the Indians gave up the lands bordering the Missouri River. "They received as an equivalent a stated amount of provisions and other necessities." This consisted of pork and sugar.

Cass County's Indian history includes not only the Omaha and Otoe, but the Winnebago, recent arrivals to the state, who often walked here from their reservation in the northern part of the state to visit relatives and friends. The sight of these travelers stayed in the memories of many a Cass County resident for a long while, but before these tribes ancient Indian peoples lived here thousands of years ago. Their flint arrow heads and tools can still be found scattered over newly plowed spring fields. They are now known as the Nebraska Culture.

The first north/south auto highway, the "King of Trails" from Omaha to Kansas City, passed through the county. It was built in 1911.

Two miles (7 miles.)

Junction with US Highway 34. To the west Highway 34 travels the length of the state. It joins highways 73 and 75 here until Plattsmouth, where it swings into Iowa.

For information about sites along this route, please see the entry for US Highway 34.

This junction is at the town of Union. For information about Union, please also see entry for US Highway 34.

Seven miles (1 mile.)

Murray, the site of the first county school, 1856.

One mile (7 miles.)

*East on this county road **one mile** to Rock Bluff.*

This is a ghost town, or better yet, a ghost field, now, since all but the school house and a few scattered sites remain of this once prosperous riverboat town. The existence of a thriving grain elevator causes some to hope that the site may once again produce a town.

The school is listed on the National Register of Historic Places. It was built in 1870, and was once a two story building. A

11

tornado took away the top floor in 1872. Further twister damage was done in 1896 and 1913. The outside of the building is a kind of historic landmark. Please do not add your name to the walls. Let us leave our legacy in the fact that we were the ones who cared about not defacing such monuments.

Seven miles (3 miles.)

Plattsmouth.

Home of the Cass County Museum, 646 Main Street. An excellent museum in a historically rich county. The Museum is open every day except Wednesday.

The Museum is also the location for the start of a short walking tour of the town. At the SW corner of 6th and Main is the Old Bank Building built around 1885. As you walk down Main Street toward 5th Street, you will pass buildings on either side of street that date from the 1880s and '90s. This one-block stretch has so many of them that one can easily get the impression that the year is 1910.

The building at 525 Main was once Pepperberg Cigar factory. Continue down Main to 4th and take a left. At the SW corner of 4th and Main is the old Waterman Opera House, built in 1882, home for the best entertainment ever seen in Plattsmouth. It housed 1,500 people and had one of the largest stages of any hall in the state. The Cass County Courthouse is catty-corner from the Opera House and was built in 1892. It is probably the best example of Romanesque architecture in the state.

The city library, at Ave. A and 4th, is a Carnegie library and was built in 1922. On the SE corner of Ave. C and 4th is the Walhaus House, built in 1886. One block farther on 4th brings you to the Heights, 1887, and across 4th street, "The Surveyor General's House."

Turn left on Ave D and walk two blocks to 6th Street. Turn left. The houses along the next two blocks date from 1885-1900. Turn left on Ave. B. On the right is Church of the Holy Spirit Rectory, formerly St. John's Convent, built in 1889.

Turn right on 5th. The church at the corner of 5th and Ave. A was built in 1897, and across the street the interesting Anderson house, 1867.

Turn right on Ave. A. Walk to 7th, turn left on 7th. You will pass several older homes and businesses, and the First Methodist Church at the corner of 7th and Main, which was built in 1903.

Turn left on Main and return to your car. See? No reason to lock your doors in this fine community!

Plattsmouth history goes back a long ways. This juncture of the Platte and the Missouri must have been a significant spot for perhaps thousands of years before the arrival of the whites. The Pawnee and the Otoes who dwelled here when the first white men pushed their boats up the river knew the area well. A Mormon, Libias Coon, ferried other Saints across the river near here in the late 1840s.

In 1853 a log trading post was established here and grew so that it soon served not only the Indians, but the new white settlers as well. The trading post was located on Indian land, and with its establishment came the first step of the Indian's eventual subjugation.

Plattsmouth was a popular river crossing spot, and so the town grew around the industry of outfitting pioneers headed west on what was known as the South Platte Trail, or Oxbow Trail, which eventually connected with the Oregon Trail just west of Hastings. The town was well established by the late 1850s and a bustling metropolis of 474 by 1860.

Try to imagine a warm day in May, 1865. On that day 125 covered wagons crossed the Missouri. The banks on both sides of the river were lined with wagons and mules and oxen and families. During that single month, a total of 2,360 wagons crossed the Missouri at Plattsmouth.

Steamboats headed up river for the Yellowstone, the Black Hills and other frontier locations filled the Missouri, using cord wood to stoke their fires. On any given day the docks along Plattsmouth were filled with sternwheelers and sidewheelers getting up a head of steam, filling the air with noise and black smoke. At that time, the river was just east of where the Burlington railroad tracks run. The river is now east of town.

In the old days a series of streams ran alongside of the boardwalks on the main streets of town. They merged and flowed into the river. Now those streams have been confined underground. The streams did serve to run several grist mills that opened here in the heyday of pioneer migration west. The first Democratic Territorial Convention was held here in 1858. One of the first automobiles in the state, (back then called a "gig") scared the horses here in 1901. It was still around in order to cross over the first wooden auto bridge across the Missouri, built in 1911. The first railroad bridge was built in 1880; it was replaced in 1903.

Plattsmouth also had an ironworks foundry, and much of the fancy ironwork that still exists in this part of the state came from there. It was in existence in the late 1800s. Another major industry here was cigars. Several factories, including the once famous "Acorn" brand, were located here.

The big annual event in these parts is the Kass Kounty King Korn Karnival, which has been held almost every year in September since 1932. One of the early Plattsmouth businesses, a clothing store, kept a tree with several monkeys in it in the store window. It was quite an attraction for miles around.

Feel a little shaky? Well, this is the location of a Nebraska earthquake. The quake started in the early morning in the spring of 1877. It was sufficiently strong to cause some cracking on the southeast corner of the brick schoolhouse, which was later rebuilt.

Many of the town's several churches date to the late 1800s.

Plattsmouth was the location for the film "Indian Runner" which was filmed here in the early 1990's. It was director and writer Sean Penn's first movie.

East on State Highway 66 nine miles then north three miles to Cedar Creek and Anna's, a restaurant built to look like a combination of the town's former one-room school house and the deck of an ocean-going ship. Only in Nebraska. . .

Continue east on State Highway 66 four more miles to Louisville, a picture-perfect town on the edge of the Platte.

Three miles (5 miles.)

The Platte River. Just east of here the Platte enters the Missouri. This is a wonderfully wild bit of land surrounded by settlement. The closest one can get to the junction without getting wet, or riding a canoe, is aboard Amtrak. The train crosses the Platte near the mouth.

Five miles (1 mile.)

Offutt Air Force Base and the headquarters for the Strategic Air Command. For those of you who would want to be first hit in a nuclear war, this is the place to stand.

The Strategic Air Command was created in 1946 in order to contend with the nuclear weapons threat, to prevent accidental firing and to plan for the use of such weapons. With the dissolution of the Soviet Union, S.A.C. ended on June 1, 1992.

At one point, S.A.C. was responsible for nearly half of the Pentagon's budget. From 1961 until 1990, S.A.C. kept a fleet of planes constantly airborne watching for nuclear attack. S.A.C. employed as many as 282,000 people and was responsible for monitoring over 4,000 ballistic missiles in the United States.

14

The monitoring continues, however, in the command head-quarters 40 feet below the surface. A new system known as Strategic Command splits responsibilities into various parts of the armed services.

The presidential plane, Air Force One, is sometimes kept here. There are actually more than one One. Look closely and you will see planes with large radar discs sitting on top. A museum on the grounds features "some of the fastest missiles and largest bombers ever flown." It is located at 2510 Clay St. in Bellevue.

It was just after 6:30 in the evening on September 8th, 1958, when Major Paul Duich sat down with his dinner at Offutt Air Force Base at S.A.C. Headquarters.

He sat with a couple of buddies. They were talking about baseball scores. Major Duich then got up to go outside to get a newspaper from a vending machine in order to find out the latest scores. He left his plate of food on the table and went outside.

As he came back from the lobby of Officer's Quarters he glanced up into the clear sky and saw what at first he thought was a vapor trail. "I have seen thousands of vapor trails, but somehow this one was peculiar. I did a double take, for suddenly it occurred to me that this short 'vapor trail' was actually a brilliant source of light. I stopped dead in my tracks and watched."

Instead of dissipating as a vapor trail would, the light grew in intensity and was motionless.

The Major called to other officers passing by. Soon there was a small crowd gathered gazing at the phenomenon in the sky.

He hurried back into the lobby and quickly called the Offutt tower. He described the object to the operator, and soon the members of the tower had it sighted, too.

The color was changing to a yellow-orange and the fuzzy outline was growing into a solid cigar-shape. One end was blunt and the other was not. The Major hurried back outside. By now nearly 20 men were gathered, looking at the object. As they all watched a swarm of black specks appeared at the lower end of the object. They looked like gnats, and after a minute or so they disappeared.

Then the object, which had been motionless, began to move. It had been in a vertical position and now swung to an angle to the side. It moved westerly, and slightly to the south.

It remained in the sky for about another 5 minutes. As it approached the horizon it continued to swing around so that it was nearly parallel with the distant corn fields. It faded from view as it moved farther and farther to the west.

The object had been in the sky for nearly 10 minutes. Toward the end a colonel had taken photographs, which were never seen by any witnesses. However, a full 25 people, including officers and civilians, saw the events of that September evening.

One mile (3 miles.)

Bellevue.

An early Spanish explorer, Manuel Lisa, who came this way trapping claimed that the area near the confluence of the Platte and Missouri rivers was a pretty view, or Belle View, hence the name of this community.

The first governor of the territory of Nebraska, Francis Burt, was sworn in here on October 7, 1854. He died two days later.

The new governor liked Omaha as a territorial capitol and moved the Legislature there. The folks in Bellevue were mad enough that they insisted they be separated from Omaha by a county line, and although the two towns were once in a single county, a new county, Sarpy, was formed and Bellevue became its first seat.

True to form, a rivalry soon developed over which town should have the courthouse. As was almost always the case, tempers rose and words and fists flew. The folks over at Papillion thought they were better suited for a county seat.

According to a newspaper account of the day, Bellevue and Papillion "measured their tongues against each other, and vituperations flew thick and fast. The air was about as sulphurous as adjectives and epithets not to be found in the grammars of the day were thrown back and forth."

Modern Bellevue offers plenty of opportunities to explore its historic past. Tours of the city start at the Sarpy County Historical Museum at 2402 Clay. The museum has hundreds of artifacts and dozens of displays illustrating how live was lived by Native Americans and early settlers.

Haworth Park on the Missouri River bank offers camping, picnics and cruises up and down the river on the Belle of Brownville, a replica of a sternwheeler riverboat.

A diesel-powered sternwheeler, the riverboat Belle of Brownville has her home port at Bellevue. The riverboat is a commercial enterprise and offers daylong cruises on the Missouri as well as moonlight dances on board.

Fontenelle Forest, 1111 Bellevue Blvd., northeast of town, offers 17 miles of hiking trails, including a Braille Trail.

Three miles (11 miles.)

Omaha.

At Omaha are the junctions of US Highways 75, 73, with US Highways 6, 275, and Interstate 80. Please see those entries for information about sites along those routes.

Omaha is Nebraska's largest city, at an estimated population of about 350,000. That makes Douglas County the most populated county in the state, hence the number one in the first digit of local license plates.

The demographics of Omaha indicate it is a fairly close representation of many Midwestern cities. The greater metropolitan area is well over a half a million in population with a median age of 31. At least 72 percent own their own homes and more than 24 per cent have been to college.

There is a lot to see in Omaha, and the city has had quite an interesting past. Below are just a few of the notable things about the city. Ask downtown for a map of the city to help you find your way around town.

Lewis and Clark reported seeing a hill with 200 Indian houses on it and some believe these were the bluffs of present-day Omaha. It was here that Lewis wrote in his journal: "The musquitors so thick & troublesom that it was disagreeable and painful to Continue a moment still." That is hardly even true anymore.

The U.S. Park Service thought about building a National Historic Park near Omaha to commemorate the Expedition, but Nebraska City won over as the site. Nevertheless, Lewis and Clark are remembered locally in a variety of ways. A group known as the Discovery Corps recreates Lewis and Clark's encampment yearly, complete with tents, flintlock guns and campfires. The river boat Belle of Brownville docks at the site and tourists are welcomed to the encampment. Ask locally, or at the Western Heritage Museum (see below) for dates and directions to the encampment.

The Omaha Indians once roamed this area in the time before the white man's arrival. The last remaining Omaha Indians who originally lived here were moved to a reservation in 1854. Their reservation is 70 miles north on US Highway 75 (see entry below for Macy).

Omaha was founded to serve as a town on the west side of the Missouri across from the town of Council Bluffs. No one thought the new town would grow, but it did quite well for itself.

In 1825, a trading post was built between 9th and 10th on

Dodge and Capitol.

The earliest large group of settlers in the area were the Mormons who had decided to go west until they found a place to live unmolested. Most of them started their journey west in caravans of hand-pulled carts from the Mississippi River. The Missouri served as a good spot to regroup and rest before the next long haul.

Their first settlement in this area was a spot just south of Ak Sar Ben, then they moved to west of present Forest Lawn Cemetery, and finally to Winter Quarters, in the northeast corner of the present city. At Winter Quarters they set up a permanent settlement to serve as a resting place for their fellow pioneers moving west toward Salt Lake City. The town was later renamed Florence and is now incorporated as a part of greater Omaha.

An excellent book on Winter Quarters and the struggle of the early settlers is Conrey Bryson's *Winter Quarters*.

The Florence Museum was built as a bank in 1856 and is the oldest bank building in the state. The Mormon Pioneer Cemetery holds countless graves from the Mormon settlement days. A visitors' center is located across the street from the cemetery and tours are available. There is no admission fee. The cemetery is located at 3215 State Street. The Florence Mills, built in 1846 by the Mormons, still stand nearby.

In 1854, Omaha was selected as the location for the meeting of the Territorial Legislature. Thus began the long battle over just where the capital city should be. The "South Platters" eventually won and Lincoln became the site, but not before the "North Platters" held a number of sessions.

Perhaps it is best understood why the capital was moved to Lincoln when one realizes that, among other activities, the Omaha Legislature succeeded in eliminating the entire criminal code, and on several occasions the sessions had to be stopped because of fist fights. In 1867, the capital was moved to Lincoln. The state seal had to be taken by force. The North Platters/South Platters dispute was quite a thing back then and nearly led to Nebraska's own private civil war.

At 9th and Douglas was the site of a two-story Territorial Statehouse, and at 22nd and Dodge, the first Territorial Capitol.

On December 2, 1863, the Union Pacific started its move west toward building the first transcontinental railroad from Omaha. Later the courts decided the railroad had to start at Council Bluffs. As a result, the Union Pacific had to build a bridge across the River.

The Union Pacific headquarters are in Omaha. They operate

a wonderful train museum at 1416 Dodge Street. It is free and open seven days a week.

Railroad supporters were quite vocal in the early days, but none so vocal as a man with the unlikely name of George Francis Train. Train lived in Omaha for a time. He was quite a flamboyant character and taken to spontaneous actions. Once, when he had a dispute with an Omaha hotel owner, he vowed to have a new hotel built right across the street in three months. His 120-room hotel opened in 90 days.

The Union Pacific Station at 801 S. 10th now serves as the Omaha History Museum and the Western Heritage Museum. The unusual building is one of the few Art Deco style buildings in the Midwest. The asymmetrical roof line, best viewed from the south, is suggestive of a locomotive. The museum houses the Byron Reed coin collection, a fine photographic exhibit and two major exhibits on Omaha's history. It is open the entire year.

Many of the trails that started in or around Omaha have disappeared under the concrete and asphalt of malls and parking lots, but believe it or not, some traces of the old trails can still be found. One such trace is located near an Omaha Public Power District substation off Old Military Road near 90th Street.

Not only did the town serve as a trailhead and the start of many railroad journeys, but by 1870 Omaha was a very busy steamboat town with trips upriver to the wilds of America leaving constantly, and trips downriver to civilization equally as frequent.

In addition to being a helper, the River often times can turn into an enemy. In April 1881 a dam of ice in South Dakota, which had held the Missouri River behind it, broke, sending a cascade of water downstream. It flooded the town. The Missouri at Omaha was 5 miles wide and was 24 feet above low water.

That record was broken in 1952 when the river reached 30 and a half feet, but by then the town had learned to take more precautions against high water. A flood in 1877 formed Carter Lake to the northeast. It took the Supreme Court to decide that since the land east of the lake was a part of Iowa before the flood, it should remain so. Consequently there is a little bit of Iowa surrounded by Omaha even today.

Omaha was always considered being on the edge of the vast American wilderness, and its history reflects that location:

—For years the Omaha Public Library displayed the scalp of a man who had survived a scalping by Indians near Lexington. Today, the beautiful main library is one of the showpieces of the modern

19

downtown, despite the fact that the scalp no longer resides there.

—The Nebraska Humane Society for the Prevention of Cruelty to Children and Animals was founded in Omaha in the 1870s. The "Children" part wasn't dropped until 1957.

—In 1890, the 16-year-old son of the meatpacking millionaire Edward Cudahy was kidnapped and held for $25,000 ransom in gold. The money was paid and the boy was returned.

Soon a former Cudahy employee, Pat Crowe, was captured. He was not tried until 1905 and by that time he had become a legend as a working man's Robin Hood. When he was acquitted the courtroom burst into thunderous applause.

—One of the last lynchings in the country took place in Omaha in 1891. A crowd of 10,000 took a black man from jail and hanged him from a street post.

Omaha's location on the edge of the wilderness made it the logical location for a base of operations for the Army. The General Crook House Museum at 30th and Fort Streets was built in 1878 to serve as a residence for the Commander of the Department of the Platte and is named after the first occupant. The museum is operated by the Douglas County Historical Society and charges a small fee.

The first performance of Buffalo Bill's Wild West Show where admission was charged was at the race track that eventually became the Ak Sar Ben track. Ak Sar Ben was formed in 1895 as a charitable organization designed to promote the best of Nebraska and its people. Each year the members crown a king and queen in a ceremony worthy of London.

Ak Sar Ben is Neb Ras Ka spelled backwards. The Ak Sar Ben track and facilities are at 63rd and Center.

The Ak Sar Ben Aquarium is sixteen miles south of Omaha via Exit 432 on Interstate 80. The 12,000-foot facility is run by the Nebraska Games and Parks Commission and is the region's only aquarium. The site includes the Gretna Fish Hatchery Museum. The aquarium is open year-round, but hours do change seasonally.

In 1898 the Trans-Mississippi and International Exhibition was held here. It was one of those grand World's Fairs where numbers of buildings were built to celebrate the American West. Included was a gigantic teeter-totter that held 200 people.

There have been many famous Omahans, but in 1911 when she died, Anna Wilson had a heart of gold and knew many of Omaha's leading male citizens in ways not even their wives knew...if you get the meaning here.

To give you an idea just how many men knew her so well,

Wilson's estate was worth $1 million, which she left to local charities. Wilson is buried in Omaha's Prospect Hill Cemetery next to her lover, Don Allen, a gambler. For years after her death, each Memorial Day people would decorate her grave. That tradition faded out until the late 1970s when a group of people, led by members of the Prospect Hill Brass Band, decided to renew the tradition. Since then, every Memorial Day 100 people or so gather at the Madam's gravesite to clap hands and sing along while the brass band plays old favorites.

Omaha has been the setting for a wide variety of unexplained phenomenon. At 4:30 a.m. on August 25, 1877, a "balloon shape" came up the Missouri and knocked over a bridge without doing damage to anything else in the area. One eyewitness said, "It disappeared as quickly as it had come." Some say it was a tornado, others claim it was a UFO.

In 1897 a group of people, including members of Ak Sar Ben, reported seeing a large flying craft in the skies above Omaha. It was 90 feet long, eliptical in shape, with four wings, two on each side. It shone with a bright light. This vehicle was also sighted throughout Nebraska and in Kansas City and Denver at around the same time.

The night after the Omaha sighting, a farmer in Kansas and his two sons reported witnessing a spacecraft descend from the sky and capture a cow. They watched a clear, cigar-shaped vessel containing six creatures hover over the cow and then capture it with a cable before the craft rose straight up and disappeared.

For other reports of UFO sightings at this same time see entry for US Highway 136 at Inavale and US Highway 281 at Hastings.

On May 28, 1966, at four in the morning two Douglas County sheriff's patrolmen saw a bright blue object, with a long orange tail, move across the sky in the western part of the county. At that same moment an employee of Western Electric saw a blue-green object in the sky. It had a long reddish tail.

One noon-day in August of 1952 a crew of workmen repairing a county bridge saw a round puff of smoke streak across the sky. It moved very quickly.

Some of Omaha's other phenomena have been explained. In 1913, a gigantic tornado touched down at Ralston and cut a 7-mile path of destruction 1,000 feet wide, from 55th and Center to Iowa. Over 2,000 homes were destroyed and 185 people were killed.

That storm stood as the worst until 1975 when a twister touched down and demolished 2,459 buildings. Thanks to early warning systems, only three died in the later storm.

The tornado of 1975 came only a month after one of the worst

21

snowstorms ever to hit the city. There were 11 inches of snow driven by 50- to 60-mph winds. The strong winds lasted for hours. The drifts from this storm were over 20 feet high.

One of the world's most famous charitable organizations is in Omaha. A Catholic priest by the name of Father Flanagan started a home for boys on the western edge of the city in 1917. The home, soon known as Boys Town, was helped by a 1938 movie and expanded to its present size. It is at 132nd and Dodge. There are many other Omaha sites to see.

The beautiful Joslyn Art Museum at 22nd and Dodge was built in 1930 and houses a vast collection of art including an extensive Western Art collection. It was named after a city founder. His home, called the Joslyn Castle, is at the site of the Omaha Board of Education Offices, 3902 Davenport.

Perhaps one of the most significant 20th Century people born in Omaha was Malcolm X. His life story, published the year of his death, 1965, tells of his boyhood in Omaha and of the overwhelming racial hatred he had to contend with in his youth. The book, *The Autobiography of Malcolm X*, is still widely circulated today. Malcolm was to become a significant contributor to the Black Muslim movement in the United States. After he announced that he had split with the movement, he was murdered.

During most of his active life, Malcolm X called for black nationalistic pride and helped to define the black nationalist movement. He called for black supremacy in order to counteract the white supremacy movements. He called for black pride and a reassessment of what it meant to be black. "I never had much feeling about being a Negro, because I was trying so hard, in every way I could, to be white. . .I joined that multitude of Negro men and women in America who are brainwashed into believing that the black people are 'inferior' and white people 'superior.'"

Malcolm X's views and speeches have been characterized as having changed black America. While many justly claim the Black Muslim movement simply added another kind of racism to our nation's ills, Malcolm himself had rejected hatred in the name of race before his death. "I no longer subscribe to sweeping indictments of any one race," he said in 1964, "nor do I subscribe to the tenets of racism. I can state in all sincerity that I wish nothing but freedom, justice and equality, life, liberty and the pursuit of happiness for all people."

Above all else, Malcolm X was a man who had the courage to challenge his own beliefs and assumptions. Above all else,

Malcolm X was a man who had the courage to grow and to change.

Among many other notable citizens, Gerald Ford, the only man who held the office of President of the United States without having to undergo the electoral process for the office, was born in Omaha. His birthplace, at 32nd and Woolworth, is now a mini-park.

Nebraska author Ron Hansen was born and raised near 33rd and Larimore Ave. As early as fourth grade his teachers recognized his writing talents. Hansen's creativity led him to a job as a cartoonist for the campus newspaper at Creighton University where he graduated in 1970. He then attended the Iowa Writers' Project and later was awarded a Stegner Fellowship at Stanford University.

Hansen spent a year in a cabin near Columbus working on a novel about Vietnam. When it didn't sell he worked as a building engineer and tended bars. For a while he was a traveling textbook salesman and spent his evenings in motels working on the draft of what would become his first published novel *Desperadoes.*

This fine writer's works include *Mariette in Ecstasy* , which finished sixth in the National Book Critics' Circle awards and a collection of beautifully crafted stories, *Nebraska.* Awards recognizing this man's talents include a Guggenheim Fellowship for writing.

Famous people seem to come from Omaha in droves. Famous people born in Omaha, in addition to Malcolm X, Gerald Ford, and Ron Hansen, include Marlon Brando, Fred Astaire, Nick Nolte, Inga Swenson, Melvin Laird, Julie Wilson, Paul Williams, Roger Williams and Buddy Miles.

Memorial Park at 63rd and Dodge streets was the site of a 1971 demonstration to legalize the use of drugs on public property. Strange times, those early '70s.

In 1966, a white Omaha policeman shot and killed a 14-year-old black girl, an act that helped touch off the city's worst riots. Since then the wounds of the city have healed, although there is much room for improving the way all races treat one another.

The unique and fine Great Plains Black Museum opened in 1976 as the largest Black American cultural institution west of the Mississippi. It features over 10,000 items. In addition to the museum, it offers facilities for community meetings and exhibitions. It is open to the public on weekdays. It is located at 2213 Lake Street.

The Historical Society of Douglas County has restored the General George Crook house at 30th and Fort Streets. Crook was a supporter of Indian rights long ago before it was fashionable. He championed native rights during the famous trial of Standing Bear.

The museum is open weekdays.

The Omaha Children's Museum is at 551 South 18th Street. It provides a hands-on experience for youngsters of all ages. It is open year-round except Mondays.

The Emmy Gifford Children's Theater at 3504 Center Street offers a long season's worth of quality entertainment for children of all ages. The professional productions and understanding of how to present live theater to children makes the theater one of Omaha's finest attractions.

The Omaha Community Theater at 6915 Cass is the largest community playhouse in the nation.

The Omaha Magic Theater is noted for its innovative productions.

Dozens of other theaters, operas, symphonies and dance troupes grace the nightlife of Omaha. Likewise, the city has a number of clubs that feature live music, including several in the Old Market area.

At 1600 Abbott Drive in Freedom Park is the World War II minesweeper the *USS Hazard*. This is the largest ship to ever make it this far inland, and serves as a monument to veterans who have fought to keep America free. Built and commissioned in 1944, it was decommissioned in 1946 after service in the Pacific. The ship is virtually intact with most systems operational. It serves as a floating World War II museum.

Omaha boasts of over 7,000 acres of city parks, which include 13 neighborhood recreation centers. The Central Park Mall, an open space in the heart of the city center, features a lagoon and waterfalls. It is adjacent to the Heartland of America Park, a 30-acre greenway along the Missouri River near downtown.

At 33rd and Dodge is the Mutual of Omaha Dome, which houses artifacts from the television show "Wild Kingdom." It is covered by the largest glass dome of its kind.

The Henry Doorly Zoo is the largest zoo in the state and is one of the nation's finest zoos. It is a natural environment zoo, which means that the animals are allowed to walk around in open spaces, and are not held in small cages. The Rain Forest building covers over an acre of land and re-creates the habitat of the world's rain forests. The zoo also has the largest enclosed aviary in North America and many other interesting sites. It is located at Deer Park Boulevard and 10th Street. It is open seven days a week. A must-see sight.

If the River made Omaha, then livestock made it big and kept it going. You can visit the stockyards at 29th and N streets. Although the Market is much smaller than in its heyday, it still features the 11-story Exchange Building and many fine steak restaurants.

One of the most unique shopping areas anywhere can be found in the Old Market area centered on Howard Street from 10th to 13th in Downtown Omaha. Great bookstores, cafes, galleries and other shops are included in an antique area still used for various sewing and other factories.

Omaha is the site for the College World Series, which is held in late spring at Rosenblatt Stadium, 13th and Bert Murphey Drive. The stadium is also the home of the Omaha triple A baseball team, the Royals.

The University of Nebraska at Omaha includes the Medical Center. The main campus is at 60th and Dodge and the Medical Center at 42 and Emile. Creighton University was founded in 1878 and is located at 24th and Cass. Along with many fine programs, the school is also noted for its basketball teams.

In 1972, Chip Davis was writing commercial jingles in Omaha with partner Bill Fries. One series of commercials, for Old Home Bread, was based on a fictional character, C. W. McCall, and a waitress named Mavis. The songwriters turned these characters into a number one record in 1975 called "Convoy," about a truck driver using his C.B. radio to outwit the police.

Davis used the profits from the song to launch Mannheim Steamroller in 1975. The largely solo effort has produced a series of best-selling albums created from the computer and synthesizer in Davis' basement studio. Davis prints out the score and hires studio musicians to record the music.

The 1984 album *Mannheim Steamroller Christmas* became a gold record in the first year of its release. That was followed in 1988 with *A Fresh Aire Christmas*. These two releases were such huge hits in the Christmas music category that they have been credited with leading revitalized world interest and sales in Christmas music during the 1980s.

Some researchers believe Davis is the most successful musician/composer to come from Nebraska.

Many fine older homes still stand all around the city of Omaha. A drive through many neighborhoods will provide a rewarding view of some of the finest homes in the Midwest. In addition, the Chamber of Commerce will provide you with information about the location of the best of these homes.

Omaha's civic pride has resulted in one of the most beautiful downtown approaches of any city. Near the river, parks, pedestrian paths, city library and office buildings offer a breathtaking and open approach to the city's core.

The Mallory Kountz Planetarium is located on the University of Nebraska at Omaha Campus at 68th and Dodge Streets.

Eleven (3 miles.)
Junction with Interstate 680.

Three miles (6 miles.)
*East on this road **two miles,** then **north for four miles.***

On top of this hill is believed to be the site of the Fort Lisa trading post established by Manuel Lisa. Lisa went up the Missouri to the Yellowstone and established a trading post near the Big Horn in 1807.

In 1812, he established this trading post to service the Indians in the area, and became the representative of the U.S. government to the Indians.

Lisa was very important to the Indians and earliest whites over the entire Midwest. His wife lived at this spot for a number of years, and died here in 1819. She was quite possibly the first non-Indian woman to ever see this area.

Somewhere near here was also the trading post of the American Fur Company, established in 1825.

This place was visited by Prince Maximilian of Germany in 1833. He wrote: "We saw a crowd of Otoe and Omaha Indians. A small brook with steep banks flows down to the river from a pleasant little wide valley in which are the corn plantations."

*A **few miles north** of here was the campsite of S.H. Long, who was commissioned by the government to explore the Platte River and the mountains beyond. The name of Long's Peak in Colorado bears the imprint of this expedition.*

Long brought along biologists, painters and geologists on his expedition. To reach this point the troupe traveled in a steamboat up the Missouri. This first steamboat to reach Nebraska had its bow carved into the likeness of a dragon, and a short smokestack was placed in its mouth. As the steamboat moved up the river the dragon breathed fire and smoke. One can imagine the effect such a sight might have had on the local native population. One recorded reaction to Long's boat from an Omaha Indian was: "The White man is a bad man, he keeps the spirit of fire chained and forces the spirit to paddle his boats."

Long camped here during the winter of 1819-1820.

Six miles (3 miles.)

Fort Calhoun.

This high and dry town used to be located on the banks of the Missouri when it was incorporated in 1858. The town has long had an importance as a trade center for local farmers, and remains unique and independent, despite its proximity to Omaha.

The Washington County Historical Museum is located in the old Fort Calhoun State Bank. The displays include a gallery containing relics and artifacts dating from 22,000 years B.C. The museum has a fine collection of Indian work and artifacts from nearby Fort Atkinson (see below), as well as many items from the county's pioneer period. One of the best collections of barbed wire in the state is also on display. The museum is open from April to December Sundays, Wednesdays, Fridays and Saturdays.

One-half mile east of Fort Calhoun: Fort Atkinson.

Legend has it that the Fort was built on the location of Lewis and Clark's famous "council" with the Indians at Council Bluffs. Truth of the matter is that no one knows for sure, or knew for sure even when this fort was built, where that meeting took place. Ask any historian and you will be bound to get a heated discussion as to the precise location of Council Bluffs.

Fort Atkinson was established in 1819 as a result of some pretty tricky international arms deals. The Hudson's Bay Company gave guns to thousands of Indians in the territory surrounding this area. They hoped to have a good chance at controlling the Northwest fur trade.

The United States passed a law that said it was illegal for any non-U.S. citizen to travel in the wilderness without a passport. To enforce this law, and to keep the British, Canadians, French, and Spanish out of the territory, a series of forts was established. The first of these was Fort Atkinson, built near the site of Council Bluffs on the Missouri River.

The Fort had a brickyard, a kiln, a sawmill, a gristmill, rock quarries, a school and a library of over 500 books. In a sense, the 1,000 soldiers, Indians, trappers, hangers-on and traders who lived here composed Nebraska's first town.

The 6th Infantry troops, who were stationed here, engaged in

27

the first of the Indian Wars when they were led by commander Colonel Henry Leavenworth upriver to the fur trading company of William Ashley, which had been attacked in June 1823. Over a dozen fur traders had been killed by the Arikara in what is now northern South Dakota. Leavenworth and 220 soldiers from the Fort attacked an Arikara village in August, initiating what would become known as the Indian Wars.

In 1825, over 500 men were sent from the Fort up the Missouri River in order to secure treaties with the Indians. Treaties of questionable endurance were made with several tribes.

The only international treaty signed in Nebraska was done at the Fort when, in 1824, representatives of the Mexican government arrived here to sign a peace treaty with the Pawnee.

Many expeditions to the Southwest and Santa Fe started from the Fort before the Santa Fe Trail to the south became the established route.

Several names famous to the west passed through the Fort during its short history. Mountain men such as Jim Bridger, Hiram Scott, Hugh Glass, Jedediah Smith and Mike Fink all stayed here. Big Elk of the Omaha and Pitlasharoo of the Pawnee came here to speak with the white intruders.

The Fort lasted from 1820 until 1827, when the entire number of troops were moved to better serve the pioneers who already were starting to move west. The troops were stationed at Leavenworth, in Kansas Territory.

Soon after the soldiers left, the Indians burned the fort to the ground. Later, in 1855, the first settlers of Fort Calhoun used what remained for building materials for their new town. Time and the elements slowly converted the last remnants of the Fort to dust. It remained nothing but a field until the 1960s when local citizens worked together to have the site saved. The Game and Parks Commission agreed to pay for half of the land.

Things really picked up during the 1970s when a series of archeological excavations began to determine the outline of the fort, and to learn more about the people who occupied it.

Under the able direction of the Nebraska Historical Society, field crews searched in the dust and dirt under the hot Nebraska sun for some trace of the earlier occupation. Through their diligent work, and the work of others, much of the life of the fort has been reconstructed.

With considerable expense and volunteer work, the Game and Parks Commission has completed a massive project to reconstruct the fort. What you will see will be their efforts at rebuilding the fort exactly as it once looked, in precisely the same spot.

A Visitors' Center has two exhibition galleries displaying items from what was known as "the Elysian Fields of the 6th Infantry" — Old Fort Atkinson.

One of the newest and most interesting state parks run by the Game and Parks Commission, Fort Atkinson is a "must see" of the area.

Five miles west of Fort Calhoun: Allen Cemetery. In this cemetery the ruts of the old Fort Atkinson Trail, which led to the Platte River trails to the west, are visible.

Three miles (6 miles.)

The former town of DeSoto, once the county seat of Washington County and now nothing more than a memory. This town once had two newspapers, a hat factory and a sizable population.

Near here the Mormon encampment at Winter Quarters (later Florence, near Omaha, see above) raised corn in order to survive the Nebraska winters before moving on to Salt Lake City.

Six miles (6 miles.)

Blair.

Blair is the home of Dana College, northwest of downtown. The college began in 1884 as a seminary for the Danish Evangelical Lutheran Church. The Danish flavor of Dana and Blair is from the largely Danish pioneers who settled here in the 1870s.

Blair is also the location of the Tower of the Four Winds. This commemorative venture is located in Black Elk-Neihardt Park near the college campus. The tower is 45 feet tall, and was constructed to promote world peace, brotherhood (and we assume sisterhood) and understanding. The tower is made from native rock. A mosaic on the east face, constructed of nearly 50,000 pieces, is based on a figure a vision of the Oglala Sioux holy man Black Elk, as recorded by John Neihardt (see entry for US Highway 77 for more on these gentlemen). In a vision, Black Elk once saw a person standing in front of the tree of life with hands outstretched: the spirit of the universe, the holy one. This tower represents that vision.

East on US Highway 30 to DeSoto National Wildlife Refuge. Please see entry for that highway for information about this and other sites in the area along US 30.

29

An interesting side trip can be had by following State Highway 91 west from Blair:

West of Blair on State Highway 91, *four miles.* Orum.
The site of the only crossroads store still operating in the county. A one-room school is preserved here as a museum.

West of Blair *15 miles* on State Highway 91 are the remains of the small village of Fontanelle. This is the site of Nebraska's first college and was originally called Nebraska University. (It did not have a football team, however.) The college was later moved to Crete and became known as Doane College.

The Fontanelle Orchard is one of the oldest continuously operated apple orchards in the Midwest. The apple juice and other fruit delights available here all year around are something like finding a bit of Nirvana in Nebraska.

Fontanelle was a misspelling of Logan Fonenelle, who was the inerpreter for the Winnebago in the 1850s.

Fontanelle made an attempt to become the territorial capital. They lost.

The Fontanelle Store was built of concrete blocks in 1906 to replace an earlier structure that had burned to the ground. The main floor was the store, and the second floor was used as a meeting hall and theater.

The Fontanelle Cemetery, south of town, has graves from the 1850s.

Four miles west of Fontanelle is US Highway 77. Please see that entry for further information on sites in this area.

Six miles (4 miles.)

Take the county road to the west to Neils Miller Cabin-Museum. This log structure, the oldest in the county, was built in 1857.

Four miles (7 miles.)

Herman.

Named for a conductor on the Omaha and Northwestern Railroad, Herman is a German and Danish settlement. On June 13, 1899, Herman was struck by a tornado that demolished every single building in town except for the school and the church, which were at opposite ends of the town.

Seven miles (4 miles.)
Tekamah.

The poetic name probably comes from an Indian word meaning cottonwood, or large cottonwood, although no one has come up with the exact meaning of the word. The name was chosen after the town was incorporated in 1855 by drawing it out of a hat.

The earliest founders of Tekamah were Swedes and pioneers from Ohio. Ben Folsom, the very first non-native settler, built a cabin near here in 1853 and wrote in his diary that "the Missouri bottoms are the richest soil imaginable with a depth from six to fifteen feet." His enthusiasm brought others to the area, which caused friction between the native population and the newcomers. In 1856, two boys were killed by Indians at the nearby town of Fontanelle (now extinct). As a result, Tekamah citizens built a blockhouse in an attempt to provide a defense for the community.

On the tallest nearby hill, known as Reservoir Hill, are the burial grounds of the earliest settlers, the Omahas. The Omahas, and later the Winnebagos, lived here for centuries. Occasionally they were raided by bands of Sioux who attacked from the north and west.

In 1918 the Spanish flu killed many residents of the town. It got so bad that schools and churches were closed and authorities ordered that there be no public gatherings of any kind.

Tekamah is the county seat of Burt County. The Burt County Museum is located in a 14-room mansion and contains many fine exhibits. It is free and open several days a week.

East of Tekamah, two miles. This is the site of an Omaha Indian Village. This village near the river was attacked by hostile Yankton and Santee on December 12, 1846. The village suffered many casualties since many of the men were on a buffalo hunt. Eighty or more of the villagers were killed. The burial ground for these Indians is just west of Tekamah.

Near here were the towns of Lyons and Oakland, settled because of their location near wood and water.

North of here, three miles to Arizona, Nebraska. Retirement center of Burt County.

West of Tekamah on State Highway 32 eight miles to Craig, which for many years had a singing school where folks would come and sing.

For more information about sites west of Tekamah please see entry for US Highway 77.

US Highways 73 & 75

Four miles (7 miles.)

Five miles west to Prairieview, where telephone poles arrived in 1905.

Seven miles (5 miles.)

Golden Springs.

This historic springs is on the face of a sandstone bluff on the west side of the road. Traces of the old stagecoach trail can still be found nearby, as this was a popular stopping place for early-day travelers. Names were carved in the rock here, and Indians claimed that some of the faintest scratchings are those of the French and the Spanish who came 150 years before the American pioneers.

Five miles (8 miles.)

Decatur.

This is the second oldest town in the state. Decatur was founded in 1855 and was an important and strategic point on the Missouri River. In 1927 a bridge was to be built across the Missouri at Decatur. As these things go, the 20 years that ensued before it was built wasn't that long. However, shortly thereafter the river changed its course, leaving the bridge a dry-land bridge. Ten years after that, in 1955, the U.S. Corps of Engineers changed the course of the river, diverting it back into its old channel, and Decatur's bridge finally became a bridge across the Missouri.

Peter Sarpy, who took over the interests of the American Fur Company in 1823 at age 19, lived near here.

Decatur was also the home of "Indian Charlie," a native New Yorker who worked his way west as a railroad brakeman. He became an Indian trader, married two women, one of whom was a Winnebago, and collected a large number of Indian artifacts. These artifacts included clothing that he displayed by touring the area with a band of Indians. His collection is now housed at the Historical Society Museum in Lincoln.

Just north of Decatur is the southern boundary for the Omaha Indian Reservation. See below for more information about the Omahas.

Eight miles (2 miles.)

*Turn off to the **east** for Blackbird Hill State Park, **three miles**.*

The story is that this area was the burial of a famous, but disliked, Omaha chief, Blackbird. When he died he was tied onto his favorite horse. The horse was led to this bluff, and then killed. The people then piled rocks and stones and dirt around the bodies until a large hill was formed. On top of the mound they placed all of the scalps Blackbird had taken, and then buried them. This was in 1800.

When Lewis and Clark came up the Missouri in 1804, they mentioned this hill. In 1832 the painter George Catlin climbed up here from the river and found a human skull, believed to be that of Blackbird. The skull was given to the Smithsonian.

*Near here to the **west** are petroglyphs on the sandstone hills including signs of the Thunderbird and Elk Hunter.*

Blackbird Hill is the site of one of Nebraska's most famous, and perhaps oldest, ghost story.

In the earliest days of this territory, two men loved the same woman. The men were best friends. When the best man, the one whom the woman truly loved, was away hunting, some disaster happened. Members of his party came back and said that he had been killed, he had drowned in the river. After a while the girl married the other man.

Some years later the best man returned, having survived the drowning, and having wandered for months. The other man, the one married now to the girl, was insane with jealousy, and fearing that his wife might return to his friend's arms, he cut her throat and jumped from the top of Blackbird Hill with her in his arms. His bloodcurdling scream could be heard for miles. Her blood spilled on the grass as they crashed down the hillside.

For years afterwards, some say to this day, no grass would grow where her blood stained the earth.

For the past 200 years there have been reports from visitors to this area who hear the faint, yet distinct scream of a man whose voice seems to carry off and over the edge of this hill.

North *of here (ask directions from a park ranger) is Indian Cave, or Robbers' Cave. Today it is nothing more than an over-used indentation in the side of the sandstone cliff, but for years it served as a hideout for river hijackers who waited for boats coming up and down river. They would attack the boats, and steal furs or supplies.*

There is good evidence that Jesse and Frank James hid out in this cave after their ill-fated and bloody attempt to hold up the bank at Northfield, Minnesota.

This area is also the southern border of the once proposed Lewis and Clark National Park. (see description in the entry for US Highway 77 for details.)

Two miles (10 miles.)

Macy.

Macy is the main center for the Omaha Indian reservation, adjoining the Winnebagos.

Long before Columbus, the Omaha lived along the banks of the Ohio River. They migrated to the Mississippi, into Minnesota, the Black Hills, and finally, into the northeast corner of Nebraska, where they had been for at least 200 years before Lewis and Clark made contact with them in 1804.

The Omaha Indians have a custom similar to what Indians in the Pacific Northwest call the Potlatch. During the annual powwow the Omaha may give away most, and sometimes all, of his prized possessions. This is an indication of spiritual wealth and strength.

The story is told of an Omaha man, Amos Two Trees, who was married to a beautiful woman, Morning Star.

Once, while Amos Two Trees was away on a hunt, a white trapper took Morning Star away. For a long while Morning Star lived with the trapper, although Amos Two Tree's heart was broken. Then, after a long while, Morning Star, torn with grief for her actions, drowned herself in the Missouri River near here.

Amos Two Trees, so distraught that his wife had killed herself, forced the trapper into the river where he, too, drowned. For the next 75 years, they say, there was no peace between the Omaha and the whites.

One of the Omahas' great leaders lived east of here on the banks of the river. Son of an Omaha leader, Big Elk, a man by the name of Iron Eyes had his home on the sandstone cliffs above the river. He eventually became the leader of the Omahas and during his term he instituted an Indian police force to serve the tribe, rather than use the BIA agents.

In addition, he wrote a monumental history of the Omaha tribe and did studies on their language, customs and rituals. His sons and daughters became some of Nebraska's leading doctors and lawyers.

One Omaha Indian in the late 1960s created quite a stir in Lincoln when he carefully plotted out a series of five foot archeological squares over several graves in the city's Wyuka cemetery. He was ready with note pad, trowel and shovel when the police took him in for questioning. His point was a good one: "If you can dig up the bones of my grandfathers, there should be no reason I cannot do the same to yours."

In 1991, there was a retribution of sorts when the bones from 106 skeletons were returned to the tribe from the University of

Nebraska where they had been stored for nearly 60 years. The remains had been removed from various Reservation burial sites and had been stored in boxes at the University. The decision to return to remains to the Omahas had been made two years earlier, but the tribe had granted anthropologists a two-year grace period to study the bones.

During their study the scientists documented lead poisoning in every one of 40 samples that were tested. Speculation about the source of such contamination, which was most probably lethal, is that the lead came from lead-based paints applied to the body, or from lead-lined cooking utensils.

Although the scientists determined most of these Omahas had a good diet, many of them died quite young. Included in the burial was an Anglo woman, a non-Omaha shaman who had been shot in the head, and other mysteries from the past.

The remains were placed in a 22-foot-long, narrow wooden coffin and buried on a bluff three miles north of Macy not far from the site of sacred fires just to the north. It was a stormy, bleak October morning, but 106 Omaha Indians were coming back home.

Two years earlier the Peabody museum in Boston returned more than 150 artifacts it had held for over 100 years. The most significant of these was a nearly 400-year-old sacred pole. The pole, which is said to have the power of life and unity for the Omahas, is 5 feet 4 inches long, wrapped in animal skin webbing, adorned with crane feathers and topped with a human scalp. Sacred ceremonies were held to bless the artifacts on their return to the tribe.

In 1991, the U.S. Supreme Court let stand a lower court's decision to throw out the Omahas' claim to over 8,000 acres of land across the Missouri River in Iowa. The Omahas claimed that the river had changed course from 1867 when the boundary of the reservation had been set, and so they filed the suit to regain the land.

Macy is the site of the annual Omaha powwow. The event, which has been held since 1804, is a chance for friends and family to get together and for the tribe to reaffirm its unity. There is not much of a formal structure to the event although there is much dancing and dance competitions as well as the giveaway ceremonies. The event, for the nearly 1,700 Omahas who live on the reservation and the additional thousand who do not, is held in August.

Ten miles (0 miles.)
    Junction of US Highways 73 and 77.

US Highways 73 & 75

You have entered the Winnebago Indian Reservation. The Winnebagos, transplanted here from their ancestral home in Wisconsin, are good friends with their neighbors the Omahas.

This is from the 1928 book *Winnebago Tales:*

Almost every Indian family lived in a lodge of the old-time oval shape made with a framework of slender poles stuck in the ground in a circle, their tops bent over the center and bound together with strong strings or cords made from the fibers of the basswood bark. This frame was strengthened by other poles placed around the sides horizontally, in as many rows as the builders saw fit to use. These poles were then covered with elm bark or mattings made of rushes which overlapped until the lodge roof was rain-proof. At the top a place about two feet square was always left open for the smoke hole. Some of the lodges were made in oblong shape with two or more fireplaces within, and even now the Indians speak of old-time lodges with as many as ten fireplaces, for Indian families were large in those days.

One half mile south of the junction of US 73 and 77, turn east on county road and travel 3 miles to a large depression, lined with trees and bushes.
This is Big Bear Hollow, named after Nebraska's version of Bigfoot, Sasquash, or the Abominable Snowman. According to legend, a large creature, half man and half bear, once lived near here. This depression, five miles in diameter, was his home. It is said that he would come into nearby villages and take off children and young girls. One time he took a young girl. The girl's boyfriend trained two bears to scour Big Bear Hollow. The Big Bear/Man ran out of a covering of brambles and the Indian killed him. Who knows, perhaps that story represents the only known killing of a Bigfoot...

The annual Winnebago powwow is held near the intersection of 77 and 73. For more information on the powwow and the Winnebago Tribe please see entry for US Highway 77.

For a continuation of sites to the north, please see the entry for US Highway 77.

36

Zero miles (13 miles.)
 Kansas border.

Thirteen miles (3 miles.)
 Pawnee City.
 Home of the Pawnee County Historical Society museum, which includes 15 buildings. The home of Nebraska's first governor is one of the buildings. Who was he? Answer at the end of the paragraph! Other buildings include Pawnee County's first school building. A barbed wire collection of considerable fame resides in the museum's collection, as do displays on early farm equipment and turn-of-the-century store goods.
 Give up? Nebraska's first governor was David Butler.
 During the severe Halloween blizzard of 1991 countless trees everywhere in the area were knocked down as were powerlines. There were so many trees in the streets that, rather then pick them up, crews simply shoved them to the sides of the road to wait for better weather. The entire county was without power and nearly every road was closed.

Three miles (15 miles.)
 Junction with State Highway 65.
 East three miles to Table Rock and the Table Rock Museum. Seven buildings make up this museum, including the 1893 Opera House, which is filled to the gills with antiques and items from yesteryear.

Fifteen miles (1 mile)
 Cross the Nemaha River, which joins the Missouri near the extreme southeastern corner of the state.

One mile (20 miles)

State Highway 50

Junction with US Highway 136. Please see the entry for this highway for information about sites along its route.

Twenty miles (7 miles.)

Syracuse. For more information about sites in this area, please see the entry for State Highway 2.

The Nebraska City Cutoff of the Oregon Trail crosses State Highway 50 at the southern edge of Syracuse.

Seven miles (3 miles.)

State Highway 50 crosses the Oxbow Trail, which connected the Missouri River at Nebraska City with the Oregon Trail, through the area near Columbus, Nebraska.

Three miles (4 miles.)

Junction with US Highway 34. For information about the sites in this area, please see the entry for US Highway 34.

Four miles (8 miles.)

Junction with S-13K. Two miles east: Weeping Water.

Somehow this quiet town with the poetic name could typify all that is beautiful and quaint about the eastern half of the state. It is located on the creek the French called L'Eau qui Pleure—The Water That Weeps—which is a translation of the Otoe name for the creek Ni-gahoe, or water that runs over a small falls. This name was confused by the French for another Otoe word that meant water that weeps.

The ground under your feet in Weeping Water, as well as a great part of the surrounding area, holds the purest limestone in the state. As early as the 1880s this stone was quarried for construction, as a feed lot supplement and for its use in paints. All around the city remnants of past quarries and the wounds of current ones can be found.

The Heritage House Complex houses the Weeping Water Valley Historical Society and museum.

The complex includes the museum with a large number of displays explaining the history of the area. Included are displays about people native to the area such as author Bess Streeter Aldrich. Special care is taken so that the displays tell a story rather than simply be a collection of objects. The museum's hours change with the seasons.

Also part of the complex is the Heritage House. The house is the oldest Congregational parsonage in the state, one of the oldest

38

dwellings in the state, and made from local limestone The original construction did not allow for a chimney. The smoke from stoves was directed into the space between the inner and outer walls, where it drifted up and out of the house.

The third building is the office of Dr. J. C. Fate, who practiced homeopathic medicine here until his death in 1929.

The final building in the complex is the City Library. The building has been called one of the most important structural and historical buildings in the state. It is an example of Early Gothic Revival architecture, and served as a Congregational Church meeting house, an academy and finally the city library.

Weeping Water is proud of its native daughters and sons. Among those from here are such folks as Ian Campbell, a reverend whose life has taken him to Turkey and India, and who was known for his love of coins. He was — and yes, there was such a position — the Curator of Coins at the Nebraska State Museum in Lincoln.

Glenn Kirchhoff made a late-life career change from farmer to artist when he turned his arc welder on old farm equipment and turned it into coyotes, eagles and gamecocks. His works began to win awards and the attention of the local press.

Marvin Kivett, a native of Weeping Water, is one of the best anthropologists and archeologists there has been. Kivett, who for years served as the Director of the Nebraska Historical Society, could walk over a field that had been searched by archeologists for a month, sniff the air, glance at the earth and point. "Dig here," he would say, and although others mumbled under their breath, shovels would fly. In a moment an entire earth lodge from a thousand years ago would slowly be exposed.

However, there was perhaps no other Weeping Waterite like Dr. Lloyd Kunkel. Earthy, gnarled, profane and profound, this gentleman's career included everything from being shot in the head by a bullet fired by Pancho Villa, to surviving a flu epidemic onboard a slow freighter carrying troops to fight in the First World War; from playing in silent moviehouse bands, to making some of the finest violins and cellos in the nation; from discovering and unearthing many of the pre-Columbian Indian dwellings of eastern Nebraska, to practicing medicine for 50 years. The noted archeologist died in 1989 at the age of 91.

The Weeping Water Heritage House Museum Complex would not be what it is today without the support and the contribution of Doc Kunkel.

State Highway 50

Eight miles (1 mile.)

Louisville.

Schramm Park Recreation Area and Ak Sar Ben Aquarium. Please see entry for US Highway 73 and 75 for more information on this fine attraction.

Please see the entry for US Highways 73 and 75 for additional information about sites in and around Louisville.

One half mile north west of Louisville is the Louisville Lakes Recreation Area. The area features modern and primitive camping sites and swimming.

One mile south and two miles west of Louisville to Platte River State Park. The park is excellent for campers, and a buffalo stew cookout can be had for a moderate price.

One miles (5 miles.)

The Platte River. The river here is sluggish and wide as it approaches its confluence with the Missouri, 15 miles east of here, after its 700-mile journey from the peaks of the Rocky Mountains.

There is growing evidence that this area was visited by Francisco Coronado in 1541. Certainly it was traversed by French fur trappers as early as1700, far earlier than any easterner (or south-westerner, for that matter) would want to believe possible of the great American desert.

Five miles (5 miles.)

Turnoff for Springfield and Richland.

One mile west of Richfield is the location of the once thriving town of Sarpy Center, one-time contender for the county seat, and thought to be the best rival to topple Bellevue as the jewel of the state.

Among the oldest fossil flowers and plants have been discovered in clay deposits near Springfield.

Five miles (1 mile.)

Junction with State Road 370, east to Papillion. Please see entry for Interstate 80 for information about this area.

One mile (0 miles.)

Junction with Interstate 80.

Zero miles (3 miles.)
  Kansas border.

Three miles (6 miles.)
  Junction with State Highway 8.

  East on Highway 8 **three miles**, **then one mile north** to Big Indian Recreation Area. The facility has boating, fishing, and picnicking.

  East on Highway 8 **less than one mile** past recreation site turnoff:

  Barneston. This town is at the location of one of the largest Otoe villages. The village stood here in the 1800s. There was once an agency here, as well as a trading post. Later this was the center of the Otoe Reservation. The reservation existed from 1854 until the end of the century, when it became apparent to most of the white leaders that

41

the Otoes would be much happier in Oklahoma.

The town was founded by a fur trader who was married to an Otoe woman.

Five miles east *of Barneston on Highway 8,* ***then north 3 miles*** *on county road to Liberty. On Cub Creek: site of early trading post around 1855. Most of the early town founders were sympathizers with the Confederacy during and after the Civil War. There is some evidence that the Jesse and Frank James gang spent time here among friends.*

The original post office was one half mile west of the present town site. The mail ran two times a week. Liberty was quite a boom town, as it was located on one of Burlington Northern's main Chicago/ Denver routes. Today it is hard to imagine that this sleepy burg was once one of the largest and busiest towns in southeast Nebraska.

Along the route of the Burlington tracks near Liberty the work crews unearthed the skeleton of a mastodon. It was 18 feet in length and over ten feet tall.

To the west on Highway 8 is Route 112 and Odell. For information about these sites, please see below.

Six miles (1 mile.)
Wymore.

Wymore started out because a man named Wymore offered part of his farm to the railroad to use as a connecting site between two railroads. The town once had a street car line, two railroad stations and one of the largest hotels in the area. Near the firehouse is a small stone building that was once the beer cooler for the old hotel. On May 26, 1900, a total of 63 trains stopped in Wymore.

Wymore is the home of Nebraska's only gold rush. A man drilling for water south of town in 1907 brought up some gravel from the shaft and there, sparkling amid the black sand, was the yellow glimmer of gold. Soon, glory-dreams of nuggets the size of a man's fist danced about a lot of heads. For the next 20 years men tried to dig deep into the earth, and several mines were started, but with no results. Finally the last of the dreamers loaded up their shovels and pickaxes and drifted off into the distance, headed for another dream-stake.

Arbor State Park near Wymore is a fine place to play baseball.

The third weekend in June, Wymore is the location of the "Little Britches Rodeo," which draws young rodeo competitors from across the nation. The town's annual Sam Wymore Days are held during the rodeo, as well.

*West of Highway 77 at Wymore **two miles, and then** 1 1/2 **miles south,** is the Lester Shalla rock house, one of the oldest structures, if not the oldest structure, in the state. It was built in 1829. It has been used as a home, a church and a school.*

Along Highway 77 is pleasant McCandless Park, your last chance to stop and rest in beautiful Nebraska if you are speeding back toward Kansas.

One mile (4 miles.)
Blue Springs. The town is located on the original trail from Marysville, Kansas, through Otoe Country to Beatrice. The Otoes once had a village at this site.
*   **One mile west** of Blue Springs is a log cabin that is over 100 years old. It is now located in the city park where it had been moved from its original location just north of here.*

Four miles (4 miles.)
Highway 77 turns sharply from the east to the north here, but those who know go south on State Highway 112 if they are going anyplace west of Kansas City, for here is one of the most widely used shortcuts in the state. Several miles can be saved by knowing just how to get from here to the Kansas border. It has happened that people get lost going this way, but people around here are friendly and are used to being asked how to get to Kansas.

*   **Six miles south** on Highway 112 is Kriter Hill, one of the tallest spots for miles. This is a spot known, for as long as there have been human beings in the area, for the beauty of the view. During the 1930s, the WPA straightened the road to the top and moved Indian Creek farther to the west to prevent flooding. The construction project was carried out with horse-drawn wagons.*
*   **One mile east** of the hill, in a pasture along the creek, the bank is still dug out where the area's best-known brick kiln once stood. The "Kriter Kiln" bricks can still be found in many of the older brick buildings in the county.*

*   After **seven miles** south along State Highway 112, the road makes a junction with State Highway 8.*
*   **Turn west on Highway 8. Three miles** to Odell. Another town created by the railroad. There is a nice and quiet city park here,*

a good place to stretch the legs and listen to the landscape of Nebraska.

The Old Odell Bank, built in 1885, is a fine example of a common early Nebraska building trait: using local limestone for local building projects. This limestone came from a quarry a few miles outside of Odell. The bank is two blocks north of the railroad tracks on the west side of the street.

Across the street from the Old Odell Bank was the Apres Bag Factory. They made canvas bags here. At one time the factory produced 250 different designs of bags in six different colors.

The short cut into Kansas goes south out of Odell on a paved but bumpy road. On this route is the village of Lanham, which started as a trade center for area farmers. Lanham is half in Nebraska and half in Kansas. Main Street is the state line.

Three and a half miles to the west *of Odell, on Highway 8, on the south side of the dam on the State Game Preserve, is the place where, with a bit of walking and some luck, you can still find some of the strange and famous "Odell Diamonds," a pink or clear stone usually with four flat sides. Unfortunately, the best site for these stones was covered with water when the dam was built, but many can still be found.*

For a continuation of this route, and of sites nearby including sections of the still-visible Oregon Trail, please see the entry for State Highway 15.

Four miles (2 miles.)

Turn off for Homesville on Homesville Road.

Take this road for **two miles, then turn north** *on the gravel road and follow the road to Iron Mountain. Keep in mind that some pioneers hadn't seen the Rockies yet and called a number of items "mountains." Still, this mountain makes an invigorating hike and the view, especially at dawn, is well worth it.*

Return to Homesville Road and continue East for five miles: *Homesville, on Cedar Creek and the Blue River. This was an alternative route for the Oregon Trail. The area was settled by several families from England.*

The limestone quarries these families started became well known during the years when so many buildings were being con-structed of the rocks of the earth. The first state capitol building in Lincoln was made of rocks from here, as were hundreds of other buildings all over the nation.

During the Great Depression, the WPA employed hundreds

of workers here to lift out the rock. The town grew to become one of the largest in the area. But the demand for the fine stone gave way to steel and concrete and plastic, and the importance of the railroad faded, so that now a glance at this once thriving town would convince you it couldn't have happened here.

Two miles (8 miles.)
Beatrice. Junction with US Highway 136. Please see entry for US Highway 136 for information about Beatrice.

Eight miles (7 miles.)
Pickrell. When the Zion Lutheran Church was built in 1917 it was said to be the largest church in open country west of the Mississippi. That's pretty easy to believe, since the bell towers can be seen for quite a distance. Some classic church art is represented at the church, including a large oil canvas, "Christ Knocking at the Door," and fine stained-glass windows.

Try to get a hold of a copy of the interesting and entertaining book that tells the church's history. The book is for sale at the church for $2.00. Pickrell was the site of an early lumber mill, and its existence is what attracted the people to start the town.

Seven miles (3 miles.)
Eleven miles east of here on State Highway 41 is the town of Adams. Near here was the first land cultivated by the whites in the area. Do you even have to ask? What else? Corn.

West on State Highway 41 is Wilber, home of the Czech festival, and DeWitt, home of the Vise-Grip. For information about each of these locations, please see entry for State Highway 15.

Three miles (2 miles.)
Cortland.

This town dates from 1884, and was first a railroad stopping place and location of a general store that attracted much local business. The creek to the west of here, Soak Creek, was given its name when a pioneer fell off his wagon and into the water. His friends named the creek, since what the pioneer called it was not really an appropriate name for anything.

Two miles (3 miles.)
Turn off to the west for Hallam.

A Lincoln businessman, Herbert Gold, tried to have Hallam

become the site of the first nuclear power plant in the country. In a close vote by the Atomic Energy Commission, a site in Pennsylvania was selected to be first. Eventually a sodium-graphite reactor was built. It operated for a single full year before "problems" forced the nuclear plant to be permanently shut down. It was converted to a conventional coal burning plant.

East for five miles to Firth. Two and a half miles south of Firth is Prairieland Park, a covered, open-air auditorium where cultural events are held during the fine-season months.

Three miles (3 miles.)

Princeton. This tiny collection of houses has had a blacksmith for as long as there has been a town here.

Three miles (2 miles.)

*Turn off to the **east** for Hickman, **four miles**. Hickman for years was the traditional campsite for a large band of Gypsies who passed through the area from time to time.*

In 1967, one of the worst tornadoes ever to hit the area tore through Hickman on June 9th, spreading destruction for miles.

***East** of Hickman **three miles** to Wagon Train Lake, a fine recreation area.*

***Three miles south** to Stagecoach Lake Recreation Area. **East** of Stagecoach Lake, **three miles** to the tiny town of Holland, where the store dates from 1900.*

These two lakes are a part of the extensive Salt Valley Lakes project created as a flood control project starting in 1958. A dozen other lakes are in the system. All permit primitive camping, while some are more developed. Waterskiing, fishing and other activities are available at many of the lakes. The State Games and Parks Commission publishes a pamphlet on the lakes.

***East** from Holland, **five miles** to Panama. Just northwest of Panama was a longtime encampment of the Otoe Indians.*

*Turn off to the **west** to Sprague, **two miles**, and Martell, **three miles**.*

***West two miles** from these villages is Bluestem Lake, another in the Salt Valley Lakes system. These lakes are open to the public for general recreation facilities.*

For years, a bench in front of the store in Martell was famous as the meeting place of every good storyteller in the county.

Seven miles southwest of Sprague was a traditional camping area for the Pawnee Indians.

The rest stop here includes a small patch of native prairie that has been preserved.

Two miles (2 miles.)
Turnoff to Roca, which had a limestone quarry used extensively to build many of the buildings in Lincoln.
The Roca area boasts berry farms where the visitor may pick strawberries and other produce.

Two miles (10 miles.)
Near here were the villages of Saltillo (**east, one mile**) and Centerville **(west, one half mile.)**
Saltillo was once a thriving town that featured two saloons, a hotel, school and a grain elevator. Saltillo had the first post office in Lancaster County. It was established in 1854. Stone foundations from the now ghostly town can be found in Lincoln's Wilderness Park near the intersection of S, 27th and Saltillo Road. The name of the town is from the Spanish and means "little leap."

The highway from here north generally follows the same route as a well-used Indian trail. The Nebraska City Cutoff crossed here, near Saltillo Road, headed east and west. There was a pony mail station about **one mile east** of here in the 1860s.

Ten miles (12 miles.)
Downtown Lincoln. For more information about the Star City, please see entry for US Highway 34.

Twelve miles (1 mile.)
Road to Jack Sinn Memorial Wildlife Management Area on the Lancaster and Saunders County line. Five hundred acres of wetlands and grasslands for the nature lover in us all.
West here eight miles to Wildwood Lake, one of the least visited of the numerous Salt Valley Lakes. Non-motorized boats only on this pretty little lake.

One mile (6 miles.)
Ceresco. Ceresco was named after the goddess of corn. It has nearly become a bedroom community for Lincoln, but is still aptly

named.

Four miles northeast of here, two twin rocks marked the Oxbow Trail. One of those rocks was destroyed and the other can be seen at the Saunders County Museum in Wahoo. (See below.)

Four miles (1 mile.)

Pioneer State Recreation Area. Primitive camping and picnic shelter near the Oxbow Trail.

One mile (4 miles.)

Junction with State Highway 63 to Ithaca and Ashland. (See entry for US Highway 6 for information about a famous UFO sighting at Ashland, and other items of interest in this area.)

Just south of this junction, on US 77 the Oxbow Trail crosses the highway. This trail ran from Nebraska City north to the Platte, and then west along the river to join up with the Oregon Trail. The route of the Trail is visible to the trained eye, although recent farm work has buried some of the traces. On the east side of the highway it comes up through a small draw of trees. On the west side of the highway the route up and over a hill is defined by the eroded rut marks of the wagons that passed here more than a century ago.

The route of the Oxbow Trail zig-zags across Saunders County, entering in the southeastern corner and leaving the county approximately where State 92 crosses into Butler County.

Five miles east on State Highway 63 to Ithaca. Indian Mound, just northeast of here, was a burial ground for Pawnee and Otoe Indians.

Four miles (2 miles.)

Wahoo.

Junction of State Highway 92, west. Please see entry for that highway for sites west of Wahoo.

Wahoo has many attractions for the visitor, despite its small size.

The Hanson house is an excellent example of classic Queen Anne style architecture. It was built in the mid-1880s, and Howard Hanson was born in the house in 1896. Tours of the house are held Sunday afternoons, or by appointment through the Women's Club of Wahoo.

The Saunders County Historical Society Complex includes the Wahoo Chicago, Burlington and Quincy Depot. It is maintained to look as it might have looked in the 1920s when railroading was nearing its peak. The depot serve a critical role in the area as it was the focus of transportation from its construction in 1886 until the mid-20th century.

The county courthouse was built on top of an Indian burial ground, and as the building was being built workers continually found pottery, bones and other artifacts. The Otoe also frequently camped here and many believe that the combination of the burial ground and the camping area makes Wahoo a particularly holy and spiritual place even to this day.

Many buildings in the town center date from the earliest days of Wahoo's pioneer history.

Saunders County Historical Museum is in Wahoo. The active and knowledgeable staff of the museum has preserved the history of the area. This includes the Ox-Bow Rock. The six-foot by six-foot quartzite boulder was once a landmark on the Ox-Bow Trail, which crossed Saunders County. The trail was used by pioneers on their way west. The rock was one of two that stood near the trail four miles northeast of Ceresco. The other rock was broken up by a farmer, but this one, rescued by a local citizen in 1992 from an Omaha landscaper who was about to use it to make Omaha prettier, now serves as a landmark for this fine museum. The museum is on the southern end of town.

Wahoo was the home of a handful of famous Nebraskans. The best known was Darryl Zanuck, who was one of Hollywood's most famous directors.

Baseball legend "Wahoo Sam" Crawford hailed from these parts. Diamond lovers can read his story and the stories of other Nebraska Hall-of-Famers in Jerry Clark's fine and loving book, *Nebraska Diamonds, A Brief History of Baseball Major Leaguers From the Cornhusker State.*

During the blizzard of Halloween 1991, visibility in the town was zero and the entire community simply shut down.

There are as many stories to explain the origin of the name of the Saunders County seat as there are citizens in this town on the banks of Wahoo Creek. Common explanations include the story that wahoo was the Otoe name of a berry bush that grew along the creek; another is that it was named after a tree with medicinal properties that was found here in pioneer days.

Other explanations for the name include that Wahoo was the name of an Otoe medicine man, that it was the mispronunciation of an Otoe word meaning "without hills," and that it is a word meaning "elm trees."

However, local inhabitants and others not from Wahoo claim that the name was an Indian joke. When the Indians, seeing that the whites were taking their land and building a town on their old burial grounds, suggested the name wahoo, which, instead of any of the above, meant something along the lines of "take it and place it where the great sun spirit will never shine."

In any event, the name...er...ah...stuck.

Two miles (5 miles.)

Junction with State Highway 109 to Cedar Bluffs. See below.

Five miles (5 miles.)

Junction with State Highway 92 east. Please see that entry for sites along this route.

Five miles (6 miles.)

Junction with State Highway 64.

Go five miles east on State 64 to Leshara. Unlike most towns in the state, Leshara was founded in this century. It was named after a Pawnee Chief, Pita Lesharu, who lived in the area with his band of Pawnee over a century before.

Just to the northwest of the village is the site of an old Indian village, probably belonging to the same band of Pawnee who lived in a large village a few miles north of here (see below).

Six miles (1 mile.)

Just south of the bridge across the Platte are markers commemorating the Pawnee villages that were located on the south Platte River Bluffs at Woodcliff.

Near here is the so-called McClean site, the location of a Skidi Pawnee village of about 80 earth lodges that was surrounded by a sod wall for fortification. The village was occupied between 1847 and 1859. It probably supported a peak population of about 250 people. It is the only Skidi village found on the Platte River and was located more than 50 miles east of the traditional lands of this band of Pawnee, who lived on the Loup River.

Just east of this point is the Pawnee Council site. In 1855, Gen. John Thayer held a council with the Pawnee chief Pita Lesharu in order to determine if the Pawnee had been responsible for stealing some cattle. The chief said that his people were not at fault, and said he personally suspected the Poncas. This was the first peace council between the white settlers and the Pawnee in the state.

Just north of here a high hill, or pahuk, as the Pawnee called it, overlooks the Platte. The hill was the holiest of five such sacred places in the area. This hill was the place where the Nahuracs lived. They were supernatural animals who helped the Pawnee and were the source of the power and knowledge of the medicine men.

This hill was considered a sacred place by the Indians, and was the locale for many of their religious stories.

Once a Nahurac bird was flying out over the Platte when he saw a horrible thing. A Pawnee man and his son were hunting, and the father killed the son with an arrow. The bird returned to this hill to ask the other Nahurac animals what to do.

A coyote said, "Do not ask us. Go to another holy place and ask there what we should do. We will do what those animals tell us."

The bird went to another sacred place, but the animals there asked him to visit yet another holy place and ask there.

The bird visited each of the five holy places, and the animals at each one told him to go to the next. Finally he returned to this pahuk and told Coyote what had happened.

Coyote waved his hand in the air. "Then you decide what to do with the boy."

The bird brought the dead Pawnee boy to this hill and the animals healed him and brought him back to life. The boy stayed with the magical animals and they taught him their secrets. When he returned to the Pawnee, the boy taught his people what he had learned. It is from this boy that the Pawnee got much of their power and wisdom.

The word for hill, pahuk, was translated into English and deformed to *pohocco,* which is the name of several local features in the area.

Take State Highway 109 west to Cedar Bluffs, so named because of the bluffs covered with cedar in the area.

Two and a half miles north of Cedar Bluffs on a county road to the site of the town of Neapolis.

In January 1858 the territorial legislature decided to move the territorial capital out of Omaha and to a place "not less than 50 miles west of the Missouri and not more than 6 miles from the Platte River." It was quite a hot topic as to what town would become the capital. Instead of selecting an already existing town, the legislature created a new town on paper and called it Neapolis. Several legislators came to the site and began to discuss the location of various buildings. The tall hill here was selected as the site for the territorial capitol building and was named Capitol Hill.

The early legislature, unlike today's governing body, quarreled and quibbled over mundane and silly issues. One such issue was the location of the capital. There were essentially two sides to this argument, those who wanted the capital to be north of the Platte River (North Platters) and those who wanted it south of the Platte (South Platters).

Although the South Platters outnumbered the North Platters, the session at which Neapolis was created was deemed illegal during the following year and Neapolis never materialized.

One mile (4 miles.)

Fremont.

Junction of US Highway 30. Please see that entry for information about sites along its route.

The surrounding hills and the Elkhorn and Platte Valleys make Fremont one of the more beautiful settings for eastern Nebraska towns. Fremont was a natural stopping point for a journey from Omaha to Kearney, and because of this the town prospered in the early days of immigrant trails and military roads that passed through here.

Early maps of the city were irregular because a wet rope was used to measure different lots and inaccuracies resulted.

At one point the Pawnee tried to scare the early settlers out of the area, but a show of force, aided by troops from Omaha, quieted the Pawnee.

Fremont was named for one of the most famous early explorers, John C. Fremont, who had the wanderlust and explored a great deal of the American West.

The Louis May Museum is located in the former residence of the city's first mayor. The home was built in the 1870s. Herein are the collections of the Dodge County Historical Society.

Downtown, the Fremont Opera House, the *Love-Larson*, built in 1888, was one of the finest in its day. The City of Fremont Performing Arts Center occupies the historic and beautiful building now.

The Oregon Trail marker at the corner of Military and D streets marks the Overland Route, which was also known as the Oxbow Trail, through Fremont to Oregon. In Barnard Park a marker commemorates the Mormon Trail, which passed this way from 1847 through the

1870s. This park was once known as "Dead Man's Park" because it was the site of the pioneer cemetery. Many of the graves were unmarked and consequently many of them remain in the park. Legends persist about the pioneer woman, wearing a large old-fashioned bonnet, who can be seen near the edge of the park on many cool, lonely nights. This apparition has been sighted by generations of Fremont citizens. The park is located at Military and Clarkson streets.

There is nothing in the entire state of Nebraska quite like the Fremont and Elkhorn Valley Railroad. The railroad was started as a scenic tourist oriented venture, and began operation in 1986. The 17-mile run from Fremont to Hooper (there are plans to expand the line for a much greater distance) is made by a 1942 Baldwin steam locomotive. The trip includes a short stopover in Hooper, which allows for a tour of the Hooper historical district (see below). On the return voyage, the train passes through Nickerson, up out of the Elkhorn drainage and into the Platte River Valley. This is a great way to tour this stretch of Nebraska. The train departs from the Old C. N. & W. depot at 1st and D Streets.

On the northern edge of Fremont is Rawhide Creek. Legend has it that a member of a pioneer wagon train through here was boasting to everyone how he was going to kill the first Indian he saw. One morning as they crossed this creek he spied an Indian and shot and killed him. The dead fellow's friends soon surrounded the wagon train and were about to attack. A truce was initiated and a discussion followed. The Indians agreed they would spare the pioneers if they handed over the man who had killed their friend. The pioneers agreed. The Indians tied the man to a tree near here and skinned him alive. Hence, Rawhide Creek.

Fremont is the location of the well-known summer relaxation and girl/boy watching spot: Fremont Lakes. For a description of this and other areas, also see the entry for US Highway 30.

Four miles (3 miles.)

Trail marker for the Major Long expedition to the Rockies. Long and his party of scientists followed an east-west Indian trail through here in the early summer of 1820.

Three miles (2 1/2 miles.)

Junction with State Highway 91. One mile east on 91 is Nickerson, which was named after its founder, a man who helped to build the railroad that passed through here.

53

US Highway 77

Two and one half miles (2 miles.)
   Two miles west of here, on Maple Creek, was the Jalapa Post Office. It was along the creek that soldiers volunteering for the so-called Pawnee War of 1859 assembled.

Two miles (1/2 mile.)
   Junction US Highway 275. Please see the entry for this highway for information about sites along its route.

One half mile (9 miles.)
   Winslow.
   One half mile north and one mile west of Winslow is the site of Logan Mills on Logan Creek. The mill was first established in 1859.

Nine miles (5 miles.)
   Uehling, founded in 1905. Near here, just on the northeast edge of the village, is a rare octagonal-shaped barn.

Five miles (1 mile.)
   Junction with State Highway 32. To the east are Craig and Tekamah. Please see entry for US Highway 73 for information. To the west is West Point. Please see entry for US Highway 275 for information.

One mile (7 miles.)
   Oakland.
   Oakland holds one of the largest Swedish festivals in the nation in early summer. It is a three-day affair and has all of the food, dancing and customs you could ever want. This town is the Swedish center of northern Nebraska, and many items from Sweden can be found in the stores.

Seven miles (5 miles.)
   Lyons. There is a pleasant campground just west of Lyons.

Five miles (10 miles.)
   Junction with State Highway 51. To the east is Decatur. Please see entry for US Highway 73 for information about Decatur.

   West on State 51 five miles.

Bancroft.

Bancroft is the Nebraska home of the late poet John G. Neihardt. Neihardt is best remembered, nationally, for Black Elk Speaks, *his report of the life and deeds and words of a Sioux holy man. Neihardt's work, however, goes far beyond this one book. Many consider his masterpiece to be* The Cycle of the West, *an epic poem about the settling of the American West.*

He was a prolific writer. In the early years of this century, he and a couple of friends took a long and leisurely boat trip down the Missouri River. While they talked philosophy and recounted stories of the then fairly recent Indian wars, Neihardt scribbled into a notebook. His articles were published in a sporting magazine and later published as the book The River and I. *This book, although hard to find, is still in print and is one of the great classic river books of modern times. He wrote many other books as well, and many of them are still read and reread by thousands every day.*

I had the pleasure to have an acquaintance with Neihardt. Often he would stay with friends in Lincoln, and there, on a number of occasions, I visited him.

Neihardt was a short man, with a great head of white hair, and eyebrows that arched above clear, cool eyes. There was little small talk with Neihardt. If conversation lagged, this man, who had written his first book on the text of an ancient and mystical religious book of India, would sit silently gazing into the air as if into a distant place.

On the other hand, when the conversation moved, as it often did with him, his insightful comments and probing questions drove to the very center of philosophy's great questions.

After my first visit, which was with a group of others, and for not much more of a reason than to have him autograph a few books, I was bound to try to see him again. Some many months later, when I did return he remembered me in an instant. "Oh yes, you were with that group of young people," he said, and then settled into the very conversation that we had started those months before.

One listened to Neihardt. Listened to his crackling voice with the faint faraway tinges of an accent from another world, and I don't mean of countries and continents, but of an age long past.

There was always talk of books and religion and the deep sure faith he had that all that happens on this earth is but a shadow to a great spiritual world all around us. "If there were only one road and that a black one, this world would not be much, but there is another road, the good red road of spiritual understanding...This good red road of spiritual understanding goes straight north across the Hoop of

55

the World to the region of white hairs and the cold of death. Where this good red road of spiritual understanding crosses the hard black road of worldly difficulties, that place is holy..." Neihardt spent a good part of his life at that crossroads.

The Neihardt Center is open during the summer Mondays through Saturdays from 8:00-5:00 and Sundays, 1:30-5:00. During the winter it is open Monday through Friday from 8:00-5:00 and on Saturdays and Sundays from 1:30-5:00.

The center features many of the personal belongings and memorabilia from the life of the Poet Laureate of Missouri and Nebraska. In addition, the center has a library and serves as the home base of the international Neihardt Foundation.

The special feature of the Center is the Sioux Prayer Garden, which Neihardt constructed from Black Elk's description of what such a place should look like. The Center is a branch museum of the Nebraska Historical Society.

Iron Eyes, considered by many to be the greatest leader of the Omaha Indians, is buried in Bancroft.

North of State Highway 51 is the Omaha Indian Reservation. For more information about the Omaha Indians and this reservation, please see the entry for US Highway 73.

Ten miles (6 miles.)

Walthill.

Walthill is the location of one of the more significant memorials in the state. The Dr. Susan LaFlesche Picotte Center is located in the building that served as Walthill's hospital starting in 1912. The hospital was built for Dr. Picotte to use and was used as a hospital for over 30 years.

Dr. Picotte was the first Native American woman physician. She graduated first in her class from the Women's Medical College in Philadelphia in 1889. She was 23. She returned to the Omaha Reservation and served the community for 26 years, until her death in 1915 at the age of 50.

Dr. Picotte was the daughter of Iron Eyes, one of the last great leaders of the Omaha, and the granddaughter of Big Elk, another great leader. In addition to Dr. Picotte, many of Iron Eye's children gained great fame. They included Susan Tibbles, or Bright Eyes, who was an Indian activist in the late 19th century, and Francis LaFlesche, a prominent ethnologist.

The Center includes the LaFlesche Family Room, a room dedicated to Dr. Picotte's life, and a gift shop. The building has been restored not only to commemorate Dr. Picotte's life, but to illustrate how her life is an ideal of dedication, learning and healing. It serves to celebrate the diversity of the local community as well as to teach the local history of both whites and Native Americans of the area.

It is said that Dr. Picotte always kept a lantern burning in a window of the building so that everyone would know that help was always available.

The town was named for Walter Hill, son of a railroad man, and not some local hill.

Walthill is at the junction with State Highway 94. East on 94 to US Highway 73.

Fifteen miles west of Walthill on Nebraska 94: Pender.

Pender is the county seat of Thurston County. Although the Winnebago and Omaha Indian Reservations had been created for the Indians, in 1884 the government opened up some of the reservation for settlement by the whites. Pender was the first town to be formed under this provision, although some of the buildings in the town had been moved from a place known as Athens, now a ghost town two miles southeast of here.

On August 12, 1977, a man claimed he was abducted by creatures in a UFO just outside of Pender. He lost his memory after seeing a ship land. The next thing he knew he was in a white room with black and white patterns of line on the walls, ceiling and floor. There were no doors or windows. A voice entered his head and began to ask him a series of questions about math and science and religion. Well, that's what he claimed, anyway.

Thirteen miles north to Emerson, the only city located in three counties in the state.

Six miles (3 miles.)

Junction with US Highway 73.

From this point northward to South Sioux City, Highways 77 and 73 follow the same route. For information about Highway 73 south from this point, please see the entry for US Highway 73.

After the Sioux uprising during the American Civil War, the Winnebago were forced into the area from their native Wisconsin. They were first placed on a reservation on Crow Creek in South

57

Dakota, but could not survive the winter of 1863 and migrated to the Omaha Reservation southeast of here. The Omaha Indians, related by blood to the Winnebago, took the tribe in and helped them adjust to the life of outcasts. Later, the Omaha sold 97,000 acres to the Government for a reservation for their homeless brothers and sisters.

Winnebago.

This is the center of the Winnebago Indian reservation.

An early pioneer, Alice C. Fletcher, wrote a book on her memories of Nebraska. She described her first experience with the music of the Indians of this reservation: "The sound was distressing, and my interest in this music was not aroused until I perceived that this distress was peculiarly my own, everyone else was so enjoying himself (I was the only one of my race present) that I felt sure something was eluding my ears; it was not rational that human beings should scream for hours, looking and acting as did these Indians before me, and the sounds they made not mean something more than mere noise."

Obviously Fletcher never sat on a hot summer evening at the annual powwow held near the junction of US Highways 77 and 73, and watched from the side of a teepee when the drummers — wrinkles and grey eyes attesting to a kind of wisdom that only comes with age - began to slowly tap out their rhythm, first one, then another.

She would have watched as one of the drummers began a low and soft humming, and then another joined the song. Their voices become a plaintive tremolo, weaving in and out of one another, dropping octaves in long and bittersweet slides. Off in the distance, a coyote, or the faint ghost of a timber wolf, lifts its ears.

The beat of the drum becomes insistent, and firm. Soon all of the drummers sing. This is the Flag Song, or the Friendship Song, or perhaps a war song.

Next the women stand, their shawls and robes about their shoulders to cut the chill that has come on with the dusk. Smoke is in the air. The fires are lit and raging. The women form a wide circle about the drummers, and stand shoulder to shoulder. They begin a slow two-step motion in time to the song. The circle begins to move. The shadows of the women fall upon the stretched skins of the teepees. Children are running about, playing tag, or clinging to their mothers' legs, trying to keep in time to the beat. Everyone, everywhere, is in motion.

Finally, the men start to dance. Slowly they appear, almost out of nowhere, and without notice they are in the center of the circle.

A knee goes high into the air. Toe down. Heel. Toe down. Heel. Ai-ye-yah-yah-yah. Toe Down. Heel. They spin and twist. Their arms mimic the secret world of eagles, the lonely life of deer, or the power of bear. Room is made for the fellow who has had too much to drink, he is not shunned, nor censored, though there is a bit of kidding as he bumps into a few of the other men.

Now all heads turn. The dancer has entered the circle. He is in full dress: thousands of feathers, all radiating out from a center of shiny metal discs, adorn his head and his rear. Long strings of them hang from his arms. There are feathers in his headdress: red and grey and white ones. He wears anklets of bells. They jingle, jingle, jingle as he steps, slowly at first, in time to the music. His feet are bare, his face is painted. Even the best of the other men clear a little space for this one. He swirls and weaves and ducks around and amid them, using the seated drummers at the center of the circle as a kind of pivot. The orange of the campfire causes his face to glow. His eyes are impassive, they are looking out beyond this world, out to a place where there is no passing of time, to a place where the winds of the prairies blow forever across open plains.

Then, suddenly, though no one is taken by surprise, the song ends. Where an instant before there was motion, sound and a beat of drums that had entered into the soul of every witness, now there is a hole in the night. The drummers smile, talk softly. The dancers drift back to their places in lounge chairs and take a sip of coffee from thermoses.

Three miles (3 miles.)
This is the Thurston/Dakota County line, which also serves as the border of the Winnebago Indian Reservation.

Three miles (8 miles.)
Homer.

One half mile northwest of Homer is the site of an old Omaha Indian village on Omaha Creek. The village predates Lewis and Clark, and when those explorers passed this way the village had already been burned to the ground. They estimated it held over 300 huts. The village, believed to have been called Tonwantonga, or Large Village, suffered the white man's invisible first conqueror: smallpox. The disease, previously unknown to the Indians, killed over 400 people here. Still, an estimated 1,000 lived here as late as 1895. Near here stood Fort Charles. The state has placed a historical marker for the village two miles north of Homer, but the village actually stood on the side of the steep hill.

North three miles, then east two miles of Homer *to the site of the town of Omandi.*

East *of Homer,* **two miles** *is Combs School, built in 1857 and used until 1964. This building has moved around the county more than some of its citizens.*

Just to the east of the school is the O'Connor House, a 14-room mansion of brick built between 1865 and 1875 and now a museum. The house is still furnished with many of the original items. Next to the house is the Museum Machinery Building, built by the Historical Society to house some of the many farm implements collected over the years. The complex is open to the public. Hours vary.

East *of the museum* **four miles** *to an abrupt cliff known as Land's End. Here the Indians came to pray and meditate, to dance and sing. The 500-foot drop to the Missouri River plain affords a dramatic view.*

Along this side of the river were campsites of Lewis and Clark. At one long-lost time, this entire region — from here south 25 miles along the Missouri river bluffs — was a proposed national park and wildlife refuge. It was proposed that the park would honor Lewis and Clark. The fact that this area was once considered to be National Park material should be enough said for the adventuresome tourist.

The area has many Indians petroglyphs. Inquire locally for directions.

Return to US 77.

Eight miles (3 miles.)
One mile east to Dakota City.

Dakota City, Nebraska, has the oldest church in the state. Emmanuel Lutheran was built in 1860 and cost $2,000 — an extremely healthy sum in those days. But this was nothing compared to the $16,000 they dropped into a grand hotel in 1858. The hotel was torn down, the church still stands. Spend a moment in the shade of the cottonwood and elm nearby and soak in the peacefulness here.

Dakota City had one of the widest main streets anywhere, as three individual roads were combined to form the street.

This place was visited by Lewis and Clark on their way to the Pacific. They reached the mouth of the Omaha Creek, just east of here, on August 16, 1804.

One of their group, Sergeant Charles Floyd, died and was buried near here. Dakota City is the county seat of Dakota County.

In the days of steamboats, the sternwheeler *Nugget* hit some snags and went down just offshore here. Her cargo was mainly whiskey, and a good many of Dakota City's best labor was to be found helping salvage what they could of the *Nugget*.

The IBP corporation meatpacking house in Dakota City was fined a record $5.7 million for violations of health and safety violations in the late 1980s. The fines, which were handed down by the government's Occupational Safety and Health Administration, were for ignoring the hazards of repetitive motions by the packinghouse workers. Such motions can lead to disabling neuromuscular disorders.

In 1987, government officials said IBP had the most flagrant violations of record-keeping about job-related injuries it had uncovered in its entire 17-year history.

The $5.7 million was the largest fine OSHA had ever handed down.

The fines were later reduced, and IBP instituted a massive program to reduce the incidents of muscular disorders.

Pottery works helped give Dakota City its start and the remains of the industry can be found throughout the town.

Because of the dams built on the Missouri River the aquifer has been lowered so that many local wells have dried up in recent years.

Three miles (0 miles.)

South Sioux City and junction with US Highway 20. For information about South Sioux City and for sites along US Highway 20, please see the US Highway 20 entry.

Zero miles (3 1/2 miles.)
Kansas State Line.

Three and one half miles (3 miles.)
County road to the east leads to Steele City and Endicott,
location of many significant sites. Please see below for a description

of the many locations in this area.

Take this county road to the **east** for **one and a half miles**, then **south for two miles**, then west again to return to Highway 15 for one of the most scenic drives in the area.

Three miles (2 miles.)
Intersection with State Highway 8 West.
Two miles west on State Highway 8, then one and a half miles south to a private mausoleum near the banks of Silver Creek.
West on State 8 seven miles to Reynolds. One and a half miles west of Reynolds is a marker indicating the site of a very early Jefferson County town called both Mark's Mill and Rose Creek City. It was founded in 1865.

Two miles (1 mile.)
State Highway 8 on the southern edge of Fairbury.

Six miles south on Highway 8 to Endicott.
Near here the oldest and most complete fossilized flower ever discovered was found in the clay at the Endicott Brick Works. The Rose Creek Flower, named after the nearby creek, was discovered in the early 1970s by paleobotanist David Dilcher. The fossil, which looked something like a cross between an apple and a rose, included flowers, stem, leaves, pollen and fruit. The fact that the specimen was so complete added to its scientific significance.

One and a half miles north and one mile east to John Fremont and Kit Carson Rock at Quivera Park. On a sandstone rock at this place are a few historic words: "John C. Fremont and Kit Carson - 1842."
There is much debate whether these signatures are authentic, although there is evidence that places the names on the rock as least as early as 1890. One misguided early historian deepened the cut of the signatures, which made dating even more difficult. In any event, this was certainly one of the inscription rocks along the Oregon Trail.
There is a great deal of difference between those pioneers scratching their names here in hopes that a loved one would come along the trail some time later and know they were alive as far as this point, and the random and egocentric scratchings of modern tourists.

State Highway 15

One mile north of Quivera Park to Rock Creek Station State Historical Park. This is a fine state park that offers the visitor many interpretations of this famous site along both the Oregon Trail and the Pony Express route.

Rock Creek Station was a company station founded originally by the Central Overland California and Pike's Peak Company. It was here on July 12, 1861, that Wild Bill Hickok, then known by his given name, James Butler Hickok, for not much of a reason gunned down David McCanles in cold blood while McCanles' young son watched. Hickok, who killed close to 200 people in his 39 years, started the bloodiest part of his career with this shooting. The two other victims of this Hickok killing spree were once buried near the East Station, but were later interred in Fairbury Cemetery. McCanles' 12-year-old son, Monroe, was attacked with a hoe, but scrambled into the brush of Rock Creek and escaped Hickok's attempts to track him down and kill him. Hickok and two others were tried for murder but were aquitted after pleading self-defense.

Rock Creek Station began as a small ranch in 1857 that served travelers on the Oregon Trail. It grew over the next decade of intense travel over the trail so that it provided supplies and feed for those moving west.

This is a fine park and, in addition to the ruts from the Oregon Trail that can be seen in the park, replicas of buildings from the Pony Express station and Oregon Trail days are here. This is one of the most significant sites of the Trail in Nebraska, and certainly one of the state's finest historical parks.

Four miles south of Endicott on State Highway 8 is Steele City. The historic district of Steele City contains many fine restored historic buildings, and gives the visitor the feeling of walking down an old western town, which is just what Steele City is. A fine small museum is located here and includes tours of a bank and a blacksmith shop. The stone Baptist Church dates from the 1880s, as do the stone blacksmith shop and the stone livery stable. They are open Sundays during the summer.

Besides its historic atmosphere, Steele City is known for the Steele City Flea Market and Old Farm Machinery Show. The annual event, held usually in September, draws thousands of visitors from all across the country. Over 100 vendors crowd the streets of the town, selling everything from crafts and antiques to soda pop and peanuts. The Old Farm Machinery Show features demonstrations of antique machinery.

Three miles east of Steele City, then one quarter mile north. This is one possible site of the famous Fremont Springs.

The Springs were named for the explorer John Fremont, who camped here in 1842. There is another, more probable site for these springs, near the Quivera Park monument. In any event, the Oregon Trail crossed from the southeast to the northwest at this point.

Go north to the next county road intersection. Then turn west and go for another half mile. This is the location of the Rock House Pony Express station. This is one of several station sites in Nebraska. The Pony Express was active for only a few years before being replaced by the railroad; however, its history is a very important part of Nebraska, since the trail cut across the entire state.

Due east of here ran the Oketo Cutoff, which was a stage-coach line in 1862. The owner, Ben Holladay, had a dispute with the leaders of Marysville, Kansas, and therefore rerouted his stage road around that town. This was the new route. The controversy was soon settled, and the Oketo Cutoff was used for only a few years.

Two and a half miles to the east was the town of Shea; now nothing but fields mark the place.

One mile (2 1/2 miles.)

Fairbury and the Junction of US Highway 136. For information about this area please see the entry for US Highway 136.

Two and one half miles (1 1/2 miles.)

Two and a half miles north of the intersection with US Highway 136 and straight west of the Fairbury Airport, on the west side of State Highway 15, ruts from the Oregon Trail are still visible. Study the land to the west and ask locally in order to best spot the ruts.

One and one half miles (1 mile.)

This is the site of Virginia Station, a Pony Express station and the location of the Whiskey Run marker. This place was unique in that there were soldiers stationed here for a time in order to keep peace between pioneers and Indians.

The story is that the soldiers took the Indians' whiskey and poured it all into a nearby creek, which gave it the name Whiskey Run.

In June of 1849, a man from Massachusetts was heading west on the Oregon Trail. He got the fever and soon was delirious. Like many other pioneers, George Winslow died of cholera. What made

65

things different was that the stone someone finally got to mark his final resting place was rediscovered years later.

Eventually it was placed inside of a larger marker by the state of Nebraska, and by Winslow's sons. The marker and grave are **one and a half miles west** of the Whiskey Run monument. The marker is on private property and if you haven't been given permission to pass through the gate, please don't do so. Trail ruts are visible just southwest of the monument.

One and a half miles west of the Whiskey Run marker, on the west bank of the Little Blue River, was a well-used springs known as Whiskey Springs.

One mile (3 miles.)

There are many interesting places west on this county road. Ask locally for additional information and directions.

Three miles west on this county road is the site of the Little Sandy Stage Station, which dates from the 1860s.

One more mile west is the sleepy town of Powell, and one and a half miles west of Powell is the site of Big Sandy Stage Station, in competition with the Little Sandy Station in the 1860s.

One and a half miles west of the Big Sandy Station site, (three miles west of Powell) is an unusual museum, dedicated to the District 10 schools, which is located on the Oregon Trail and the Pony Express Trail. This site is eight miles west of State Highway 15 and just south of the Alexander State Recreation Area. It is open Sunday afternoons.

Three miles (6 miles.)

Junction with State Highway 4.

This is the site of the former town of Bower.

Eight and a half miles east of here is the site of the former town of Old Plymouth, and **four miles to the west** of here, the site of the former town of Helvey. Please see entry for State Highway 4 for more information about sites along this road.

Six miles (2 miles.)

West of here is the town of Western. There is a debate whether this town was named because it is western, or after a man named West.

Two miles (4 miles.)
>   Turn off for State Highway 74.
>   **Eight miles west** of here to Tobias.

>   *Don't pass through Tobias without stopping at a fine small museum run by the Tobias Community Historical Society and located in the former Citizens State Bank building. The bank building was saved in the 1891 fire, which destroyed much of the town. Other displays are in the original Tobias Print Shop.*

>   *Tobias was founded in 1884 as a railroad town and to be a market town for an area of the county not easily served by other places.*

>   *Tobias was formerly called Castor, but the name change was to avoid confusion with Custer and Closter.*

>   *In the early days, Main Street had bookstores, hotels and hat stores as well as a race track and roller skating rink.*

>   *There are still buildings standing that date to the town's first decade.*

>   *Over half of the town was burned to the ground in 1891. The fire was caused by arson.*

>   *Alice, a notorious horse, ran in races around here often. Alice was a mare who always seemed to win her races. Sixteen loads of corn were won in a race she once ran. She ran on a lot of tracks in the state, but was most frequently seen here. She died in Utah from eating loco weed.*

>   *One story from Tobias' early days was that at a candy and fruit shop three men began to argue over a bunch of bananas that had come in. They decided that they could eat the entire bunch in one sitting. One man ate 20, another 30 and another 34. No report survives about what they did the rest of the day.*

>   *The Tobias Cemetery was laid out in 1884. The oldest grave is dated 1876. The site was selected after much debate with a farmer who deeded the land. His concern was that it be placed in such a manner that his family would not have to pass a cemetery every time they went to town. The site selected is south of town.*

>   *The Community Church, formerly the Baptist Church, was built in 1886.*

>   *The bar is a friendly typical Nebraska bar with stalls along the bar and good food on short order.*

>   *Old pioneers say of the area that the Indians didn't give them much trouble, but that they had to beware of the Gypsies.*

State Highway 15

The first appendectomy in the state was performed in Tobias, in 1896.

Tobias has a nice small museum located in the Tobias print shop. Memorabilia, newspapers, antiques and photographs are all on display here. Volunteer operated. They'd appreciate donations.

Tobias is the home of the 1959 Nebraska High School Basketball champs. (Class E) They beat Wilsonville 45-36.

The historical marker on Highway 74, east of Tobias, is for Sgt. Leodegar Schynder, who served in the Army for 53 years, longer than any other non-commissioned officer. He was stationed for a long while at Fort Laramie during the peak years of travel over the Oregon Trail. In a way, he was a kind of landmark for thousands of travelers, just as Chimney Rock might have been. He witnessed much of the Old West's famous events, but, unfortunately, he did not keep a diary and he did not like to talk much about his life. He was among 42 people left at the fort after the start of the Indian Wars brought on by the events of the Grattan massacre and the Battle of Blue Water (see entry for US Highway 26). He fought in the Seminole War and other Indian engagements. He was a resident of Tobias.

Sgt. Schynder lived two miles north of town and is buried at the Atlanta Center Cemetery, which is located four miles north and one mile east of Tobias.

If there could be anything else you would like to know about Tobias, just ask around.

Four miles (2 miles.)
Junction with State Highway 41 east.

Two miles east on State Highway 41 is Klacel Hall, site of an old dance hall.

Eleven miles east of State Highway 41. Wilber. Wilber is the Czech capital of Nebraska. It celebrates its Czech heritage nearly every day of the year, but especially during the two-day-long Czech Festival the first weekend in August. There is nothing, absolutely nothing, that can compare with turning the corner on to Third Street and suddenly being swept up in the bright colors, the deep-settling smells of Czech foods, and the bright music that clutters the street. The arts and crafts for which the town is noted are on display and the visitor can almost get a year's fill of kolaches, Polish sausage and beer.

The Festival includes accordion jamborees, parades, Czech

heritage demonstrations and dances, as well as a Czech historical pageant.

Hotel Wilber, near Second and Wilson streets, was built in 1895 and has recently been renovated. It features a fine Czechoslovakian cuisine. In the hotel's import shop is a display of heirloom jewels from the old country.

There are many other fine arts and crafts shops in the town. The Czech Museum is located at 102 W. 3rd and features doll and quilt collections as well as many other exhibits of early Wilber history. The museum is open in the afternoons from May through November, and at all other times by appointment. Admission is free.

The Dvoracek Memorial Library was built and given to the city by the Milo Stastnys, an unusual single contribution for a worthy cause. It includes a Czech Ethnic Room with books and cultural artifacts.

Just north of the city (sniff, sniff) is one of the area's largest pork processing plants.

Return to State Highway 15, or continue north on State Highway 103 to Crete and US Highway 6.

Between Crete and Wilber is the Czech Settler's monument, to commemorate Czech settlements in the Blue Valley, which date from 1865. The first of these settlers walked here from Nebraska City, following a wagon loaded with supplies.

South of Wilber *on State Highway 103* ***seven miles*** *to DeWitt. DeWitt carries the unusual history of having its first church built with money paid in order not to have the new town named Dennison. Dennison was one of the early founders of the town, and when it came time to name the town, many of the locals wanted to name it after this gentleman. He, instead, preferred that the town be named after a minister from his hometown back East, DeWitt Talmage. In order to ensure his anonymity, Dennison paid $500 toward the construction costs of the Congregational Church.*

The Methodist church was built in 1873.

Every home handyman or handywoman in the world has a special reason to visit and pay homage to DeWitt, for it was here, in 1929, that the Vise-Grip was invented and is still manufactured. The Vise-Grip wrench is a tool so useful, some say, that the object it is used on will often lose its usefulness.

Near here was the location of the once sprawling village of Swan City. Swan City, which covered thirty acres, but probably never

69

had a population of more than 60, was located on the south bank of Turkey Creek, one mile west of DeWitt. For a short while, Swan City served as the county seat of Saline County. Until recently, pilings, which once supported a mill, could be seen in Turkey Creek. The mill burned to the ground in 1891.

Two miles (3 miles.)

Junction with State Highway 41 west.

Eight miles west *of the intersection and at the junction of Highway 41 and Tobias road: Old Quaker settlement in "early days." It was called Triumph. It was located two miles west of Atlanta Center Cemetery.*

Three miles (7 miles.)

During a blizzard on March 29, 1976, wet snow and high winds brought down hundreds of power lines near here like dominoes, putting power out up to ten days in a 16-county area.

Near here the first brood of pheasant chicks was released in Saline County around 1910. If you don't hunt, this information may not be of extreme historical interest to you.

Seven miles (3 miles.)

Junction with US Highway 6. Please see the entry for US Highway 6 for more information about sites in this area.

Three miles (5 miles.)

Dorchester. Site of the Saline County Museum.

Please see the entry for US Highway 6 for information about Dorchester.

Five miles (5 miles.)

Just after entering Seward County and on the north side of the West Fork of the Blue River, follow county road east to the confluence of the West Fork with the Big Blue. A quiet and beautiful natural spot.

Five miles (4 miles.)

State Highway 15 turns north. Continue east on US Highway 6 in order to go to Milford. See entry for US Highway 6 for information about Milford.

Four miles (5 miles.)

Junction with the Interstate of Nebraska: 80. Please see entry for Interstate 80 for information along its route.

Five miles (5 miles.)
Seward. Please see entry for US Highway 34 for information about Seward.

Five miles (2 miles.)
West 4 miles to Staplehurst.
This town dates from 1873 when the earliest settlers built dugouts along the banks of Lincoln Creek. The area was settled by Germans, Danish and English. The first Lutheran church in Staplehurst was built in 1882 and was moved south of Seward some years later. It can be seen from the Interstate, just east of the Seward exit.

A dam was built on the Blue River in 1912 to provide electricity for the village, and every August since then the town celebrates the occasion. The Staplehurst Bank has been robbed a number of times. Once so much dynamite was used to blow up the safe that pieces of metal were found two blocks away.

Three and a half miles west of here was a trading post known as Marysville. There was a mill and a post office located there on a well-traveled mail route.

Two miles (14 miles.)
Two miles east to Bee.
Bee was founded in the late 1880s with the coming of the railroad. This area was settled by the Irish initially, and later by the Czech and the English.
In recent years this area has become noted for the use of corn-burning stoves to heat houses. Several homes in the area have been using the stoves, which produce a clean-burning and efficient means of keeping out the Nebraska winter chill.

Fourteen miles (5 miles.)
Junction with State Highway 92. Please see that entry for sites along this route.

Five miles (1 3/4 miles.)
David City.
David City celebrates its heritage each year with Vaudeville Days. The event, usually held in late June, centers on Thorpe's Opera

House. The opera house, which was built in 1889, was at one time the largest opera house in the state and provided seating for more than 1,000. In later years, the balcony was removed and now the theater holds about 300. The feature attraction of the celebration is the vaudeville show put together by local citizens.

The town's annual event also commemorates the life of David City native Ruth Etting, who was a Ziegfeld Follies girl, singer and movie star. At one time, Etting was Nebraska's most famous native as her hit songs "Shine On Harvest Moon" and "Ten Cents a Dance" became national favorites. She was born in David City in 1897 and died in 1978.

David City is the county seat. The county of Butler was named after the first state governor, David Butler. Inappropriately enough, David City was not named after David Butler, but an early settler.

Butler County is also home to towns with names such as Rising City and Surprise.

The Oxbow Trail passed this way. The Oxbow Trail, which connected Nebraska City with the Platte River near Columbus and eventually the Oregon Trail west of Hastings, passed through what is now Butler County. It crosses State 15 about 1 3/4 mile north of David City. It crosses State 64 about 3/4 of a mile before the Polk County line. It crosses State 92 twice, first just as the highway enters Butler County from Saunders, and again one mile farther west.

In general, the trail makes a winding route from southeast to northwest through the county. Traces of the route can still be seen in some areas. Ask locally.

One and three fourths mile (3 miles.)

The Oxbow Trail, which connected the Missouri River travelers from near Omaha with the Oregon Trail, crosses the highway here.

Three miles (6 miles.)

Junction with State Highway 64. On State 64: Bellwood. For information about Bellwood and its unsung hero of Arbor Day, please see the entry for US Highway 81.

Site of the town of Savannah, once a county seat, and Presentation Catholic Church. Please see entry for State Highway 92 for information about these two sites.

Six miles (1 mile.)

Junction with Highway S-12.

Seven miles on S-12 to Linwood. Linwood is located on the *banks of Skull Creek, which flows into the Platte. Skull Creek was the location of an old Indian battlefield and burial ground, hence the name.*

*The county road to the **west** at this intersection follows the Platte River and makes for a nice and quiet drive.*

One mile (4 miles.)

The Platte River.

Just across the Platte, the highway crosses the route of the Mormon Trail, which followed the north bank of the river.

Four miles (3 miles.)

Schuyler and the junction with US Highway 30. Please see entry for US Highway 30 for information about Schuyler.

Three miles (19 miles.)

The Benedictine Mission House.

The Benedictines are the oldest monastic order in the Catholic Church. They were founded in 529 in Italy. Their mission is to develop the monastic life and to share in the common work of the Church.

To this end, the dozen or so monks who inhabit this earth-sheltered monastery live a life of contemplation and work. Their work includes gardening, teaching or ministering to patients in the Schuyler hospital and local nursing homes.

The Mission House contains a wide assortment of artifacts collected from other Benedictine Houses throughout the world. Of special interest is the large collection of rosaries.

The facility is open to the public, but should not be considered an ordinary tourist stop. The solitude and peacefulness one can find inside these doors is a special treasure to be protected.

The Mission House has been located on this site since 1935, when the first members of the order came here to escape Nazi persecution. The new Mission House was opened in 1979. The windowless chapel is lit by skylights above the altar. Statues and terra-cotta plaques grace the walls.

The modern house is built into the side of a hill and looks out over the surrounding Platte Valley with serenity and grace. The Benedictine House coordinates fund-raising activities for all Benedictine missions around the world.

Nineteen miles (8 miles.)

Junction with State Highway 91.

State Highway 15

Leigh, Clarkston and Howells are three small burgs along the northern edge of Colfax County. All three were founded in 1887. These small communities share many of their activities and yet retain a sense of pride and identity of their own.

Howells, **three miles east on 91,** is located on the banks of Maple Creek. It was nearly destroyed by a prairie fire in 1875 and by an 1884 flood.

The town has a nice park on the northern edge of the village.

Clarkson, **three miles west on 91,** had its share of disasters as well. The blizzard of 1888 inflicted a lot of damage here. The railroads, both passenger and freight service, were once the lifeblood of the town. Clarkson has been suffering ever since they withdrew in the early 1960s.

Eight miles (4 miles.)

Junction with State Highway 32.

Take Highway 32 for **eight** miles to junction with State Highway 57, then **north eight miles** to Stanton.

Stanton. The county seat for Stanton County. The original townsite was to the east of the business district, but moved when the railroad tracks were placed here.

Bet you think the town of Stanton was named after the county of Stanton, which was named after the Secretary of War in President Abraham Lincoln's administration. Wrong! The city was named after the maiden name of the founder's wife. Not everything is always as it seems it should be. The town was founded by Germans from Wisconsin in 1869.

The Kirche der Evangelische Gemeinschaft at 8th and Kingwood is a historically significant frame church built in the 1890s. This church was an important link in establishing German-American culture.

The United Methodist Church at 10th and Jackpine is a well-preserved brick church.

At 10th and Ivy is a building typical of the style built for banks at the turn of the 20th century.

Nearby, at 10th and Hickory, this structure was built originally to house a brewery.

Stanton has many fine examples of the Queen Anne style of architecture. These private residents are at: 804 Jackpine, 4th and Ivy, 801 14th St., 500 10th St., and 1103 7th St.

Two miles north of Stanton is the Maskenthine Recreation Area, one of the largest lakes in the area. It was built on the lower Elkhorn system for flood control and recreation. Surrounding the lake is a 300-acre wildlife management area. On the east side of the lake is an arboretum maintained for growing trees, grasses and other natural and indigenous plants of the area. The lake is stocked with a wide variety of fish. Camping is permitted, although no set facilities are available.

Four miles north and then two miles east of Stanton to the District 13 School House. Built in 1900, it is a well-preserved example of the hall-type school building so typical of that era of history.

One mile west and then eight miles north of Stanton to the Bega School, a brick building where many Swedish pioneer children were educated.

One and a half miles west and one mile south of Stanton to a 1902 farmhouse, which is a good example of the spindlework subtype of the Queen Anne style of building.

You may return to State Highway 15 the way you came or take the county road east out of town to Pilger.

Four miles (8 miles.)
The Pawnee and Sioux fought over the use of the Elkhorn Valley for hundreds of years. Generally, the Sioux won the rights to these hunting grounds.

Later homesteaders from a wide variety of places — Germans, Czechs, Bohemians, Scandinavians and others — settled this area. Many of the farms in this area are examples of the intensive livestock production farms that were common in the early 1900s.

Eight miles (1 mile.)
Pilger.

Pilger was the home of Bud Tinning, who pitched for the Chicago Cubs in the 1932 World Series against the New York Yankees. He struck out Babe Ruth, Lou Gehrig and Tony Lazzari in the series, although New York won. He later played for the St. Louis Cardinals.

Pilger's Old Farmers Bank Building can be seen at 2nd and Main. It was built in 1901.

The old blacksmith building, with the false front so typical of old western towns, can be seen at 2nd and Stanton.

Take the county road **east** of here **nine miles** to Stanton (see above).

One mile east of here to the 1911 Heckendorf farm, which includes a large Tudor-style house.

Just northwest of Pilger is the location of the first town in the county, which was built on Humbug Creek.

Two miles north of here is Pilger Recreation Area with a pretty, 40-acre lake.

One mile (4 miles.)

Junction with US Highway 275. Please see entry for this highway for more information about sites along this route.

For 2 miles State Highway 15 follows US 275.

Four miles (13 miles.)

Since State Highway 15 turned north and broke away from US Highway 275, you have been traveling on the county line between Stanton and Cuming Counties. Cuming County, you might like to know, calls itself the livestock capital of Nebraska.

Thirteen miles (10 miles.)

Wayne.

Home of the internationally famous Wayne Chicken Show. Now, this is something to crow about, something that Wayne likes to think makes folks roost here. The event, usually held in midsummer, has been featured on Johnny Carson's "Tonight" show, on "Good Morning America," and in *USA Today* and the *Wall Street Journal.* This is a celebration of the oft-neglected chicken and its talents. SEE the international competitive egg toss! SEE the Chicken Art Show! HEAR the Cluck-Off Competition! TASTE the Chicken Feed! (no, not the feed the chickens eat, but the food we eat made from chickens.) SAVOR the Omelet Feed! All right here in lowly seeming Wayne, not eggsactly the center of the world.

Just so no one thinks we're simply taking a cheep shot at Wayne, chickens and eggs *are* important to the area. Wakefield's Waudbalm Inc. produces more eggs than any other place in the country. You might want to stop by and take a peep at the place.

Wayne State College dates back to a Lutheran school started in 1881. The 130-acre campus is now a part of a state arboretum. The friendly and hard-working faculty and staff at Wayne State include some of the best and best-educated professors in the country.

Wayne is the location of the Wayne County Museum, located in a large mansion built in 1901.

Also located here are the Bumble Bee Gardens and Iris Country, two of the largest gardens of perennials in a ten-state area. The area is full of nurseries and gardens.

About the turn of the century, a boy named George Heady saw a bright star fall from the sky and land somewhere south of town. He went out the next morning and searched the area. What he eventually found was a strange doughnut-shaped circle of burnt grass in the middle of a field. There was a slight depression in the earth. He found a large piece of metal or stone nearby and took it back into town. He began telling people that he had found a piece of a star that had fallen to earth. Everyone laughed at him and his story until finally, someone went with him back to the burned field. Slowly the people of Wayne began to believe George's story. He kept the rock all of his life until finally, an old man about to enter a nursing home, he gave the stone to a friend. For a long while the friend kept the rock, but finally the stone — an oval about 17 inches in diameter — was used as a marker to commemorate George Heady. When folks tried to carve words of honor to Heady in the stone, all of the tools broke on its incredibly hard surface. Instead, they placed a granite stone to mark Heady's passing. The commemorative marker is near the entrance to the Wayne Cemetery on the western edge of the city.

Ten miles (5 miles.)

Junction with State Road 116.

*East on 116 **one mile** to Concord. For over 30 years the "Owl Band" played concerts at the local band shell and for various functions elsewhere in the area. Local merchants furnished benches for the concerts. The county fair is held in Concord and Gurney's nursery started here.*

Two miles north of Concord *on 116 to Dixon. The annual Dixon Picnic held on or near August 15 has been celebrated every year since the town's founding in 1890.*

*Continue **north 5** miles to US 20, or east nine miles to Allen, home of the Dixon County Museum. See Entry for US 20 for more information.*

Five miles (3 miles.)

Laurel. This tiny hamlet was the birthplace of a big star. The fine Hollywood actor James Coburn was born here.

State Highway 15

Junction with US Highway 20. Please see entry for US Highway 20 for information about sites along this highway.

Three miles (9 miles.)

Junction US Highway 20, State Highway 57 and State Highway 15.

Two miles north of this intersection on State 57 is the location of the old town of Norris, abandoned after it was bypassed by the railroad. Three miles east of the site of Norris and a quarter mile north is the location of the old Norris Cemetery.

Please see entry for US Highway 20 for sites along that route in this area.

Nine miles (9 miles.)

Coleridge. Yes, this is named after the man who wrote such lines as "Water, water, everywhere, and not a drop to drink," and who gave us such phrases as having an albatross around one's neck — the poet, Samuel Coleridge.

The most famous feature of Coleridge, the town, is the bird zoo. Ask around for its location.

Nine miles (7 miles.)

Hartington.

This is the home of the Cedar County Museum, a fine museum in the old Lammers' home built in 1900. The four-story house has 21 rooms, and many of the rooms have been turned into display rooms for the museum. The caretakers of the museum live here as well. The museum includes a library, dress shop and military room, as well as quilt displays — often with members of the local quilting society present to answer questions. The lawn chairs and tables are for your use. Feel free to relax at this fine museum for a good long while.

Seven miles (2 miles.)

Junction with the historic State Highway 12. Please see entry for this road for more information about the sites along its route. State Highway 15 ends at this junction, however; continue east on State Highway 12 one mile to State Road S-14H.

Turn **north** on State Road S-14H.

Three miles north on State Road S-14H.

One mile west of here is the brick house of the Lammers. They are the only remaining early-day pioneer family in the county.

78

The house is located on the original homesteading site and is 120 years old. The bricks were made on the property.

On the southeast corner of this intersection is the St. Helena Catholic Cemetery. It is the 4th oldest cemetery in the state and there are graves that date from the early 1860s. One mile farther north on State Road S-14H to St. Helena and the site of the Felber Tavern. For over a century, this was the center for information, comfort, supplies, gossip, cardgames, booze, neighborly conversation and news.

West one quarter mile *of St. Helena, then* ***north*** *on graveled road for* ***one and a half miles,*** *then* ***west for two and a half miles.*** *On the northwest corner of this intersection is the site of the Bentz Hill Massacre. Dr. Lorenzo Bentz was killed here by Indians in 1864 as a warning to other settlers who might be so silly as to try to settle in this area.*

See entry for State Highway 12 for a map of this area and further information.

Zero miles (4 miles.)

The Kansas border.

Chester.

It was in a dark, snow-covered field in Chester on Christmas Eve 1985 that the body of a young boy was found. The unidentified body was clothed in a set of blue sleepers. It took several years and an article in *Reader's Digest*, but eventually the boy's father was found guilty of abandoning a body and concealing a death. The father said he found his son's body in the back of the car, became frightened and left it in the field. Before the father was arrested, the case gained national attention and the unidentified boy was nicknamed "little boy blue" because of the blue sleeper he was found wearing.

Four miles (6 miles.)

During the Halloween blizzard of 1991 this and other sections of the highway were covered with snow and closed to traffic. Snow-plows could not move because of the deep and blowing snow and because nearly everywhere the storm reduced the visibility to zero. Trees and powerlines dropped like blades of grass all across southeastern Nebraska.

Six miles (1 mile.)

Hebron is just west of the highway. Hebron was founded in 1869 by a group of pioneers associated with the Disciples of Christ. It is the county seat of Thayer County and is built on the banks of the Little Blue River.

In 1953, a tornado destroyed a six-square-block area of town. The town's peak population of 2,000 was reached that same year. It has declined only slightly since then.

The Post Office was built in 1937 and includes good examples of the murals commonly painted in post offices during the 1930s.

The Hebron library was built in 1921 and is a well-preserved example of the Renaissance Revival style.

Two miles (4 miles.)

At the intersection with this county road is where the Oregon Trail crosses US Highway 81. A marker is on the northeast corner of the intersection. Bear in mind that the trail was not like the straight, narrow roads of today. Instead, in most places, the trail was a general direction with landmarks to keep travelers on course. Don't look for specific routes for many places along the Trail, but remember that the wagons might have been spread out over a half mile either side of this general location.

Three miles west of here on the county road is the site of the Hackney Ranch, an important settled spot on the Oregon Trail. Three miles east on the county road, and then one half mile north to an Oregon Trail marker and the location of Millersville Station on the Pony Express Route. The Pony Express Route generally followed the same route as the Oregon Trail.

Four miles (12 miles.)

Turn off for the tiny village of Belvidere.

Belvidere is the location of the Thayer County Museum.

Take county roads east of Belvidere 15 miles to Alexandria Lakes State Recreraction Area just north of the Oregon Trail and Pony Express routes. Ask locally for directions to sites along this section of

US Highway 81

the Oregon Trail.

Alexandria has a former livery stable, built in 1875, still standing. It is a frame structure on top of limestone and cement blocks. The town has many other fine older buildings.

Twelve miles (8 miles.)

Junction with State Highway 74.

East 13 miles to Tobias, where a small but active Community Historical Association operates a museum. See entry for State Highway 15 for further information about Tobias.

Eight miles (15 miles.)

Geneva, the county seat of Fillmore County (named for Millard Fillmore), is known for the Girls' Reformatory just west of town. It is somewhat disconcerting to stand at the collection of clean buildings and gaze out on the pastoral setting and realize that this place was founded for the reform of delinquent girls and younger children.

The town was named after Geneva, Switzerland.

Fifteen miles (5 miles.)

McCool Junction...which sounds as if it was named after a failed TV show from the early 1960s. The fact of the matter is no one is quite sure how the town got its name. It is located on the cool banks of the west fork of the Big Blue River.

Six miles east and two miles north of here on the banks of the West Blue River is the first frame house built in the county. It was built in 1869 from lumber milled at least three days' ride away. The house still stands, although it is on private land.

The site of the first homestead in the county is another five miles east of this site.

Five miles (1 mile.)

Intersection with Interstate 80. Please see the entry for Interstate 80 for more information about sites along that route.

One mile (2 miles.)

The Nebraska City Cutoff of the Oregon Trail crosses US 81 at this point. This cutoff was a popular alternative route for the westward migration. The Trail passes through the width of York County. From this point westward the Trail parallels the Interstate. East of here the Trail swings to the southeast toward Beaver Crossing in Seward County.

Two and a half miles east and one mile north is a marker that designates the burial sites of the first two men killed and buried in York County. One of the men, the driver of a stage, was very drunk and threatened the owner of the Stage Station. The air grew quiet, the two men faced off, guns were drawn and in an instant, the stage driver was dead.

The other burial is of a man who was struck and killed by lightning. All he had on his person was $500. To this day he remains unknown. For years, ruts from the Trail could be seen in this area.

In 1868 the Pawnee, Omaha, Ponca and Otoe united to fight their common enemy, the Sioux. Although no white settlers were hurt, the warfare made times rough for finding food and raising crops. Luckily that was the same year that a large herd of bufallo wandered into the area, and provided food for the pioneers. That was the last year buffalo appeared in York County.

Two miles (1 mile.)

York. York, the county seat for York County, is the home of York College, which was founded in 1890 as a seminary school for the United Brethren in Christ.

York has several fine parks and a golf course.

When the railroad split the town in two folks began to refer to the sections of York as North York and South York.

Shortly after the railroad arrived in town a new community started up on the outskirts of town and was named, logically, New York. New York is now a part of York, that is to say, New York is a part of old York, unless you are talking about the old New York, which is in New York, named after York, which is not here at all, but over in England...oh, never mind.

Landmark Hildebrand Drug and Soda Fountain operated in York from 1876 until it closed in 1990.

In 1964, when the government enforced its morals on the population even more then it does today, county workers took away a single mother's four children and put them in foster homes. The county believed the woman couldn't raise them without a husband. For the next 28 years, the son serached for his true mother. Then in 1992, at a video store in York, the son, now approaching middle age, overheard a woman give her name to the clerk. By pure chance the two of them had been living in York for about two years. Theirs was certainly a remarkable chance reunion.

US Highway 81

One mile (12 miles.)

Intersection with US Highway 34. Please see that entry for information along this highway.

Twelve miles (4 miles.)

Stromsburg. This town is the boyhood home of C. H. Morrill, whose pioneer work in archeology and paleontology played a significant role in the modern theories of those sciences. Morrill Hall, the grand museum at the University of Nebraska in Lincoln, was donated to the University by Morrill and is dedicated to his memory. Nebraska writer Loren Eiseley worked for Morrill on several digs in the western part of the state and wrote about Morrill in several of his essays.

Stromsburg was settled by Swedes who found the spot on the banks of the Big Blue appealing. The Big Blue is one of the state's trickiest rivers. It has its headwaters just a mile from the Platte river, west of here in northern Hamilton County, and yet swings a couple of hundred miles to the south before joining up with the waters of the Republican river and eventually the Missouri at Kansas City.

The Blue was an important route for both prehistoric and historic Indians and pioneers, and although few modern roads travel along its banks, traces of those early travelers can still be found in many places. The Blue drainage system flows within 20 miles of Lincoln, although many Lincolnites would not be able to trace its course on a map for love or money. As is the case with many other rivers, civilization has turned its back on the Blue, but it just keeps slowly moving along its lazy way to the sea.

Four miles (3 miles.)

Intersection with State Highway 92 west. Please see entry for State Highway 92 for more information about items of interest in this area.

Three miles (6 miles.)

Osceola. At one time Osceola's name was known nationwide for its fine brooms, which were produced from local broom corn, a variety of corn with a stalk used in the making of brooms. However, Osceola could not make a clean sweep of the market and consequently was brushed aside by other companies wanting to stand on their own.

The town won the county seat away from nearby Stromsburg by distributing a county map made of cardboard with a pin stuck in Osceola. On the back side were instructions for the finder to place

84

their finger on the pin and see how the entire piece of cardboard balanced perfectly. This proved, the promotion claimed, that Osceola was indeed the center of the county and should therefore be the county seat.

In the grasshopper invasion of 1874, Osceola was particularly hard hit and the local paper reported that it was impossible to step outside for even a brief moment without being hit in the face with several of the pests.

Six miles (3 miles.)
Shelby.

Shelby was the birthplace and the adult home of Regionalist artist Terence Duren (1907-1968). Please see entry for State Highway 92 for more information about this fine artist.

Three miles (10 miles.)
When the highway turns north, you will be riding down the county line between Butler and Polk counties. State Highway 92 continues to the east. Please see that entry for more information about sites along this highway.

Ten miles (5 miles.).
Junction with State Highway 64.

Seven miles east on 64 to Bellwood. The founder of this town, Jesse Bell, owned a section of land here and started his own beautification project by planting thousands of trees. His first trees were planted parallel to the roads that surrounded his section, but later he and his family began to plant more and more trees. The folks who lived here since have continued to plant flowers and shrubs and trees. Only Arbor Lodge in Nebraska City has a wider variety of trees in the state. J. Sterling Morton had money and power, while Jesse Bell had simply his love for beautiful trees to sustain his work.

Five miles (1 mile.)
Cross the Platte and then the Loup Rivers, which join just below here.

The Spanish explorer Coronado is alleged to have erected a cross along the Platte River in 1541 west of here near Monroe, but no evidence survives to prove the visit.

However, this was the probable site of a fierce battle between other Spanish conquistadors and Pawnee Indians. In 1720, another caravan from Santa Fe had come north in an attempt to colonize the area. Traveling with Comanche guides, the Spaniards decided to get the Osage to fight against their enemies, the Otoes. The Spaniards revealed this plan to a group of Pawnee they had mistakenly assumed were Osage. The Pawnee played along. They gave a big feast for the Spaniards and celebrated late into the night, while secretly amassing up to 2,000 warriors. At dawn, the Pawnee attacked while the Spaniards slept. They killed all but one man. The survivor, a monk, was allowed to escape in order to tell the story to others.

This place marks the most northeasterly exploration by the Spaniards.

For more information about this and other sites in the area please see the entries for State Highway 92 and US Highway 30.

One mile. (6 miles.)

Columbus.

The Oxbow Trail, which connected Nebraska City with the Platte River near Columbus, and eventually the Oregon Trail west of Hastings, passed here on the north banks of the Loup, as did the Mormon Trail.

In general, the Trail follows the Loup through Platte County. Traces of the route can still be seen in some areas. Ask locally.

For more information about Columbus, please see the entry for US Highway 30.

Six miles (15 miles.)

Junction with State Highway 22. This road parallels the Loup River for 15 lovely miles. For more information about this area, please see the entry for State Highway 14.

Fifteen miles (5 miles.)

Junction with State Highway 91. Just to the southwest is the town of Humphrey, located in Tracy Valley. Tracy Valley was named for a man who, in 1870, came upon the stream in flood. Instead of waiting for the water to subside, the man took off his boots, threw them to the other side, and swam the torrent.

Five miles (5 miles.)

The Shell Creek Cattle Trail paralleled US Highway 81 about 16 miles west of here. The trail was used to move cattle north to railheads and toward the Black Hills in the late 1800s. It went through the town of Newman's Grove, located 16 miles west on county roads.

This is the heart of a very productive agricultural area.

Five miles (14 miles.)

Madison.

This is the county seat of Madison County, despite the fact that well over half of the county's population lives in Norfolk. Like Norfolk, this town was settled by a colony of Germans in the late 1860s.

After the early settlers returned to their homeland to pack up the rest of their families and belongings, they came back to find that their land had been taken over by another party. Rather than start a fight, they took up the land adjoining and the community began.

An early resident of Madison, Doctor John Quincy Adams Harvey, got his medical degree by self-proclamation. Once, when called on to inspect a pioneer who had frozen to death in his cabin, the good doctor peeked in the door, jumped back out and told the surrounding people, "He's deader 'n hell."

The windbreaks and trees you see in this area date back to 1881 when local farmers planted thousands of bushes and trees.

Fourteen miles (6 miles.)

Norfolk.

Junction with US Highway 275. Please see entry for US Highway 275 about sites along this route.

A life-long Norfolk resident, Orville Henry Carlisle, was known worldwide for his mastery of fireworks and rocketry. He invented the world's first model rocket for the hobbyist, but lost the patent to a model-rocket company on a technicality. His rockets are on display at the Smithsonian and he held card number one in the National Association of Rocketry.

You need not go to Washington to see his fine works. Carlisle created the only fireworks museum in the world from his vast collection. It is located next to Carlisle's Shoes in downtown Norfolk.

Norfolk may have more city parks than any other city of its size anywhere. Activities available at these parks include canoeing, archery, go carts and a variety of other recreational wonders.

Norfolk is world famous as the hometown of Johnny Carson. Carson lived most of his boyhood here and graduated from Norfolk High School. For 29 years, Carson served as host of NBC's Tonight Show. His talent as a comedian, talk-show host and comic actor is unlikely to be surpassed in television history. The familiarity of his Midwestern smile will not soon be forgotten by millions. Ask locally for directions to Carson sites.

Norfolk was founded by a large colony of Germans who, in 1866, settled the fertile area of this stretch of the Elkhorn River valley. Their grist and saw mills marked the first buildings in town. They had selected the name North Fork, but the U.S. Government, in its infinite wisdom, shortened it to Norfolk.

If anyone has ever read the pulp novels about "Diamond Dick" published in the early years of this century, this is hallowed ground. Marksman and owner of the first Model-T, author Dr. Richard Tanner was a citizen of Norfork.

In 1926 a local boy, Fred Patzel, won the National Hog Calling Championship. When Fred was asked to reproduce his bellow for the local radio station he blew out the microphone and temporarily put the station off the air.

Norfolk was the home of George Carlson, whose book *Studies in Horsebreeding* has outsold any other book on the subject.

The site of St. Paul's Lutheran Church was the location of the hunting campsite of the Pawnee. They camped here as late as 1870.

In 1891, the construction of a sugar beet factory was a big boon to the town.

The temperance movement was big in Norfolk, as was its opposition by beer-drinking Germans.

The Native Americans called this place "koxie comie" or Place Where the Crows Gather.

Six miles (7 miles.)

Junction with State Highway 13.

Near here in 1870 the Pawnee had one of their last big buffalo hunts.

Near here was the frequent gathering place for Standing Bear and his band of Poncas.

Nine miles north on Highway 13 to Pierce.

Pierce. This is the seat of Pierce County. The town was named for President Franklin Pierce. Trivia Question: When was he president and what party did he represent? (Answer at end of this description!)

Pierce is also the home of a fine museum complex that includes the Chicago-Northwestern Railroad Station, a schoolhouse, blacksmith shop and a building that houses many historical machines. The museum is open all summer.

The first settlement in this area was made by a man named J.H. Brown who built a sod shanty on the banks of Willow Creek in 1870. Before long his structure not only served as a home, but as a hotel, post office and courthouse as well.

CAUTION: it is illegal to play baseball on Main Street and has been since 1885. Five dollar fine.

Pierce was the home of author Lynn Montross, acrobat Inez Lucas and early movie producer Phil Goldstone.

Pierce was also home to "Nebraska's Giant" a man who stood a mere 7 feet tall, hardly even NBA material these days, but that height and his 275-pound frame were big back in 1880.

Pierce's dentist for a number of years was also the town's blacksmith. Note: this is no longer the case. . .

On the courthouse lawn is a piece of native granite that was placed here in 1936 in memory of the pioneers. On it is this poem, written by Elsie Hartman:

> *Live on! Oh, Spirit of the Pioneers,*
> *Our heritage throughout the years!*
>
> *Dauntless courage to face the trackless dawn*
> *Of unknown perils, and e'er marching on*
> *With Hope as outrider in shining cloak*
> *And Faith serenely perched on oxen yoke,*
> *Ever Onward, with eyes on western stars—*
> *Your goal achieved, what matter then, the scars.*
>
> *Live on! Oh, Spirit of the Pioneers,*
> *Our heritage throughout the years!*

Give up? Franklin Pierce was the 14th president, right between such favorites as Millard Filmore and James Buchanan. Pierce served from 1853-1857. A Democrat from New Hampshire, Pierce, at 48, was the youngest man to serve as president up until that time.

Seven Miles (2 miles.)

Junction with State Highway 98 West. Five miles on 98 to Pierce. For a description of Pierce, see above.

Two miles (9 miles.)

Junction with State Highway 98 East to Wayne. For information about Wayne, please see entry for State Highway 15.

Nine miles (7 miles.)

Junction with US Highway 20. Please see entry for that

highway for information about sites along this road.

Seven miles (3 miles.)
Junction with State Highway 59, please see entry for State Highway 14 for information about sites along this road.

Three miles (7 miles.)
Intersection with county road. Turn east for Coleridge, 10 miles. Please see entry for State Highway 15 for more information.

Seven miles (8 miles.)
Intersection with State Highway 84. West to Bloomfield and the Wild Horse Holding Facility. For more information please see entry for State Highway 14. East to Hartington and the Cedar County Museum. Please see entry for State Highway 15 for more information.

Eight miles (8 miles.)
Junction with State Highway 12. Please see that entry for more information about sites along this route.

Eight miles (1 1/2 miles.)
Turn west, follow paved road **four miles** *to a scenic overlook for Gavins Point Dam and Lewis and Clark Lake, which is well worth your stop. The dam is the last dam on the Missouri before it reaches the Mississippi. There are several camping and picnicking sites along this lake.*

Turn east off of 81 at this same intersection for site of Bentz massacre, Fort Jackson, St. Helena, Wynot and other sites. For more information please see entry for State Highway 12.

One and a half miles (0 miles.)
The bridge over the Missouri into Yankton, S.D.

Zero miles (5 miles.)

Superior. This quaint farming town on the banks of the Republican River is in Nuckolls County.

In 1871, William Louden built a dugout on this small creek just north of the Republican River and became the first white resident of the area. A few years later, when he built a log cabin to replace the dugout, others were attracted to the area so that by 1879 the town was incorporated.

His original cabin was donated to the town and moved to Lincoln Park in the 1930s.

Louden was responsible for saving the lives of four men during a blizzard in 1873. He had placed a lantern in a window of his cabin so that travelers could be guided. Four men who were in the area stumbled into his cabin nearly frozen to death after wandering aimlessly in the storm for hours.

When the Republican River flooded in late May of 1935, it hit this area very hard. The flood, which came just 3 months after the

State Highway 14

worst dust storms ever to hit the area, was responsible for wiping out farms, houses, railroads and roadbeds in Nuckolls County.

The neat and modern Nuckolls County Museum has displays of Indian artifacts, circus items and dioramas. A one-room school house sits on the grounds of the museum.

Superior shops include one devoted to fashions for dolls. Doll restoration and doll making is done in the shop as well.

Five miles (4 miles.)

For the next 4 miles State Highway 14 and US Highway 136 are the same road.

Four miles (4 miles.)

US Highway 136 heads to the east. See entry for US Highway 36 for more information about sites in this area.

Four miles (1 mile.)

The small town of Nelson is near the divide between the Republican and Blue River drainages.

The town was founded in 1873. The log cabin in the city park dates from the late 1800s.

One mile (6 miles.)

One mile north of Nelson, take the county road east ten miles to Oak. It is hard to believe that this little town could have as much history as it does, but it is true. Much has happened here. For one thing the Oregon Trail passed right smack-dab through the center of what later became the village. A map to help you get oriented is located in the northeast corner of the city park.

In addition to the pioneer sites described below, near Oak is the location of what some scientists claim is the best sample of Ice Age life in the region. A retired school custodian from Oak, Albert Ahrens, discovered fossils at the site that now bears his name. Well over 100 species of backboned animals have been unearthed here and include parts of ancient horses, giant beavers, stag moose antlers, cats, birds, deer, camels, musk oxen, plants, trees, mastodon, you name it. The site is located along the banks of an extinct, Ice Age stream bed where the animals lived over a half a million years ago. Ask locally for directions.

Four and a half miles east of here in 1864 a stagecoach and its nine passengers barely escaped a massacre. The driver saw

Indians waiting in ambush in some trees along the Little Blue. He spun the stage around and, under heavy gunfire, sped back to a large wagon train some miles to the east.

*   ***One and a half miles east** of Oak is the site of the Comstock Ranch massacre. On August 7, 1864, several ranch buildings north of here were raided by warring Sioux and the residents killed. The buildings were destroyed. Also near here was Oak Grove Station, a station on the Pony Express route.*

*   ***One and a half miles north, then one mile west** to the overlook for the Narrows. This place was a bottleneck where wagons, oxen, pioneer and horse had to squeeze between the Little Blue River and a bluff. Near here was the place where 16-year-old Laura Roper, a woman named Mrs. Eubanks and her four-year-old daughter were captured by the Cheyenne. Mrs. Eubanks had taken several children across the river to pick grapes when the Cheyenne attacked their cabin. Mrs. Eubanks pushed the children into a thicket. One of the children cried out when they saw their father being scalped and the Indians found them. Several older children were killed trying to escape and Mrs. Eubanks, the four-year-old and 16-year-old Laura Roper were captured.*

*   The fear and horror of facing such a wilderness inhabited by the hostile owners is no more clear than in Laura Roper's eyewitness account of the massacre. In her 80s, the woman was interviewed by the editor of the* Nelson Gazette *in 1929. Although this account was nearly 65 years later, her matter-of-fact account with its tiny details gives a precise image of the day's events.*

About one p.m. on the seventh day of August, 1864, I left my home on the Little Blue River to spend the afternoon with a neighbor by the name of Eubanks. I rode with my father's partner, Marshall Kelley, and J. H. Butler who were going to Nebraska City for supplies.

About three weeks before, Indians had stolen some horses from my father and had committed other depredations around the country which of course had caused the people to have some fear of them. This being the case, my father told me as I left to be sure and not come home along as the Indians might be lurking around.

I spent the afternoon at Eubanks until about 4 p.m. at which time Mr. Eubanks, his wife and two children and myself started for my home which was about one and one half miles away. We had gone about one half mile when we came to a place in the road which was called the "Narrows" because the road was so narrow in that place. Mr.

State Highway 14

Eubanks was barefooted and got a sliver in his foot and said he would stop and get it out and for us to walk on; he would overtake us. We had gone about 50 yards around the bluff when we stopped to wait for him. Just then we heard terrible yells. I said I thought it was Indians so we turned and ran back until we came in sight of Mr. Eubanks who was running toward the house. Just as he got to the edge of the sandbar the Indians shot and killed him. His two brothers that were in the house started to run up a drawn and they were both killed. His sister started to run toward us; they had tried to take her prisoner and she fought them so they stabbed her in the head and killed her.

By this time we had gotten into the timber; the Indians had killed every one at the Eubanks' house and we started for my father's house. As they passed they saw us, whirled their horses and came right to us. I had taken off my slippers and was carrying them in my hand. The first thing they did was to snatch my hat off and my slippers out of my hand. I had a signet ring on my finger and they took it off next. Then they took us by the hand and told us to come; they picked us up and put us on the horses and took us back to Mr. Eubanks' house. On the way back we saw Mr. Eubanks' sister lying beside the path a hundred yards from the house. We could see where they had stabbed her; she was not quite dead but threw her arms over her head as we passed. In a few minutes another Indian came riding up with this girl's scalp on a spear dripping with blood; he was yelling like a madman.

They put us off the horses and began destroying everything in the house; they broke the stove, dishes and guns; emptied the feather beds, taking the ticks with them. During this time about an hour they let us wander around and seemed to pay little attention to us. About six o'clock they put us on the horses behind them and started south. We travelled all night; all the next day and night. About three o'clock the following afternoon we camped and ate a wild turkey they had killed on the way. While riding we had only dried buffalo meat to eat. Only seven Indians had taken part in our capture; by now five more joined the party.

I was put on a horse by myself instead of riding behind an Indian on one horse. The next day we came to a band of about 50 Indians. Then they all painted their faces, put feathers in their hair and put on their war paint and regalia. Then we rode on for one and a half hours when we came in sight of their main camp of about ten thousand Indians. I was treated very nicely; one of the old squaws took me under her care. The camp moved westward traveling steadily until within a few day's ride of Fort Lyons, Colorado.

Here we camped and a few warriors went on to attempt to

bargain with the soldiers that came part way out to meet us. Both sides mistrusted the other; finally I was given to the soldiers in exchange for some other prisoners. I was taken into Denver where a strong wagon train was soon made up and we started back for my old home at Nebraska City. I arrived safely there and from there we went to Pennsylvania, my people's former home.

In 1929 at age 81 Laura Roper Vance returned here at the invitation of the State Historical Society and, with a crowd of 150 following, identified the spot where the massacre took place.

Shortly after the actual event, a captain in the military was one of the first non-natives to visit the site of the massacre:

I met a party of freighters and stage coach passengers on horseback and some few ranchmen fleeing from the Little Blue Valley. They told me a terrible story that the Indians were just in their rear and how they had massacred the people west of them, none knew how many. All knew that the Cheyennes had made a raid into the Little Blue Valley striking down all before them. Next day I passed Eubanks' Ranch; found there little children from three to seven years old who had been taken by the heels and swung around against the log cabin, beating their heads to a perfect jelly. Found the hired girl some 15 rods from the ranch staked out on the prairie tied by her hands and feet, naked, body full of arrows and horribly mangled. Not far from this was the body of Eubanks, whiskers cut off, body most fearfully mutilated. The building had been fired — ruins still smoking.

In all four men and two children were killed at the Eubanks ranch. During the spree there were a total of 23 people killed.

Just a few hundred yards south of the Roper site is an unmarked grave of a 16-year-old boy and a wagonmaster. The boy's job was to keep the oxen prodded and moving. Growing weary, he sat and rested. Unable to rise at the wagonmaster's request, the master took out his rifle and shot the boy. A posse hunted the wagonmaster and hanged him at this site. Both were buried on a small hill to the south of the Roper site.

Two hundred yards northwest of this place is the probable location of the Little Blue Station, one of only two stations in the 200 miles between Julesburg, Colorado, and Kiowa, Nebraska, to have survived the Indian uprisings of 1864.

One mile north and one mile west of Roper/Narrows site: Just to the south of this point is the grave of Parson Bob, also known as Phill Landon, who was a frontier scout for George Armstrong Custer and later romanced with Calamity Jane. A trail camp also was here known as Camp Kane.

North one half mile and west one mile *to Angus. A reconstructed sod house is in Angus.*
Return nine miles west to State Highway 14.

Six miles (4 miles.)

Six miles north of Nelson, intersection with State Highway 4.
Ten miles west *on State Highway 4 to Lawrence, home of the Cow Chip Gold Tournament held the second Sunday in June. The tournament's name does not come from cows attempting to make chip shots to the green, but rather the unusual divots found frequently on the course, which sometimes also serves as pasture for local bovines.*

Four miles (2 miles.)

The highway crosses the path of the Oregon Trail and the Pony Express route.

Two miles (10 miles.)

West 4 1/4 miles on S-18C *to the intersection with county road on the south. In the southwest corner of this intersection, just north of the town of Deweese, was the Liberty Farm. This station for travelers along the Oregon Trail stood on the small knoll. The trail went in a northwesterly direction, following the north bank of the Little Blue River. This station was destroyed in the Indian wars of 1864.*

Continue west from the Liberty Farm 3/4 mile and then swing south for a quarter mile. Continue west for 4 miles. *Along this stretch you will pass an older cemetery with tombstones dating back to the early pioneer days.* **Turn north and go for three and a half miles** *to the site of Pawnee Ranch. This ranch, or station along the Oregon Trail, replaced Liberty Ranch when it was destroyed by Indians (see above).*

Continue north one half mile. *Turn west. In 3/4 mile the road forks. Straight here one quarter mile, then south across the Little Blue for one half mile. A half of a mile to the west, in this field, is the grave of Elizabeth Taylor, only one of three women to be lynched during the Oregon Trail days. Return to fork in the road. Take northern branch of fork. As soon as the road turns north again, stop.*

One hundred yards to the west stood the Spring Ranch, a stagecoach station and trading post during the pioneer days. One report has the trading post located at the confluence of the Little Blue with Pawnee Creek, about a mile southeast of here.

Return to State Highway 14.

Ten miles (4 miles.)

Clay Center.

One system that the railroads employed to name towns was to name them in an alphabetical sequence. Clay County is a good example of this. It has the towns of: Deweese, Edgar, Eldorado, Fairfield, Glenvil, Harvard, Inland and so on.

Clay Center was formed when the usual county dispute on what town should have the county seat was finally settled by deciding to build an entirely new town to serve as the seat of government. They found a spot as near to the center of Clay County and named it, well, yes, Clay Center. The courthouse was built in 1918 at a cost of $100,000.

The Clay County Historical Society and Museum is open Mondays, Tuesdays and Saturdays.

The town's annual Old Trusty Days is held the first weekend after Labor day. It is known for its large flea market and display of antique farm machines.

Five miles west of Clay Center to the Roman L. Hruska US Meat Animal Research Center. Yes, there is such a thing supported by the government with your tax dollars. But heck, wouldn't you rather have more meat on the table and less bull in Washington, anyway? The Center is the largest animal research facility of its kind in the world. A staff of 250 studies 12,000 cattle, sheep and hogs to develop new technology for the industry. The 35,000-acre Center offers guided tours.

Four miles (3 miles.)

Intersection with US Highway 6. Please see this entry for more information about sites along US 6.

Three miles (8 miles.)

State Highway 14 leaves US Highway 6 and turns north toward Hamilton County. For more information west and east of here, please see entry for US Highway 6.

State Highway 14

Eight miles (1 mile.)
Just before the northern bridge of the Big Blue: near here on the fork of the Blue River, Jarvil Chaffee made the first homestead claim in Hamilton County in May of 1872. The Chaffee family had traveled to Nebraska from Wisconsin (a wise choice) and constructed a 10 X 12 foot dugout in which to live.

Mrs. Chaffee died in 1871, just before their homestead claim became official. The few scattered neighbor women were distraught at the thought of this fine woman being buried in a plain pine box, much less at such a remote place. Before the final words were said over Mrs. Chaffee's remains, the women gathered wild grapes, crushed them and used the dye to stain the box to give it a darker, richer color.

One mile (7 miles.)
Just to the north of the Big Blue River is the turnoff for. Stockhom, a tiny burg *four miles east.*

East of Stockhom five miles to Farmers Valley Cemetery.
This small cemetery, "receiving back into the bosom of Mother Earth the sons and daughters she gave to the first settlements along the Blue," is bordered on three sides by the river.
The remains of many of the area's finest and earliest settlers are here including such folks as the Wescotts, the Lauries and Buckskin Charlie White. The original school house is nearby.

Seven miles (4 miles.)
Read this monument to the Oregon Trail. It may be a bit misleading since the main Oregon Trail was actually about 35 miles south of here. However, in 1861 the Nebraska City/Fort Kearny cutoff was established in order to save time for travelers and freight from Nebraska City. It is the cutoff that crossed this site.

Seven and one half miles west, and a half mile south of here will take you to the site of the Deepwell Ranch, which saw its heyday from 1865-1868. Since a long segment of the Nebraska City Cutoff road had no station, two confederate soldiers, recently freed from a Chicago prison, built a sod house, and dug a well 60 feet deep. It became one of the best-known stops on the trail, and many stopped to sip its cool, clear waters. The monument is an attempt to reproduce what the well looked like.
P.S. The ranch's well was not made of concrete and stone.

98

P.P.S. The ranch's well had water in it.

One mile (3 miles.)
Intersection with Interstate 80.

Three miles (5 miles.)
Aurora. For information about this fine and historic community, please see entry under US Highway 34.

Five miles (7 miles.)
Cross the Big Blue River. The headwaters of this river are a few miles to the west in the low bluffs along the Platte River. Although the Blue starts within sight of the Platte, it flows away from the larger river, southward, eventually joining with the Republican and joining the Missouri several hundred miles south of where the Platte joins the mighty Mo at Plattsmouth.

Seven miles (2 miles.)
The Oxbow Trail, which ran from north of Omaha to join up with the Oregon Trail 20 miles west of Hastings, crosses the highway at this point. There isn't anything left to see, but with a good imagination one can still picture the oxen pulling heavily laden wagons along this pretty stretch of Nebraska.

Two miles (3 miles.)
Before this concrete and steel structure was built, a mile-long timber, plank and pole bridge once spanned the waters of the wide Platte. The bridge that crosses the Platte was one of the longest wooden bridges in the country.

Three miles (5 miles.)
Central City. A place rich with history and fame. For more information on Central City, please see entry for US Highway 30.

Five miles (12 miles.)
Intersection with State Highway 92. Near here is the route of the Mormon Trail. For information about this and other sites in this area, please see entry for State Highway 92.

Twelve miles (1 mile.)
The Loup River. This river and its many tributaries drains a large portion of the Sandhills region.

State Highway 14

One mile (2 miles.)
 Junction with State Highway 22 West at Fullerton.

Two miles (6 miles.)
 Junction with State Highway 22 East.

For an interesting sidetrip, **Genoa is 14 miles east** *on State Highway 22.*

*   **Genoa.** *Located on the Mormon Trail, Genoa was founded by the Mormons as a trail camp in 1857.*
   Location of Looking Glass Meadow Massacre. On August 17, 1864, a settler was killed at his hay farm when it was attacked by a Sioux war party. Adam Smith was killed by eight arrows. His wife lived over 30 more years despite being hit by 5 arrows. Their son hid in a haystack and witnessed the entire attack. Years later he retold his account to a local newspaper.
   This is the location of the last great concentrations of Pawnee before they were removed by the treaty of 1876. A very large Pawnee village stood one and a half miles west of here at the time the treaty was signed. The village was nearly 250 years old. It was north of the highway about half a mile, at the highest point of land at the juncture of the Beaver and Loup Valleys. Over 3,000 Pawnee once lived here. In one house 54 bodies were found during an excavation. There is some evidence to suggest that Spanish explorers from the Southwest, searching for the City of Gold, Cibola, made it as far as this Indian village in the early 1700s.
   At one time a Pawnee Reservation covered most of what is now Nance County, Genoa moved its location when the reservation was formed so as not to be a part of it.
   After the treaty was signed in 1876, the government built the Pawnee Industrial School for Indians, only one of 16 such Indian boarding schools in the nation. The school operated for 50 years, finally closing in 1934. At its peak over 600 students were enrolled, representing several of the major tribes in the country. The school once sprawled across 160 acres, providing help, as Yellow Knife of the Nez Perce once said, "to teach us how to cut our Mother the Earth's breast." The whites believed the best way to treat the Indians was to educate them in the white ways of the world. This meant the Indians were forced to speak only English and to abandon all traces of their native rituals, customs and clothing. As one of the former

100

students put it, "They told us to forget the Indian."

In the late 1980s a monument was erected to commemorate the 24 students who were known to have died while attending the school. Some died of the flu, some died while trying to escape. Most are believed to be buried on the grounds, although no cemetery has yet been discovered.

Today the shop building has been restored and is open to the public.

Genoa was once site of a large Pawnee Indian Reservation, and the museum in Genoa has one of the largest collections of Pawnee artifacts anywhere in the world.

Six miles (7 miles.)
Junction with State Highway 52.

Seven miles (8 miles.)
Junction with State Highhway 56.
Eight miles west. Cedar Rapids, Nebraska. Are there rapids here? You'll have to take the side trip to find out!

Eight miles (9 miles.)
Albion.

In 1872 when this town was first being settled the subject of a name for the burg came up. The two leading contenders were Albion, after the hometown of one man — his hometown in New York — and the home town of another, Manchester — after the city in Massachusetts. This disagreement almost came to blows and gun-play, but instead the concerned parties decided to have a game of euchre on it. The town is called Albion for the winner of that famous game, but in the spirit of gentlemanliness, the township is named Manchester.

Albion's fate, like that of a great many towns in Nebraska, rested with the railroad. For a while Albion was the only shipping and supply point for most of the surrounding counties, and the town prospered.

The Methodist Church is one of the oldest structures in the city. It dates from 1878, when it was built for a cost of $1,400.

There is general sentiment around here that the people in Albion are the friendliest in the nation. This fact is little known, but widely appreciated by those who have relied on that goodwill. Ninety-six percent of the streets in Albion are paved. The city library is one of the best in the area. And if that's not enough to impress you, check out the Boone County Historical Museum, open year-round, but mostly in the summer.

Albion is the county seat of Boone County, and yes, folks, it was named after Daniel Boone.

Nine miles (6 miles.)

Just after the road swings to due north, to the west is Beaver Creek. It was at this site where the famous Omaha Indian squaw man, Logan Fontenelle, son of a French fur trader and an Omaha Indian woman, was killed in a battle with the Lakota Sioux in the summer of 1855.

The Sioux had drifted down from their territory to the northwest in order to raid the Omaha who traditionally hunted in these areas during the summer. The Sioux raiding party included a young teenager named Curly who would later have a great vision and gain great fame after taking his father's name of Crazy Horse. The Sioux had attacked the Omaha a few days earlier (see entry for US Highway 281 for a description of that battle) and taken many of their horses. The Omaha had trailed the Sioux for several miles, and finally doubled back down Beaver Creek to resume their buffalo hunt. At that point the Sioux also doubled back, swung out around the Omaha and met them in a surprise attack at this site.

They met two Omaha out hunting for elk. One fled, but the other dropped to the ground and tried to fight off the advancing Sioux. After killing one young Sioux warrior, the Omaha was hit and killed. The Sioux discovered that the man wore the clothes of a trader, and other garments that indicated he was highly regarded among the Omaha. The man was Fontenelle. The Sioux then engaged the band of Omahas in a fierce battle along Beaver Creek that lasted over three hours. Because they feared retribution from the army, the Lakota did not widely publicize the killing of Fontenelle.

Many people credit Fontenelle with preserving peace between the Indians and the whites as he traveled throughout the area and spoke with the native tribes in their own language, trying to explain why the whites were taking over the land. Others have different opinions about the man. In either case, bow your head a moment here, for his ghost surely stalks those fields along the creek.

Six miles (4 miles.)

Petersburg.

The first homesteader in these parts staked a claim in 1871 near the present town of Petersburg. The county has the distinction of being in a kind of transition area, not too sure whether it belongs best to the corn and grain lands of the eastern part of the state, or the cattle and Sandhills of the western.

Four miles (5 miles.)
> Turnoff to Raeville, one mile east, and a must-see church, a cathedral in the wilderness of rural Nebraska.

> Nestled in the valley in the small village are the twin spires of St. Bonaventure Catholic Church, a Romanesque structure built in 1919 and designed by J. M. Nachtigal of Omaha. This is no small-town church. The expansive building seats 600 and is adorned with artistic masterpieces painted on the ceiling and frozen in the stained glass windows.

> The town had two churches prior to 1919 that were torn down to make way for the new one. The wood from those churches was used to build the rectory. Plans were that Raeville would be a major Catholic community and residents built a church to match their expectations. In 1886 a priest helped pass a law that forbade any railroad within three miles of the town. The priest believed that the train would be a demoralizing influence on the parish. The town was not demoralized, but as a consequence it never grew, either.

> South of the church is a cemetery with a wrought iron fence and a German blessing *Rehet in Frieden* (Rest in Peace). Since 1882 the church has held a processional on the second Sunday after Pentacost from the church to the neighboring land in order to bless the land.

Five miles (11 miles.)
> Elgin, a small but hardy collection of memories on the edge of Nebraska's least populated area to the west.

Eleven miles (15 miles.)
> Neligh, county seat of Antelope County and home of the Neligh Mills. Near here is the Tintern Monastery. For a description of these and other sites in the area, please see the entry for US Highway 275.

> As the road climbs up and out of the Elkhorn River Valley it enters the more orderly fields of the northern half of the county. Look for yucca plants along the roadside for indications of the western feel this county harbors.

Fifteen miles (10 miles.)

State Highway 14

Intersection with US Highway 20. *Ten miles northwest of here is the fascinating Ashfall Sate Historical Park, where the remains of several prehistoric beasts have been unearthed. For a description of this site, and others in this area, please see entry for US Highway 20.*

Ten miles (8 miles.)

Intersection with State Highway 59. To the east are the towns of Creighton and Bazile Mills. See below for more information.

Eight miles (11 miles.)

Verdigre. This town's kolaches are so good they even have an entire event set aside to celebrate the fact each summer. If you do not know what a kolache is, immediately turn yourself in to the nearest State Police officer and revoke your Nebraska citizenship.

For an interesting side trip, continue east on State Highway 84 to Bloomfield and on Highway 13 to Bazile Mills.

__East 9 miles__ on State Highway 84 to Center. The center of the county, and county seat of Knox county. This was a town formed because of the dispute over which of the existing towns should be the county seat. After the usual bloodshed and violence, surveyors located the center of the county, bought the cornfield from local farmers and started the town. For a short sidetrip swing __south on State Highway 13, two miles__ east of Center to Bazile Mills. See description below.

__Seven miles east__ on State Highway 84 and five miles west of the town of Bloomfield is the Wild Horse Holding Pens. It is a government-run operation that serves as a temporary holding pen and reconditioning center for wild horses taken off range lands. Over 3,000 horses are held here each year before being shipped to adoption centers around the country.

__East of Bloomfield six miles on 84, then south, seven miles on State Highway 121__ to Wausa. A Swedish village with Swedes still making up the majority of the population. Good food and pastries here. Throw the calorie counters away.

Return west on 84 to State Highway 13. __South on 13 six miles__ to Bazile Mills, so named because of the mills that were once located on Bazile Creek. This included both flour mills and woolen mills.

Eleven miles (0 miles.)

Niobrara. Please see the entry for State Highway 12.

NEBRASKA
U S
281

Kansas Border (1 mile.)

The sights of Webster County are many, from the rolling land along the divide between the Republican and the Little Blue watersheds, to the quaint country towns like Inavale and Guide Rock, but far and away Webster County is known for the town of Red Cloud, and that town for its most notable citizen, the great writer, Willa Cather.

One mile (4 miles.)

The Willa Cather Memorial Prairie. This 610 acre strip of land has never been broken by a plow. Many native grasses, some found nowhere else for many miles, flourish here. It may be hard for some people to share the excitement of others as they demand the driver of their car stop, and they rush out to smell, taste, feel and inspect the land here, but if you are one of those drivers, please tolerate them and give them as much time as they want in this place. It may be that without people like them the quality of all our lives will suffer. The

US Highway 281

Prairie is preserved by the Nature Conservatory.

*East of the Memorial Prairie, **4 miles** to site of the Pike Pawnee Village. Zebulon Pike and his 21 men camped on the "commanding hill" in 1803 on their way west. Across the way was a large Pawnee village.*

The story is that some weeks before Pike's arrival here the Spanish had arrived at this large Pawnee village and convinced the Indians to fly the Spanish flag. After Pike's arrival he offered the Indians the American flag and they promptly tied it next to the Spanish flag.

Pike spent four days trying to convince the Pawnee leaders that it was pointless to fly two different flags (perhaps the Pawnee were convincing Pike it was pointless to fly even one...). Finally, the story goes, the elders of the village took down the Spanish flag and gave it to Pike, thus ending the brief Spanish domination of Nebraska.

Much archeological work has been done here by professionals and nonprofessionals alike. Remember, it is a crime to violate important historical sites. In short, take nothing but photographs, leave nothing but footprints.

Four miles (1/2 mile.)

The Republican River. This important river traverses the state's southern border and served as an important water source for the Pawnee, Sioux and other tribes of Indians, as well as for the large buffalo herds and Texas cattle drives. Until the 1940s the Republican was a threat to residents because of flooding. A large flood in the mid 1930s killed over 100 people and sent a wall of water down the river valley.

One particularly beautiful description of this river is in Willa Cather's short story, "The Enchanted Bluff" where a handful of children, at the end of a summer vacation, daydream about buried treasure and distant lands while basking in the setting sun of the prairies.

One-half mile (1 mile.)

On the east side of the road, off a bit from the road is the site of the mansion Cather used for the setting of her short novel *A Lost Lady.* The house burned down not long ago.

One mile (21 miles.)

Red Cloud and the junction of US Highway 136. For many world citizens, Nebraska's most famous town. For a description of

106

Red Cloud please see entry for US Highway 136.

Twenty one miles (8 miles.)
>Blue Hill.
>On the high flatlands above the Little Blue drainage, Blue Hill was settled in 1878 by German immigrants. Located here is an early flour mill. It is easy to see how the beauty of this area might have influenced the writer Willa Cather.

Eight miles (1 mile.)
>Junction with State Highway 74. Please see entry for State Highway 74 for more information on sites along this road.

One mile (2 miles.)
>State Highway 74 continues east, and US Highway 281 turns north.

Two miles (2 miles.)
>Cross the Little Blue River. Imagine a blacksmith shop, wells, stores and a couple of saloons. The town of Millington once stood here.
>*Thirteen miles west of the Millington townsite is the still alive village of Holstein. Ask at Holstein for directions to the Einspahr Sod House Museum, **about 4 miles west of the village.** This is the only sod house still standing in Adams County. Tours by appointment. See also the entry for US Highway 6 for more information.*

Two miles (3 miles.)
>*One tenth of a mile east: Site of Smith and Simonton Wagon train burial site. Eight men were killed by the Sioux here on a hot, dry Nebraska August day in 1864. They are buried at this place, and were members of a wagon train working its way over the Oregon trail.*
>*A mile to the northwest of here was the frontier town of Brickton. For a delightful side trip into the heart of the Oregon Trail country continue as described below.*

>*Continue east for one mile, then go south for 3/4 mile. Ruts of the Oregon Trail are visible on both sides of the road. They are southeast of a cattle pond.*
>*Continue south 1/4 mile from ruts, turn east, go one mile, turn south, go one mile, turn east and go 1/4th mile. Just to the south, along the north bank of the Little Blue River, was the campsite*

of John C. Fremont on June 25. 1842. Fremont gave up trying to float the Platte after dragging his boat for miles. He chose the Little Blue instead. Some say that Fremont had to be crazy anyway to want to explore such a wilderness. Fremont was one of the most versatile and well-traveled of the West's early explorers.

*   **Continue east one half mile.** The Oregon Trail here crosses the county road. Just to the east of the trial, and to the north of the county road, is the site of Lone Tree Station. This station on the Pony Express line and Oregon Trail took its name from the single lone cottonwood tree which stood on a hill and was visible for miles around. All right, so it wasn't any Chimney Rock, Longs Peak or Scottsbluff, this tree was an important landmark to pioneers moving west. In those days to see a tree anywhere outside of a creek bed was something.*

*   Return to Hiway 281 if you can find your way...only kidding, go west three miles and you are there. If not, boy are you lost!*

Three miles (3 miles.)

*   **West 4 miles on gravel road, then south 1/4 mile** to the site of 32 Mile Station. This place was so-called by travelers on the Oregon Trail because it was 32 miles SE of Ft. Kearney. The Oregon Trail cuts Adams County diagonally in half going from the southeast to the northwest. The Pony Express route followed the Oregon Trail route in this part of Nebraska.*

Three miles (14 miles.)

Junction of US Highway 6. For information about sites along US Highway 6 please see entry for US Highway 6.

Hastings.

Famous Hastings citizens include Barney Pearson, who lived until the early 1940s, was known as "Colonel Idaho Bill" and was a good friend of Buffalo Bill. Colonel Idaho Bill's feature attraction during the performances of the Wild West show was being able to capture a wide variety of strange and wild creatures with his lariat.

Sandy Dennis, Academy Award winning actress was born in Hastings. Other famous Hastings citizens include Carolyn Renfrew, an author, and Adam Breede who was an author, explorer and archeologist. Hastings was the location for the first interstate radio broadcast in the state of Nebraska.

During the 1930s Hastings Municipal Power had the distinction of selling its power at a rate 50% lower than that of the rest of the nation. Hastings has always been a prosperous and pretty Nebraska town, and with the recent improvements to the downtown area it seems to be aware of that distinction. Adams County's first white settlers were Englishmen who came to take advantage of the homesteading act. One of them, Walter Micken laid out the town of Hastings in 1872.

Hastings, like many of the towns in Nebraska, was a railroad town, and was named after a man who graded the last section of the St. Joseph and Denver railroad into the townsite. Hastings once boasted three individuals railroad stations. Now Amtrack serves one of the few remaining passenger stations in the state.

There was an early debate over whether Hastings or the town of Juaniata to the west should be the county seat. The issue was settled when a group of men went to Juaniata at night and stole a wagon full of public records and brought them back to town.

Over sixty percent of the bricks used in the state of Nebraska come from Hastings.

Those with a culinary slant should know that the Jerusalem artichoke was developed in the Hastings area. It is today commonly used as a vegetable some parents threaten children with, but at one time it was used not only as food, but as feed and for the manufacture of fuel alcohol as well.

For those with less refined tastes, Kool-Aid was invented by a man from Hastings.

Hastings Museum is at the **intersection of Highway 281 and 14th streets** is a good place to start your tour of Hastings. Built in 1938, the building was constructed of bricks from the old Morton School which once held the museum's collection. The museum encompasses not only local history, but a wide assortment of other attractions as well.

The museum's Native American collection features interpretive displays demonstrating the day to day life of the Plains Indians and their conflicts with the immigrants.

Items of local and regional history are here through the efforts of the Adams County Historical Society. The tools and lifestyles of the pioneers are displayed here as well.

The Hastings Museum is quite expansive, far beyond what would be expected in a museum for a town the size of Hastings. The staff is quite proud of its natural history collection, which includes a large collection of fossils donated by Brett Kent a zoologist. Kent grew up in Hastings and credited his interest in zoology to the trips he took through the Hastings museum as a child.

The J.M. McDonald Planetarium features a changing schedule of sky shows throughout the year. One of the newer additions to the museum is the Discovery Center which allows visitors to have a "hands-on" experience with history.

This is a fine museum. The Hastings Museum charges an admission. Hours are from 9-5 Monday through Saturday and 1 to 5 Sundays and holidays.

From the Museum south on US Highway 281 three blocks: One of the older cemeteries in the area is located at 13th and Burlington. The Highland Park Cemetery contains the graves of many of the area's first pioneers. East on 14th about 1 mile: The Crosier Monastery Museum at 14th and Pine contains a collection of wood carvings and artifacts from the Asmat people of New Guinea. It is open by appointment only.

The Jacob Fischer Rainbow fountain located **east on 12th to Denver Street** was erected as part of the electrical exposition for the 1932 Adams County Fair. The fountain with eight water jets, twelve lights and the wizardry of 1932, produced various forms for effect.

East on 12th street road, 4 miles. Provancher Cemetery site marker. This was the site of a French Canadian cemetery during the late 1800s.

East on 7th one and a half miles: Hastings College campus. A pretty and quaint campus typical of those state colleges in Nebraska. The oldest building was built in 1883. The college was created by the first meeting of the Synod of Nebraska Presbyterian Church in 1873.

There is a college museum on campus which includes collections of rocks and minerals, animals and paleontological specimens from Nebraska. Before many of these buildings were built, the first airplane to land in the city of Hastings used the fields about the campus as a landing strip.

West on Fifth to Chesnut in Hastings is a relic of the State's intellectual past, a Chautauqua pavilion. Chautauquas once were the major attraction of any town's summer entertainment. The idea of a traveling caravan for intellectual stimulation originated in upstate New York in the early 1800s. At that time the term was used exclusively to denote a series of lectures of a religious nature, but as the phenomenon spread Chautauquas encompassed larger and larger definitions.

By 1907, when this pavilion was built, the events included

110

lectures, discussions, short plays, music and often large picnics. People came from everywhere to participate and to learn. In recent years many states have attempted to revive the Chautauqua by staging traveling events, often sponsored by the state arts and humanities commissions. In recent years a Chautauqua was begun with help from the University of Nebraska. That Chautauqua traveled with a large tent, and used local halls to present its shows.

In 1992 an arsonist destroyed about half of the Pavilion. An immediate public outcry resulted in an effort to rebuild the landmark and match the original color and design of the structure.

Brickyard Park, developed from an old brickyard, is the home of the annual Cottonwood Prairie Festival. The park serves as a center for outdoor entertainment and cultural arts.

Hastings is the home of a unique museum. The museum for the Nebraska Military Historical Society is located on the grounds of the former Naval amunition depot. The collection includes artifacts from wars dating to the Civil War and the Indian Wars. It includes items from World War I on through to the present. Although the collection is large, the museum displays mostly feature vehicles. Halftracks, command cars and armored cars are kept in working order. Museum volunteers make many of the repairs on the vehicles.

Intersection of 3rd and St. Joesph Streets is a historical marker denoting the site of Liberal Hall and the Olive Trail.

At 1100 Block of West 2cd Street a marker draws attention to the first well in the Hastings area.

East on Second to Kansas Ave: The first church in Hastings, the First Methodist, was built at this location in 1873.

No entry about Hastings could be complete without a word or two on the sad story of Andy th Goose. In the late 1980s Andy was born a normal goose except a birth defect left him without feet. Through the careful kindness of his owner, Andy's webless legs were fitted with baby shoes and he learned to walk. The people of America knew a story when they heard one. The world's environmental crisis, the dissolution of the Soviet Union and the growing national debt were set aside for news about Andy. Soon he appeared on "The Tonight Show," and the grey goose with the white shoes was pcitured in magazines all over the country.

Late in 1991 someone stole Andy from his owner's home in Hastings. His headless, wingless body--although still wearing the shoes, was found in the park ending his short and happy life.

US Highway 281

At Hastings US Highway 281 and 34 are joined for several miles north, to Grand Island, where they go their separate ways once more.

Fourteen miles (3 miles.)

One half mile east: Doniphan.

West of here two miles, then north 2 1/2 miles to Campbell Monument.

In 1867, during the peak of the Sioux hostilities, a small group of Indians made a raid on the Peter Campbell farm. The adult men were not at home, and the Indians killed a woman and her son, and kidnapped four children, including the Campbell's twin sons. The Indians moved on to a neighboring farm and killed the German farmer who lived there. At a later time the government traded an Indian woman and her child, who had been captured at the battle of Elm Creek for the four children.

Near here was a fine early farm. The legend is that two sons of this farm were pinned together by an arrow as they rode double on a horse, trying to escape an Indian raid.

Three miles (4 miles.)

The Platte River. In 1878 four "tramps" were hung here for no other reason than being on the lam. The Grand Island *Independent* reported "we are opposed to mob violence under all circumstances, still we fear that justice to law abiding citizens may require it." The *Independent,* one of the finest small town daily papers in the nation may no longer be quite so independent, but then their editorials don't speak from both sides of the mouth any longer as this one did.

Just to the south of the bridge the Oxbow Cutoff of the Oregon trail crosses the highway. This was a side road of the main Oregon Trail and connected those crossing the Missouri River at Nebraska City with the main trail near present day Kearny. The route of the Oxbow follows the south side of the Platte River to near Columbus, where it then heads southeasterly toward Nebraska City.

Four miles (4 miles.)

Down the Tom Osborne Parkway into Grand Island. Three US Highways (281, 34 and 30) come together here, as well as the major State Highway 2. You will find Grand Island sites listed for the entry for US Highway 30. Also see the entries for State Highway 2 and US Highway 30 for information about locations in this area.

112

Four miles (11 miles.)

Intersection with State Highway 2. Please see this entry for information about sites along this major State Highway.

Eleven miles (2 miles.)

Turn off for St. Libory an earlyday pioneer town. Now mostly memory.

Two miles (9 miles.)

West on State 58 20 miles to Boelus and a small quaint campground near the confluence of the south and middle forks of the Loup.

Nine miles (3 miles.)

St. Paul.

St. Paul is the county seat of Howard County and was founded when James Paul (along with Major Frank North) came up the Loup river and was taken with the beauty and potential of the area around the forks in the river.

Later Paul consulted with his brother, and with leaders in his home country of Denmark, and settlers began to move to the area. The town they founded was originally named Athens, but was later changed to St. Paul. A good part of Howard County was settled by Danes.

The Danish Land and Homestead Colony from Wisconsin was responsible for settling the communities west of St. Paul at Farwell, and Northwest of town at Elba. To the southwest is the small community of Dannebrog, named after the Danish flag, and settled by Danes and Swedes.

The Indian attacks on early settlers, as well as storms and grasshopper plagues kept settlement low. Eventually Ft. Hartsuff, 55 miles upriver, was established to protect homesteaders from the Native Americans and the county's population began to grow. See entry for State Highway 11 for more information about the Fort.

When the railroad reached St. Paul in 1881 the town began to boom since the farmers now had an outlet for their crops. Other Danish communities sprang up including Nysted, west of Dannebrog, and Dannevirke in the northwest part of the county.

At one time the Danish population was 25% of the entire county. It is believed that Howard County has more Danish descendants living in it today than any other area of the state.

113

US Highway 281

Three miles (8 miles.)

Cross the North Loup River at a State Wayside Area.

Eight miles (5 miles.)

Eight miles west of here is the Big Wash. The Big Wash is a scenic area located on Leonard Well's ranch. It is two miles north and three miles east of the town of Cotesfield. Ask for directions, locally. For information about this unusual accidental man-made canyon, see entry for State Highway 11.

Five miles (3 miles.)

This was the tiny railroad town of Brayton, settled in 1888.

Three miles (4 miles.)

Nine miles west on 22 to Scotia.

For information about Scotia, please see entry for State Highway 11.

Four miles (5 miles.)

Greeley.

One early pioneer woman, who left a beautiful home in Boston, came in sight of the early town of Greeley, mostly tents and lean-tos alongside a barren set of railroad tracks. She turned to her husband and burst into tears. "Is that Greeley?" she screamed.

The town has come along some since those days. The Greeley County Historical Society Museum is located in the County Courthouse and is open 5 days a week.

It seems the more isolated and sparsely populated an area is, the more interest they have in preserving their history, and Greeley is no exception. In 1939 a small history of Greeley County was published, and this book was handsomely reprinted in 1977 by the local historical society.

Greeley was settled in the 1870s largely by the Irish, who were fed up with the British control of their land and immigrated to the United States. Many of the earliest settlers in this area came from Ireland via Boston. The earliest settlers came upon the land by accident. Disgruntled Irish pioneers were about to return to Boston when a surveyor told them of the good land along the creekbeds in an area he had just finished surveying. They inspected the land near here and the first white settlers of the county were soon building their sod houses.

When the railroad reached Greeley it brought a bit of the

outside world with it. In the railroad camp just south of town the stable boss got in an argument with the night watchmen who stabbed him in the heart. The watchman was never caught. This was at a time when there were nearly as many saloons as there were people in Greeley. Bank hold-ups and highway robbers were common in those days of the late 1880s.

County couthouses are known for strange characters, and Greeley has had its share. Greeley had one who was known as the eccentric judge. This judge, who presided over the bench at the turn of the century, was never predictable. Once he made a favorable ruling in a lawsuit, and the successful lawyer, knowing the judge's ways, immediately wrote down the words of the decision in the docket so that he would be able to refer to it again should the need arise. Just that very next day a friend stopped by his office. "Heard you lost that case," the friend said, "too bad."

"No," the lawyer said, "I won it."

"Not the way I heard it. The judge was over to the saloon last night and re-tried the entire case. This time he ruled in favor of the defense."

The lawyer rushed to the courthouse and pulled out the docket of the case. The entire page where he had written the judge's words had been torn out.

During a single week in the month of July, 1894 a total of 328 wolf pelts were delivered to the courthouse and the owners were paid the bounty of $3.00 for each pelt. There were no wolves reported in Greeley County much past the turn of the century.

Seven miles west of Greeley on Wallace Creek once stood the town of Horace. Some railroads built small communities to service the line every seven miles. Horace was one such town.

One mile east and one mile south of Greeley is the site of Jacksonville. A small town of a school, saloon, church, blacksmith shop and post office stood here on the banks of the creek in 1878.

Three miles east of Greeley on State Highway 56 and two miles south. Site of O'Connor. The Church of the Visitation is on the National Register of Historic Places.

O'Connor was first laid out as a settlement of the Irish Catholic Colonization Association, which was to be an association of Catholics in the new world.

This town gained a lot of good press, and in the 1880s many hundreds of Bostonians moved here from the east, as well as many others. The Sisters of Mercy opened a school here on the hill near the church. The convent was home to a school, musical academy and retreat house.

During the blizzard of 1888 a snow drift completely covered a barn near here. The owner cut steps in the drift and then sawed a hole in the roof of his barn in order to feed and water his livestock.

East on State Highway 56 fourteen miles, *near the county border. This area is traditionally a cattleman's land, and the cattle industry here dates back to the earliest white settlers in this vicinity, around 1877.*

Five miles (5 miles.)

This area was one of the hardest hit areas in the entire country by the deadly blizzard of 1888.

There is a legend here of a ghost dog who still roams the hillsides looking for his master, a seven year old pioneer boy who had been attacked and killed by wolves.

Late at night the lights of cars passing on this isolated stretch of road fall on its ghastly form and the dog's empty eyes glance up in terror and anger.

Five miles (2 miles.)

Turn off for State Highway 91 to Spalding.

To the west here was unclaimed land for a long while. The first homesteaders to claim land in this area did not stake their claims until 1909, and only then did others come to join them. The land, locally known as the "Sandhills" part of the county, or the "Homestead" area, is still sparsely populated.

Ten miles east on State 91.

Spalding. This town almost ceased to exist shortly after it was founded when the Great Grasshopper Invasion of 1874 wiped out every blade of vegetable matter for miles around.

Just west of here a man was captured by the Indians in 1877 when he and his two companions were attacked by Indians while hunting along Cedar River. He was buried two miles west of here.

Just south of Spalding, across the Cedar River, was the site of a large, temporary Pawnee village in 1880. Several hundred teepees were pitched in a circle on a bank above the river. The site covers 35 acres and artifacts from the location can still be found.

The Sisters of Mercy, who had already started a school in O'Connor (see above) started a small school in Spalding as well. Spalding was another town founded by the Catholic Colonization Association.

The Union Pacific built a line to Spalding. The hope was that the railroad would build a line further up the river. This was never to be the case.

One of the greatest prairie fires of the history of Greeley County started near here on a July day in 1890 and over the next few days spread as far south as O'Connor and Greeley and beyond, an area 15 miles square was destroyed.

Two miles (2 miles.)

Cedar River. Excellent fishing to be had here, say the local experts. Also a safe and scenic river for canoe trips.

Two miles (2 miles.)

One mile east: *Lake Pibel Recreation Area. The most beautiful lake in miles. Recreation facilities available.*

Two miles (7 miles.)

Junction with State Highway 70 west.

Northeast *of here in the summer of 1855 a young Brule Sioux known as Curly, killed an Omaha woman during a battle. It was his first kill in battle. He did not take the woman's scalp, it was said, because the thought of it turned his stomach, even though taking a woman's scalp was considered a great honor. The young man would later become known through out the world by his adult name, Crazy Horse.*

The battle took place after the Sioux had stolen some of the Omahas' horses. When many of the Omaha warriors left their hunting camp to track the stolen horses, the Sioux, who had been hiding in the hills waiting for the moment, swept down on the camp. The Lakota Spooted Tail was said to have had one of his bravest battles here as he swept through the Omaha camp at least three times counting coup.

After the battle the Omaha followed the Sioux out of the valley until they were certain they had withdrawn. Instead, the Sioux circled back and attacked the Omaha once again on Beaver Creek where they killed the famous Omaha trader Logan Fontenelle. See entry for State Highway 14 for more information about the Battle at Beaver Creek.

Seven miles (17 miles.)

US Highway 281

Bartlett sets out in the sun and the wind and the storms and the snow and seems like a long ways from any other place in the world. There is some truth to this as there isn't much else in the way of what some people would call civilization for a few miles in any direction. A pop machine maybe, maybe a pay telephone, but aside from a few ranch houses, Bartlett is it.

Bartlett is the county seat of Wheeler County which is a county that has places where people live with names such as Gritty Ridge, Headquarters, Buffalo Flats and Dry Cedar Creek.

When the first settlers came to this area the only trees were a few (very few) scattered in the river valleys. Since then much timber has been planted in the river valleys and on the sandhills and despite what it may look like out your window this is much greener than it was when the pioneers settled this area.

Wheeler County has a number of streams passing through the county but out of their valleys the land becomes typical of the sandhills region.

Seventeen miles (8 miles.)

Turn off to the east for the town of Bliss and Goose Lake, a one-time state recreation area which has some of the best fishing in these parts. Inquire locally.

Eight miles (18 miles.)

Junction with State Highway 95.

Twenty two miles to Swan Lake, but look for trout, not Tschaikovsky.

Eighteen miles (27 miles.)

O'Neill and the junction with US Highway 20 and 275. See the entry for US Highway 20 for more information about this area.

Twenty seven miles (9 miles.)

Spencer. Frontier Acres, a museum on the northern edge of town on US 281 houses farm machinery and a complete old post office. It is open seven days a week in the summer months, and not quite as often during the winter.

Junction with State Highway 12. Please see that entry for information about this beautiful and seldom-traveled road.

Nine miles (0 miles.)

South Dakota border.

118

Zero miles (4 miles.)
Intersection with Interstate 80 at Exit 300.

Four miles (1 mile.)
Wood River. State Highway 11 follows US Highway 30 for a mile or so, and then swings north. For information about this location, please see entry for US Highway 30.

One mile north of US 30 (1 mile.)
*Take county road **two miles east** to the bank of the Wood River.*

On a morning in January 1862, a local farmer by the name of Anderson set out after his neighbor, Smith, who had gone ahead to the Platte to fell trees. Smith had gone out in the early morning with Anderson's son and two of his own sons. Anderson had planned on meeting them at the Platte with another wagon to help load the timber for the return to the farms.

State Highway 11

When Anderson reached here he found his neighbor's blood-soaked wagon. The horses were gone. He slowly climbed down off his own wagon and searched among the willows. He soon found Smith's body face-down in the river, clutching the hands of his two sons.

Anderson found his own son a few feet further on. He had been riddled with bullets. The bodies of all four were filled with arrows. The Sioux hostilities were beginning and would last until after the end of the American Civil War.

One mile (4 miles.)

East 4 miles to Schauppsville. The town of Wood River, a few miles distant, was already established in 1874 when Mr. John Schaupp built a flour mill at this site. Its location about midway between Wood River and Alda, and along the Mormon Trail, enticed settlers to move to the land around the mill. Soon a town flourished here.

Schaupp could never quite make things work the way he wanted them to. He wanted to build a canal from the Platte to the Wood River in order to increase the flow of the Wood and to provide more water for local farmers. The voters saw it as a way to increase water power for his mill and denied the funding for the project.

In this river bottom land he next decided to drill a well in order to find coal. The coal in Nebraska would make him rich, he decided. It is an indication of his success to say simply that the town of Schauppsville eventually faded into obscurity.

Four miles (3 miles.)

West two miles to the site of Cameron and Cameron Cemetery.

In 1876, when the post office was started here, farms often sold for about $6 per acre. The area had a school, post office, G.A.R. Hall and other niceties. In those days there was a different kind of spirit about things, a kind of community that exists only very rarely these days. Imagine holding a community gathering on Christmas Eve in this day and age of closed-up houses and frightened hearts. In Cameron, Christmas Eve meant coming from miles around to gather in the school house to recite poetry, sing songs, read aloud from the latest novels and watch for Santa Claus' arrival.

Three miles (4 miles.)

One and a quarter miles east to the site of Berwick, a small farming community that thrived during the 1880s. Berwick had an

120

*interesting social organization in 1886 known as the Berwick Eating
Society. The group gathered every few weeks to, well, eat and enjoy
one another's company.*

The Berwick cemetery is just west of the town site.

Four miles (5 miles.)

Cairo. Please see entry for State Highway 2 for information
about Cairo.

Five miles (12 miles.)

Intersection with State Highway 58.

Dannebrog. Home of writer and folklorist Roger Welsh,
whose appearances on CBS television's "Sunday Morning" news
show featured many sites in Nebraska. Welsh also collects stringed
instruments. His collection includes a zither donated to him once long
ago by this author.

*Five miles west of here, near Boelus, is a nice campground
at the junction of the South and Middle Forks of the Loup River.*

Twelve miles (5 miles.)

Junction with State Highway 92.

Howard County was settled by Danes and is believed to have
the highest concentration of Danish descendants of any county in the
state.

Five miles (6 miles.)

Elba.

Elba was so named because a bend in the railroad track
reminded people of an elbow. There might be sillier reasons to name
a town, but if there are, this one would give them stiff competition.

Just north of Elba on the banks of the North Loup River were
several important Indian settlements that dated to pre-Columbian
times. North of Elba the highway follows the pretty and lazy Calamus
River for the next 45 miles.

A sign on the road announces that this is the birthplace of
Grover Cleveland. Perhaps, but not the Grover Cleveland who was
the 22nd individual to serve as President of the United States. That
Grover Cleveland was born in New Jersey.

Six miles (8 miles.)

Cotesfield.

State Highway 11

Two miles north and three miles east of Cotesfield is the Big Wash, on private land.

The Big Wash was created overnight when a farmer made a drain from a table-land lake into the Calamus River drainage. Overnight, a canyon one hundred feet deep and over a mile long was created by his mistake.

Today, Mother Nature has patched things up a bit, and the canyon is full of vegetation and is a haven for wild birds and animals. In the spring the hills are covered with bluebells and other wild flowers.

The Big Wash runs through large rolling hills with oak and cedar trees on the fringes. Ask for directions and permission to visit the Big Wash locally.

Eight miles (1 miles.)

To the west of the highway and below the hill known as Happy Jack Peak is a chalk mine.

The state bought the land, sealed the mine and placed a few picnic tables here for a wayside area. The mine opened in 1887 and the chalk was used in building construction and in the manufacturing of paints.

Happy Jack Peak was named for an Indian scout who climbed the hill to watch for pioneers moving up the valley. When he spied some he would climb down and give them food. The peak offers a wonderful view of the valley and is worth every calorie-burning step up.

One mile (2 miles.)

Junction with State Highway 22.

One mile east to Scotia.

Scotia, by many accounts, should be the county seat of Greeley County, instead of Greeley. The reason it is not the county seat becomes one of those fine Nebraska county seat war stories.

Seems that Scotia won the election to become county seat fair and square. However, as the ballot boxes were being transported from one place to another, 61 additional ballots were added, which swung the vote in favor of Greeley. Since the election had taken place just days after the great blizzard of 1888, lawyers for the town of Scotia had trouble reaching the trial of the two men who were supposed to have been responsible for protection of the ballots. Eventually a judge ruled that there was no proof that the ballots had been tampered with and the new vote, that of Greeley as the county seat, was officially adopted.

Later court cases revealed that a mysterious stranger "riding in the direction of Scotia" had altered the ballots in favor of Scotia. By the time the case was settled enough suspicion and doubt existed between the two towns that gunfire and fisticuffs broke out. Eventually, an armored wagon pulled up to the temporary courthouse in Scotia, and the armed men loaded up the county records and moved them to Greeley under heavy guard, where they remain to this day.

The Chalk Building on the east side of Main Street near the lumber yard is the only remaining chalk building in the state.

On November 3, 1958, ten-year-old Roger Groetzinger was milking his family's cows on a farm at Scotia when he noticed an object circling near his barn. It was an oval-shaped object, flying low and giving off a humming noise. He wanted to stand, but to his horror he discovered he was paralyzed. The object slowly moved up and away from the barn, and as it did Roger found that he could move again. There was a funny smell in the air.

When his mother returned an hour later, Roger was nearly out of his wits. She believed his story.

Two miles (14 miles.)

North Loup. This, dear reader, is the popcorn capital of the world. The village of North Loup has attested to this fact every year since 1902 by celebrating Popcorn Days.

Those factory buildings are for processing popcorn. As they say here, thanks for popping in.

North Loup is near the junction with State Highway 22 west. *Twelve miles west of here State 22 connects with the route outlined in the entry for State Highway 10.*

Fourteen miles (6 miles.)

Ord.

Ord, built on the south banks of the Loup, is the county seat of Valley County. It was named after a general who, at the time of the town's founding in 1874, was commander of the military department of the Platte.

The town of Ord boasts that it is "the throbbing center in an exciting area." The town is a major shopping and service center for a wide area of the Sandhills. There are a nine-hole grass greens golf course, swimming pool, tennis courts and hospital in Ord.

Perhpas the town's finest feature is the North Loup River, which offers tranquillity and good fishing. It cuts through the Sandhills, and a drive or a walk along its banks provide dramatic views of the

State Highway 11

valley. There is a small campground here on the north bank of the river. See also the entry for State Highway 10.

Six miles (9 miles.)

Elyria and the turnoff to Fort Hartsuff State Historical Park, **four miles north.**

On the north bank of the Loup River, just on the Valley/ Garfield County line, is Fort Hartsuff State Historical Park.

Fort Hartsuff was in operation from 1876 to 1881, when it was closed and replaced by Fort Valentine. This fort was instrumental in the settlement of the state, as soldiers from here protected the pioneers from the native population who had roamed Valley County for thousands of years. The plan of the fort was typical of those of the 1870s, with most of the buildings fronting a parade grounds.

A fine state historical park is located here and many of the original buildings have been restored. Unlike some other state parks, many of the original buildings still remain. The restoration as well as the isolation of this place give the visitor a good feel for what life might have been like here.

Still, the employment opportunities here drew settlers from miles away and the dances, celebrations and parties that such a population provided made the fort one of the most pleasant duties in the entire Department of the Platte.

The duties of the fort were to scout the Loup and Cedar rivers for hostile Sioux and chase horse thieves and train robbers. A detachment also escorted prospectors headed for the Black Hills gold fields, to protect them from attacks by the Sioux, on whose land they were trespassing.

The most significant battle in which soldiers from this fort participated was the Battle of the Blowout, in April 1876. See below at Burwell for a description of that battle.

In 1881, the fort was abandoned, and its preservation is owed, in part, to the fact that the buildings were purchased by the Union Pacific Railroad, which intended to use them for future development. When that didn't pan out, the railroad sold the site to local farmers, who eventually donated it to the state.

The park is open seven days a week during summer for self-guided tours.

Nine miles (28 miles.)

Burwell.

Burwell is the county seat of Garfield County and is one of the

124

prettiest but least visited county seats in the state. Careful planning has made this town of over a thousand an attractive and comfortable place.

For a long while Burwell has served as an important market and shipping center for the Sandhill region. Cattle and crops come through Burwell on their way to and from market. Quarterhorse ranches are one of the area's claims to fame. Burwell sits at the edge of the eastern farmlands of Nebraska, and at the start of the isolated and beautiful Sandhill country.

The town boasts a good number of authentic cowboys and ranchers who may not all wear cowboy hats and spurs, but know their *riatas* from their *remudas*.

At the south end of town is Nebraska's Big Rodeo Grounds, a National Historic Site. Each July these grounds are very active with a professional rodeo and the Garfield County Fair. Nebraska's Big Rodeo has given spectators a traditional, first-class rodeo for over 60 years.

The junction of the North Loup and the Calamus rivers is here, one of the two most beautiful small rivers in the entire American West. It was near this confluence that an early settler was killed on Pebble Creek in 1774 by Teton Sioux, which led in part to the formation of Fort Hartsuff.

Several tours of local sites have been designed by residents of Burwell. Ask locally for directions.

For the next fifty miles State Highway 11 passes through the lonely but beautiful Sandhills region. Make that gas and pop stop now.

Six miles northwest on county roads to Calamus Reservoir. Boat ramps, fishing, camping, picnic area at this 5,000-acre reservoir on the once free-flowing Calamus River. Valleyview Flat area, on the north shore, is situated at the site of the town of Valleyview, founded in the early 20th century on the never-completed Lincoln and Black Hills railroad.

Nebraska's largest fish hatchery is just beyond the dam itself. Since Calamus was one of the last large reservoirs built in the state, this hatchery will likely be the last large fish hatchery, since those facilities need large volumes of water to function. The hatchery produces over 50 million fish every year in 50 rearing ponds connected by raceways and tanks.

Near here is the site of the Battle of the Blowout. In April 1776, a detachment from Company A, 23rd Infantry, was sent out from Fort

125

State Highway 11

Hartsuff with orders to respond to complaints that a party of Sioux warriors had been harassing settlers. Company A found the Sioux warriors and a short but intense battle was fought with the Sioux at the hollowed-out hillock of a blowout. While the number of Sioux dead is not certain, one infantryman was killed. See also entry above for Fort Hartsuff.

Twenty-eight miles (4 miles.)

Swan Lake, a natural comfortable lake with good fishing just south of the South Fork of the Elkhorn. Inquire locally.

Four miles (19 miles.)

Turnoff for State Highway 95 and the small ranching community of Chambers (**twelve miles east**). This road follows the South Fork of the Elkhorn and connects with US Highway 281.

Nineteen miles (27 miles.)

Junction with US Highway 20/275, at Atkinson. See entry for US Highway 20 for information about this area.

For the next 27 miles the highway zig-zags through the northern half of Holt County, entering Boyd County at the Niobrara River.

Twenty seven miles (6 miles.)

At the Niobrara River is the beautiful Kit Wade Canyon. If this isn't "out west" then there is no such place.

Six miles (2 miles.)

Butte.

The county seat of Boyd County, Butte was named for the Harvey Buttes just south of town. This makes a nice picnic spot, and, if so inclined, an ideal location for a little roadster romance.

The buttes in this area of the state are of the same formation as the Black Hills in South Dakota. One geological theory is that they were formed by glaciers that deposited a part of their load of rocks as they retreated. The soil on the floor of the valley and the rock of the buttes are of two distinct origins.

Butte is the location of the junction with State Highway 12. Please see the entry for State Highway 12 for information about sites along this road.

Two miles (5 miles.)

126

The tiny village of Anoka, which is Sioux for "on both sides." There is nothing here for Anoka to be on both sides of, however.

Five miles (0 miles.)
Just at the South Dakota line is Scalp Creek, named for...well, you figure it out. This is one of the best local fishing spots.

Zero miles (3 miles.)
> Kansas border.

Three miles (2 miles.)
> *East five miles* to Lookout Mountain, a limestone hill with a cap. Climb to the top of Lookout Mountain and you will be overlooking an Indian village known as Reams Village. Up until the 1930s several Indian houses still stood at this place and pot sherds and arrowheads were everywhere.

Two miles (2 miles.)
> Intersection with county road. This road parallels the south bank of the Republican River for the entire east/west length of Franklin County. It is a treat to drive.

Two miles (14 miles.)
> Franklin. For information about Franklin, please see entry in

section on US Highway 136.

Fourteen miles (2 miles.)
Intersection with State Highway 4.
For the next eight miles State Highway 10 gradually rises as it approaches the headwaters of the Little Blue River.

Two miles (12 miles.)
West five miles to Hildreth. Hildreth is the home of the nationally known Hildreth Tractor Pull competition. In addition, this tiny burg is the location of the Superbowl of six-man football. The Nebraska six-man Football All Star game is held here.

Twelve miles (10 miles.)
Minden. Home of the famous Harold Warp Pioneer Museum and much more. For a detailed description of Minden, please see entry for US Highway 6 and 34.

Ten miles (1 mile.)
Junction to the west with State L 50. Please see entry of US 30 for information about Platte Station, Fort Kearney, "17 Mile Station" the Pony Express and Oregon Trail and other sites along this beautiful road.

One mile (5 miles.)
Platte River. At the Platte is Hook's Ranch, or Dogtown, a stage station and trading post at the junction of the Oregon Trail and the Ft. Kearney Trail from Nebraska City. An early pioneer wrote, "Dogtown is the first settlement west of Marysville and an ugly one at that." This is also the location of Valley Station, a later day stage stop, and Lowell Cemetery an early day cemetery.
West of here four miles to Ft. Kearny Historical Park, at the site of the old Ft. Kearny. See entry for US Highway 30 for a description of this fort so important to early day settlement.
Along this stretch of the Platte is the best place in the state to see the migration of the sandhills cranes which might include a sizable number of the 112 or so remaining whooping cranes.
In 1978 a non-profit trust was set up in order to protect the migratory bird habitat along the Platte River. The trust was formed as a result of a $7.5 million endowment granted via a federal court settlement involving three power companies and the building of a Wyoming dam.

State Highway 10

The Platte River Whooping Crane Habitat Maintenance Trust has purchased thousands of acres along the river, restored wildlife habitat, conducted water quality and wildlife quality research, established a data base on the diversity of the wildlife, continued restoration of crane roosting habitat and fought to establish minimum flow levels for the river.

Much of this work was accomplished under the leadership of Executive Director John VanDerwalker, who served the trust during the 1980s. VanDerwalker left the trust in 1991 to take a job with the State Department in Washington, D.C. Before he left, however, he said that state officials have been indecisive in their role of protecting the Platte for future generations. He said the river was being managed for one purpose, and one purpose only, irrigation. Domestic water use, recreation and wildlife preservation are accomplished only by way of default to the financial interests of irrigation companies like Central Nebraska Public Power and Irrigation, VanDerwalker said.

In response to his remarks, politicians and bankers across the state pointed their fingers elsewhere.

The population of at least two endangered species is on the verge of disappearing from the river because of lack of a minimum flow level.

"If the state does not protect instream flows," VanDerwalker said, "the Platte River will be lost, period."

Five miles (1 mile.)

Just south of the intersection with US Highway 30 the Mormon Trail crosses Highway 10.

One mile (7 miles.)

Intersection with US Highway 30.

Seven miles (15 miles.)

Kearney. For information about Kearney and this area, please see entry for US Highway 30. State Highway 10 leaves US 30 at Kearney and heads north.

Fifteen miles (9 miles.)

Pleasanton. Named after the pleasant view of the valley of the South Loup, known locally for decades as Pleasant Valley.

Nine miles (6 miles.)

Hazard and the junction with State Highway 2. Please see

130

entry for State Highway 2 for information about this area.

Six miles (12 miles.)

East 8 miles on State 68 and **then south seven miles** on State Highway 58 to a small and beautiful campground at Boelus, near the confluence of the Middle and South Forks of the Loup River.

Twelve miles (10 miles.)

Loup City. This quaint town of over a thousand souls was named because of its location in the Loup River valley.

The Loup River did not get its name because of a misspelling of the word loop, but rather in a roundabout way from the wolf, which once, long ago, roamed its banks. The Pawnee who lived along the river's edges were known as the Skidi band of Pawnee. Skidi was the Pawnee word for wolf. The French fur trappers, in their attempt to name things so that they might be able to recognize them when they next chanced upon them, called the river where this band of Pawnee lived *Loup,* French for wolf. So the Loup River is the French translation of the Indian translation of the word in English, wolf.

Loup City is known as the Polish capital of Nebraska. In the late 1980s the historical society opened a museum celebrating the area's Polish history. The museum, located in a refurbished house on nearly 3 acres of land, has displays in nearly every one of the nine rooms. A one-room school house is included at the museum. The town's once popular Polish Days festival is making a comeback.

Loup City is the county seat of Sherman County. It is the location of Bowman Lake Recreation Area, which offers camping and boating facilities.

From Loup City **seven miles to the northeast** *is the large Sherman Reservoir and State Recreation Area. This large area encompasses the entire reservoir and offers hiking, fishing, boating and concessions.*

Just northwest of Loup City, the hills rise to over half a mile above sea level for the first time in the long ascent to the Rockies. Loup City has a museum which, among other exhibits of local history, houses some items from India and Africa.

At Loup City is the junction with State Highway 92. Please see entry for State Highway 92 for sites in this area.

Continue north on State Highway 10 which is joined at Loup

State Highway 10

City with State Highway 58.

Ten miles (5 miles.)

Turn off for Arcadia at State Highway 70.

Six miles west to Arcadia, "simple pleasure and quiet." Tornadoes have ignored this interpretation of the name and ruined the village three times.

Every fall, well after tornado season, the town celebrates its Fall Festival with talent shows, parades and a rodeo. It is held the first weekend in September.

Five miles (9 miles.)

Junction with State Highway 22 to North Loup and Scotia. See entry for State Highway 11 for further information.

Nine miles (0 miles.)

Ord. A thriving, albeit small, Sandhills community. The North Loup is very pretty here and is well worth a walk. Ord is close to a number of historical and recreation sites.

See State Highway 11 for further information.

Zero miles (7 miles.)
     Kansas border.

Seven miles (21 miles.)
     Alma.
     This is the heart of the great buffalo hunting grounds of the
Old West. From here, west to the Rockies, millions of bison roamed
the plains. Early settlers were drawn to this area partially because of
the great herds.
     The Republican River was known to local Indians and early
settlers by the more earthy version of "Manure River" because of the
great numbers of buffalo that ate, slept and...er...lived near its banks.
     Alma is located on the shores of the Harlan County Lake, one
of the largest man-made lakes in the state. The lake was created when
the Republican River was dammed in 1952.
     The dam was conceived after a terrible flood in 1935. An

eight-foot wall of water moved down the Republican, destroying property and taking 104 lives in its path.

On a bluff on the south shore of the lake is a cave where, as legend has it, Buffalo Bill used to camp. He once spent 27 days there after suffering a broken leg. During this stay, Sioux Indians found him and took his food, but left him alone.

Alma is one of the oldest towns along the Republican. It was founded in 1871 and is the county seat of Harlan County.

In late 1984 or '85 a citizen of Alma was walking along the south shore of the Harlan County Lake and saw some bones sticking out of a bank. He contacted some officials and then the Kansas University Museum of Natural History, and before anyone could bat an eye, the scientists from the neighboring state had arrived and carefully removed the remains of a "30-foot reptilian creature." The museum has nicknamed the creature, which lived at least 63 million years ago, the Kimono Dragon.

In 1871, Buffalo Bill Cody ran for state representative for the 26th District, which included Harlan County. He filed as a Democrat in the predominantly Republican district. However, the Buffalo Bill name and fame went a long way and he was apparently elected by the narrow margin of 44 votes.

He then added the moniker "The Honorable" to his name, but failed to show up in Lincoln at any time to fulfill his duties as a representative. After all, he had better things to do.

His opponent in the election, shocked that he could be beaten, began to investigate the election. As it turned out, an error in counting the votes had taken place in Alma. The Harlan County clerk had goofed and sent his count to Lincoln, rather than to North Platte. The additional vote count swung the election in favor of Cody's opponent by 42 votes.

Cody was informed of this mixup and went on about his business without much of a change. He hadn't bothered to go to Lincoln anyway, and he never dropped the "Honorable" from his name after that.

As you travel north out of Alma toward Holdrege try to imagine the vast herds of buffalo that once grazed these rolling prairies.

Twenty one miles (2 miles.)
Holdrege. For more information about this pretty town please see the entry for US Highway 6.
Two miles (3 miles.)

Phelps County Museum. A large (34,000 square feet) museum with every item imaginable, and some that are not. The museum is also the home of the active Phelps County Historical Society and the Sod House Society.

For more information please see entry for Holdrege on US Highway 6.

One mile north and seven miles west, or follow State Highway 23 out of Holdrege to Loomis. Several historic cemeteries are near this small community:

Loomis Cemetery, on the west side of town, is no longer in use. Started in 1898.

Platte Valley Cemetery is 11 miles north and a half mile east of Loomis and dates from 1881. Local author Edla Larsen Gourley's 1940s novel Homestay traced the lives of a pioneer family. Many of the people she based her characters on are buried here.

Williamsburg Cemetery is 12 miles north, three miles east and a half mile south of Loomis. Oldest burial is 1885.

Three miles (3 miles.)

Two miles west on county roads to the site of the former town of Phelps Center. Once the county seat, before that honor was stolen from it by the citizens of Holdrege, Phelps Center was at the crossroads of several important local trails and roads. The town once had two newspapers, stores, blacksmith shops, banks, schools and churches.

In 1888, a local minister took three orphans into his home and raised them, starting the Orphans' Home. In 1923, a new building was constructed and is still in use by Christian Homes, a care facility headquartered in Holdrege.

Three miles (10 miles.)

West of here six miles a huge stratospheric balloon crashed to the ground in 1934. The balloon flight, sponsored by the National Geographic Society, was designed to study the upper altitude. The passengers survived by parachuting to the ground, but the balloon was destroyed. The event captured the attention of the nation.

East of here five miles to the Magill Cemetery dating from 1881.

Ten miles (1 mile.)

Before you reach the Platte river, *turn west and go three*

US Highway 183

miles. This county road, which parallels the Platte, roughly follows the route of the Oregon Trail. In three miles is Sandy Channel Wayside Area along the Platte River. Near here was the westernmost ford of the Platte River, which connected the Council Bluffs section of the trail with the St. Joseph Trail. This was also the location of Craig Station of the Pony Express and Oregon Trail routes.

For more information about sites in this area, including information about one of the state's bloodiest massacres at a place called Plum Creek, please see entry for US Highway 30.

One mile (2 miles.)

Cross the Platte River. Hard to imagine that this sluggish river, littered with rusted cars and concrete blocks, was so important in American history, isn't it?

Two miles (14 miles.)

Junction with US Highway 30. Elm Creek is one half mile east of here. See entry for US Highway 30 for more information on this area.

Fourteen miles (7 miles.)

Junction with State Highway 40 at the tiny village of Miller, named after an Omaha businessman who bought land in the area. In the deed to his land, Miller stipulated that if the railroad were to come this way, and if a town were formed, it had to be called Miller. Look around, this is his legacy.

The highway crosses the Wood River.

Seven miles (18 miles.)

The highway crosses the South Loup River, and as it does the land seems to perceptively grow wilder and more remote. Ahead lies the heart of the great wilderness of Nebraska, the sparsely settled and little-known Sandhills.

Eighteen miles (9 miles.)

Ansley. This village was first settled in 1886 and was named after a woman who invested in the area.

Junction with State Highway 2. Please see the entry for State Highway 2 for more information about sites in this area.

Junction with State Highway 92, east. Please see the entry for State Highway 92 for more information about sites along this route.

136

Nine miles (2 miles)

Westerville. Westervillians argue that their town is the oldest in the county. While Sargent will give them a good fight on this issue, many hints of the town's age still stand.

*West of Westerville **12 miles** to Broken Bow. Please see the entry for Broken Bow in State Highway 2.*

Two miles (8 miles.)

Cross the Clear Creek. This is the site of the most noted feud between ranchers and homesteaders in the state.

In 1878, homesteaders Luther Mitchell and Ami Ketchum were fed up with ongoing troubles with cattle rancher Print Olive. His cattle broke into their fenced corn time and again, and his cowboys continually made trouble for the sod-busters.

It was here where a gun battle broke out between the two factions. A brother of rancher Olive was killed. The homesteaders Mitchell and Ketchum were arrested for murder.

On their way to the trial they were ambushed about 10 miles southwest of Broken Bow by Olive and his men. The farmers were hanged and then their bodies were burned. Olive was not arrested.

Eight miles (6 miles.)

Junction S-21 C .

*Seven miles **east** to Comstock. This town started in 1901 and has many rustic buildings still standing. The general store was purchased by the historical society and now serves as a museum. Just south of here is the Dowse sod house, built in 1900. It has been restored.*

On the same county road and before reaching the house a marker commemorates the site of Fort Garber. It was built and stationed by local citizens during the Indian scare of the 1880s.

Six miles (1 mile.)

Still visible on a hill about one mile south of Sargent on the west side of the road are the mounds of a mysterious encampment made by some early inhabitants of the area. They were probably Indians, as this place was already covered with grass when the first white settlers arrived. The mound has 108 pits, arranged in the shape of a large crescent encompassing 6 acres.

Local legend has it that the Indians buried gold in this area, after having robbed a train carrying gold dust and nuggets. The land is in private ownership and the owners would not appreciate anyone tearing up their property to try to find mythical gold.

Others believe that the shape of the ruins indicates that the Indians were trying to form a large ceremonial hill in the shape of some creature. Some of those believers then speculate that this was in order to communicate with beings from outer space.

One mile (8 miles.)

Sargent. Sargent is the oldest town in Custer County (unless you are from Westerville). It was settled in 1880 by Polish settlers. There are several sod houses in this area and many owners will let you have a look. Ask locally for directions.

Six miles west of Sargent is the site of an old flour mill. Ask locally for directions.

Sixteen miles east of Sargent to Ord and Fort Hartsuff Historical Park, a wonderfully restored fort well worth the visit. See entry for State Highway 11 for more information.

Eight miles (15 miles)

Junction with State Highway 91, and Taylor. Taylor is the county seat of Loup County and was named after a local pioneer. It is located on the southern bank of the North Fork of the Loup River.

Near here, on the banks of Sioux Creek in 1873, Sioux Indians attacked settlers in a short but furious battle. Over $1,500 worth of horses were captured by the Sioux. The infuriated whites complained enough so that the incident helped convince the government that a fort was needed in this area of the country. A year later, at a cost of $110,000, Fort Hartsuff was built 15 miles east of here. Ask locally for directions to Sioux Creek.

The population of Taylor, by official statistics, increased by 2 between 1930 and 1980. At this rate, Taylor's population should reach 500 by the year 7490. Keep at it, Taylorites!

West of Taylor on State 91 ten miles to Almeria, a town founded in this century. The drive between Taylor and Almeria through Cheesebrough Canyon is considered by many to be the most beautiful place in all of Loup County.

East of Taylor on State 91 8 miles, then north to Calamus Reservoir, a large and well-developed state recreation area. The lake can be reached by traveling north on US 183 15 miles to marked turnoff. See entry for State Highway 11 for more information.

East of Taylor is the site of the Battle of the Blowout, the location of an intensive battle between Teton Sioux and soldiers from nearby Fort Hartsuff. See entry for State Highway 11 for more details about this battle.

Fifteen miles (8 miles.)

Turn off on marked road for Calamus Reservoir, a well-developed area with good fishing and boating. See entry for State Highway 11 for more information about this area.

The highway north of this point parallels the beautiful and peaceful Calamus River for a number of miles. There is little traffic here, and every passing car seems to have a driver willing to slowly raise an index finger off the steering wheel as a friendly greeting. Try finding someone who will do that in Omaha or Lincoln!

Eight miles (15 miles.)

On the banks of the Calamus River, just as the highway leaves it to swing more directly north and near the Loup County line, were several Indian villages as recently as a century ago. Remnants of many of these villages can still be easily found. The villages were home to the Pawnee and the Arikari. Fishing along the Calamus is reported to be some of the best river fishing in the state.

Fifteen miles (18 miles.)

Rose, a small, almost blown away building or two.

Eighteen miles (10 miles.)

A county road heads east ten miles to the lake country of Rock County. Pony Lake, Smith Lake and others offer fine fishing and beautiful, isolated scenery. Ask locally for directions and road and fishing conditions.

Ten miles (12 miles.)

Bassett, and junction with US Highway 20.

Bassett, the county seat for Rock County and, as is typical for this part of the state, a center for a large area of sparsely populated ranches. There is no significant population center for another 60 miles south of Bassett. However, the trip south along US 183 is particularly beautiful given its isolated nature.

The highway passes through what many consider to be the most beautiful section of Nebraska's unique Sandhills region. There are few trees, but many perfectly rounded hills of grass and yucca.

Bassett was named after an important Nebraskan and local

citizen who, in 1871, brought the first herd of cattle into the Sandhills and started one of Nebraska's most important financial resources: cattle raising.

Rock County is not without other villages, however, and their names would do justice to a Louis L'Amour novel: Horsefoot, Mariaville, Pony Lake, Skull Creek and Rose.

The long hill that forms the town is one of the attractive features of the community. Bassett is a pretty town that serves as a shipping point for much of the cattle and hay produced in the area.

The downtown area was once the hangout of such Nebraska desperadoes as Doc Middleton and Kid Wade. Wade, who was a rustler, gambler and leader of a notorious gang of outlaws called the Pony Boys, was eventually caught and hanged in 1884 just east of town by a group of vigilantes.

Twelve miles (14 miles.)

US Highway 183 and US Highway 20 are the same road for these 12 miles west of Bassett. For information on this section, please see entry for US Highway 20.

Fourteen miles north of US Highway 20 (3 miles.)

North on US 183 to Devil's Gulch, a steep canyon where many fossils have been recovered. There were once woolly elephants and camels in Nebraska, and if you believe that you'll believe that Nebraska had a native-born son in the White House and addressed as "President."

Three miles (2 miles.)

East and south on county roads to the site of the ghost town of Riverview. This is said by many to be the most beautiful spot in the state, especially in the spring when the area is in full wildflower bloom. The road sits high above the river and provides the inspiration for the claims of beauty.

Near here in 1991 two employees from the Nebraska Department of Roads were working in a state-owned pit when they found the skull of a stegomastodon, a large elephantlike creature. The fossil is now at the State Museum in Lincoln.

Two miles (5 miles.)

Springview. This is the county seat of Keya Paha County. The county with the most beautiful name in the state, Keya Paha is a Sioux word meaning Turtle Hill. It was the name the Indians gave to the river, and the whites gave to their county. It probably originated because of the many rounded, turtle-shaped hills in the area.

Springview is the haying and trade center of a wide area. The county has never had a railroad, and may be the only county in the state with such a distinction.

When this town was first formed, a spring flowed not far from the central square. Story has it that the founder of Springview, a pioneer with a bad back, actually was hauling buckets of water to the site in order to make settlers believe such a spring existed. Soon after the town was incorporated, the spring dried up and the founder's back condition improved vastly.

Springview is at the junction with State Highway 12.

Please see the entry for State Highway 12 for more information about sites west of Springview.

Five miles (7 miles.)

Junction with State Highway 12 east. Please see entry for State Highway 12 for information about sites east of here.

Seven miles (0 miles.)

The border with South Dakota.

Zero miles (13 miles.)
   Kansas Border.

Thirteen miles (12 miles.)
   Beaver City.
   The earliest white traveler in these parts was so taken by the beauty of the area that he vowed to return here and settle. He kept his word and 1872 the town was born.
   Beaver City was given a boost when the railroad came this way in the 1880s, but the blizzard of 1888 left houses and barns buried in snow. The town seems to have had its share of bad luck ever since. In 1915 the smallpox scare closed the place down. That was followed by a severe drought in 1934, dust storms in 1935, floods and more blizzards.
   Still, there is plenty of reason to fight out the bad times here. Beaver City is rightly proud of the central city park, which was a part

143

of the original design for the town. It was built as a memorial to the Union soldiers of the civil war and, according to local sources, is always a favorite play-spot for family gatherings, checker games, egghunts, watermelon feeds, parades and Union church services on Sunday evenings.

The courthouse has two marble tablets in the lobby which trace the history of Furnas County. Part of that history was stumbled on in the 1970s when a log cabin with dove tail construction was discovered beneath the walls of a frame house in town.

The fairgrounds are located north of town on the Civilian Conservation Corps campgrounds. The Corps was active during the 1930s.

Beaver City is located on Beaver Creek which was named for the beaver that lived there. It is the county seat of Furnas County.

Twelve miles (20 miles.)
Arapahoe.
See entry for US Highway 34.

Twenty miles (6 miles.)
Elwood, the county seat of Gosper County.

Eight miles (3 miles.)
Johnson Reservoir, and the popular Johnson Lake State Recreation Area. There are several state wildlife management areas in the vicinity and they make for good, patient bird-watching sites.

Three miles (4 miles.)
Just before the highway swings to the east the Oregon Trail crosses the road. Near here are several important sites of the Oregon Trail. See entry for US Highway 30 for more information about these sites.

Four miles (0 miles.)
Lexington. US Highway 283 ends at Lexington. For information on Lexington, please see entry for US Highway 30.

NEBRASKA
U S
83

Zero miles (14 miles.)

Kansas border.

Ranchers got their start in this area by rounding up stray cattle that roamed from the large herds passing north from Texas on the Texas Cattle Road. That road, which led from Texas to Ogallala and north, passed west of here. Throughout the entire Red Willow County, and especially in these open areas, the Pawnee and the Sioux hunted buffalo. Some of the largest herds were in this section of the state on the southern side of the Platte. The largest oil field in the state was discovered near McCook in the late 1950s.

One mile south of McCook is Barnett Park. Barnett Park was formed after several people cleared tons of debris left here by the flood of 1935.

Fourteen miles (10 miles.)

McCook.

For more information on McCook see entry for US Highway

145

6.

Ten miles (30 miles.)

Hugh Butler Lake. A state recreation area formed when Red Willow Creek was dammed.

Hugh Butler Lake in Frontier County is noted for excellent fishing in a remote, yet accessible spot.

Thirty miles (8 miles.)

Junction with State Highway 23. A short way down this road is the favorite spot of "Evil Doc" Carver, one of the state's notorious bandits. Near here is also the comfortable Strunk Lake. Depending on your time, a variety of interesting sidetrips are available on this route:

One mile east of US Highway 83.

Maywood. Maywood is a small community on the way to Hugh Butler Lake and McCook (see below). Mayfwood holds an annual event known as The Spring Rites.

Seven miles east of US 83

Curtis, at the juncture of State Highways 23 and 235, celebrated its centennial in 1987 and owes its existence to the railroad and the cattle industry.

Be sure to visit the Hansen Memorial museum while in the area. It contains artifacts, paintings and furniture of pioneers who settled the area of Frontier County. It includes a small county schoolhouse, which is furnished exactly as it had been on the last day of school in 1948.

You might as well stop by the campus of Nebraska College of Technical Agriculture while you're at it. The school is located on a 400-acre farm that serves as the field lab for classes.

A few miles north of here, the largest mammoth skeleton on display at Morril Hall at the University of Nebraska was discovered in a canyon of loess and red clay. Ask locally for directions to other places with prehistoric artifacts.

The area around Curtis and Curtis Creek is known for its wild fruit, and, consequently, some of the kinds of birds not often found in most parts of the state, including the magpie and several types of hawks.

East of Curtis on State Highway 23: (all mileage is from Curtis.) Ten miles:

146

Morefield is a small town that boasts both a post office and a grain elevator.

Twelve miles *to the junction of State Highway 47 to Interstate 80 and Gothenburg.*

Twenty miles:
Eustis. Eustis was one hundred years old in 1987 and was founded as a result of the railroad that was built through the northern part of Frontier County. It was settled by German pioneers and still has a Wurst Tag, or, for you non-informed, a Sausage Day, during the late summer.
A silica mine once operated just west of town.

Twenty-one miles to the junction with US Highway 283.

South of Curtis on State Highway 235:

Seven miles south of Curtis: *Frontier County was founded in 1872 when a pioneer named Henry Clifford raised his Sioux teepee on the banks of Medicine Creek. Clifford and his Sioux wife, Eena Teglake, had found the only reliable water between the Platte and the Republican River and made their stand.*
Medicine Creek cuts the county diagonally from the northwest to the southeast, and since it was such an important water source throughout history, many artifacts can be found along its course. In addition, many prehistoric Indian villages were located on the hills along the valley and canyon of Medicine Creek.
The area has several reservoirs for sportspeople, swimmers and gazers.

Ten miles south of Curtis:
Stockville.
A nearly deserted town (don't mention this to the 40 remaining residents) but with many of the buildings from more prosperous days still standing. Stockville, which is competing with Brewster in Blaine County as one of the smallest county seats in the nation, has a county courthouse that was built in 1888 and is still in use. The previous building, also made of wood, was built in 1872, and burned to the ground in 1884, along with most of the county records to that time.
This is considered the oldest city in southwestern Nebraska.

Stockville lost its luster when the railroad passed it by, in favor of a more northerly route across Frontier County. Frontier County would like you to know that 22 men have been sent to the state Legislature from near here.

One and a half miles north of Stockville *to Dancing Leaf Earth Lodge. Possibly the most unique commercial lodging in the state, Dancing Leaf (a Native American name for the cottonwood tree) caters to those wishing to believe they can live as the Upper Republican culture of Native Americans did 600 years ago in this area.*

For a fee, the visitor may experience the intense heat and steam of a sweat lodge to "purify mind, body, heart and spirit," as the owners claim, or learn primitive living skills such as tool making, pottery, hide tanning and basket weaving, or visit "spiritual bonding points" — "Special isolated places set aside for individuals who wish to get in touch with the renewing power of nature and learn more about their own spirituality."

Prices are established by the length of the stay and range from a two-hour tour to overnight stays. The overnight accommodations are provided in — what else? — an earthen lodge. Meals provided include buffalo stew and "traditional Indian meals."

Three miles south of Stockville, *along the road that parallels Medicine Creek:*

The favorite spot of Dr. W. F. "Evil Spirit of the Plains" Carver. At the age of 14, Carver lived with the Indians of Minnesota after his father booted him out of his family in Illinois. He left Minnesota and ended up in this part of the frontier, hunting and trapping as a loner. When the Sioux War started in 1862, Carver was named as a scout for General Henry Sibley.

After the war he came back to this area. One of his favorite camps was this spot on the Medicine. He became known as one of the great buffalo hunters. He also became known as a dentist. The two occupations still seem to have some kind of a relationship.

Carver knew many of the legendary Wild West characters, including Buffalo Bill, Wild Bill Hickok, Texas Jack Ojomondro and Kit Carson.

In May 1883, Carver and Buffalo Bill jointly opened the Wild West Show. Carver was one of the best rifle shots of his day and held a record for a long while. He managed to shoot at clay balls tossed into the air. Out of 6,000 balls, he missed only 650. The first performance was in Omaha.

148

Carver's main act was known as The Great Rifle Shot and involved him shooting glass balls the size of quarters, which had been tossed into the air. A hard enough task, but Carver did it while riding horseback.

On a bad day, when Carver's shot was off, he became disgusted with himself and show business and turned his act over to Buffalo Bill and stormed off. Soon after, the partnership was dissolved. Later Carver started his own rival show, and he and Buffalo Bill became enemies and remained so for the rest of their lives.

Carver's shows toured off and on until his death. His last great act, touring the year he died, was a troupe of diving horses, which would leap from a platform into a large tub of water. Carver's shows never became as popular as his rival's, however. Carver died in 1927 and is buried in Illinois.

Ten miles south of Stockville, *on Coon Creek, two divisions of soldiers camped for the summer of 1872.*

Fifteen miles southeast *of Stockville is Harry D. Strunk Lake, a fine recreation area created by a dam on the once wild Medicine Creek. You can buy bait, soda pop and treats here, and boat, fish and relax.*

On the way to this lake, and in the surrounding hillsides, you might get a feel for what this area of the state once was like. Not too long ago this land between the Platte and the Republican Rivers was teeming with wildlife. Buffalo, wolf, fox, wildcat and bear roamed these hills.

Eight miles (6 miles.)

The tiny spot on the road known as Wellfleet, which was named after a "whale fleet." Don't even ask how a town here got named after a fleet of whaling ships...

Six miles (15 miles.)

Junction of State Highway 23. See entry for the highway for sites west of here.

Ten miles (5 miles.)

*Ask locally for directions and road conditions. Take the county road to the **east** for about **four miles** to the 3,200-foot hill known as Sioux Lookout. This hill served as a lookout for the local Indians as they watched for buffalo and for the whites moving along*

149

US Highway 83

the Great Platte River Road. From this vantage point the Indians could signal a hunting party or warriors to attack. A statue of a proud Sioux in a double war bonnet was erected on the top of the hill in 1931, but vandals have destroyed much of the structure. Although the statue stands on public land, most of the routes up the hill are on private land. A move is under way to have the entire hill made into a state historical park.

Five miles (3 miles.)

Turnoff for Maloney Reservoir, one mile to the west. This state recreation area has fishing and boating for all types of crafts. Camping is available and includes hookups and pads for RVs.

Although fishing is good here, nothing quite matches the prehistoric human leg bone found sticking out of the ground by a McCook fisherman one September morning in 1991. Archeologists noted that this area was an important area to Native Americans for at least a thousand years.

Three miles (2 miles.)

Just before the highway becomes a four lane road the Oregon Trail crosses it. Just to the west, about three tenths of a mile down a small road, is the site of the Cold Springs Pony Express and Stage Station. It was of adobe construction and also served as ranch buildings.

Two miles (21 miles.)

North Platte. Please see entry for US Highway 30 for information about North Platte.

For the next 23 miles Highway 83 is joined with State Highway 70. Together they lazily climb into the grassy slopes of the start of the Sandhills. This is beautiful and isolated land. Stop the car a moment, turn off the engine and step outside. The quiet and the beauty here can melt the ice of any sorrow or boredom.

Twenty one miles (4 miles.)

Junction with State Highway 92, east. Highway 92 splits off and continues east of this junction to Arnold. For information about sites along State Highway 92 please see that entry.

Four miles (18 miles.)

Stapleton.

This is the county seat of Logan County, and like 99.97

150

percent of all of the counties of the state, there was a battle to get the courthouse and its fine workers here instead of elsewhere. The most recent elsewhere in contention was the small Logan town of Gandy. This particular battle was settled in the courtroom in the 1930s and Stapleton won.

The small town of Stapleton, hovering around a population of 350 houses, is the only school district in the county. Children are bused here from all of Logan County and from parts of McPherson and Lincoln counties as well. Even drawing from this wide area, the district enrolls only 215 students. The mural on the side of the Veterans Building along State Highway 92 through town was finished in 1976 and depicts scenes from the life of the county.

In the Senior Citizens' building, also along Highway 92, the Logan County Museum is starting to grow. This museum is a new venture and any assistance from the outside visitor to help this community effort would be appreciated.

State Highway 92 leaves US Highway 83 here and heads west. For information about sites along its path see entry for State Highway 92. Many of this county's citizens have roots that extend over 200 years in Logan county.

Two miles southeast of Stapleton.
Gandy. The outlaw Parker was captured here in the late 1880s. Gandy tried to increase its stature by legally attempting to become Logan County's county seat. It lost.

Eighteen miles (3.5 miles)
Thomas County/Logan County border.

The great Prairie Fire of the 1890s, which burned thousands of square miles, passed by here, destroying barns and livestock. Other more recent fires have stopped just short of destroying the National Forest lands. A fire on March 6, 1972, burned 100,000 acres in a path 32 miles long and 12 miles wide. It destroyed many ranches in the county.

Three and a half miles (9 miles.)
The Dismal River, which flows through Thomas County, is still successfully trapped by local ranchers. Mink, muskrat and beaver still frequent the banks of the river.

In this area in the 1930s a rancher started growing sugar cane and started a molasses plant. It was a sticky business...

During the dry years of the 1930s this area of the Sandhills suffered many natural disasters. The storms that did come were intense lightning storms, and many people lost their lives because of them. When the rivers to the south dried up, snakes moved farther and farther north. Thomas County was plagued by the influx of many varieties of snakes during the drought years. The dust storms crossed the county as well, bringing the earth from hundreds of miles away in tall black clouds and raging winds.

Nine miles (5 miles.)
Four miles west on county and private road. The Pearson sod house and school.

Thomas County, like the rest of this isolated part of the state, had many one-room schools. Now that the population has declined, and larger and larger ranches occupy the land, one-room schools are nearly extinct. Likewise, there are still sod houses, now mostly melting back into the hills, or used as cow sheds and storage barns. One fine example can still be seen here. The only remaining two-story sod house in the county, it is now abandoned. It dates from at least 1917, and perhaps earlier. It is on the Pearson ranch and permission is required to view the house.

Five miles (21 miles.)
Junction of State Highway 2. Just to the west of this junction is the county seat, Thedford.
Thedford.
Cattlemen from the Thedford Livestock Association were directly responsible for the last great settlement of the American West. They petitioned the U.S. congressman to introduce legislation to allow homesteaders to claim up to two sections of land as opposed to the old limit of 160 acres. With the support of the Livestock association, Congressman Moses P. Kinkaid passed the new homesteading law, which allowed homesteaders to claim up to one section of land. The Kinkaiders, as this new breed of homesteaders was soon known, settled the last great open areas of the American West.

Thedford, when first founded, had no trees. For a long while a lone cottonwood tree, outside a homesteader's house, was the only tree. Later pioneers planted apples and other trees.

The Timbers Claim Act required that each owner plant a certain number of trees on each 160 acres, and the results of this act can be seen all over the county.

One of the most famous stories to come out of Thedford was the story of the missing Haumann girls.

152

In May of 1891, two young girls, ages eight and four, went for a short walk between their house and another. They left their house just north of Thedford at five, and when they had not returned by six, the mother went looking for them.

After nightfall men from the town mounted up and began to look for the girls. By morning the only ones left in town were the postmaster and the depot agent. Finally a faint trail was found. At times the searchers crawled on their hands and knees to try to follow the trail. Usually the two sets of footprints were side-by-side, but often there was only a single set: the older girl was carrying her sister.

On the fourth day of the search one of the girls was found, still alive, although barely. When finally she could speak she told how her sister and she had gotten lost while picking wildflowers to bring to their mother. At nightfall the first night they had heard people calling, but her older sister would not let her go to them for fear it would be Indians.

In a few more days the older child was found near Dunning, Nebraska. She had taken off her coat and spread it on top of some wild rose bushes, and then crawled under the shade to sleep. She never woke up again. It was estimated that they had walked 75 miles. By this time the national press had picked up the story, and the newspapers across the nation carried reports.

After the girls were found letters came from all over the world. They became subjects for poems, stories and remembrances. The girls' father for years afterwards would ride about the county in his wagon and give children rides home, warning them sternly about playing too far from home. Trinkets made from the hair of the dead girl began to appear almost immediately all over the county. Many residents still have locks of hair purported to be from her tiny head.

The post office delivered mail by horse every day for a number of years. The 50-mile trip required three changes in teams.

The Cowpoke Inn is well-known around these parts for its food and conversation.

The Thedford Vicinity Womens' Club was organized in 1919 and today serves the area as the main civic organization. In addition to collecting local history, the Club is active in a wide variety of charitable causes.

And it isn't as if there isn't any culture in Thedford. The Thomas County Library, for example, received the national Dorothy Canfield Fisher Award for having made the greatest contribution in library service. In addition, the Thedford Art Guild meets often and offers workshops and art shows. The Thedford Catholic Church was built in 1922 from concrete blocks made on a local ranch.

The Thedford Park was nothing more than a couple of cedar trees until 1951, when a retired rancher made it his personal responsibility. Carl Wiese planted hundreds of trees and shrubs and flowers and hand-watered them from several cream cans loaded into his truck, to keep them growing. Through the additional efforts of others-the park gained playground equipment, and a well-lighted ball field.

The Hillcrest Cemetery was originally formed when an early pioneer was laid to rest on a hill overlooking the Middle Loup Valley. A sign posted over the grave proclaimed, "this is hallowed ground." Today, it is the largest cemetery in the county.

On a February morning in 1934, the Chicago, Burlington and Quincy Depot was robbed on horseback, probably the last robbery performed with such a getaway device in the United States. The robber wore a kerchief over his face and brandished a six-shooter. He got $17 and was caught within hours — not because he used a horse, but because he was a local boy whose voice was easily recognized.

Before 1940 there was no north-south highway, and although North Platte is only 70 miles distant, many people never visited the town prior to the completion of US 83.

Twenty-one miles (20 miles.)
Five miles to the small burg of Brownlee, near Swan Lake, one of the area's most beautiful natural lakes.

Twenty miles (19 miles.)
Near the roadside picnic area is the site of Simeon, which was a post office established at a ranch with the same name.

You are now in the center of Cherry County's vast Lake Group, a part of the Valentine National Migratory Wildlife Refuge, a vast 70,000-acre refuge for a wide variety of wildlife. Within easy reach of here are many lakes with good fishing spots.

The refuge preserves several thousand acres of Nebraska's unique Sandhills. Millions of years ago, when the inland seas receded, winds rushed across the dry sea beds, lifting sand into the air and depositing it here. Later, Indiangrass, big and little bluestem, prairie and sand lovegrass shielded the sand from erosion and gave it some stability. A high watertable in many areas provides the grass with a fine source of water and produces the area's many lakes. Although early pioneers attempted to drain may of the lakes to provide additional land for their crops and livestock, recent efforts have attempted to bring the area back to its natural condition.

154

The refuge's headquarters are located on State spur 168. The turnoff for 168 is in another eight miles, 11 miles south of the junction of US Highways 83 and 20. No camping or power boats are allowed in the refuge, and so a good hike is the best way to view this area, which contains some of the last remaining stands of mid- and tallgrass prairie in the United States. More than 200 species of birds have been sighted here, and during the fall and spring migrations as many as 300,000 ducks are here. Mule deer, whitetail, coyotes and antelope are also residents of the refuge.

Several public access trails leave from Highway 83. Some travers the entire refuge while others deadend at lakes and marshes.

The lakes' names read like a kind of western poem:
Trout, Red Deer, Hackberry,
Long, Willow and Dewey.

Ballard's Marsh
Marsh Lake.

Pelican and Dad's Lake.
Beaver and Big Alkali.

Nineteen miles (5 miles.)

Junction with US Highway 20. Please see entry for US Highway 20 for information about sites along this route.

Five miles (10 miles.)

Valentine. See entry for US Highway 20 for information about the Valentine area.

Ten miles (0 miles.)

South Dakota border. The area between here and Valentine is one of the most productive areas in the nation for finding fossils.

This highway begins at North Platte.

Zero miles (31 miles.)

North Platte. See entry for US Highway 30 for information about North Platte.

Go north on US Highway 83 two miles and then take Highway 97. For the next thirty miles this road winds into the Sandhills of Nebraska, and a few lonely looks back at the town of North Platte are invited since for the next several hundred miles the traveler enters one of the most sparsely populated areas of the state.

Thirty one miles (29 miles.)

Tryon.

Tryon, Nebraska, is the county seat for the sparsely populated McPherson County. Tryon itself has a continually shrinking population, but manages to hold onto the county seat by virtue of the also shrinking populations of its closest competitors, Flats and Ringgold.

This is not to say that the county is uninhabited or that it did not at one time have a larger population. In fact, the county has many ghost towns to serve witness to those former residents. Nearby Brighton, for example, was located in the Brighton Valley near Tryon.

In the northeastern part of the county the remnants of the village of Omega can still be found. Omega was so named after the phrase in Revelations, "the Alpha and Omega, the beginning and ending." Since the location of this burg was nearer the Omega of everything rather than the Alpha, it was so named.

Speaking of names, one story on how Tryon got its name is still apt today. When selecting a name for the new community, some residents felt that the town itself was not worthy of a name. A local booster kept saying, "Lets keep tryin' to have a town." Tryon is still tryin'.

There are many interesting sites east and west of Tryon on State Highway 92 including ghost towns, ranches and good fishing spots. Please see entry for State Highway 92 for information about these and other locations along that route.

Twenty nine miles (5 miles.)
Take the narrow paved road leading off to the west. **Down this road 15 miles** *to the banks of the North Fork of the Dismal River, cross the river and continue another* **eight miles** *to the banks of the South Fork and the site of the North and Cody Ranch.*

This grassy expanse of hills was once the range of thousands of buffalo, antelope and deer. In 1877, William F. Cody, who would later become world renowned as Buffalo Bill, along with Major Frank North, purchased a herd of cattle at Ogallala and spent a good part of their summer driving them to this range land. Here the men started a ranch that would become known as the North and Cody Ranch. Not much is known about the success of this ranch, or Buffalo Bill's part in it, but for years the ranch was made welcome to any traveler who happened this way. In later years, many dignitaries were entertained here. Today, the quiet and peaceful river flows through beautiful country of grasslands and thickets along the banks.

Five miles (35 miles.)
Mullen.
Junction with State Highway 2.

State Highway 97

For information about Mullen, see entry for State Highway 2.

Thirty five miles (5 miles.)

Narrow paved road leads 20 miles east to the near ghost town of Brownlee, on the banks of the North Fork of the Loup river. Eight miles beyond Brownlee the road connects with US Highway 83.

Five miles (8 miles.)

Gravel road (S-16B) heads **east** into the Sandhills toward the lake country of the vast Cherry County.

In five miles this road becomes surfaced and in another ten connects with US Highway 83 south of Valentine.

Under most weather conditions the road is passable, although it might be a bit washboardy in spots.

Eight miles (2 miles.)

Merritt Reservoir. Forty-four miles of isolated shoreline are available on this beautiful oasis in the Sandhills. It is considered by many to offer Nebraska's premiere fishing opportunities. Walleye, crappie and bass are common, and catfish lurk in the shadows in the Snake River arm of the reservoir. Primitive camping sites are available overlooking the lake with spectacular views of the surrounding hills.

Three miles (2 miles.)

Turn off west for Snake River Falls.

The state's largest (although not highest) waterfall. This beautiful falls is easy to get to as walking trails lead along the ridge above the small canyon, as well as wind down the canyon sides for those wishing to get a closer look at the 22-foot cascade. Worthy of "must-see" status. A small store provides cool drinks and bait for the fisherman.

Two miles (21 miles.)

Samuel R. McKelvie National Forest.

A drive through this National Forest can be one of the most rewarding drives in the state. The Samuel McKelvie National Forest area provided some of the hideout spots for the state's most famous outlaw, Doc Middleton (see entry for US Highway 20 for a details about this famous bandito).

158

Turn left on the access road and follow it west 15 miles through the sparsely wooded hills of the forest. Grouse, deer and elk are common here. In recent years mountain lions have been confirmed in the Sandhills. The beauty of the hillsides and valleys along this stretch is not easily matched. Highway S-16F on the west side of the forest goes north 20 miles to connect with US Highway 20 at Nenzel.

Twenty-one miles (0 miles.)

Valentine and the junction with US Highways 20 and 83 and State Highway 12.

For a description of Valentine see entry for US Highway 20. For other sites in the area, please see the entry for one of the above highways.

Zero miles (15 miles.)

Kansas Border.

This moonscape landscape of interesting rock formations and canyons is where hundreds of fossils have been found, including those of many prehistoric turtles.

Fifteen miles (8 miles.)

Trenton.

Supply center for those headed for Swanson Reservoir. Intersection of US Highway 34. For further discussion of Trenton, see entry for US Highway 34.

Eight miles (7 miles.)

Intersection of US Highway 6. See entry for US Highway 6 for a discussion of the sites along this road.

Seven miles (8 miles.)
> Junction with 25A (west).
> ***Six miles on 25A to Palisade.***
> *In 1867, George Armstrong Custer went from Fort McPherson to Kansas in order to take part in the Sioux Indian Wars. Custer, as well as many other famous fighters, crossed Hayes County, and by their passing, created a much-used military trail. The trail crosses Highway 25A at Palisade, and more or less follows Highway 25 north through the county.*
> For other items near Palisade, see entry for US Highway 6.

Eight miles (5 miles.)
> Hayes Center.
> There were many battles around these parts in the pioneer days. The Pawnee and the Sioux fought with the pioneers so much so that the battles became known as the Sioux Wars. In addition, the Pawnee often fought against the Sioux for land possession since it was near here that their homelands overlapped.
> Hayes Center was known as the windmill city as each family once had their own windmill and tanks. The public windmill was at the hill on Main Street and was a famous landmark for a long while. This water supply was free to anyone in need of it.
> This is the location of the Hayes County Historical Society, and the museum is located in the old newspaper building.

Five miles (3 miles.)
> From here, stretching 70 or more miles to the west, was the front line of probably the greatest prairie fire in recorded history. The fire reached Hayes County on April 1, 1893. The wind was near tornado force, and drove the fire across thousands of square miles of western Nebraska, Colorado and Wyoming. Drifts of ashes piled up like snow against houses and fence posts. The sun was blacked out. It is estimated that this great fire moved at about 15 to 25 miles per hour.
> The fire's eastward movement was held near here, but it is not clear how far it moved to the south before it burned itself out. Despite the severity of the fire, and its great extent, only two lives were lost.

Three miles (6 miles.)
> East of here is Grand Duke Alexis' recreation ground on 140 acres, with a 100-acre lake. The lake is well stocked with fish.

State Highway 25

In 1873, Grand Duke Alexis, 22-year-old brother of the Czar of Russia, was the main attraction of a hunting party led by Buffalo Bill Cody. Gen. William Sherman went along for the ride, as did several others.

They camped on the Big Blackwood, 8 miles NE of present day Hayes Center. It was at this place that the Sioux Chief Spotted Tail and 100 warriors showed the Indian method of hunting and gave a realistic demonstration of a a war dance.

The Duke killed several buffalo, which wasn't much of an accomplishment since the animals are not very smart and will stand around while others near them are shot down.

The famous campground of this famous hunting party is commemorated by a locally made marker at the spot. Buffalo skulls were found at this site as late as 1973. Ask locally for directions to the site.

Six miles (10 miles.)

Near here the Military Road of 1867 (see above) swings to the east toward Fort McPherson, 55 miles away. It roughly follows Route 25 south to the Kansas border.

Ten miles (23 miles.)

Intersection of State Highway 23.

West on 23 to Grant, in Perkins County. Please see entry for State Highway 61 for information about this area.

East on 23 to US Highway 83. Please see that entry for information about sites along its route.

For the next 23 miles the State Highway 25 winds through the little traveled stretches of Nebraska ranchland.

Twenty-three miles (0 miles.)

Sutherland. See entry for US Highway 30 for information about Sutherland.

162

Zero miles (5 miles.)
Kansas border.

Five miles (18 miles.)
Benkelman. See entry for US Highway 34 for information about the sites in Benkelman.

Eighteen miles (7 miles.)
Six miles west on this road to site of Hiawatha. The Society of Friends, or Quakers, organized Hiawatha Academy in 1888, which served as the hub of education in the area for years. Unfortunately, the economic crisis and crop failures of the 1890s forced the school, and the town, to close down.

The buildings of the academy stood until the 1920s. Since then a school and the cemetery are all that remain of this once thriving community. The great prairie fire of April 1, 1893, swept past this area fueled by a dry previous summer's worth of grass and a powerful wind.

The fire burned a stretch at least from the South Platte River to the Republican and many believe the area was much more extensive than that. A widow woman was killed near here when she became curious about the fire and left her dugout to climb a small hill to watch the flames. The wind whipped the fire right across the top of the hill and she was burned to death. Her name, ironically enough, was Burner. She is buried in the old United Presbyterian Church cemetery six miles north of Parks. Another man was saved when he burned a little circle of grass around his wagon and horses when he saw the fire coming. He stood in the burnt circle while the fire swept past him. From that point onward this man was never known to travel without matches in his pocket.

To the east, on back roads are the spectacular canyonlands of Nebraska. Ask locally for the routes and the conditions of the roads since many of these roads are impassable after rain.

Seven miles (1 mile.)

One mile south of Enders dam is near the location of Box, or Inscription Canyon. To reach the canyon go one mile south of the dam on Highway 61. Walk from Highway 61 near the northeast corner of a field to a quarter mile to the southeast. The canyon is located in section 16.

One mile (9 miles.)

Enders Reservoir, and along its edge, the tiny Chase County village of Enders.

Chase County is known for its wheat, corn, horses, alfalfa and sugar beets.

For the next nine miles State Highway 61 and US Highway 6 are combined.

Nine miles (27 miles.)

State Highway 61 turns north and away from US Highway 6 just east of Imperial. See entry for US Highway 6 for information on Imperial.

For the next fifty miles or so the highway roughly follows the route of the Texas Cattle Road of the 1880s. Along here large herds of cattle were driven north from Texas to be shipped east out of Ogallala. This is the territory Larry McMurtry wrote about in his wonderful novel *Lonesome Dove*.

Twenty seven miles (18 miles.)

Grant. The county seat of Perkins County. This is the home

of the Perkins County Museum, located in one of Grant's fine old mansions. If you don't find the museum open, just call the posted phone number and make arrangements to view the many fine exhibits located there.

Near Grant are the well-known Wild Horse Springs, so named in the cowboy days for the wild horses seen near here. Ask locally for directions to this lovely spot.

Eighteen miles (1 mile.)

One mile due south of Ogallala, and just west of the road, was Gill's Station, a Pony Express and military supply station. Both the Oregon Trail and the Pony Express Trail crossed the road approximately one half mile south of the Interstate exchange.

One mile (2 miles.)

Ogallala. See entry for US Highway 30 for information about Ogallala.

Two miles (10 miles.)

Junction with US Highway 26. Please see the entry for that route for sites along US Highway 26.

Ten miles (3 miles.)

The dam. The big one. And behind it the big Mac. Lake C.W. McConaughy. There are camping spots, fishing spots, boating spots, parks, wildlife and just about anything else around here for the tourist. For more information about Nebraska's largest lake and the surrounding area, please see entry for US Highway 26.

East eight miles on county road on the north side of the North Platte River to Keystone.

Keystone is known for its unusual church, built in 1908 at a cost of $1,000. This is the only known church built to be used by both the Catholics and Protestants. Special dispensation was given by the Pope himself to allow dual services in the building. The church was used by both faiths, and later also by the Lutherans for a number of years. The Catholic altar is at one end, the Protestants' at the other. The backs of the pews are hinged so that they can flip over and be of service to either faith. The stove, bible and organ date to the dedication. The church is no longer in regular use, but is open to the public Sunday afternoons and by special request.

The road to Keystone from Highway 61 follows the Mormon

State Highway 61

Trail, and traces of the Trail extend eastward from here.

Three miles (9 miles.)

Junction with State Highway 92, west.

See the entry for that highway for information about sites along this route.

Keith County has been captured beautifully in John Janovy Jr.'s wonderful book *Keith County Journal.*

Twelve miles (13 miles.)

Arthur County line. Arthur County was the home of many large cattle camps during the heyday of the cowboys. Buffalo Bill Cody, John Bratt and others drove their cattle up this way to feast on the grass of the Sandhills. There were stores at places with names like Lightning Valley and Lena to serve the handful of early pioneers, and with the coming of the Kinkaid Act, Arthur County flourished for a time. In 1913 a large tract of land in the western part of the state, which had been set aside to become a man-made forest preserve, was opened to homesteaders.

The county has had a difficult history of being able to maintain its self-esteem. Several times it has disappeared from the maps of the state, usually being swallowed up by the larger McPherson County to the east. The problem was that Arthur didn't have enough people to organize into a county and make it stick. Finally, by 1920, and thanks to an act by the Legislature, Arthur County became official.

Thirteen miles (10 miles.)

Arthur.

The tiny town of Arthur, with a population of under 125, is the largest metropolis in the county. It is the county seat of Arthur County, and was named after Chester Arthur, who was President in 1881. The county population is somewhere slightly over 400, making it the sixth least populated county in the nation.

The smallest courthouse in the United States, built in 1914 and used until the early 1960s, is now the county museum. It is indeed small. One hopes that the county government officials got along with one another, as it doesn't appear there is much room for disagreement.

Arthur is also the home of the only baled hay church in the world. The word "only" is used here in case you think that the good Lord has allowed other churches to be built out of baled hay in other parts of the world. If He has, then you may substitute the word "first"

166

for the word "only" and thank the good Lord you are in Arthur, where the first one was built. It looks a bit as if it were made from adobe bricks, since the bales have been stacked, and then plastered over inside and out. It was built to be the home of the Pilgrim Holiness Church in 1927. The original interior had hand-made pews and pulpit and metal sheeting that served as the ceiling. In 1967, a new building was hauled in to the area to serve the needs of the people and the baled hay church sat unused until it was purchased and renovated by the Arthur County Historical Society.

The Martin-Monhart house is also made from bales. Ask locally for directions.

There is some real concern that with the declining population, Arthur County may cease to exist. The only real industry here is cattle ranching, and if you are born here and do not have a ranch, there may not be much reason to stick around. Still, this is a place where there are still some traditions such as round-ups on ranches that range up to 50,000 acres, complete with chuck wagons and canvas tents.

Then there are those who want to turn Arthur County and a good part of the land from here to Canada into a giant preserve for buffalo. Others say the government should concentrate funds on communities that have a real chance of making it, rather than those, like Arthur, that they say can't survive into the 21st Century.

The population may be small, but folks around here have had a long tradition of surviving where people said they couldn't. Let's hope that will be the case once again.

Junction with State Highway 92. East of here are several sites of interest. For information, please see entry for State Highway 92 at Tryon and the entry for State Highway 97.

Ten miles (22 miles.)
There are still log cabins and sod houses in this area. Local friendly residents might be able to steer you toward one or two.

A bounty of $25 per pelt was placed on grey wolves in Arthur County at the turn of the century. Forty-seven pelts were collected, and the last bounty was paid in 1901 for, presumably, the last grey wolf taken in the state of Nebraska.

Before you leave Arthur County, pause a moment to reflect on what life must be like for the residents of this area. Breath deeply. Smell that clear air, see those gentle hills rising in the distance? There is a kind of love for the land that fewer and fewer of us experience. The folks around here know all about that love — that's why they stay in what others would call a God-forsaken place. They'd tell you that God hasn't forsaken Arthur County.

Eight miles (12 miles.)
Eight miles east of here up Spring Valley, located on the east side of Spring Valley Lake in a grove of trees, is a small cemetery. Marked with two headstones are the burials of three children, who died between 1923 and 1933. This fenceless land held tens of thousands of cattle in earlier years. As many as three wagon outfits worked roundups that roamed this area in the not-so-distant past.

Twelve miles (12 miles.)
Hyannis. See entry for State Highway 2 for information on Hyannis. It is 67 miles from here to the small town of Merriman in Cherry County. This is one of the most isolated stretches of road in the state. WARNING: Do not travel it unless you seek isolation and beauty.

Twelve miles (55 miles.)
Dr. Plummer's home on the Dumbbell Ranch. Built in the 1890s, this home was to serve as a maternity hospital. It is hindsight that is 20-20, and so it might be more obvious to today's traveler that the sparsely populated Sandhills would not be the ideal place to build a maternity hospital. The name for the ranch came after the good doctor hit his thumb with a hammer while building the house/hospital. He said, "Only a dumbbell would do something like that."
Dr. A.J. Plummer built this house with six upstairs bedrooms and four downstairs. The size of the house caused the Plummer spread to serve as a community center for years. The good doctor bought out more and more of his neighbors and the Dumbbell Ranch grew to 52,000 acres. This was good for cattle ranching, but bad for ensuring patients for the doctor's practice. He later sold the ranch and moved to Montana. The house was built in the 1910s.

Along this stretch of Highway 61 are many small cemeteries and graves.

Five miles west near here is Mother Lake. It was here, after the devastating blizzard of March 13-15, 1913, that 600 dead cattle were found. They had wandered into the lake and had frozen to death.

Fifty-five miles (1 1/2 miles.)

Merriman and the intersection of US Highway 20. Please see the entry for US Highway 20 for information about sites in this area.

One and a half miles (3 miles.)
Two miles east to the Arthur Bowring Sandhills Ranch State Historical Park.

Arthur Bowring began ranching in 1894 near Merriman and expanded his land by purchasing Kinkaid homesteads that were being abandoned by their owners.

Soon Arthur married, but his wife died in childbirth. For the next 20 years, he lived alone until he met and married a traveling saleswoman from Lincoln. Eve Bowring brought her three sons from a former marriage to the ranch.

Eve Bowring's story is a portrait of a woman overcoming the obstacles placed before her by a male-dominated society. Not only did she put in long hours making her isolated cattle ranch into a productive business, but served in a variety of public service positions. Perhaps her greatest service was when she was appointed by Governor Robert Crosby to become a U.S. Senator after the death of a Senator. After that term expired she was appointed to the Federal Parole Board by President Dwight Eisenhower.

Arthur Bowring was active in civic matters as well. He was a state legislator, a county commissioner and a deputy of the Game and Fish Commission.

The Bowrings' greatest service, however, was the donation of their 7,200-acre Bar 99 ranch to the state. Eve Bowring's only stipulations were that the property continue to generate taxes for the county, that her home and its collections be maintained as a museum, and that part of the ranch's Hereford bloodline be kept intact.

As a result, the park is a working cattle ranch, preserved as a living history museum. It now includes the Eve Bowring Visitor Center, which contains displays on the geology and history of the area.

There are no camping facilities at the park.

Three miles (0 miles.)
South Dakota border.

This state highway begins off US Highway 30, seven miles east of Chappell in Deuel County.

Twenty miles north of the junction with US 30 (2 miles.)
      Just south of the North Platte River, in the northwest corner of the junction with the county road immediately south of the river, is the grave of John Hollman, who died on the Oregon Trail in 1901. An old state of Nebraska Trail marker, placed in 1914, still stands.

Two miles (17 miles.)
      Oshkosh. See entry for US Highway 26.
      For the next 50 miles State Highway 27 becomes a remote, aggregate surfaced road that leads through the sweeping hills of golden grass known as the Sandhills. These miles are perhaps the most remote in the state and offer a tranquillity and beauty all their own.

Seventeen miles (9 miles)

State Highway 27

Take the left fork when the routes divide to continue toward Lakeside.

From here northward the road passes through the area with the greatest number of wetlands in the entire Sandhill region. These natural lakes in the grass-covered hills provide excellent habitat for an amazing variety of migratory species.

In nine miles the right fork leads to the eastern section of the Crescent Lake National Wildlife Refuge (see below) and in another 28 miles to State Highway 2 near Hyannis. See entry for Highway 2 for further information about this area.

Nine miles (25 miles.)

Crescent Lake National Wildlife Refuge. One of the largest refuges in the state, Crescent Lake is home to many species of birds and is the birder's paradise. Crescent Lake is one of the largest natural lakes in the state.

As the road winds to the north, paths of questionable navigational quality lead to the west toward some of the numerous lakes that pepper this region of the Sandhills.

Twenty five miles (8 miles.)

Junction with State Highway 2. For information about sites along this route, please see entry for State Highway 2.

A mile to the west is Lakeside. World War One potash was mined here, making this a temporary boom town. State Highway 250 goes north from here to Rushville. For a description of sites along that route, please see entry for State Highway 250.

In June of 1897, three companies of Black enlisted men tried to make their way from Montana to St. Louis on bicycles. They were a special division of the Army cavalry, and were being used to try to prove that bicycles would bring the Army into the 20th Century.

Each man had to carry 40 pounds or more of supplies. Once they reached the Sandhills they could not move, not even over the faint lines of wagon roads. The sand bogged them down. At this point they got on the Burlington railroad tracks and bounced their way east. They made a total of 2,000 miles in 41 days, and the worst of those days were right along here.

For the next 8 miles east Highway 27 follows Highway 2.

Eight miles (7 miles.)

Ellsworth. Once the headquarters for the gigantic Spade

171

Ranch. At Ellsworth, Highways 27 and 2 divide. Highway 27 continues north out of Ellsworth.

Morgan's Cowpoke Haven Museum and Tack Shop. You are not a true traveler of the wilds if you pass up a place with such a name.

Seven miles (20 miles.)

An increasingly rare sight in the modern world: a sod house. This is known as the Hunsicker Sod House.

You are entering Old Jules Country, Mari Sandoz country, land of a kind of beauty that was fortunate enough to find a voice of considerable talent. Best known for the book that told the story of her father, *Old Jules*, Sandoz wrote in a unique and gifted voice of the people of Nebraska.

She was born on her family homestead in 1896 and raised in this wild and isolated land by her strict and domineering father. She taught school for a while and eventually made it to the University of Nebraska, where she became friends with the budding literary men and women of that town, including Loren Eiseley and others. Her writing career began with the publication of *Old Jules*, which had been rejected by scores of publishers before it finally won the Atlantic magazine's non-fiction award in 1935.

Before her death in 1966, Sandoz wrote over 20 books, most of them about the plains and its people.

Her greatest gift was in capturing the voice of her characters. In her best work that talent creates the feeling that the reader is witnessing history as it happens. In what is perhaps her masterpiece, *Crazy Horse*, a biography of the Brule Sioux leader, she is able to sustain a narration that seems as if it is being told by a Sioux holyman around a smoky campfire on one of these surrounding hilltops.

The University of Nebraska at Lincoln houses the Mari Sandoz collection, which includes tens of thousands of items including most of the research notes for her works of history and fiction.

An excellent biography of Sandoz is Helen Stauffer's *Story Catcher of the Plains.*

Her works have been read all over the world. Many local bookstores contain a more complete collection of her works than you are likely to find anywhere else. To the east on a dirt road from the sod house is where Mari Sandoz lived while teaching.

Between here and the turnoff for Smith Lake Road, Highway 27 passes the turnoff for Spade Ranch, on the National Register of

Historic Places, and a historical marker commemorating Mari Sandoz.

Twenty miles (1 mile.)

Just south of Smith Lake Road, near the state historical marker, on the east is a three-mile-long dirt road to the grave of Mari Sandoz. "It had always been that the dead returned to the earth which fed them, as the flowers returned, and the tree and the buffalo and all living things go back."—*The Buffalo Hunters.*

The official-looking sign at the highway gives way to signs that have an increasingly friendly tone, directing the dedicated to the final resting place of this Nebraska writer. As the road thins to mere faint traces in the grass, a sign simply points the way with a hand-lettered arrow and "Mari."

The path fades to mere guesswork as it reaches a large orchard on an easterly sloping hillside. Those driving cars with low frames best walk from here. Rain-washed ruts lead around the southern side of the orchard. Follow these to the far side of the trees and the small fenced area of Sandoz's grave. The view from here is about as peaceful and beautiful as anyone could ever want. In the quiet, gazing out at the orchard and distant hills, the voice this woman perfected in her prose seems to seep up out of the sandy soil with whispers of the generations who have loved this land: the Cheyenne, Sioux and the heedless pioneers.

Below the hill is the ranch of Flora Sandoz, who, if she is free and sees you here at the grave, may walk up for a chat. Old Jules' house is among the ranch buildings.

One mile (8 miles)

Smith Lake Road.

Turn west on this road for a self-guided tour around the locales from Mari Sandoz's books.

The trees along this road were planted by the local fans of Nebraska's fine writer.

In 13 miles this road intersects with State Highway 250 at Hooper Ranch and Smith Lake. See entry for this highway for more information. Good fishing here, along with a campground and a playground.

At Highway 250, turn North to go to Rushville, or South for Lakeside and Alliance.

Eight miles (9 miles.)

State Highway 27

Mari Sandoz Rest Area.

For years this rest area was kept beautiful by local citizens with flowers, grass and trash pickup. In recent years, with the population of the hills dwindling to almost nothing, maintenance has been less regular. Take care here to pack out your own trash. Better yet, pick up some of the trash left behind by others as well.

The small cinderblock building contains a few artifacts from Mari Sandoz's career. These included a re-creation of her New York City apartment, complete with many of her household items. Due to vandalism, the museum is no longer open.

The ranch road here heads east on a washboardy surface to the house of Mari's sister, Caroline Sandoz Pifer, herself a writer. At the house is the Sandoz Books Free Museum. Pictures, research material, memorabilia and personal items are housed here. Open by appointment, "or if someone is at home."

Nine miles (12 miles)

Cross the Niobrara River. Many consider this Nebraska's finest river.

Near this crossing in 1991 two canoeists from Gordon found the jawbone of an ancient elephantlike creature at the base of a cliff. When scientists came to remove the bone, a photographer from the Gordon Journal went along. While he was digging a foothold into the cliff to steady himself he kicked loose a second jawbone.

The jawbones are now a part of the State Museum's collection in Lincoln.

Twelve miles (15 miles.)

Gordon. See entry for US Highway 20 for a description of Gordon.

Fifteen miles (0 miles.)

South Dakota border.

The entry for this road begins with the junction with State Highway 2 at Lakeside in Sheridan County.

Zero miles (25 miles.)
Traveling north out of Lakeside off State Highway 2, the traveler soon starts to come to a long string of beautiful Sandhills lakes. Thompson is first, then others by the hundreds, it seems: Peter Long Lake, Diamond, Albrecht, Twin Lakes, Cravath and countless others offer some great fishing.

Twenty-five miles (4 miles.)
Intersection of Smith Lake Road, which goes to the east. East of here is the heart of Mari Sandoz country, one of the state's finest writers. See entry for State Highway 27 for more information about

State Highway 250
Sandoz sites, and what to look for along Smith Lake Road.

Four miles (6 miles.)
   Smith Lake.
   A nice spot to stop a spell, enjoy the Sandhills and take a break for lunch.

Six miles (12 miles.)
   South of the Niobrara River is the turnoff to the west for Old Jules Trail.

   Old Jules Trail.
   Three and a half miles down this road is the pioneer Swiss Beguin Cemetery in the valley of Oxbow Country. Mari Sandoz's uncle Emile was killed by a hired gun near here. The thinking at the time was that the killer, who shot Emile Sandoz in the back, had been hired by the Smith family, who wanted the creek and the two Sandoz homesteads for their cattle operation.
   This road was the old freight trail and was traveled many times by Sandoz's father, Old Jules. Continue on this winding road another mile and a half and along the river to the site of many Indian encampments, which lasted even into Mari Sandoz's lifetime.
   In another 3 miles, just before the road swings to the north, is the site of Old Jules' first homestead, known as River Place to those who have read Old Jules. The Catholic Church, in another 3/4 miles, dates back to pioneer times. For more information about these sites, see below.
   Intersection with State Highway 87 See below for information about State Highway 87.

Twelve miles (0 miles.)
   Rushville. Intersection with US Highway 20.

Zero miles (10 miles.)

This entry begins 16 miles north of Alliance at the intersection of US Highway 385 and State Highway 87. For information about US Highway 385, please see that entry.

Ten miles (4 miles.)

Just as the road turns more directly north is the site of the

State Highway 87
school house.

Four miles (1 mile.)
The well site, where, according to Mari Sandoz, her father fell to the bottom of a well and broke his leg. He then tried to crawl his way to Fort Robinson, 40 miles distant. The story can be found in Sandoz's book *Old Jules*.

Intersection with county road, known as **Old Jules Trail,** *east to State Highway 250, and the Sandoz River Place, the Swiss Cemetery and other sites. Please see above entry for State Highway 250 for details.*

One mile (13 miles.)
Sacred Heart Catholic Church, built on land donated by Old Jules so that the priest, who admired Caesar and collected stamps, would continue to visit the nearby Sandoz homestead for conversation.

As the highway crosses the Niobrara River: this was the location of a large fossil quarry excavated by the American Museum of Natural History in New York back in the 1920s.

Thirteen miles (4 miles)
Hay Springs. A fine tour of the back-country starts here, north out of Hay Springs. See entry for US Highway 20 at Hay Springs for more information.
From here **east** to Rushville State Highway 87 is combined with US Highway 20.

Four miles (7 miles.)
South on marked road to Walgren Lake, the site of Nebraska's only known water monster. In this lonely and isolated lake numerous people have seen a serpent-like creature rise up above the tranquil waters. Others, walking by the shore, have heard a gigantic splash and have turned in time to see a large wave rushing toward shore. Mari Sandoz mentions the monster in her book *Old Jules*.
For a while there was talk of making people pay to see the lake (and maybe the monster) but the attempt failed. The visit is free. Check the camera for film, and don't let the dog or the kids get too close to the water.

178

Seven miles (20 miles)

Rushville. See entry for US Highway 20 for further information on Rushville. Highway 87 continues north, just on the west side of Rushville.

Twenty miles (3 miles.)

Just before Highway 87 crosses Patton Creek, about 3 miles south of White Clay, is the site of the last known Sioux sun dance, 1881. For a description of the sun dance see the entry for US Highway 20 in Dawes County just west of Chadron. The road west from here can connect with the tour north out of Hay Springs. See entry for Hay Springs on US Highway 20.

Three miles (0 miles.)

Whiteclay, just south of the South Dakota border. This town is on the Pine Ridge Indian reservation, what is left of the land once owned by the Sioux.

NEBRASKA
U S
385

Zero miles (3 miles.)

Sidney.

Please see entry for US Highway 30 for information about Sidney.

For the better part of the distance between here and Bridgeport, the highway follows three significant trails. A cutoff, and less-traveled branch of the Oregon Trail, known as the Upper California Crossing is to the east of the highway until the town of Gurley, and then it crosses to the west. The Deadwood/Sidney Trail and the Pony Express route are just to the west of the present road.

Three miles (8 miles.)

Old district 77 school house. This school was built in 1916 and is still in use today.

Eight miles (6 miles.)

180

A marker commemorates the first oil well in the area, drilled in 1949.

Six miles (5 miles.)

Dalton. Located here is the well-known Prairie Schooner Museum, a quaint but interesting spot.

Two miles due west of here is Yellowstone Cliff, a famous local landmark. (They are yellow cliffs, made of stone.)

Two miles north of Dalton is the Morrill County line.

Five miles (14 miles.)

Go west on the county road, one mile, and then turn right, to the site of Mud Springs, an old stage station on the Deadwood/Sidney trail. There wasn't much of a springs here, just buffalo wallows, which were usually muddy. In 1865, the Sioux attacked the station and everyone at the place was killed. This was also the stomping grounds of Nebraska's most famous outlaw, "Doc" Middleton (see description for Gordon in entry for US Highway 20 for details about this notorious outlaw).

Fourteen miles (8 miles.)

Just a quarter mile after the highway swings west in order to begin to parallel the North Platte River, and an eighth of a mile to the north of the road, is the site of Amanda Lamin's grave. Two miles to the west are the famous Oregon Trail landmarks of Jail Rock and Courthouse Rock. See description of US Highway 20 at Bridgeport for more information.

Eight miles (35 miles.)

Bridgeport. See entry for US Highway 26.

Thirty-five miles (16 miles.)

Alliance.

Home of the Knight Museum of High Plains Heritage at 908 Yellowstone.

Alliance has the feel of an exciting town, with plenty of hustle and bustle. Its large size and isolated location have made it a center not only for local and regional business, but for many tourists passing through the area to the Black Hills or Yellowstone. Hang around town a while and you are likely to see plates from every state in the Union.

In the mid-1980s, in what was once an unassuming wheat field outside of town, a man named James Reinders made national news by placing old automobiles to look like Stonehenge. During a family reunion, Reinders arranged cars, an ambulance and other artifacts of the 20th century in the same configuration as the ancient stone monument in England, 5,500 miles due east of here. He then painted his creation a kind of foggy-glass grey.

Reinders said that his monument "is something to gaze at. It is a very intriguing monument. Hopefully someday it will have some kind of historic value."

While not everyone agreed with him, it didn't take long for the town to realize that the hundreds of people stopping at the site everyday meant tourist dollars. Many of those folks began to think Carhenge was an all right place.

Some people of the area have other opinions, while still others formed a "Friends of Carhenge" to seek funding in order to keep the work open and free to the public. On summer solstice, in 1991, the Friends group placed an automobile outside of the circle, to mimic the heel stone of Stonehenge.

One citizen was quoted in national publications on the educational value the monument might have for some Alliance citizens: "I never heard about Stonehenge until Carhenge got me interested."

To judge for yourself whether this is an education, a work of art, a spiritual monument, or a pile of junk, ask anyone in town how to find Carhenge, or simply continue north on 385 two miles.

Junction with State Highway 2. See entry for that highway for information concerning sites in the area.

Sixteen miles (9 miles.)

Junction with State Highway 87.

Please see entry for State Highways 250 and 87 for information about sites along this road into Mari Sandoz's Old Jules country.

Nine miles (8 miles.)

The Niobrara river and the turnoff for Box Butte Reservoir

Eight miles (16 miles.)

Road to Dunlap. A ghost town in the best sense. Spirits are said to linger here in the old buildings and haunt the banks of the river. The mill was built in 1884 and a few years later a man was shot near its paddle wheel by a jealous husband. Although the town of Dunlap grew up, expanded, and then finally died when the highway passed it by, many a lonesome traveler has reported hearing the moans of a man coming from the weeds and brush along the river's banks.

This scenic road leads to Deadhorse Canyon, Deadman Canyon and eventually to State Highway 2. Please see that entry, and the entry for US Highway 20, for further information.

Sixteen miles (10 miles.)

Chadron State Park. Fine campgrounds, horseback riding, and recreation area. Included on the grounds is a lake, and trapper demonstrations by the park personnel. This is Nebraska's oldest state park, established in 1921.

The park includes campsites as well as cabins, which are available for rent. From Look Out Point the view to the north and west includes Pine Ridge, the Black Hills and Crawford.

The southern trailhead for the isolated Pine Ridge Trail is in the park, as well as other, shorter hikes.

The children will long remember riding in the paddle boats in the cooling evening of a long summer's day, and falling asleep under the dome of stars to the chorus of frogs and of nighthawks in the sky.

Ten miles (5 miles.)

Dawes County Museum. For more information on this fine museum and several nearby sites, see the entry for US Highway 20 at Chadron.

The Dawes County Museum, which is run by the efficient and well-organized Dawes County Historical Society, is located just off 385. It is open every day during the summer months, and many weekdays during winter.

Down (north) Chadron Creek from the Dawes County Museum one half mile is the site where the great Sioux Chief Red Cloud was captured in his camp in 1876. (See below)

This is also the location where Northern Cheyenne Indians under Dull Knife surrendered to the Army in 1878.

The story of Dull Knife and his band of Northern Cheyenne is one of vast courage. It is a story that serves as an example of the broken promises, misunderstanding and sometimes genuine human kindness of the whites as well.

After Crazy Horse was killed (in 1877 at Fort Robinson, west of here. See entry for US Highway 20 for the story of Crazy Horse) many Northern Cheyenne had come into Fort Robinson expecting to be allowed to live on the Pine Ridge reservation. The whites, citing their interpretation of the Treaty of 1868 to mean that the Cheyenes should live on the reservation of the Southern Cheyenne in Oklahoma, insisted the people be moved south. In addition, one of the Cheyenne leaders claimed going south was a good idea. Although the whites listened to him, this man apparently had been speaking in order to get in good graces with the whites. His views, however, did not represent the wishes of the rest of the Cheyenne.

Besides, General George Crook assured Dull Knife that they could return north if they did not like the southern reservation.

In any event, the Northern Cheyenne, under the leadership of Dull Knife and others, and traveling under military escort, went south in the summer of 1877. After three months, and the deaths of 35 of their members, they reached the southern reservation.

Instead of buffalo on the plains they found bleached piles of buffalo bones, even then starting to be scavenged by some whites to be sold for their calcium content. Instead of plenty of food, they found their southern relatives starving. Despite urgent letters from white commanders, the government in Washington sent only enough supplies to keep the heartiest from death. One such commander wrote to his superiors complaining that the beef the government was sending was not usable for *anything*, much less food.

There was no food. There were no blankets. There was a single medical officer, but no medication. In Washington, the Secretary of the Interior thought the complaints of the Cheyenne were a plot by their leaders to get them to revolt.

The Northern Cheyenne spent the cruel winter of 1877-78 in the south, but when spring came Dull Knife and others asked permission to return north, just as General Crook had promised them they could.

Permission was denied.

In the early morning darkness of September 10, 1878, Dull Knife and another leader, Little Wolf, led 297 men, women and children and a handful of starving horses north. They were followed by soldiers who caught up with them along the Cimarron River in southern Kansas. The soldiers engaged the Cheyenne in a place known as Cedar Breaks, but the Cheyenne were able to hold them off and escape northward.

During the next five weeks the Cheyenne moved as fast as they could, stealing fresh horses to carry their people. By now a total of over 1,500 soldiers and volunteers were chasing the small remaining band of the once powerful Cheyenne. On five different occasions soldiers and volunteers caught up with them and each time the Cheyenne managed to escape, driven and pulled north toward the land that held the bones of their mothers and fathers.

In mid-October, the band split in two. Little Wolf took about half of the band and headed north toward the traditional hunting grounds along the Tongue River in Montana. The other half stayed with Dull Knife, who had decided to try and seek refuge with the Sioux leader Red Cloud at his agency.

On October 23 at this spot, time ran out for the Northern Cheyenne. During an intense blizzard, cavalry appeared and surrounded the Cheyenne. After talking with his leaders, Dull Knife had his people disassemble their best weapons and disguise the pieces as necklaces and beadwork, and then he surrendered.

The Cheyenne were locked up once they reached Fort Robinson. They asked to be allowed to go to Red Cloud on the new Pine Ridge reservation in South Dakota, but the government said they would have to return to Oklahoma.

"There we found a Cheyenne cannot live," Dull Knife said. "You may kill me here, but you cannot make me go back. We will not go. The only way to get us there is to come in here with clubs and knock us on the head, and drag us out and take us down there dead."

The government insisted they return south. It was the 9th of January — the temperature hovered near zero.

At nine o'clock that evening the Cheyenne made their final attempt at freedom. They reassembled the guns they had hidden. Marksmen huddled around the small windows of their prison and then shot at the six guards standing outside. In the confusion the Cheyenne ran out of the building and into the howling January darkness.

The soldiers soon followed on horseback. In the first hour of fighting over half of the Cheyenne warriors had been killed. The soldiers killed many women and children as well. By morning all but 38 of the Cheyenne had been killed or recaptured. Thirty-two of those were followed northward and then attacked. Only nine survived that attack.

Dull Knife and five members of his family had stayed hidden in the canyons outside Fort Robinson. Those six made their careful way to Pine Ridge reservation. When they arrived they were taken prisoner.

Meanwhile, Little Wolf's band had spent the winter hiding in the tributaries of the Niobrara east of here. The next spring they, too, surrendered.

After over a year of being held prisoner, Dull Knife and the

185

surviving members of the two bands were given a small reservation on the Tongue River in Montana.

Mari Sandoz told the story of the Cheyenne in her book *Cheyenne Autumn.*

For further sites concerning this tragic story in American history, see entry for US Highway 20.

To the west of the golf course is the military road. (see entry for Chadron State College in chapter on US Highway 20.)

Later this was the site of a ranch and another town with the name of Chadron.

Near here is the trailhead for a fine hiking tour of the area. Ask locally about routes and conditions for The Pine Ridge Trail, located here at the Spotted Tail trailhead. It traverses rugged Kings and Strongs Canyons before reaching Chadron State Park, ten miles south. The trail is less traveled than the much better known trails around Fort Robinson to the west, but no less beautiful.

Just beyond the city of Chadron reservoirs, to the southeast was the site of Chartran's Trading Post. The reservoirs are located on the site of the cabin of Hurbert Rouleau, who was a trapper mentioned by Francis Parkman in 1846.

Directly north of here, just where the highway crosses the valley, is the location of Quick Bear's Brule Sioux camp, which was captured by Pawnee scouts in 1876, under the Command of the Eagle Chief Three Fingers Mackenzie. On this same day, the Army fought and captured Red Cloud.

A month earlier at the Red Cloud Agency, a dozen miles west of here near Fort Robinson, Red Cloud and other Sioux had been told that if they did not sign an agreement giving away the Black Hills their children would not be fed. Since gold had been discovered there the American government was eager to secure the land. Many of the Sioux leaders were kept under guard and not allowed out until they signed. Although Red Cloud signed, and many Sioux subsequently curse his name even today, a treaty signed years earlier in 1868 provided that the Black Hills land could not be given away unless three-fourths of all male adult Sioux voted to do so. This clear violation of the 1868 treaty and the illegal seizure of the Black Hills is an historical reality that still reverberates in the Sioux nation of today.

Unknown to Red Cloud or Quick Bear or the others, General

George Crook had ordered that the army seize the Sioux horses and guns as soon as they had been forced to sign the agreement. This may have been due, in part, to the fact that Custer had been defeated only two months earlier. In any event, it was here that some of the last free Sioux were captured and placed under the directed supervision of the US governent.

This area was the location of an elaborate plan to form a monument to the great Sioux Nation. Sculptor Gutzon Borglum's plan was to create an entire tribe of Indians using the natural rock buttes in the distance, as well as the boulders from Mount Rushmore. "We'll make them 14 to 16 feet tall and reproduce them as our forefathers saw them...wild and carefree." He planned to have additional statues at various important Indian sites throughout the region. Borglum's plan gathered much support throughout the region as well as the nation. His death in 1941, however, stilled the idea.

The dirt road that takes off to the east is the old King's Canyon Trail, a beautiful, but nearly impassable route. It connects with the Bordeaux Road.

East four miles is the site of the annual Bordeaux Creek Fur Trade and Muzzleloading Association's Rendevous, held each summer. See entry for US Highway 20 for more information.

Five miles (2 miles.)

Just to the east on US Highway 20 is Chadron. Please see entry for US Highway 20 for more information.

Two miles (5 miles.)

Location of the original town of Chadron, before the railroad came in 1884 and persuaded the town to move to its present location.

Five miles (10 miles.)

Cross the White River. On the north side of the river is the Fort Pierre-Fort Laramie Trail. The use of this route, which went from the North Platte River in Wyoming to the Missouri in what is now central South Dakota, may date to prehistoric times. Some historians believe that the route may have served as an ancient trans-continental highway, providing Native Peoples with a route from the Great Lakes to the Pueblos of the Southwest.

This route became important to white fur trappers as an overland passageway to the steamboats on the Missouri. From 1837 until the early 1850s, more than a quarter million buffalo robes and tons of trade goods passed over this trail. The trail was in general use until the 1880s, when the arrival of railroad routes made transportation easier. The trail follows the White River in Nebraska to near Fort Robinson where it drops south to the Niobrara, and from there southwest toward Wyoming. Ruts can still be found along the route, including sections near Agate Fossil Beds and along "Corkscrew Road," west of Fort Robinson. Please see entries for State Highway 29 for Agate Fossil Beds and US Highway 20 for information about "Corkscrew Road."

Ten miles (0 miles.)

Take the county road west. In about a mile you will see a pile of concrete sitting in the middle of a field. This pile, once a bank vault, is about all that is left of the once thriving community of Wayside. The highway you just left bypassed Wayside, and one by one the residents moved. The bank vault, long since empty, was left behind.

Ten miles west of the site of Wayside, in 1892, a find that was to shock the scientific world was discovered. Bill Rossiter and his two sons unearthed a "petrified man" from the badlands of this area. The man was anatomically correct and was exhibited for a while in Chadron, where the Rossiters began to gain a bit of fame and wealth from their find. Bill then decided to take it to the Chicago World's Fair for exhibition. Bill eventually sold the petrified man to a local doctor who then took the man on a tour of eastern Nebraska, Iowa and Kansas. He, too, got people to pay for the wonder of seeing what a man frozen in the limestone of ancient Chadron may have looked like. Eventually someone noticed a bit of wire and plaster of Paris showing through one of the petrified man's kneecaps. The Rossiter boys smiled sheepishly and shrugged. No one knows what happened to the petrified man after that.

Zero miles (15 miles.)
    Colorado border.

Fifteen miles (12 miles.)
    Kimball. For information about Kimball, please see entry for US Highway 30. See also entry for Interstate 80.

Twelve miles (13 miles.)
    Banner/Kimball County line.
    Banner County was named by someone who believed it would one day be the "banner of the state of Nebraska," and the "brightest star in the constellation of Nebraska counties." Today Banner County has only a single town, Harrisburg, in the entire county. But don't let these facts steer you away from the place. First of all, although perpetually in running for the least populated county in the state (in 1980 it had 1,000 people...down from 2,500 in 1890),

State Highway 71

Banner's thousand people are some of the friendliest, most good-natured folks alive. What's more, many believe this place is in the running for the most beautiful county in the state.

Banner County was once peppered with sod houses at every section and quarter section. This was partly due to the fact that there was speculation that a railroad was to be built through the county. The railroad never happened and the banner of Banner ceased to flap so hopefully in the high prairie wind. However, there were some benefits to the place. What cattle and summer-fallow wheat didn't bring in, the more than 200 oil wells that still dot the countryside did.

Two miles (8 miles.)

At the top of a hill 12 miles to the west of here is what many claim to be the highest spot in the state. No one ever wants to call this a mountain, because there aren't supposed to be mountains in Nebraska, but if someone from, say, Connecticut, were to learn that there is a place in Nebraska 5,430 feet above sea level they would call it a mountain.

Eight miles (2 miles.)

Near here to the west is Lover's Leap. Legend has it that this was the place where a beautiful Indian princess, a daughter of a Sioux Chief, jumped to her death. She was upset over the pending marriage her father had arranged with a man from the Ogallala tribe, and wanting to remain faithful to the mysterious man she loved, took a hike, and then a jump.

Two miles (1 mile).

Harrisburg Turnoff.

Four miles west, Harrisburg.

Brochures from Harrisburg boast that the town is unincorporated, has no mercantile, no restaurant, no major highway, no newspaper and no TV or radio stations. But don't let that stop you. If you've come this far, you MUST stop and see this town. Harrisburg's modern courthouse is all paid for, and the town does have churches, schools, a fire department and one of the best museums in the western Nebraska, if not the entire state. The Banner County Historical Society and Museum complex includes several buildings, which contain a vast collection of professionally displayed exhibits and exquisite restorations. The museum has pioneer artifacts, cattle brands, Indian artifacts, and other items. The museum can boast one of the few operating (and they fire the baby up once a year, so they know it is working) Case steam threshers. An entire building houses this monster and several other machines. In addition, the grounds contain a log school house, a sod house, a pioneer church, a log house and a picnic shelter for you to spend a moment or three in the shade. One block south of the museum is the old Banner County Bank building, established in 1889.

One mile (9 miles.)

Junction with State Highway 88:

In the distance, southeast of the Junction of Highway 88 is Big Horn Mountain, 4,713 feet, called He Sha (white mountain) by the Cheyenne. There once were big horn sheep here, in case you couldn't figure it out from the name.

In 35 miles, Highway 88 leads to Courthouse and Jailhouse Rocks, important sites along the Oregon Trail. For a description of these and other sites in that area please see the entry for US Highway 26.

East five miles. Near here a local rancher by the name of George Bennet discovered a major deposit of mastodon bones. He led Nebraska writer Loren Eiseley to this deposit in 1931 while Eiseley was working for the state museum.

Eiseley wrote about this find-of-a-lifetime in his wonderful book Night Country in which he used the fictional name Pa Mullens for Bennet.

Nine miles (3 miles.)

Wildcat Hills State Park.

This is a lovely area that makes you realize what a wonder the American West is. The State Game Reserve includes a herd of buffalo, elk and deer. It provides the traveler with fine picnic and camping facilities.

Three miles (5 miles.)

At the first four-way intersection north of Wildcat Hills, turn west. Go one mile and then turn south. Continue one mile to the site of Fort John. This was not really a fort at all, but a trading post to service, first, the America Fur Company, and later the gold rush prospectors and the pioneers. There is a small monument 200 feet west of the road, directly under the power lines. There are several unmarked graves around here, including that of a famous French trapper, Pierre Papin, who died here in 1853.

Five miles (6 miles.)
Gering and Scottsbluff.

Here are several sites of historical importance, and several modern-day entertainments and sights. Please see the entry for US Highway 26 at Scottsbluff for further information about this rich area.

Six miles (7 miles.)
Turn off for Minatare Lake. (10 miles east). A fine lake with plenty of good fishing and swimming, and a lighthouse to boot!

Seven miles (47 miles.)
Before the ranchers were here, this was the land of the Sioux. In 1878, four outfitters got their start in this county and became the first ranchers for a good long ways. On an early scouting trip through the area to find the best land, one of these men reported that he had ridden on horseback for six weeks without seeing another human being. Not much different from today, an Easterner might say.

Some of the early ranches were actually part of Texas ranches. The ranchers of Texas would send cattle up this way, fatten them on the sweet grass of Sioux County, and then sell them to the Indians and soldiers in South Dakota.

Cattle ranching the old way: round 'em up in the spring and in the fall, brand 'em, sort 'em, ship 'em or turn them loose to fatten up for the next round up. One of the most famous cattle ranches in the county was the N Bar Ranch, which lost about 8,000 cattle in an 1879 blizzard. Other big ranch operations were the Bar T, the TOT, the TAN and the Anglo-American Cattle Company, which purchased the other three to form the largest single operation in the state. The operation ranged nearly 50,000 head of cattle over a good part of Sioux County.

The glory days of the big ranches declined as the price of cattle dropped and modernization, railroads and other markets began to take their toll. The last of the great roundups was in the spring of 1898. At least 10,000 cattle were herded in one bunch after a sweep of the area by cowboys from Sioux County.

The highway winds 47 miles through the heart of the Sandhills to the junction with State Highway 2. Turn north on State Highways 71 and 2, nine miles to Marsland, and Crawford via the old Deadwood Trail. For more information about sites along this route, please see entry for State Highway 2.

Forty-seven miles (0 miles.)

Junction with State Highway 2. For a continuation, please see the entry for State Highway 2 at the junction with State Highway 71.

This route begins at Mitchell in Scotts Bluff County and goes north to the South Dakota border.

Ghost towns are abundant in Sioux County, as the once prosperous ranching and pioneer towns faded away to the speedy and efficient modern ranches. Glen, Andrews and Montrose are three such towns.

Zero miles (38 miles.)

Mitchell. For information, please see entry for US Highway 26.

Thirty-eight miles (22 miles.)

194

Agate Springs. The ranch building and house are those of Captain James Cook, who gave up leading a cowboy's life on cattle drives from Texas and New Mexico in the 1870s to start his own ranch at this place. At this house he entertained his good friend, the Sioux leader Red Cloud. Red Cloud visited this ranch many times during his life, especially in his later years. The house, in a shady oasis of the upper Niobrara River, is still in the Cook family and is not open to the public.

Cook did donate part of his land for the Agate Fossil Beds National Monument, and his collection of Red Cloud's belongings are on display in the visitors center (see below).

Turnoff for Agate Fossil Beds National Monument.

Three miles east *to visitor center of Agate Fossil Beds.*

Fossils, agates, ancient mammals, tiny rhinoceros, and other strange creatures from a time long before mankind have been found here.

The fossil beds were discovered in the late 1800s by local rancher Jack Cook (see above), and excavations began in the early 1900s. Although many remains have been quarried, scientists believe less than 25 percent of the fossil-bearing hills have been excavated. Most of the remains found are from creatures who roamed this area 19 million years ago during the Miocene Epoch.

Helpful rangers and amazing exhibits make this worth your journey. The 11,000-square-foot visitors center, which included interpretive displays along a self-guided tour, was built in the 1990s. Over $1 million in exhibits grace the facility. Of particular interest is the Red Cloud collection.

The Sioux leader Red Cloud became friends with local rancher, scout and Indian fighter James H. Cook and gave the man many of his belongings. Over 700 artifacts are a part of the collection and include clothing, photographs and war clubs.

Except for restrooms and a small gift shop, the monument has no facilities.

One of the most delightful backroad trips in the state begins here. A winding, breathtaking jaunt across sandy washes and over crests of pine-swept ridges snakes its way north and east for 30 rugged miles to US Highway 20. Part of the route follows the Fort Pierre-Fort Laramie Trail. For a description of the route please see the entry for "Corkscrew Road" west of Fort Robinson on US Highway 20.

Twenty-two miles (0 miles.)

195

State Highway 29

Harrison.

Harrison has a swimming pool at the Grade School Park, and nothing is sweeter than jumping head first into its waters on a hot summer afternoon. On Main Street is the Sioux County Museum, which will orient the traveler to Sioux County and its heritage. The Sioux County Fair is the first weekend in August and boasts a rodeo and a fine county fair.

North out of Harrison on county road:

Five miles to Gilbert Baker Recreation and Wildlife Area.

This area encompasses the headwaters of Monroe Creek, one of the finest small creeks in the state. Its waters support one of the few naturally reproducing trout populations in Nebraska. Monroe Canyon offers a view of unique geological features. From the ridge of Monroe Canyon one can look to the north for a view of the Black Hills, if one is so inclined to look into a vastly inferior state.

*Beyond the Recreation Area, by about **three and a half miles,** just as the road takes a sharp curve to the east the Old Fort Robinson Military road crosses the blacktop.*

*If you continue on this road for **another 17 miles** you will reach the ghost town of Montrose, after passing through the Ogallala National Grassland. At Montrose, old settlers' fortifications are easily visible in the grass around the site.*

To the northeast is Warbonnet, or Hat Creek.

Black Elk was a 13-year-old Sioux when he and a band of Sioux and Cheyenne attacked a wagon train of settlers near this site in May of 1876. Black Elk used a "six shooter" given to him by a relative to fight in his first battle. He rode bareback, hanging onto the horse's neck and leaning under the beast's head to shoot at the wagons. The wagon train had circled its wagons and placed the oxen in the center for a defense. The wagon train consisted of prospectors headed to the Sioux land in the Black Hills in search of gold. Black Elk's band was headed to the Rosebud to join up with Crazy Horse. They had left Red Cloud's band because they believed he had sold out to the whites by signing a treaty relinquishing the Black Hills.

A month later Black Elk would be present to watch Crazy Horse and others wipe out Custer at the Little Big Horn in Montana. Black Elk's story can be found in John G. Neihardt's Black Elk Speaks *and Joseph Epes Brown's* The Sacred Pipe. *The best book on Crazy Horse is Mari Sandoz's* Crazy Horse.

A month later another battle took place here.

Just to the northeast of Montrose on the east bank of the

creek is where Buffalo Bill had a fight with the Sioux Chief Yellow Hand in July 1876 during what became known as the Warbonnet Battle. He claims to have scalped Yellow Hand and proclaimed it was "the first scalp for Custer," who had been massacred just weeks before. This is before Bill became a legend in his own time.

Just north of the church on a small cone-shaped hill is a monument to Colonel Wesley Merritt and the troops of the 5th Cavalry. They stood here and fought off a band of 800 Cheyenne. The Cheyenne were attempting to join up with the large band of Indians that had fought Custer at Little Big Horn and were then encamped in northeast Wyoming. An eyewitness account of this skirmish, along with the part Buffalo Bill played in this era of Nebraska history, can be found in Campaigning with Crook by Charles King.

This same hill was used as a "fort" by the citizens of Montrose to "protect themselves" from the possible attack by the Indians of the Ghost Dance cult at Wounded Knee. Turns out there was nothing left of the Indian Wars anywhere in America after that.

Montrose is a T intersection in the road. Either turn north to head into South Dakota (who would want to do that?) or turn south for a circle back to Harrison.

Zero miles (5 miles.)

Missouri Border.

Rulo.

Rulo was named after the wife of Charles Rouleau, on whose land the town was built. Sorry, but as usual, history has not deemed it necessary to give any credit to this woman other than being Charles Rouleau's wife. Charles was a Frenchman who came west with John Fremont's expedition, married an Indian (Mrs. Rouleau) and took up land on what was then known as the "Half-Breed Treaty."

People who were children of French and Indian parents were not allowed the protection of laws of the Frenchmen, while on the other hand the laws governing the Indians could not be applied to them either.

In 1857, the United States government decided to set aside 127,000 acres of land for those with mixed ancestry and for Indians with no tribe. As a consequence, a triangular piece of land west of the Missouri, from Rulo to the Nemaha, was deemed "Half-Breed Tract" by the government and Indians alike.

Half-breeds were allowed to settle here, and unlike other reservations, which were owned communally, land on the half-breed reservation was deeded directly to individuals. That meant the land could be bought and sold, and many of the initial inhabitants gladly sold their property. As a result much of this land was never settled by half-breeds, but by those who bought the land.

The very first person to be deeded land, for example, sold his piece three days latter to land speculators. The speculators were partially banking on the hope that a railroad bridge would one day be built near here and greatly increase the value of their land.

This half-breed reservation was the only one of its kind in the nation.

The town of Rulo, thanks to Mrs. Rouleau, a half-breed on whose tract the town grew, was on the edge of the reservation.

Lewis and Clark Trail passes nearby to Rulo, the route the explorers took on their way west and their way back east.

Rulo was the location of perhaps the most gruesome crime in the history of the state.

In August 1985 police found the graves of a five-year-old boy and an older man who had been mutilated north of Rulo. As the search for the killer or killers continued, a bizarre story unfolded that involved a survivalist cult and their charismatic leader. The leader claimed that God spoke to him, and said that a birth at the commune was from an immaculate conception.

The first-degree murder trial against the leader of the cult was the first in the history of Richardson County. While the trial was just starting an arsonist burned down the farmhouse where the cult had its headquarters. The caves that the cult dug to prepare for Armageddon mostly have been filled in by local farmers to discourage sightseeing.

Before the story left the nation's headlines, stories of the cult's strange acts and beatings were splashed over newspapers from coast to coast. Talk of movies based on the incident and publication of books about the strange incident have plagued Rulo for years.

The story is so well-known, however, that visitors still ask at local gas stations for directions to the cult's farm. It is a part of their history most folks in Rulo would just as soon forget, but like the violent actions of the Old West, the Rulo slayings are now a part of the area's history.

South of Rulo one mile on county roads. Near here was a large Indian Village still in existence in historic times. A small town of pioneers once also stood near here.

South of Rulo three miles to the northern edge of the Iowa Indian Reservation, which borders the Sac and Fox Reservation to the west. You are now very close to the lowest elevation in the state of Nebraska.

On the banks of the Missouri River just east of here you are at a mere 850 feet above sea level, or roughly 4,600 feet lower than a spot in the Panhandle that is the highest point in the state.

If you are the odd sort who wants to be one of the few people who have stood in the precise southeast corner of the state, follow this road for another mile. There you will find the Iron Monument, which represents the first surveyor's stake planted to mark the boundary between Nebraska and Kansas, at 40 degrees latitude. This was done in 1854.

Five miles (3 miles.)

A small road leads **south two miles** to a tiny village. When this town was founded it was called Bluffton and then Sac, in honor of the Sac Indians of the area. Later a pioneer suggested the town's name be changed to Preston to honor his hometown in England. Guess who won.

The Sac and Fox Indian Reservation is one of Nebraska's six Indian reservations, although a large portion of this reservation is in Kansas, where this tribe once roamed. The other reservations are: the Iowa, just east of here; the Winnebago and the Omaha, both in Thurston County, 70 miles north of Omaha; the Santee in Knox County; and a small piece of the Pine Ridge reservation in north central Nebraska.

Three miles (0 miles.)

Falls City. US 159 joins US 73 here and swings south into Kansas. For information about Falls City, or sites along US 73, please see entry for US Highway 73.

West of Falls City, *three miles.* Just to the south of the road is the site of the first oil well ever dug in the state of Nebraska.

Zero miles (9 miles.)

Nemaha County.

If there were a single county that offered everything from one of the oldest communities along the Missouri, to what many consider to be the state's finest state park, to one of the most beautiful and yet undiscovered villages in the world, to a steaming, puffing steamboat, to a steaming, puffing nuclear power plant, it would have to be Nemaha County. The county was named after the Otoe Ni Maha, or muddy river.

Brownville.

Brownville may be Nebraska's richest historical location. Though crumbling in recent years, many of the town's residents still recognize the area's unique and important place in the settlement of the American West.

Before the Whites came, the Otoe Indians held these lands. They surrendered the lands in a treaty in 1854. The reservations of the small Indian tribes of the Fox, the Iowa and the Sauk at one time extended to near here. These tribes, which were brought to Nebraska by the government resettlement plan, are still located in the extreme southeastern corner of the state.

Brownville had high hopes in its early years. Founded by Richard Brown and Joel Wood, who crossed the Missouri in a canoe, the settlement began and the first Christian Church in the state of Nebraska was organized in 1854. It quickly became the main shipping point for trade up and down the Missouri and steamboats docked on the banks of the Missouri, and travelers bustled about the town of 5,000's busy Main Street.

Brown started to operate a flatboat ferry across the Missouri to Nemaha County and soon a road stretched between Brownville and the Marshall's Trading Post near present-day Beatrice. During a single week in 1855, 50 families crossed the river to settle here. The boom was on.

One of the state's earliest and most influential newspapers, *The Nebraska Advertiser*, was started at Brownville in 1856.

The first telegraph line in the state, from St. Joseph, Missouri, to Brownville was strung in August of 1860. *The New York Times* announced that the telegraph now reached "the half peopled wilds of Nebraska." The first message sent out on the line was addressed to the "States of the Union."

A small college, Brownville College, existed here for a short while.

By the mid-1860s at least a half dozen ferries were operating on this stretch of the river, ferrying pioneers and settlers to Brownville. One, the Belle of Brownville, was large enough to carry 22 wagons and their teams.

Importantly, a brewery was begun and over 3,000 barrels of beer a year were made, most of which was consumed by the citizens of Brownville. The remnants of the brewery cave can still be seen at the end of Main Street.

The town became the county seat of the newly formed

Nemaha County and had high hopes of becoming not only the largest and most prosperous city in the territory, but the capital of the new state as well.

Then came the railroad, passing up Brownville for other cities. Those cities began to grow and to attract the river traffic that had made Brownville bloom. By the mid-1880s, the decline of this once-thriving metropolis was on, and by the economic woes of the 1890s Brownville had dwindled to a single block of ragtag businesses.

But the town was far from dead. Although it floundered for a long while as a tourist curiosity, Brownville today is home for over 200. The town's historic atmosphere has attracted arts and crafts people and has given the location the cultural feel of a town a hundred times larger.

The *Meriwether Lewis* is a sidewheeler steam boat that has been converted into the Museum of Missouri River History and is run by the State Historical Society. In addition to being located on a steam boat, the museum features exhibits that highlight the historical significance of the Missouri River. The museum is open seven days a week April 1 through November 15.

The Brownville Museum was organized in 1956 by the Brownville Historical Society and has permanent exhibits in the Bailey House, the Carson House, the Dentist Office, the Railroad Station and the Main Street Museum. The museum also operates other historic buildings and homes. The museum facilities are open all afternoons in summer and on weekends and selected other days during the winter months.

The Brownville Village Theater is a repertory theater that offers fine productions during the summer months.

Cruises of the Missouri River on board the *Spirit of Brownville* are available through a local private company.

Many of the fine old houses are built of native brick, which was made at Brownville's brickyards.

The Methodist Church, once used to house part of Brownville College, was built in 1859 and is the oldest continuously used church in the state.

Walnut Grove Cemetery, up Cock Robin Hollow to the forks, then left, is one of the oldest cemeteries in the state. It is the final resting place of Civil War soldiers, Indians, pioneers, river boat people and Governer Robert Furnas, who founded both the state board of Agriculture and the Nebraska Historical Society. The tombstones here date back at least to the 1850s.

East from the cemetery to a high hill known as Lookout Point, once an Indian lookout, which offers a fine view of the surrounding area.

Perhaps many area residents remember the height of the Old Time Fiddlers contests held in Brownville from the 1960s on. Brownville had gained a considerable reputation as having one of the best and most authentic Old Time Fiddlers gatherings in the country. On a warm afternoon the streets of the sleepy village would be packed with cars and people and dogs and music. Music was everywhere. To walk down Main Street was to experience a constantly changing menu of great music. Banjos, guitars, autoharps and, of course, fiddles were brought out of cases and men and women who had been complete strangers moments before now sat or stood in circles grinning and laughing and sharing their lives with music. The entire life of true folk music got its blood and its soul from places like Brownville and the thousand people who gathered there as a single family to share the universal language: music.
At its peak in the mid-1970s the contest drew as many as 30,000 people to this tiny town. The festival was cancelled, then restarted on a less grand scale. The rebirth of the festival was designed to attract a smaller, more polite crowd. It worked, but the smaller crowd made it more difficult for the organizers, the hard-working Brownville Historical Society, to break even financially on the event. In the late 1980s, the event seemed to have finally died, as the organizers said they could no longer sponsor it. The best bluegrass in the region, perhaps in the country, could usually be heard on the banks of Whiskey Run Creek.

Brownville is well known for its two annual flea markets, tours of historic homes during the Christmas season and an annual re-enactment of scenes from the Civil War.

One reason Brownville came back to life was because of the

US Highway 136

efforts of a world famous artist who also happened to be a Nebraskan. Regionalist Terence Duren (1907-1968) promoted the town in his later years and used it as the subject of some of his paintings and drawings. (For more information about Duren see entry for State Highway 92 at Shelby.)

Just south of town, along the Missouri River, is one of two Nebraska Nuclear Power Plants. The Cooper Plant, built during the early 1970s at a cost of nearly a half billion dollars, went "on line" in 1974. The boom in nuclear power plants has largely faded due to the increased costs of building and financing the construction, as well as the fallout from such disasters as Three Mile Island and Chernobyl. The plant is run by the Nebraska Public Power District.

The land south of Brownville, from here to the extreme southeast corner of the state, was designated a half-breed reservation in 1880. For more details on this, please see the entry for US Highway 159.

What many consider is Nebraska's prettiest state park is just a few short miles south of Brownsville, and the most beautiful city in the state, Peru, just a few miles north on these side trips:

Four miles south of Brownville on State 67, *Nemaha City.*

Nemaha is near the mouth of the pretty Little Nemaha River. The town was formed in 1855.

In 1891 the citizens of this tiny town got together to hold a picnic as a celebration of community spirit and togetherness. They've been holding the picnic every year now since then, and although the town's population has shrunk alarmingly close to under 200, the Old Settlers Picnic is held every August and includes contests only folks who trust and know each other would enter in front of one another: pie eating, beautiful baby and watermelon eating, to name just a few.

Five miles south of Nemaha, *then five miles east on S-64E to Indian Caves State Park.*

Indian Caves State Park.
This 3,000 acre State Park is considered the favorite state park by many lifelong residents of Nebraska, and it is easy to see why. The park gets its name from the huge sandstone embankment at the

southern end of the park, which houses the only particular petroglyphs of this kind in the entire state. The origin of the glyphs, ancient Indian paintings etched into the walls, are still a mystery to archeologists. The pictures depict the animals of importance to the Indians who left these signs, but many are of unknown creatures and shapes. Unfortunately many of the pictures have been obscured by modern vandals who believe their names and current loves warrant as much importance as these mysterious and beautiful ancient drawings. Please discourage anyone from defacing the sandstone.

At the other end of the park the state has reconstructed a portion of a river settlement known as St. Deroin. It was named after an Otoe half-breed whose father was French, and whose mother was an Otoe woman who owned the land where the town stood. The park maintains a small reconstructed log cabin at the old town site and rangers there can tell you more about Joseph Deroin, the town's founder, who among other things, it is said, was buried sitting on top of his horse in the town cemetery. A great flood in 1911 washed most of the town away, except for a few buildings.

The park also offers 20 miles of trails for backpackers, cross country skiers, horseback riders and just plain walkers. Bank fishing in the Missouri is available for those who believe there is no danger in taking fish from 6 miles below a nuclear power plant outlet. The catfish taken from the bank in the park have been pretty large, however. . .

An interpretive program about the area is presented every Friday and Saturday night during the summer. There is plenty of camping for groups, trailers, and backpackers.

The park is home to a wide variety of animals and plants. It is located on the Central Flyway for migrating birds, which include the bald eagle. Even turkey vultures, which are somewhat rare in Nebraska, have been seen at the park. In addition, there are coyotes, foxes, turtles, wild turkey and flying squirrels. There is quite a debate about which season is the best for visiting the park. Some say spring, when all of the many wildflowers are in bloom, while others swear by autumn, when the foliage is a rainbow of color. In any event, Indian Caves State Park is a prize for the state and deserves to be treated as such.

US Highway 136

Take the paved State Highway 67 north, just east of Brownville for the winding and beautiful drive 10 miles to Peru.

Peru is perhaps the most beautiful village in the entire state of Nebraska. Its brick, tree-lined streets, sleepy downtown and quaint college atmosphere make it the most underrated, undiscovered jewel around. It was founded in 1857 on the banks of the Missouri and soon the Nemaha Valley Seminary and Normal Institute was founded in 1860. It was the forerunner of Peru State College.

The campus, the oldest school still operating in the state, is known as the Campus of the Thousand Oaks and is the alma mater for thousands of graduates. On campus is a glacial boulder that was found south of town and brought to campus in the 1920s. It was deposited by the ice sheets that once covered Nebraska (No, not last winter...!)

Peru State College is the location of Nebraska's claim to western literary fame. The annual reunion of cowboy poets is held on the campus each year. Contact the college or the Brownville Historical Society for details.

Just west of Bluff Road is a hill known as, and I'm not kidding, Nebraska's Pike's Peak. The slopes of this hill are steep, sure, but whoever gave this hill such a name may not have seen the real Pike's Peak in a long while and had forgotten what a peak was all about. In any event, since we are in Peru and not Colorado Springs (one thing to be thankful for) try to climb up to the top of this Pike's Peak. It was used as a lookout by the Indians, and local legend has it that the trail up the hill was the Indians' route as well.

Just northwest of the Peak is the site of several Indian houses, probably dating back to historic times.

Just south of the Peak, at the school site, is the location of an Indian Burial ground. For some reason the original settlers chose the burial ground as the place to start the community. They may have been on to something, as the peaceful and special atmosphere of Peru may be because of the spirits of those long-ago Indians.

The town has a hiking and nature trail and a viewpoint of a four-state area of the Missouri River Valley.

Take some time here — it will be a town that you will dream about retiring to.

Because of a change in the river's course, a teardrop-shaped part of Nebraska is across the Missouri directly northeast of Peru. It is completely surrounded by Missouri, but is a part of Nebraska.

Nine miles (10 miles.)
Auburn.
For a description of the sites in and around Auburn, please see the entry for US Highways 73 and 75.

Ten miles (10 miles.)
Just north at the junction of State Highway 105 is the town of Johnson, founded when a homesteader named Johnson used a part of his land to start a town. It is located in the pretty rolling hills between Auburn and Tecumseh.
For a lovely private park north on State Highway 105, please see the entry for US 73/75.

Ten miles (6 miles.)
Tecumseh.
Tecumseh, the county seat of Johnson County, is also the home of the Johnson County Museum at 3rd and Lincoln Streets. It is open most days of the week during the summer and autumn months. An old church, a country school and the town's jail are all a part of the museum.
The courthouse is on the National Register of Historic Places and many of the town's old and historic buildings are still in use.
The town was named after the Shawnee Indian, who never set foot in Nebraska.
The ABC TV mini-series "Amerika," which attempted to show what the country would be like under Soviet domination, was filmed in and around Tecumseh.
During the early winter storm on Halloween 1991, most roads in Johnson County were closed. The road crews would no sooner clear a road than it would drift over.

Six miles (9 miles.)
North on county roads four miles to the tiny town of St.

209

US Highway 136

Mary's, which once went by the rather proud name of Smartsville.
Northwest five more miles on State Highway 41 *to
Sterling. Parts of the television mini-series "Amerika" were filmed in
and around this town of 500. The town was named after J. Sterling
Morton and has a small but vocal fan club promoting its finer
attributes.*

Nine miles (7 miles.)

Just off US 136 is Crab Orchard. The name no longer applies,
if it ever did. There may be some crabs here, but there are few
orchards.

Seven miles (4 miles.)

Filley.

Two miles south of here via county roads is the Filley Stone
Barn, which was built in August of 1874. Since the farmer was fed up
with grasshoppers, he wanted to build a barn that would not only keep
the pests out, but would hold the produce of the good seasons once
the plague had moved on. The barn is three stories tall, and built
against a bank. It was made from local limestone and rock, and the
plank floors came from Nebraska City. When they finished work in
November, folks from as far away as fifty miles came to the big dance
in the barn. The petition to place the barn on the National Register of
Historic Places read in part: "This is one of the most magnificent barns
in the state, and the largest known limestone structure."

Four miles (8 miles.)

Rockford, a once thriving town, nearly blown away by neglect,
has begun to come out from a long sleep thanks to the state recreation
area just **three miles south** of US Highway 136. The area has a man-
made lake good for fishing, camping, swimming and picnicking.

Eight miles (9 miles.)

Beatrice.

Whether you are *not* from around here and call it Be-IT, or
know better and call it Be-AT, this small city has much to offer.

The town was founded in 1857 and named after the daughters of one of the founding pioneers.

Beatrice *is* indeed the original home of the nationally known
Beatrice Foods, just in case you weren't sure.

Its location on a ford of the Blue River and its proximity to the

210

Oregon Trail were the features that originally caused people to settle here.

Beatrice still has a fine park named for its use as the site of the old traveling education and entertainment programs: Chautauquas. This park started as a place to train Sunday School teachers. Its original tabernacle and gatehouse have been preserved on the park grounds. Also in the park is a log cabin, originally located on south Fifth Street in the city. The park is located on the southern edge of the city, off Sixth Street.

The Paddock House at 1401 N. 10th was built in 1870 and looks pretty much as it always has. It is named after Algernon Paddock, one-time senator of the state from 1875-1881, who lived here. This is a private residence and is not open to the public.

The Gage County Historical Museum is located at Second and Court. It displays the historic artifacts from all towns in the county, as well as displays on rural life, and a part of the old train depot. It is open Tuesdays through Sundays. Hours vary. Is free.

Sixth and Grant. Gage County Courthouse. This building was built in 1890 and is on the National Register of Historic Places.

The Martin Luther home at 804 S. 12th is one of the best care centers for folks with developmental disabilities. It was established in 1925 and has since gained a national reputation for its programs for children and adults.

Beatrice celebrates Homestead Days, a four-day celebration of the pioneer history of the town, are held the last weekend in June. The festivities include a rodeo, Chautauqua lectures and other events.

Beatrice was the birthplace and boyhood home of one of literary America's most mysterious talents. Weldon Kees, whose father owned the Beatrice manufacturing factory, gained minor fame in the early 1950s as a poet and painter as a part of the post-World War II literary Renaissance. Kees was close friends with Jackson Pollock, Truman Capote and other such well-known figures.
Kee also wrote fiction but decided his work was no good and destroyed most of it in a bonfire in San Francisco in the early 1950s.

In 1955, he disappeared into a thick fog and mist under the Golden Gate Bridge. Most people assumed he committed suicide, although some believe he actually changed his identity and moved to Mexico. In any event, some of the work by this Beatrice native and graduate of the University of Nebraska is still in print, including his brilliant satire of academic life, the novel *Fall Quarter*.

The F.D. Kees company, which made lawn mowers and other equipment, was the state's oldest continuously operating industry before it shut its doors late in 1992 due to changing economic times. A few months later, the company started up again with new stockholders and the incentive of orders for new equipment.

According to research done by author Renee Sansom-Flood, another Beatrice resident, General L. W. Colby, gained a certain kind of fame when he went to Wounded Knee, South Dakota, four days after the 1890 massacre as a part of a burial detail. Miraculously, three infants survived the attack and four days in the snow. Two of the infants died, but the third survived. Colby wanted the baby to serve as "my living curio," and after taking it from surviving Sioux who tried to hide it, Colby returned with the six-month-old baby to Beatrice.

Colby's wife, Clara was quite active in the suffrage movement and she cared for the child, named Zintkala Nuni, as best she could. The child, whom the Colby's called Margaret, stayed with Clara after the Colbys were divorced.

Her life was not a happy one. She married several times, battled health concerns her entire life and eventually took a job in Buffalo Bill's Wild West Show.

Colby was elected to the state Senate, and there he is credited with creating the Nebraska National Guard. He became its first colonel. The Guard had been called to South Dakota after the massacre.

The story of the tragic life of Zintkala Nuni can be found in Sansom-Floods' book *The Lost Bird*.

During the severe Halloween snow storm of 1991, a 1,500-square-foot section of the roof of a foodstore collapsed under the weight of the snow.

Beatrice is justifiably proud of its efforts in building one of the state's finest town libraries. The old structure, a Carnegie building constructed in 1903, had become a maze of narrow lanes between overstuffed shelves and a mish-mash of clutter. It was one-fourth the recommended size for the number of volumes it held.

Through a well-organized community effort, a modern, beautiful building was constructed to serve the town. The old building was to be preserved for other uses. Ask locally for directions to the library.

Homestead National Monument: 4 1/2 miles NW of Beatrice on State Highway 4.

This National Monument was created to serve as a memorial to the hardships of the pioneers who cultivated the civilization of the American West. At this spot, Daniel Freeman made the first claim to a homesteading site under the provisions of the original Homesteading Act of 1863. Although in recent years there has been some controversy whether he was indeed the first, all loyal Nebraskans have no doubt that he was. The property remained in the Freeman family until the Government purchased the homestead and created this Monument.

There is a fine display in the center, and a short self-guided walking tour of the monument.

Across from the Homestead Monument is the brick Freeman School, which was built in 1871 and used continuously as a school until 1968.

Nine miles (10 miles.)

During the surprise snowstorm known as the Halloween Blizzard of 1991, visibility on this part of the highway was at zero for hours. Roads were closed and many trees and power lines fell in the heavy, blowing snow.

Ten miles (3 miles.)

Jansen.

There are many points of historical interest in this area. The Oregon Trail passed through Jefferson County, and it is one of the few areas in the eastern part of the state where sections of the original ruts can still be seen.

In addition, this area is where such legendary western men as Wild Bill Hickock and Kit Carson roamed.

For information about the specific location of these sites please see the entry for State Highway 15.

Three miles (3 miles.)

US Highway 136

Oregon Trail markers are in the school yard of the District 39 school house. There are ruts still visible to the west of this school. The school was built in 1904.

Three miles (22 miles.)
Fairbury.
Junction with State Highway 15. There are many interesting sites north and south of town on 15, including areas where the visitor can see the ruts of the Oregon Trail, which passed through here. For more information, please see the entry for State Highway 15.

Fairbury was built on the site of an Indian trail. An Otoe Reservation was once east of town.

The Jefferson County Courthouse on the south side of the square was built of native limestone and is on the National Register of Historic Places. Inside are six ceramic tiled fireplaces, and many of the antique furnishings are from its earliest days.

The courthouse was dedicated in 1891. One hundred years later the copper box sealed in the cornerstone was opened as a part of the celebration of the building's 100th birthday.

Inside were items someone long ago believed would serve as indications of life in 1891 Fairbury: a penny, newspaper articles about the building of the courthouse, weather reports, articles about the attempt to raise sugar beets in the county, deeds, and articles about two county commissioners who were convicted of bribery during the construction of the building.

The centerpiece of the items, however, was a letter written to "the unknown and unborn" written by a Fairbury doctor, L. Humphrey: "I am a physician practicing medicine. Settled in this city in 1880. Never was drunk, nor gambled, am a member of the First Baptist Church."

His words painted a portrait of life in this town over a century ago, how the status of crops and the fragile balance of weather were central to the quality of life. "The year is one of great abundance of all fruits, grains, vegetables of all varieties, all in abundance never before equaled in this state. Never did a people have so much to be thankful for. General health prevails. Last year was a poor year for agriculture owing to insufficient rainfall."

Dr. Humphrey's remarks and the other items were resealed in the box, along with items from the 1991 celebration, and placed back in the cornerstone.

The town was founded in 1869 and named after a town in

Illinois, which was the former home of one of the early pioneers. Like many towns in the state, Fairbury owes its existence to the railroad, which came up the river in 1872.

Russian settlers came to this area and established a colony on 27,000 acres near here. Many of the descendants of those settlers still populate the town of Fairbury.

The fine museum in this town is on the west side of the town square. It is open Mondays, Wednesdays and Fridays in the afternoons.

The town's annual celebration, Germanfest, is held the third weekend in September and features German arts, crafts and food as well as other activities.

An old log cabin, originally built on a homestead of the 1860s, is preserved in Fairbury's Park.

The town had mostly brick sidewalks until as late as 1981.

On April 4, 1933, Ma Barker and her gang robbed the First National Bank. The outlaws were posted all around the outside of the bank with machine guns. Traffic was stopped while the robbery was in progress. The employees and customers were told to lie on the floor and the inside of the building was riddled with bullets. A deputy sheriff and others were injured during the stickup.

The gang took two women as hostages, and they were later released unharmed. As they made their getaway, the gang littered the highway with carpet tacks, so that the cars that chased them out of town soon all had flats.

Fairbury was the home of the Campbell Brothers Circus, which performed over the Midwest in the 1890s. The circus consisted mostly of human acrobats.

Take the River Road northwest to the restored Smith Limekiln and house built in the early 1870s. The limekiln was built in order to fire limestone until it became lime. The lime was then used as mortar and sold to places as far away as Denver and Kansas City. The house of the original owner still stands and contains displays about this little-known industry. This kiln was not the only kiln in the area, as there were others who tried to make a living from the booming of

215

faraway cities. However, the Smith kiln is the only survivor from that era. Such burning of lime is still practiced, however more efficient kilns are in operation at many cement plants and sugar plants. The limestone exposed in many parts of Jefferson County contains many sea fossils. The museum is run by the local historical society and is open Sunday afternoons, or by appointment.

Five miles east of Fairbury to Rock Creek Station on the Oregon Trail (see entry for State Highway 15 for more information).

Twenty two miles (1 mile.)
Junction with US Highway 81.

North, one mile to Hebron. Hebron is home to the world's largest porch swing, which holds 25 people. Gives you an idea what folks around here do on nice summer evenings. . .
The Oregon Trail crossed Thayer county north of here, and there are many sites in the area connected with that route. For more information on the Oregon Trail and other sites in this area, please see the entry for US Highway 81.

One mile (7 miles.)
Junction with US 81 south. Please see entry for US Highway 81 for information about the sites in this area.

Seven miles (7 miles.)
Junction with State Highway 5.
Just south is Deshler, home of the Thayer County Fair. On the fairgrounds is an unusual octagonal barn used to show livestock.
The town has a number of limestone buildings and houses.
Dreshler's roller mill was built in 1890 and looks essentially the same as when it was built.

Five miles north on 5 to the Little Blue River. Just on the north side of the bridge, diagonally across the "T" intersection, some ruts from the Oregon Trail are visible. The Trail followed the Little Blue to near Hastings, where it crossed a small divide to the Platte.

Continue north 1/2 mile from the bridge. Turn west and go one mile. Turn north and go 1/2 mile. Turn west again and go 1/2 mile. Here, on the north side of the road, is the location for the Kiowa Station, which survived a series of violent Indian raids in 1864.

216

Continue west 3 miles, *a quarter mile past the Oregon Trail marker just west of the Thayer County line in Nuckolls County. This is the Emery Trail marker, which commemorates an incident in 1864 when a number of Indians tried to ambush a stagecoach. The driver spotted the Indians at this point, turned his rig around, and outran them.*

Continue west 1/2 mile to "T" intersection, then south for 1/ 2 mile, then west for 1/2 mile to the site of the Bowie ranch, where a rancher and his wife were not as lucky as the stagecoach driver. They were killed the day before the stagecoach incident by raiding Indians.

Continue west and take the first left turn. Turn left and go 3/ 4 mile to the site of the Comstock ranch, which was attacked and burned to the ground by the Cheyenne during the August raids in 1864.

Continue west to Oak. Oak is a delightful town rich with history. For a more complete description of the many additional sites in and around Oak, including what has been called the best Ice Age fossil site in the state, please see the entry for State Highway 14.

You may retrace your steps, or continue west from Oak to State Highway 14, and then south, four miles to US Highway 136, or go south on county roads six miles to US Highway 136.
For eyewitness accounts of the Cheyenne raids of August 1864 please see entry for State Highway 14 at Nelson.

Seven miles (11 miles.)
Ruskin.
North of here, six miles on county roads to Oak and many sites from the time of the Oregon Trail and sites of prehistoric Ice Age life in Nebraska. For more information about this area, see above and also the entry for State Highway 14.

Eleven miles (4 miles.)
Junction with State Highway 14. For more information about sites in this area, please see entry for State Highway 14.

North here five miles, and then west eleven miles to Oak. Oak is a small town with a lot of history. The Oregon Trail brought both the pioneers and the Indians. Buffalo roamed these parts in gigantic herds. You may visit Oak and then continue east 9 miles to State Highway 5, and then return to US 136 by driving south on 4 for a nice loop trip of this area (see above).

For more Information about this wonderful location, please see entry under State Highway 14

Four miles (6 miles.)
Junction with State Highway 14, south to Superior. Please see entry for State Highway 14 for more information.

Six miles (8 miles.)
Take this county road south to cross the Republican River and then continue west on county roads that parallel the river for a delightful break from the hot asphalt. Return to US 136 via State Highway 78 in eight miles.

Eight miles (10 miles.)
One mile south of State Highway 78 is Guide Rock. The town has preserved a stockade from earlier days before expensive county jails were the thing to do. Guide Rock is so named for the rocky hill southeast of town, which served as a landmark for centuries. This place was a holy spot for the Pawnee Indians. It was one of several places where the earth was connected to the sky...a place where the great spirits who watch over all, and the great mother the earth, were connected. It is possible, for those non-Pawnee who are very still and very devout, to feel the holiness of this place. There are not many such places left in the world. Say a prayer just for that.

Continue south on State 78 across the Republican River and take the first county road east for a delightful detour off of the hot US 136 along the banks of the Republican River. In eight miles turn north across the river and return to US 136. (see above.)

Ten miles (5 miles.)
Red Cloud.
An article in an April 1985 *New York Times* said, "The marvelous thing about Red Cloud is that it has preserved itself utterly unspoiled, hardly changed since the early days of about 100 years ago...here is a place with the charm unbroken, the spell still upon it..."
One of America's most popular and sensitive writers, radio

personality Garrison Keillor, brought his entire radio show company to Red Cloud in 1991 to give what many consider among his best performances. The show centered on a respect for Red Cloud's best-known citizen.

What draws people from cosmopolitan New York, Chicago, London and Paris to this small town is the writings of Willa Cather, Nebraska's best-known and most widely read author.

Cather was not a native of Nebraska but was born in Virginia, where she lived for the first six years of her life. Then, in 1884, her family moved to the open prairies of southern Nebraska. Although Cather was only to live here from then until 1890, she returned to the area for the rest of her life, and, as readers of her works know, the open prairies and the prairie spirit are what make her books so timeless.

Cather said of that period, "The years from eight to fifteen are the formative period in a writer's life, when he unconsciously gathers basic materials. He may acquire a great many interesting and vivid impressions in his mature years, but his thematic material he acquires under fifteen years of age."

Cather's appeal has never faded from view, and in recent years she has gained in significance, if one can judge by the number of scholarly and popular biographies that have appeared. Cather's modern lifestyle, strangely blanketed with an old-fashioned restraint, is subject of scrutiny these days, but what remains pure and wonderful are her books.

If you have never read Willa Cather's *O Pioneers* or *My Antonia* you have missed a very wonderful part of American literature, a very wonderful part of being able to read. These two books most clearly capture the essence of the prairie life and times. For Cather, unlike most writers, was able to let the land itself — the very place — become a dominant character in her work. The open plains, the prairies and fields of her homeland rise up out of the pages of her books and come alive.

Others of her books are also set in Nebraska, and except for one or two books, all of her 12 novels are near masterpieces. Her best of many beautiful works may be a short novel called *The Professor's House*. Citizens of New Mexico still line up at bookstores to buy copies of her historical novel of the Southwest, *Death Comes for the Archbishop*. People still weep at the close of *A Lost Lady*.

Willa Cather died in 1949 and is buried in New Hampshire, a distant and foreign landscape from the land she brought to life in words.

Red Cloud and Webster County have preserved many of the sites mentioned in Cather's books, or important in her life.

The Farmers' and Merchants' Bank, which was also known as the Garber Bank, was built in 1888. The founder of this bank, Silas Garber, appears as a fictional character in several of Cather's works, most notably as Captain Forrester in *A Lost Lady*. The bank now houses the museum and interpretive center as well as a fairly substantial archival collection of materials on Cather. Begin your visit in Red Cloud at this special and unique Nebraska State Historical Society Museum.

The entire downtown area of Red Cloud is divided into historic districts. The Main Street district has been preserved because so many of Cather's stories and novels have significant scenes that occur here.

The Seward Street District, with its churches and courthouse, also figures in many of her works.

The Elm Street area is significant because in Cather's day, this area was the "wrong side of the tracks" of Red Cloud, and less-fortunate folks lived here. Cather wrote with an awareness and sensitivity about such people, and the area serves as a setting in her works.

The Railroad Addition District is significant not only in Cather's works, but to an entire group of towns whose very existence is owed to the railroads.

In addition to the museum, The Willa Cather Pioneer Memorial and Educational Foundation has a book store and art gallery on Main Street, and offers guided tours of the surrounding countryside and the sites Cather portrayed in her books. The Foundation is known around the world as an excellent source of information and research about Cather. In 1991, for example, a rare diary of a World War I troop ship doctor was donated by the doctor's family to the Foundation because of the institution's fame at serving Cather scholars. The diary is important because Cather borrowed it from the doctor and used information from it as the basis for her Pulitzer Prize-winning novel *One of Ours*. The doctor lived in Jaffrey, NH, where Cather often visited.

The Cather childhood home (338 N. Webster) was built around 1879, and the Cather family rented the home from 1884 until 1904. This is the home where Cather grew up, and where she gathered many of the materials for her later fiction. The house is open for tours seven days a week during the spring and summer months, and five days a week during the winter.

The Burlington Depot was built in 1897, and moved to its present location in 1966. The railroad played an important role in Cather's life and in her writings, as it did for so many of the towns in the Midwest.

St. Juliana Falconieri Catholic Church was built in 1883 and figures in *My Antonia, Song of the Lark* and other works. Grace Episcopal Church (it is now the Church of Christ) was a frame church built in 1884, although a brick veneer was later added to the structure. Cather was raised a Baptist and became a member of this church in 1922.

Spend some time in this delightful town and you will certainly begin to feel Cather's power and insight come alive all around you.

Five miles (7 miles.)
The Narrows. The Republican River squeezes through a couple of bluffs and creates quite a pleasing view in this pretty county.

Seven miles (6 miles.)
Inavale. Inavale suffered greatly when the Republican River flooded in 1935. Today, Inavale is a sleepy, quaint Midwestern town. Inavale was long noted for its excellent cheese factory.

On February 6, way back in 1897, a group of people returning from a prayer meeting in Inavale saw something they could not explain. They looked up into the night sky and saw a bright light directly overhead. They said it was an airship, a cone 50 feet in length with two sets of wings on each side. A few days earlier hundreds of people in Omaha watched as a bright light flew over the city. The Omaha UFO was described as resembling a canoe. No explanation for this rash of sightings was ever found.

North of here eight or so miles on the divide lands between

221

the Platte and the Republican River watersheds is the land that Willa Cather wrote about in many of her novels. Catherton, a small ghost town founded by her relatives, is here, as are many of the farms and farmhouses, some still standing, which she included in O Pioneers, My Antonia *and other works.*

Tours of the countryside Cather made famous are organized in Red Cloud. See above entry for Red Cloud for more information.

Six miles (6 miles.)
Riverton, on the banks of the Republican River. There is some evidence that Spanish explorers visited this area as early as 1541. Artifacts from that period have been found near here.

Six miles (4 miles.)
Location of the townsite of Grant. Grant was started after the Civil War by a colony of freed slaves who named Lovely Creek, started a brickyard and planned a courthouse. Since the colony had only a single team of horses to share between several people, the colony disbanded after two years of hardship.

Four miles (5 miles.)
Franklin. Yes, named for Benjamin Franklin, this quaint town was once called Franklin City. For a while, Franklin was home to a small college founded by the Congregational Church. It lasted from 1881 until 1922, when it closed due to lack of enrollment. The area was made into the city park.

In 1882, Jesse James read an ad in a Lincoln paper and wrote to Franklin asking about land that was for sale. He said he planned on moving to Franklin, but he was killed before he could make the transition.

During the destructive 1935 flood of the Republican River, many bridges in the area were taken out. Franklin was the location of the Red Cross headquarters for relief aid. The flood killed over 140 and did an estimated $8 million in damage.

The town was founded by Civil War veteran Colonel Van Laningham. His enthusiastic letters back east led others this way.

Many Franklin residents had never seen a train, so when one finally arrived here in 1879 many people ran away when it roared into town.

In the 1940s, the town was host to the state Cornhusking Championships. Men picked corn in the fields while the women back

in town husked the ears from the trucks the men had loaded.
Franklin is the location of the Franklin County Museum.

A fine, well-maintained road follows the banks of the Republican River on the south side of the river, so get off the lazy and boring US Highway 136 and try it out.

Junction with State Highway 10. For sites along this route, please see entry for State Highway 10.

Five miles (6 miles.)
Bloomington. Here you can find a long-abandoned cemetery, old land office from the 1880s and a mill built in 1882. Ask locally for directions.

Six miles (5 miles.)
One half mile south, toward the tiny village of Naponee, is the site of Camp Cameron. Here in 1871 a camp was established by soldiers from Fort Kearny to protect settlers against Indian raids. The camp, which was located on Turkey Creek, proved to be unnecessary.
At Naponee is the Naponee Museum housed in an eight-sided structure that was once a church.
Naponee was the hometown of actor David Janssen, who was best known for the role he created of Dr. Richard Kimble for the television drama "The Fugitive." The show, which was about a man on the run who had been wrongly convicted of murdering his wife, was popular from 1963 until 1967.

Five miles (7 miles.)
Prisoners from the Atlanta POW camp used to harvest corn near here in the 1940s. A farmer had to pay 12¢ per bushel for the service and 40¢-50¢ an hour for other labor. Some of this money went to the local co-op. The local paper gave advice for the farmers: "Everyone is cautioned not to fraternize with the prisoners."
For more information about the Atlanta POW camp see the entry for US Highway 6.

Seven miles (6 miles.)
Alma. Junction with US Highway 183.
Alma is headquarters for the vast Harlan County Lake, built as a flood control project after the devastating Republican River flood.

For more information about the lake and the area, please see entry for US Highway 183.

Six miles (12 miles.)
Orleans.

Orleans was settled as a part of the Catholic Colonization Association in 1872.

Just south of Orleans, the Sappa Creek enters the Republican River. It was here, in 1869, that the Republican Sioux attacked a party of surveyors and killed them all. This massacre led to a series of battles with the Sioux that are known as a part of the Nebraska Sioux Wars.

On August 1, 1955, several people in Oxford saw a formation of a dozen white lights in the sky. This phenomenon, still unexplained, was also observed at Oxford and Arapahoe at the same time.

Seven miles west of Orleans on State Highway 89 to Stamford. Stamford's Pork Days, held each fall, features an old time community barbecue. Over a thousand locals come by for food and fun.

Twelve miles (8 miles.)
Oxford. Oxford, on the Furnas/Harlan County line, goes hand in hand with another Furnas town named Cambridge. However a ford of the Republican River near here was locally called Ox Ford, and that is the likely derivation of the town's name.

On August 1, 1955, several people in Oxford saw a formation of a dozen white lights in the sky. This phenomenon, still unexplained, was also observed at Orleans and Arapahoe at the same time.

Eight miles (2 miles.)
Edison. No, not after Thomas, but after a local rancher with the first name of Eddie.

Two miles (0 miles.)
Junction with US Highways 6 and 34. US Highway 136 ends here and the route west is taken over by these two other great American roads. Please see the entry for US Highway 6 for information about the route west of here.

NEBRASKA
U S
6

This Highway enters the state at the Missouri River in downtown Omaha and travels the entire length, leaving the state on the high plains of Colorado.

Zero miles (13 miles.)
Omaha. For a description of the many sites in Nebraska's largest community, please see the entry for US Highway 75.

Thirteen miles (14 miles.)
Boys Town. For a description of Boys Town, please see the entry for Omaha on US Highway 75.

Fourteen miles (6 miles.)
Gretna. A beautiful small city overlooked by many who prefer the sightless Interstate for their travel between Omaha and Lincoln.

South of Gretna ten miles to the beautiful Platte River State Park.

Near Platte River State Park is the Ak Sar Ben Aquarium at Schramm Park State Recreation Area. Located at the site of Nebraska's first fish hatchery, the aquarium is the only one of its type in the region. The main fish tanks holds nearly 1,500 gallons of water. A very small admission is charged and the aquarium is open seven days a week during the summer, and during most weekdays during the remainder of the year.

For more information about this area please see entry for US Highways 73 and 75.

Ten miles northwest of here to Mahoney State Park (see below entry for Ashland.)

Six miles (1 mile.)

Linoma Beach on the east bank of the wide Platte River.

Hard to believe this was once the most popular recreation spot in the eastern part of the state. Here, before the days of television and state recreation areas, thousands from Omaha and Lincoln would gather to celebrate and cool down in the summer months. Those were the days when the waters of the Platte flowed a bit clearer. There are still those who spend time here and the quiet spot makes for a nice break.

Southwest of here five miles to the Platte River State Park (see above, and entry for US Highways 73 and 75).

One mile (2 miles.)

Just across the Platte River is the junction of US Highway 6 and State Highway 63.

There is a kind of quiet and solemn feel about this area, wouldn't you agree? Now that the Interstate has taken so much of the traffic away from this once busy road, the distance between Omaha and Lincoln seems to have once again returned to the isolated lonely countryside it once was.

There may be more than just a strange feeling about this spot, for this is the location of one of the most famous UFO incidents ever reported. The story has been retold around the world because of the way it has a particular validity.

For one thing, it happened to a police officer.

In the early hours of December 3, 1967, Herbert Schirmer drove past a barn on Highway 63, near the intersection with US 6. Outside the barn in a corral a bull was kicking and throwing himself against the fence. Schirmer stopped to make sure the fence would hold.

Once outside, he noticed that the cows in the barn were kicking at their stalls and bawling.

After making sure things were secure he got back into the patrol car.

He drove toward the intersection.

At first he thought it was a truck. A row of blinking lights were shining in the road about a quarter of a mile ahead of him, but as he watched, the lights began to flash very quickly and then rose straight into the air.

The story is that Schirmer returned to the station and filed a report. In the log he wrote: "Saw a flying saucer at junction of 63 and 6. Believe it or not!" This was what the newspaper picked up on in the next few days. As he entered this information in the log he noticed that it was 3 a.m., much later than he thought it should be. It was this nagging fact that led investigators to persuade him to undergo hypnosis.

Some weeks later Schirmer was hypnotized. He was taken back to that dark night at this very spot. What his conscious mind had kept hidden from him was laid open under the influence of the researchers.

Schirmer began to tell the rest of the story.

After the football-shaped object rose into the air he drove farther on toward the intersection and watched as it moved toward a mud field.

He turned the patrol car up the mud road to the field.

The lights were very bright. They were flashing above him in the field. He reached for the radio to make a call for help, but the radio was dead and the car had stopped.

The object hung over the field. It had a silver glow all about it, and the lights continued to flash rapidly.

As he watched, tripod legs extended from the craft and it settled to the ground.

He tried to get out of the car, but something was preventing him. Something in his mind kept him from moving, although he tried to fight against it.

As he watched, a form came out of the craft and moved toward the patrol car. He tried to reach for his revolver, but again, he couldn't move. The being drew out some object, pointed it at the car and a green gas soon filled the air. There was a sudden bright flash of lights and he passed out.

What seemed like an eternity later he woke up and rolled down the window.

Now there were several beings about the car. In Schirmer's own words, one "had a very high forehead and a long nose. His eyes were like ours, round, but they were sunken in. Their pupils were not round, but sort of like a cat's: like the small letter a. Their complexion was grey. The mouth was a sort of slit."

The creature reached through the open window and touched him on the neck. He felt an intense, deep pain, and the creature withdrew.

Although the creatures did not speak, Shirmer "heard" their words in his head.

"Are you the watchman of this place?" they asked.

He said that he was.

"Watchman, come with me."

He could not resist. They took him toward the craft, all the while asking him questions about the surroundings. They asked about the Platte River water supply, and about the Lincoln Electric generator near Ashland.

He was taken inside the craft, where it was explained to him that they get energy for powering their craft by reversing electrical and magnetic power. In order to keep going, he was told, they take electrical power from power plants and electrical lines. He was told they draw power from water, as well.

After a while longer he was told that he was to report only that he saw a UFO and watched it take off from the highway, and nothing more.

He was taken outside again, and from his patrol car he watched as the craft's legs were withdrawn, a humming noise began and an orange light was added to the bright and flashing lights. In an instant the craft shot straight into the black sky.

Fantasy?

Maybe so, but Herbert Schirmer was evaluated physically and mentally and his friends and family all checked out. He was a flawless witness: honest, dedicated, straightforward and not the kind to come up with such a story.

Schirmer claimed the beings told him that they would return twice more. One year later to the day, a family from Lincoln was passing by Ashland on Interstate 80 and reported seeing a "beacon that was hovering about 200 feet above the ground. It was shaped like a flat oval. It made no sound."

Yes, maybe a fantasy. You judge for yourself, as you sit here near the very spot where Schirmer saw the craft land.

Two miles (13 miles.)
Ashland.

Ashland is noted as being the home for some Lincoln water works, but the town is worth a stop, for it contains many interesting older buildings.

St. Stephen's Episcopal Church was built in 1872 at what was then the edge of town. It is an example of Gothic Revival architecture.

The Israel Beetison house was built between 1874 and '76, close to the Oxbow Trail, of limestone quarried at Plattsmouth.

The National Bank building was constructed in 1889. It served as a bank building until 1948 and since then has had a variety of uses.

Ashland's Carnegie Library building was built in 1911 at a cost of $7,000. It is typical of the designed favored by the Carnegie Corporation with a single story, raised basement of brick. The style is an example of the Jacobethan Revival form.

The Oxbow Trail passes through Ashland on the west side of town. It cuts across US Highway 6 from the southeast toward the northwest. Where the trail crosses Salt Creek was known as Saline Ford. The trail crossed here because the solid limestone creek bottom at this spot was the only natural bridge on the entire trail. Because of the natural bridge, this spot became a depot where supplies could be shipped west. Freighters and settlers gathered at this spot and eventually founded the town of Ashland.

North of Ashland on State Highway 63 to *Stambaugh House. The house was built in 1876 by the first permanent white settler in the area. His original dugout was southwest of the current building. He had built this Italianate brick house onto his sod and log cabin.*

By the early 1980s local folks had purchased the house and surrounding land for farmland and began renovations of the Stambaugh house. Their unique design incorporates the old house with a considerably more modern one. The house contains open stairways, a museum, an intercom system, a sauna, leaded glass arches, a wide cornice along the roof, an atrium with etched wheat leaves in the glass, a sun porch, a pantry and built-in furniture. The home is a private residence and not open to the public.

Continue north on State Highway 63 seven miles north of Ashland to Memphis.

The Armour Ice House once located here was one of the largest ice houses in the nation. It served railroad cars carrying beef east and west across the nation.

The house and adjoining 40-acre pond were constructed in 1897. Each fall the pond was filled with water diverted from Silver Creek. In the winter ice was cut from the pond. A channel was cut and kept open to provide access to the ice elevators that entered the lake. Cakes 40" by 20" were marked and sawed eight inches thick. They would be poled to the elevators and then loaded into the ice rooms. The ice was very pure because of the care taken to clean the pond each season.

The ice house was a forty foot high building that was 200' by 735'. There were 20 rooms to store the ice. A steam-driven engine provided electricity for the house.

As many as 24 railroad cars were filled in a day. The ice house burned down in 1921, although ice continued to be harvested until refrigerated railroad cars made such an operation unnecessary.

For further information about sites in this area please see entry for US Highway 77.

*   **Southwweast of Ashland, three miles** to Mahoney State Park, a 500-acre masterpiece of a modern state park. Don't come here planning to rough it, as the park includes miniature golf, a water slide, heated and air-conditioned cabins, RV hookups, paddleboats and a lodge. Designed to serve over a half million people each year, the park draws visitors from Interstate 80. Please see that entry for more information about this Disneyland of a state park.*

*For a more subtle park, continue **south of Mahoney ten miles** to Platte River State Park, near Louisville (see above entry at Gretna).*

Thirteen miles (9 miles.)
Waverly.
The original Burlington Depot still stands in town.
A log cabin that for years stood here was recently moved to

230

a farm six miles west of Lincoln on A Street.

The Old Mormon Trail, an alternate route west for Mormons coming through Nebraska City, passed two miles south of Waverly. Ruts from this trail are still visible at that spot. Ask locally.

One half mile west on US Highway 6, and one mile south to two cedar trees with a boulder between them, which marks the old freight trail that passed through here in the 1860s.

Nine miles (8 miles.)

Lincoln. For a description of the sites in Lincoln, please see entry for US Highway 34.

Eight miles (3 miles.)
Emerald.
Near here in 1902 a Burlington train was held up. The robbers got $32,000.

Two miles to the south of town is the location of a one-room schoolhouse located on a private farm. The owners of the property purchased the building at an auction and had it moved to their farm because they collected antiques. The 1894 building was built on the James Lane farm four miles west of Agnew, some 20 miles from here. The school closed in 1962 but was also used as a church and a community clubhouse. Also located on the farm is an old filling station and an antique outhouse. The building is a museum and is open by appointment only. Ask locally.

Five miles to the south is Conestoga Lake, one of the several recreational lakes in the Salt Valley system. Four miles beyond Conestoga to the south is another lake, Yankee Hill. Both are open to the public.

Seven miles south of here to Denton. Southwest of Denton the ruts from the Nebraska City Cutoff to the Oregon Trail are still visible. They are three miles south and one and a half miles west of the village. Ask locally for directions.

Two miles northeast of Denton, just northwest of the school, was a well-used encampment for the early Indians in the area. Children attending the school in the early years would walk along the

231

creek bed in order to avoid being seen by the Indians.

Denton was located on an old cattle trail that brought cattle up from Texas around 1871. Near here as well was the last open range in Lancaster County. The last open range closed in 1879.

It was near there that three early-day pioneers chased three Indians they claimed had stolen a cow. A fight followed on a hillside near Emerald. One Indian was killed, and a pioneer, Jeremiah Garret, was hit in the ribs by an arrow. Garret pulled the arrow out with his own hands and then collapsed.

Three miles (2 miles.)

One half mile south of here is the Burd School, a small school that has served the area for over a century in the same building. There are children attending this school whose great, great grandparents sat in the same room to learn their three Rs.

Two miles (9 miles.)

Pleasant Dale.

In clay pits near here were found some of the oldest fossilized plants known to science. The plants resembled a cross between an apple and a rose.

On October 14, 1959, two people driving down the road late at night saw a UFO here. It made a siren-like sound and the bright light traveled in an arc to the horizon.

Nine miles (8 miles.)

Milford.

The Milford Rest Home, east of town, was built in 1888 as an Industrial Home. The first automobile highway west from Omaha, then known as the Omaha-Denver Road, went through Milford.

The Ponca Indians camped here after they surrendered their homeland and were being forced to march to the reservation in Oklahoma. The daughter of the Ponca Chief Standing Bear, Prairie Flower, is believed to have died here of a broken heart and is buried somewhere in the area.

The Shogo Litha Springs produced bubbling natural water (California had nothing on Milford!) that was shipped to Lincoln and bottled as Shogo Soda Pop. The Community College is built near the site of the springs.

The Amish-Mennonite Church was here from 1878 on, and a sizable Mennonite population still inhabits the area.

Milford wanted the county seat so badly that the argument between Milford, Camden (a ghost town north of here) and Seward became heated enough to produce physical violence. Seward won, at least for the time being.

Old buildings dating from the earliest years of US Highway 6 still dot the area. Most date from the 1920s and '30s. Likewise many of the trees planted in rows along the highway date from those early years. The government had a highway beautification project, which involved planting trees. There was also some belief that green trees would produce rain in the drought-stricken area.

Eight miles (1 mile.)
Just north of the bridge across the West Fork of the Blue River, take county roads east to the confluence of the Fork and the Big Blue River. Many consider this to be the prettiest place two rivers come together in the state. Ask locally for directions.

One mile (3 miles.)
Blue River Recreation grounds. The timber here is native and nature-planted.

Three miles (9 miles.)
Dorchester.
This is the location of the Saline County Museum, which has thousands of exhibits in nine buildings including an old school, a train depot and a post office. It is open Sunday afternoons, or by appointment. The secretary of the historical society is there every day, weather permitting, since she walks the six blocks every day to the museum.

The weather wouldn't have permitted during the Halloween storm of 1991. The early winter storm closed many roads in Saline County, and ice downed powerlines.

Just west of Dorchester is the site of West Mills, built in 1859, and Pleasant Hill, the location of Saline County's first county seat. Inquire at the museum for directions to these locations.

Junction with State Highway 15. Please see that entry for information about sites along this route.

Seven miles east of Dorchester on State Highway 33 to Crete.

Crete.
Near an exquisite older mansion, known locally as "The Maples," is the first cabin built in Crete. It was constructed in 1864. Both places are open to the public the third Sunday of the month, or by appointment.

Tuxedo Park was the home of the first Chautauqua Park in the state. The Chautauqua was a traveling event that featured cultural and religious lectures and demonstrations and was popular at the turn of the century.

Crete's annual celebration, known as "Coming Home Week-end," is the fourth weekend in July.

Doane College in Crete is the first liberal arts college in the state. It was established in 1872. Doane is known for its excellent English as a Second Language program.

Crete received a tiny bit of national fame in the late 1960s, at least with the young. In a popular song called "Tarkio Road" by a couple of Missouri boys named Brewer and Shipley the opening lines mentioned "riding into Crete, Nebraska..."

South of Crete 10 miles to Wilber. Please see entry for State Highway 15 for more information.

Nine miles (3 miles.)
Friend.

Friend contains many relics of the heydays of US Highway 6 when it served as one of the first transcontinental highways. Cabin camps were the forerunners of motels. Small cabins could be rented. Most were small single rooms, sometimes with a bathroom, sometimes not. Occasionally, cabins would include some cooking facilities so that the traveler could cook a meal.

What else need be said about a town with the name of Friend?

Three miles (5 miles.)
North on S-76 A four miles to Cordova.

Cordova's most famous landmark, a windmill at the center of town, was built in 1916 and for many years was the main source of water for all the inhabitants.

Cordova is the home of Michael Bristol, who works from photographs to paint portraits of people's houses. Usually owners hire him to create watercolors of their homes. Bristol was written up in "The New York Times," which called his work "meticulously detailed and set in their proper surroundings of trees, bushes, lawns or city sidewalks."

Five miles (8 miles.)

Exeter. An alphabetical name assigned by the railroad. Poor visibility and roads packed with snow and ice caused many problems near here in the Halloween storm of 1991.

Eight miles (1 mile.)

Fairmont, founded in 1871. As was the case in this area, many towns were named by the railroad. The railroad had a simple solution as to what to name the towns that sprang up along their routes. They simply selected a batch of names, put them in alphabetical order and started with the A's. This spot was the sixth town to be named. It was first named Hesperia, which was sixth on the list. The citizens changed the name to the more localized Fairmont.

Fairmont has a small museum located in the former office of the town's doctor.

Fairmont was the home of Fairmont Creamery, which expanded to become the nation's largest food processor: Fairmont Foods.

Many scholars believe that Fairmont is the setting for Stephen Crane's masterful short story, "The Blue Hotel."

One mile (8 miles.)

Junction with US Highway 81. Please see entry for that highway for information about sites along its route.

Eight miles (8 miles.)

The pretty brick Catholic Church two blocks north of the highway dates from the early 1920s.

Eight miles (8 miles.)

Sutton.

Dating to 1880, Sutton is the oldest settlement in Clay

County. The area was originally settled by Russians and Germans.

Eight miles (3 miles.)
Junction with State Highway 14, north. Please see entry for that road for information about locations along its route.

Three miles (3 miles.)
Junction with State Highway 14 south. Four miles south on State Highway 14 to Clay Center.

See entry for State Highway 14 for information about Clay Center and other sites along Highway 14.

Three miles (1 mile.)
Just north of here is Harvard. Don't laugh, Nebraska also has a Cambridge and an Oxford.

One mile (5 miles.)
On the south side of the road is the University of Nebraska's Agricultural Research Center.

Five miles (1 mile.)
Those symmetrical hills on the south side of the highway are leftover ammunition depots from the Second World War. Hidden and protected from potential enemy airfire by earth and grass, many of these are now abandoned, while others are used for storage by a variety of state and private businesses.
One mile south then one mile east to historic cemetery.

One mile (2 1/2 miles.)
Large series of concrete buildings on the south side of the road is the research facility for a commercial seed company.
Two and a half miles (5 miles.)
To the north is an ethanol manufacturing plant where combustible alcohol is produced from corn. On the south side is a local power plant.

Five miles (6 miles.)
Hastings.

Junction of US Highway 281. For information on Hastings and along US 281, please see the entry for that highway.

Junction with US Highway 34. For information about sites along this road, east, please see entry for US Highway 34. Highway 34 joins Highway 6 for the next 135 miles until west of McCook.

Six miles (2 1/2 miles.)

Junction to Juniata, which is 2 miles north.

Juniata is the oldest town in the area. Named for the Juniata River in Pennsylvania. The first court house in Adams County was located at 9th Street. It was used from 1871 until 1878.

The park at 8th and 9th streets was the site of the GAR Hall.

Until the 1950s, Juniata still had a public well, surrounded by a bandstand, in the center of town.

At 4 miles west of town where the road crosses Muddy Creek was the Muddy Creek Stage Station on the Oregon Trail and Pony Express route.

At Highway 6 and Juniata Junction, go 2 miles south on county road to an Oregon Trail marker.

Two and a half miles (5 miles.)

At the intersection of the highway and county road, the route of the Oregon Trail crosses here.

Five miles (1/2 mile.)

Turn south to get to the village of Holstein and the Einspahr Sod House Museum. See entry for US Highway 281 for directions and further information.

One half mile (1 mile.)

Turn off to Kenesaw on S-1A.

One and a half miles north: location of a Pony Express station, which was mostly a dugout that rose only a few sod feet above the earth. There was a springs here as well. The place was called Summit Station. The station master here was almost lynched because local settlers thought he had stolen their horses.

One and a half miles more to Kenesaw. Many people envy Coloradans, who can find the elevation of their towns listed instead of populations as you enter the town. For those of you longing for the Rockies, Kenesaw is at 2,051 feet above sea level.

Kenesaw has the Edward Ziebarth Museum, which contains collections of fossils, pioneer artifacts and other items of interest. While it is open by appointment only, a trip into Kenesaw is worth your effort, as someone is usually around to open the place up.

US Highway 6

For an interesting side trip into the past, follow this route out of Kenesaw:

Go north one mile *at the northern edge of Kenesaw, then go west 3.5 miles, turn north one mile. Turn east, go one mile where a knoll overlooking the Platte Valley is the site of the Susan Hail grave marker.*

Susan Hail, traveling along the Oregon Trail in 1852 with her husband and other pioneers, drank water from a well supposedly poisoned by the Indians, and died here. She was buried in a coffin her husband put together from the lumber of his wagon. He left the other pioneers and went to Omaha, where he purchased a granite marker. He returned to this site carrying the stone in a wheelbarrow. This is not the original stone, which has long since been looted by nameless tourists. No one knows the location of her husband's grave.

Return to US 6.

One mile (7 miles.)

Just south of here is the Blevins Cemetery, a pioneer burial ground where 40 people found their final rest during the 1870s and 1880s.

Seven miles (10 miles)

Though mostly deserted, almost all of this once-beautiful town's buildings are made of local brick.

Ten miles (9 miles.)

Minden and junction with State Highway 10. Also please see entry for State Highway 10.

You can't drive through the state of Nebraska without knowing about Minden's Harold Warp Pioneer Village.

The enormous museum's motto, "There is nothing like it anywhere...," is quite accurate. Dozens of buildings and over half a million items bombard the visitor's eyes and ears. Everything imaginable, and some items not imaginable, can be found here. An entire building of 100 old automobiles, original land office, the Lowell Depot, replicas of sod houses, kitchens (the kitchen from 1950 looks just like the one many still use), and countless other displays are too much to see in a single day.

The museum is one of Nebraska's best-known attractions if

for no other reason than the large billboards along the Interstate that announce Pioneer Village for a thousand miles in any direction. The museum is not free, and it is not devoid of other tourists, but if you have never seen the place, you owe it to yourself and anyone you can take with you to see it.

The Pioneer Village is not the only attraction in Minden. At Christmas time, for example, the Minden pageant is performed with the cooperation of over a hundred citizens. It is presented the first two Sundays in December and includes the pageant and the lighting of the thousands of lights. The pageant celebrates city lights commissioner J.W. Haws who, in 1915, decided to surprise the city by lighting the courthouse dome. Every year thereafter until his retirement, Mr. Haws hand-dipped light bulbs and strung them about the city.

The Minden Square, with the Kearney Courthouse, is a landmark visible for miles.

At 106 S. Colorado is a house that is a fine example of Second Empire style architecture.

The house at 743 E. 4th was built for George Kingsley, a well-known early Nebraskan, and is an example of modified colonial style.

At 842 E. 6th is the boyhood home of longtime Nebraska Senator Carl Curtis.

At 9th and Minden is the 1913 Burlington Northern depot.

The former Nichol Hotel is at 535 North Minden.

On the north side of the square at 5th and Colorado is the opera house built in 1891.

A fine example of the bungalow style of house can be found at 540 N. Brown.

The fine Georgian Revival house at 225 N. Brown was owned by a doctor who was noted for his 1,600-mile roundtrip bicycle trip to a convention in Chicago. The house was built in 1911.

Another fine home built at the same time is close by at 219 N. Brown.

At 137 N. Brown is a Greek Revival style house that was constructed in 1893 during the heyday of the Victorian style craze.

Nearby at 115 N. Brown is another example of the Victorian style house.

The Kearney County Historical Museum, overlooked by those seeking the flash and glamour of the Pioneer Village, is one of the more interesting local museums in the area. It includes three buildings, including the original school house in Minden. It is located at the corner of Sixth St. and Nebraska Ave. If the museum is closed, local arrangements can be made for a tour.

North of Minden, 10 miles to the Platte River. This is the heart of the very narrow migration route for the Sandhill Cranes. During March and early April each year a half million of the birds, the entire population, pass through a ten-mile-wide strip of land. Best viewing is near the State Highway 10 bridge across the Platte. Stay in your car, as it makes an ideal blind. For more information on this and other sites in the area please see entry for State Highway 10.

Nine miles (3 miles.)

Axtell. Axtell is the home of Bethphage Mission, located just north of town. The mission was founded in the late Nineteenth Century as a school for disabled folks. The clean and quiet buildings of the mission are an important addition to the Lutheran church in Nebraska. There is a museum with displays about the mission on the grounds.

Just west of Axtell is McBride Sanctuary, which includes a 1-mile-long hike and bike path.

Three miles (5 miles.)

Turnoff for the Sacramento-Wilcox Wildlife Management Area.

South of here eight miles to the tiny town of Wilcox. Just west of Wilcox is the wildlife area and the haunted town of Sacramento (see below.)

Five miles (3 1/2 miles.)

Funk, Nebraska. And there were those who thought there was no funk in Nebraska. Get down!

Three and a half miles (1 1/2 miles.)

Turnoff for Sacramento.

Three miles southeast to Sacramento, and location of a ghost known as Faceless Fred. According to Glen Thompson of Holdrege, a man named Fred lived in Sacramento in the late Nineteenth Century and ran a roadhouse to provide services to folks headed west.

Although married, Fred enjoyed the company of women other

240

than his wife, including a woman who was a member of Buffalo Bill's Congress of Rough Riders.

The start of the end for Fred came when he grew attached to a local prostitute named Goldie. Fred's wife decided she had had enough. She took a large butcher knife and killed her husband one night when he returned home. She then used the knife to cut off most of her husband's face. She dragged his body to a dry well and dropped it inside.

The wife was never convicted of the murder and the prostitute soon left town, but that was not the end of the story.

Fred's roadhouse served a number of other purposes over the coming years. It became a general store, a feed store with an added elevator to lower feed sacks, and eventually the building was used as a speakeasy during the years of prohibition.

It was during the Depression that Fred's spirit began to appear on a regular basis.

In the mid-1970s a restuarant was started at the site of Fred's original roadhouse. Before long strange things started to happen there. One longtime employee got frustrated when the door of the walk-in cooler would swing shut on her. When she realized that it wasn't caused by any of her fellow employees she started to get nervous.

One night she got the feeling that something was closing the door. When she looked up she saw a man wearing a checkered flannel shirt. . .but the man had no face.

Other employees have claimed to have seen Fred. A waitress saw a man she described only by the fact that he was wearing a checkered shirt. Others have seen shapes in the mirror, or have discovered all the knives in the kitchen have disappeared.

Fred has been reported hitch-hikling on this road. The description is always the same: a checkered shirt and a face no one can quite make out.

Continue southeast another two miles *to the Wilcox-Sacramento Wildlife Management Area. One of several areas state-wide, this wooded land is home to many of Nebraska's species of birds. Included in the 2,313 acres is a Canada Goose restoration flock. Camping is allowed in designated areas.*

One and a half miles (7 miles.)

Holdrege and junction with US Highway 183.

Holdrege was founded in 1883 just before the railroad arrived . Like dozens of other frontier towns, Holdrege became the county seat by less than honorable means. Early on, the county records were stolen from Phelps Center and hidden in Holdrege until a courthouse was built.

Phelps County started getting a non-native population in the 1850s as stage stations and trading posts sprang up along trails west. Today 338/348ths of the county is farmland watered by wells and irrigation ditches.

Grain dealer C.E. McConaughy led the early battles for irrigation. His efforts eventually yielded results. The Central Nebraska Public Power and Irrigation District began in the 1940s with Holdrege as its hub. McConaughy's name now graces the state's largest reservoir north of Ogalala.

While the district provides water for over 30,000 acres from the Platte and other river sources, the limited supply of water and other demands for its use have put the district in the spotlight. The state of Wyoming, for example, claimed the district was using water irresponsibly. The state were joined by environmental groups that objected to the district's application for delivery of water. Part of the problem came after the district admitted that it had been transferring water from farmers who no longer wanted it to farmers who did without authorization from the state of Nebraska.

Wyoming's objections also stem from a dispute involving both states over a dam project near Casper, Wyoming.

This legal battle is between those who see the Platte as a source for water and energy to serve mankind's needs. Unfortunately, the Platte's other uses — namely as a habitat for endangered species, as a supply of drinking water, and as a part of the delicate balance of nature — must wait in line for what is left over once the big powers are finished fighting.

Holdrege has beautiful residential streets. The streets leading to the downtown business district are lined with stately houses and comfortable family homes. Sixty-five acres of parks provide fishing, tennis, golf and swimming. City Park, on the southeast corner of the junction of US Highways 6 and 183, is a large open area with picnic tables, swimming pool and other facilities. The health of the city's park budget, however, can be told by the varied condition of the playground equipment.

Swedish Days are held in and around Holdrege every year in mid-June. The two-day-long event includes ethnic foods, parades, musical and dramatic programs and the crowning of a king and queen.

The town is proud of a bronze statue "Promise of the Prairie," which was created by the internationally known sculptor George

Lundeen especially for the town's centennial celebration in 1983. The statue is located at North Park at the northern edge of the city on US Highway 183.

Holdrege was home to obscure author Edla Larson Gourley, whose novel *Homestay* traced a pioneer girl's story.

On a steamy August day in 1989, a Holdrege police officer clicked on his flashers and indicated to the rental van ahead of him to pull over. Instead, the van swerved and rammed into the police car. Shots rang out from the van.

The officer called in reinforcements.

Soon the rental van was racing through the normally quiet residential streets of the town with several police cars in close pursuit. Those in the van continued to fire at the police. One police car tried to stop the van by cutting in front of it.

The van crossed the median and hit a tree. Four people jumped from the van with guns in their hands and ran across a neighboring yard. The police opened fire. Soon the four surrendered, but not after one of them had been injured in the hand.

Thus ended one of the town's most dramatic moments. The next day, folks learned that the four were fugitives from an equally dramatic prison escape in Colorado. Two women had hijacked a helicopter and flew into the prison yard at Ordway to grab the two inmates, and then fled in the van.

The highlight of a visit to Holdrege is a trip to the Phelps County Museum, located on US Highway 183 two miles north of the intersection of 183 and 6.

The museum is one of the most comprehensive county museums in the state. The museum's philosophy, "To display as many items as possible so they can be viewed and appreciated by the donors, their children, grandchildren and guests," is well-served by the vast 34,000 square feet of floor space in the gigantic complex.

The museum includes scale models of area churches, dioramas of pioneer life, Indian artifacts, stuffed examples of a wide variety of American wildlife, nearly 50 cars, buggies, trucks and farm implements, including a like-new 1915 Case steam engine for powering mills and threshing grain.

There is a room devoted to over 100 old radios, a room displaying the history of the Atlanta POW camp, tools, slot machines, 30 television sets, and lots and lots of old toys.

There is even a display of spark plugs — yes, spark plugs.

If you were wondering where your child's collection of ceramic horses ended up, you can probably find them here, alongside a fine collection of real-life saddles made by such famous masters as R.T. Fraizer, T. Flynn, Fred Mueller, Collins Morrison and N. Porter.

Nowhere else can one see such a large collection of mortar and pestles, or washing machines, or stoves, or shoes and boots, or cut and pressed glass, or quilts, or cameras.

Most Phelps County towns have rooms devoted to their history as well.

The museum includes the George W. Johnson collection. Johnson was a member of Buffalo Bill's Wild West show from 1896 to 1899.

In the yard are some of the donated objects too large to fit inside. They include a church, a windmill and a schoolhouse.

The museum is free but will accept donations. It is open six days a week and Sunday afternoons.

Please see information contained in the entry for US 183 for more information about sites in the Holdrege area..

Seven miles (21 miles.)

Atlanta.

Atlanta is and always has been a temperance town, never having had a saloon serving the demon rum, or Bud. The town's highest population has been 300, which has nothing to do with the fact there are no saloons.

Just west on US Highway 6 is the site of a large prisoner of war encampment from World War II. Over 3,000 prisoners were imprisoned here, most of them captured in North Africa and Italy. The camp was the headquarters for a large number of smaller camps in the Platte Valley.

The Atlanta camp consisted of over 70 buildings and a dozen streets. Over 700 security personnel were housed here as well. Many of the prisoners were used to help local farmers with harvesting and planting.

The chimney and the silo-shaped water tower, visible from the road, are virtually all that remain of the buildings. However, an extensive display on the camp can be found in the Phelps County Museum on US Highway 183 just north of Holdrege.

Other area POW camps were at Weeping Water, Hebron, Hastings, Alma, Elwood, Indianola, Hays Center, Palisade, Benkelman, Lexington, Kearney, Grand Island and the town of Cornhusker, near Grand Island.

Six miles west of Atlanta on county roads to Rock Falls, on *private land.*

This small waterfall was once the center of the community of Rock Falls on the banks of Spring Creek, a stream that comes entirely from water from a variety of springs. By 1886 the area had developed a resort and attracted local and distant visitors. The area included boating, rope swings, a dancing platform and a circular swing.

The current owner is jusifiably concerned that the area be trated with respect. Permission must be granted in order to visit the site. Ask locally for the phone number of current owners in order to obtain permission.

Twenty-two miles (6 miles.)

Junction with US Highway 136. Please see that entry for information regarding sites along this route.

Six miles (6 miles.)

Arapahoe. Junction with US Highway 283. Please see that entry for information about sites along its route.

Our Lady of Fatima Shrine was built by Father Henry Denis, a Polish priest who, as a prisoner of war in a Dachau Nazi camp, promised to erect such a shrine in thanksgiving if he was liberated. He became the pastor of the local Catholic church after the war and kept his promise.

The Arapahoe public library is the site of the Howard Browne Literary Collection.

Arapahoe is the location of the Furnas County Historical Museum.

Arapahoe is a trading center for this busy highway and rural area.

On August 1, 1955, several people in Arapahoe saw a formation of a dozen white lights in the sky. This phenomenon, still unexplained, was also observed at Orleans and Oxford at the same time.

South of Arapahoe 12 miles to Beaver City. See entry for US Highway 283.

Six miles (1 mile.)

Holbrook.

A trading post for the Indians once stood here on the banks of the Republican River and on the Buffalo Bill-Fort McPherson Trail. It was named after the local river feature, Burton's Bend. Actually, the man who ran the trading post was named Ben Burton, so the full name of the curve in the river is Ben Burton's Bend. Boy!

The Trading Post, built in 1871 was also known as "Indian Bend" and pioneers could find "a square meal, and a little Benzine, in case of snake bites or frosted limbs."

Pioneer veterinarian Pete Phillipson practiced 75 years in the town of Holbrook. A history of the science can be found in the Dr. Phillipson Vet Hospital, which is maintained in its original condition.

One mile (8 miles.)

Marker commemorating the Fort McPherson Trail, which went from near here to the Platte River from 1863 to 1880.

Eight miles (8 miles.)

Cambridge.

The Cambridge Museum, one block north of the highway, has a surprisingly large collection of firearms, furniture and other items in a tidy, modern facility.

Cambridge has been called Pickleville, Northwood and Scratchpot. They settled on the best, don't you think?

North of Cambridge, mastodon remains have been unearthed. In 1931, Nebraska writer Loren Eiseley and archeologist Bert Schultz worked at the site.

Near the site is the Medicine Creek State Recreation Area.

Eight miles (6 miles.)

Bartley. East of here is Richmond Canyon, where in the late 1800s a 15-foot wall of water swept down on a wagon train making its way west. One man rescued two of his children, but 17 other pioneers were swept away. Only 5 bodies were ever found, and these are buried in the Cambridge cemetery.

South of Bartley 13 miles to Lebanon. Near here was one of Red Willow County's five flour mills. There are none left in the county.

Six miles (8 miles.)

Indianola.

The city park on the north side of the highway is the burial site of an unnamed Pawnee woman who died from injuries suffered at Massacre Canyon. She had been taken in and cared for by a local pioneer family, but died a few days later. See entry for US Highway 34 near Trenton for information about the massacre.

246

In 1944, Indianola was the site of a German prisoner of war camp. Over 5,000 prisoners were held here and worked on nearby farms. The prisoners soon painted pictures on the walls of the camp. Most all of these were destroyed; however, some sections were salvaged. They make up one of the most popular displays at the High Plains Museum in McCook, where they are now housed. (See below entry for McCook.)

Eight miles (2 miles.)

Harry D. Strunk Park for travelers. Often you can find some local folks giving coffee away here.

Near here in the Medicine Creek drainage was found a vast collection of fossils and tools from a band of nomadic people who lived here 10,000 years ago. Scientists say they most likely roamed after herds of buffalo and gathered wild foods as they moved. Their diet was more diverse than just buffalo, however, as they ate elk, shellfish, birds and deer, too.

The site was exposed after a flash flood in 1947 ripped away 60 feet of sediment. It was excavated and then covered by water from Strunk Lake.

Two other significant sites dating from these prehistoric times have been discovered in the area.

Two miles (1 mile.)

Karrer Park, under the auspices of McCook. This fine little park was built for the traveler. It features picnic tables, showers and local information, and during some summer months local citizens serve as hosts to the park.

One mile (11 miles.)

McCook.

McCook began life as a small pioneer community on the banks of the Republican River in 1879. The town really started to grow around its third birthday when it became a division point for the railroad. During a single month in 1882 over one hundred buildings were built. Soon a land office opened here and new settlers began to arrive.

During the 1920s McCook was one of the fastest growing communities in the country. Its population increased over 50 percent.

In 1935 the devastating flood on the Republican River destroyed hundreds of homes, and several people from McCook were among those who perished. During the flood a shortage of boats in the

McCook area contributed to the loss of life.

The discovery of oil fields in the area made McCook a temporary oil boom town during the 1950s.

McCook is the county seat, and yes, it won the dubious honor in a long-fought battle with other towns in the county.

Nebraska's best known and most respected politician, Senator George Norris, had his home in McCook. Norris was born in 1861 in Ohio, where he became a member of the Ohio bar. He moved to Nebraska in 1885 and entered politics. He served three terms as county judge and then was elected to the House of Representatives in 1902. He was re-elected six times and then ran for US Senator. He was re-elected to the senate a number of times. Norris was registered as a Repuiblican, but his independent ways earned him the respect of many people. He died in 1944.

Although best known as the father of the Tennessee Valley Authority, Norris also wrote the amendment to the Constitution eliminating the lame duck session of Congress, and wrote the amendment to the Nebraska Constitution that created Nebraska's unique unicameral legislature. He was a staunch advocate of public ownership of power companies, and created the Rural Electrification Administration. He was an advocate of women's suffrage.

The Norris Foundation, a non-profit corporation, has been formed to give people information needed to choose rural America as a place to invest their lives. In addition, the foundation hosts workshops, essay contests and other activities.

The US Senate has called him America's greatest senator. His home is a National Landmark, administered by the Nebraska Historical Society. It is open to the public. It is located in the 700 block of Norris Avenue.

The McCook Townhouse on Norris Ave. in downtown McCook is the former Keystone Hotel.

During World War II, an airport serviced B-29s, which would leave McCook with their deep droning engines roaring on their way to Japan.

The old Army base, including the old control tower, is being partially restored by the Air Base Historical Society.

The McCook Community College is the oldest junior college in the state. It was founded in 1926.

McCook is the smallest city in the country to have a complete

YMCA facility.

The town was named after a major general who fought for the Union in the Civil War.

If you were trying to get from Omaha to Denver, and somehow found yourself in McCook, you are now halfway there.

The Museum of the High Plains is located at 421 Norris Avenue and contains a fine collection of local history exhibits. Those exhibits include the D.A.R. Room, a recreation of an old-style drug store, based on items donated by Hendley, Nebraska, home of the man who invented Kool-Aid. The remains of one of the first dwellings built by white pioneers are contained here, as well as fossils, dresses, military items, local regional history, a re-created general store, blacksmith shop, business office, dental room and other items.

One of the more unusual displays in the museum are sections of a wall that had been painted by German prisoners of war who had been housed at nearby Indianola (see above entry for Indianola.) Most of the wall had been destroyed, but these sections were salvaged by the Bureau of Reclamation.

The museum's new building was constructed in the late 1980s and is located next to the unusual Spanish-style Carnegie library building.

At the corner of F street and Norris, a few blocks to the north of the museum, is a home designed by the famous architect Frank Lloyd Wright. The house was built in 1907 and is one of Wright's few homes west of the Mississippi.

Just to the north of the museum is the old Carnegie Library building, the former home of the museum. It has been placed on the register of Historical Sites for its unusual Spanish-style architecture.

On the upper center islands of Norris Avenue a nine-block area becomes Santa Claus Lane during the Christmas season. Life-size statues inhabit the street and help spark the wonder of the season for the local children, and for children of all ages passing through the town's snow-lined streets.

The old McCook post office, built in the 1910s, is a fine building, despite the fact it has virtually no heat or insulation. The old post office now holds shops.

Just so you know that this fine city, which sees itself as the metropolis of southwestern Nebraska, hasn't lost all of its country roots, in 1992 a woman threatened she would go to jail rather than to give up her pet pig, Jerry, which she was raising inside the city limits. A half dozen other pig lovers defended her stand. The city council had to consider whether or not to outlaw hogs, or just the breeding of hogs, within the city limits. The woman said she would plead guilty to having a pig, but not to having a hog.

Junction with US Highway 83. For information about sites along this route, please see entry for US Highway 83.

One mile south of McCook is Barnett Park. Barnett Park was formed after several people cleared tons of debris left here by the flood of 1935.

Eleven miles (3 miles.)

Culbertson. When the great flood on the Republican happened in May of 1935, the river was two miles wide here.

For a long while this town was the end of the railroad and hence a shipping point for many surrounding areas. The railroad worked its way slowly up what is today US Highway 6 and reached Palisade, 27 miles northwest of here, in 1891.

Three miles (8 miles.)

Junction with US Highway 34. From here east to Hastings the two routes are together. For a continuation of sites west of here on US 34, please see the entry for US Highway 34.

Legend has it that ranches in this area started when early pioneers gathered stray cattle from the Texas cattle drives that passed through here.

Eight miles (5 miles.)

When the highway crosses Red Willow Creek: near here on the old Walker ranch, two "claim trees" held the bodies of two Sioux warriors for years until they were finally buried. A post office was on this farm, called "Thornburg."

Grasshopper plagues were common in this area. The pests not only killed off all of the green and growing items in the area, but covered houses, pets, animals and humans.

Five miles (2 miles.)

On Stinking Water Creek the first non-sod school house was built of stone and still stands on the A.J. Irvine ranch. Ask locally for directions and permission to visit.

Two miles (7 miles.)

Palisade. The trail that George Armstrong Custer followed from Fort McPherson to Kansas, in order to take part in the 1867 Sioux Indian Wars, crosses the Highway here. This trail was often used in the years that followed.

Seven miles (1 mile.)

Hamlet. The Texas Cattle Road of 1880s passed through here on its way up the Stinking Water Creek on toward the shipping yards at Ogallala.

Throughout the county are still some sod houses on private ranches and farms.

This area was a part of one of the largest buffalo ranges in the country. Buffalo Bill Cody, Doc Carver and other historic figures hunted buffalo here for the railroad in 1868-69. By the late 1880s there were no buffalo to be found here at all.

Stinking Water Creek, which is just three miles north of Hamlet, got its name from the thousands of buffalo carcasses left to rot on its banks. During the 1870s this was a sportsman's paradise for hunting buffalo. Doc Carver claimed that it was in Hayes Co. where he killed his 30,000 buffalo. For more information on Carver, who was one of Nebraska's most interesting historical figures, see entry for State Highway 23.

North of Hamlet is a small pioneer cemetery that is located on a hillside and is reachable only by a footpath. Ask locally for directions.

One mile (6 miles.)

This canyon was one of the difficult crossings for the Texas Cattle Trail. The cattle had to walk the narrow flatland with canyons to the west and east of them. Once, the story goes, a couple of cowboys had been feuding most of the way up from Texas. One of the two, a black man, brought the cattle too near the western edge of the trail and the other, a white man, thought he was getting them too close to the edge. A fight broke out and the white cowboy killed the black cowboy and his body fell into the canyon.

Six miles (7 miles.)

The legendary cowboy and Texas outlaw Robin Hood, Sam Bass, said on his deathbed that he buried $10,000 worth of gold he had taken from a railroad train in a holdup "on the Frenchman River, west of the Falls." No one has found it yet.

The Frenchman River flows alongside of the highway from Hamelt to the Chase County line. The Pawnee called the river the Frenchman after a lone trapper who lived seven miles west of here on what is now the county line between Chase and Hayes counties. The Sioux called the river White Man's River after the same trapper.

The story of the French trapper is a mystery. No one knows much about him except for the amazing number of personal items that have turned up near the site of his cabin. He owned a gun and a rifle. He had no horse, and had to carry everything he used up river from St. Louis, probably by dugout canoe. He was probably killed by Indians during the Sioux War, but perhaps after cutting off the hand of one of his attackers. The bones of a human hand were found in the burned out shell of his cabin in the 1880s.

A half mile to the south of his cabin on the Frenchman was a large Pawnee village of 40 to 50 tepees. This village was probably attacked by the Sioux at the same time the Frenchman lost his life.

Ask locally for directions to the historical marker indicating the approximate location of the cabin.

Seven miles (9 miles.)

Wauneta, in the SE corner of Chase County, was named after the song Juanita, and given an Anglicized spelling. There's no reason to go to Colorado to find a town that seems to be in the mountains. Wauneta's setting gives one the feeling of being somewhere in the Rockies and without all the tourists from Nebraska!

One block from the center of town was a waterfall — a small but an important historic site as, in the early days of settlement, several people hid in the rocks of the ledge of the falls from raiding Indians.

The Sioux chief Whistler was camped at the falls when surveyors came through in 1872. He told them the land they were surveying was his. The whites retreated, but returned and continued to work with armed guards at their side.

The falls was blasted out in 1951 as a result of a questionable Bureau of Reclamation decision.

The Wauneta Roller Mill, founded in 1925, is one of the few flour mills remaining in the state. It is the only family-owned mill still in operation.

The well-known and well-used Texas/Ogallala Cattle Trail split Chase County right in two from the northern edge to the southern. During the 1880s this trail was used by cowboys bringing cattle up from Texas to the railheads in Nebraska. Some of the men drove the cattle farther and found suitable range in the Sandhills and the Dakotas further to the north.

Twenty miles north is the Lovett site, an excavated Indian village. See below for description.

Eight miles (1 mile.)

Junction with State Highway 61, south. Please see that entry for sites along this route.

Near here is Inscription Canyon. The canyon is located one mile south of Enders dam. Walk from Highway 61 in the northeast corner of a field toward the southeast for a quarter mile.

One mile (3 miles.)

Enders. A tiny community on the edge of the popular recreation lake, Enders Reservoir. There's good camping here.

Three miles (5 miles.)

Turnoff for Saloon Tree Monument and Lovett site.

*Just as Highways 6 and 61 turn sharply west, go **east two miles**, then turn **north and go 1/2 mile**. Monument is on the east side of the road in a field.*

*Return to paved road 1/2 mile south and **continue east another three miles**. The Lovett site, where an entire Indian settlement has been excavated, is in a field northwest of feedlot.*

Five miles (6 miles.)

Imperial. This is the county seat of Chase County. Here is the headquarters of the local historical society, although the museum is in Champion. (see below.)

US Highway 6

Junction with State Highway 61, north. Please see entry for State Highway 61 for information about sites along this route.

Eight miles to the SE on state road s15A is Champion. Here are the county's two main attractions for the history buff. Champion Mills was the last water-powered mill in the state. Using the water from the Frenchman River, this mill was in operation until recently. Thanks to the State Game and Parks Department, the mill has been turned into a small tourist attraction.

The trip to Champion is made twice as good since the Chase County Historical Society bought a former high school in 1963 and started a museum. The society modestly will tell you that the museum consists "mostly of machines." The history of ranching and farming in the southwest corner of the state is spelled out in the steel building that houses a good part of the society's collection.

Six miles (11 miles.)

One mile south on gravel road and then walk 1/2 mile east and south into a pasture. In this ravine were once a mud springs and stream that served as a frequent campsite for Dr. W.F. "Evil Spirit of the Plains" Carver. Carver used this camp on his many buffalo hunts.

Eleven miles (3 miles)

Just as the highway angles to the northwest, west of here is Three Buttes, an important local landmark for the past 1,000 years. There are no roads to the buttes.

Three miles (5 miles.)

Lamar, just off the road to the north. Lamar was named for Lucius Quintus Cincinnatus Lamar, Secretary of the Interior under Grover Cleveland. Good thing they stuck with just the last name.

Near Lamar is the home of one of Nebraska's widest read and least known writers. Wayne C. Lee has written dozens of books set in the Old West, full not only of adventure and suspense, but historically accurate, and infused with a love of the land that speaks to us all. His books may be a little hard to find, and you may not be used to reading "westerns," but you will not be disappointed in picking up one of Mr. Lee's creations.

Five miles (0 miles.)

Colorado border.

254

US Highway 34 enters Nebraska at Plattsmouth. From there until Union it follows the route of US Highways 73 and 75. Please see the entry for US Highways 73 and 75 for information about this section of Highway 34.

Zero miles (4 miles.)

Union. Union is a small town at the "T" intersection of Highway 34 and 73/75.

There are still some small and falling-down traces of the incredible beauty this small burg once had.

When you turn onto Highway 34, heading west, you may not know it, but there are those who claim you are now on the longest road without a turn in the world. You can set your car on automatic pilot and not turn the wheel an inch for the next seventy or more miles.

Another faction claims that this highway is a gigantic sun dial, and that on each summer's and winter's solstice the sun rises and sets at each end of the road.

Highway 34 was a ribbon of white for the dual freak storms of the winter of 1991-92. The first was a freak storm not only because it came so early in the season, but also because it hit on Halloween 1991. The 60-mile-wide band of snow, pushed by winds up to 50 mph, buried much of the state.

Fourteen inches fell at Hastings, 11 at Grand Island and 8 at Omaha. Before the snow fell freezing rain locked up most of the state's highways in a straitjacket of ice. The combination of snow and ice caused roofs to collapse and forced many mayors to cancel Halloween trick-or-treating. Interstate 80 was closed and travelers jammed area motels.

The rest of the winter was unusually mild until the second freak storm hit the state.

This storm hit at the other extreme of the season. On April 20, 1992, an intense low pressure area, combined with a southerly swing of arctic winds, dropped up to 14 inches on Brownville and 13 inches in Omaha. Budding trees and flowers were capped with crowns of white. It was the heaviest snow ever so late in the season.

Four miles (6 miles.)

Turn off for Nehawka, a town of quaint sentimental beauty and wonder.

Nehawka is home to perhaps the nation's only log cabin library. The building was built in 1934 by the Women's Club, which organized a network of donated items (including the logs) in order to build the building.

The library now serves mainly as a place to archive some of the village's history. There are books, but town's shrinking population took a bite out of the Women's Club's ability to finance the purchase of new items. There are no regular hours, but calling a phone number posted on the door will reach someone who has a key and can let you in to browse.

Six miles (1 mile.)

South one mile to Avoca.

Location of the studio of artists Kenny Walton, a glassblower, and Karen Kunc, who creates wonderful color woodblocks. Ask locally.

Queer, but this quaint and quiet community quickens its quality by a quantum when it quells the quondam quest for quiet by

256

commissioning a quality **Great American Quack-Off Duck Race,** *quickly 'cause it's cold,* **every Jaunary.** *A queue of vehicles with the quasi-curious, combined with the quintessence of quality quackers from across the county, qualm the quandary of the querulous quizzers who quarrel and can't comprehend the quote, quixotic, unquote, competition between all but quadrupeds. But the quibblers are quieted and quarantined as the quorum claps for the quackers, who — quills quavering quartzlike _ quickly quell the quislings, providing Avoca's quarterly quota of all kinds of quacks.*

(p.s. Please, no quirts or quails.)

One mile (2 miles.)

Turnoff to Weeping Water. Please see entry for State Highway 50 for information about this town rich with history.

Two miles (6 miles.)

Junction with State Highway 50. Please see that entry for information about sites along this route.

Six miles (6 miles.)

Turnoff for Elmwood, the writer Bess Streeter Aldrich's home. Location of Bess Streeter Aldrich Museum to commemorate the best-selling author. Aldrich was not born in Nebraska, but spent a number of years here.

Her best-known book may be the novel *With a Lantern in Her Hand.* That novel tells the story of three claim jumpers who were caught, hanged and buried in a mass grave near here.

The museum is housed in the Elmwood Public Library and contains original manuscripts, memorabilia and other items.

Six miles (4 miles.)

Eagle. In 1891, Major Pembleton performed here. The good major was able to play six instruments at once while Indian dancers danced to his music.

You stand in what many consider to be the center of the cornhusker land. Eagle for years held cornhusking contests each fall. The world's record is held by Monroe Barryman, who during an eleven-hour period on November 20, 1891, husked 130 bushels. If you have to ask what cornhusking is, go back to New York.

Eagle is the location of the MoPac Recreational Trail, part of a nearly continuous 25-mile-long hiking and biking trail, which begins in Lincoln and goes through the villages of Walton, Elmwood, Wabash and Eagle.

Four miles (2 miles.)
From this hill is a view to the west of Lincoln and the State Capitol Building.

Two miles (6 miles.)
Turn off for Walton, **one mile south.**

Walton is a tiny community about to be swallowed by Lincoln, yet holding on to its own identity. Southwest of Walton is a tiny burial plot containing the remains of one pioneer-era family.

Two miles north *of here and a mile east the old stagecoach line road crosses the county road. Traces of the road are still visible. Ask locally.*

Two and a half miles north *of here a well-used Pawnee trail crosses the county road.*

Walton is located along the 25-mile MoPac Recreational Trail. See above entry for Eagle for more information.

Six miles (8 miles.)
Lincoln.

Lincoln is the juncture of US Highways 34 and 77, Interstate 80 and State Highway 2. For more information about sites along those routes, please see the entry for those highways.

Any tour of Lincoln must start at the Capitol Building. This is one of the most beautiful man-made objects you are likely to see.

In 1919, the fourth capitol building was crumbling and the Legislature decided to spend some money and make a statehouse that would last.

A capitol commission organized a nationwide competition, and eventually the design of architect Bertram Grosvenor Goodhue was selected.

Goodhue's design was a unique and, some said, outrageous tower that rose from a square base. It looked more like some kind of a monument rather than a building with usable office space.

In 1922, the groundbreaking ceremonies, done with a plow pulled by oxen, signaled the start of construction. The new building was built around the old capitol so that the state government would not have to move to temporary offices. As new offices were completed, the workers simply moved out of the old and into the new, and then the old building was demolished.

Ten years after work began, the building was finished. The cost was $9,800,440.07. The building was paid for by the time it was completed.

Today, well past the half-century mark, the building shows little signs of wear. The flesh-colored stone walls are thick and stately and rise to a climax on the golden dome visible for miles. A statue of a sower, pointed northwesterly toward the greatest expanse of the state, sows his seeds into the vast expanse of the prairie winds.

The sower was designed by New York sculptor Lee Lawrie. The figure stands on a 12-foot pedestal of wheat and corn. It is nearly 20 feet tall and is made of inch-thick bronze. He sews seeds of life to the winds, facing northwest toward the fertile farmlands of Nebraska.

On the west side of the building the figure of Abraham Lincoln stands in a pensive pose. The statue was created by Daniel Chester French, who also did the statue of the seated Lincoln, which adorns the Lincoln Memorial in Washington, D.C. Lincoln's Lincoln predates the construction of the current building.

The north side of the building was once the site of a statue of William Jennings Bryan. The statue had been placed there by the Democrats under protest from the Republicans in the non-partisan government of the state. The Democrats kept saying the statue would only be temporary. The "temporary" statue was placed in concrete and stood there for decades. The Republicans finally won out, and the statue now stands at Bryan's Lincoln home, "Fairview" at 4900 Sumner (see below).

In 1932, the Governor had been successfully petitioned to light the tower at night. Since then, depending on the cost of electricity and the state's level of environmental awareness versus civic pride, the lights have sometimes been on at night, sometimes not.

A sampling of inscriptions from outside and inside gives an idea of what Nebraskans believe a good government and a good state should be:

"The Salvation of the state is watchfulness in the citizen." H.B. Alexander (over main, north entrance.)

"As onward we went
Thinking of our children
Many trails of buffalo we behold
Many trails of life" Pawnee Song.
     (north stairs.)

"Arise with the dawn

US Highway 34

Bathe in the morning sun
Sleep when the birds no longer fly
Awake when the first faint dawn appears." Sioux saying
(north stairs.)

"Political society exists for the sake of noble living." Aristotle
(south parapet.)

The mosaics in the Great Hall were added in 1967 as a part of the state's centennial celebration. They tell the story of the Blizzard of 1888, of planting trees, of the first railroad and other events in the history of Nebraska.

A walk through the rotunda and a ride to the observation deck on the 14th floor make up the usual tour for most people, but a far better plan is to take the guided tours, which are offered almost hourly throughout the year.

The West Chamber is the gathering place of Nebraska's unique, one-house, non-partisan Legislature, which was created in 1934. That chamber, along with the governor's offices, the Supreme Court, the Law Library and the Hall of Famous Nebraskans, are among the beautiful wonders of this building. In addition, the building is like a maze, with little tucked away corners of carved wooden doors, twisting halls and spiral staircases.

Lincoln's year-round walking event, Volkswalk, was named among the region's best walks by the editors of a walking atlas. One good way to enjoy the city is to take a walking tour of some of the fine old mansions.

The Ferguson House, just across from the Capitol at 700 S. 16th, is restored to the elegance of the 1915 era. Nearby at 1627 H, the Kennard House has been restored as a statehood memorial. It was the home of the Secretary of State when Lincoln became the capital city. Some say Kennard built such a stately and long-lasting home to show that he was confident the state of Nebraska and the capital city would be around a while. Both of these buildings are sites administered by the State Historical Society. Closed Mondays.

The Harris house at 1630 K Street is open for inspection. Other stately homes in the downtown area are private residences or commercial businesses.

The First Plymouth Congregational Church at 20th and D

streets is second only to the Capitol building as the state's most noted architectural site. It was designed by H. Van Buren Magonigle and features a 100-foot bell tower and a combination of architectural designs from around the world.

Lincoln was founded by pioneers who discovered salt flats just northwest of the present downtown. They thought these flats indicated large deposits of the precious commodity and began to promote their new town. By the time it was discovered that the salt flats were just the deposit of an occasionally flooded creek, the town had already started to grow.

Because of the way it started, Lincoln is one of the few cities in the state not located on a major river course. Tiny Salt Creek is the most significant waterway, and it barely floats a canoe.

The first non-Indian settlement was at the mouth of Oak Creek where it flows into Salt Creek. That was in 1857. The first Lincoln log cabin, built by Luke Lavender in 1863, was at the intersection of 14th and O streets. A marker commemorates this site on the southeast corner of the intersection.

The early days of Lincoln were filled, much as they are today, with the childish squibbles and squabbles of politics. In 1868, for example, an Iowa postmaster came to town to organize the Democratic Party. After announcing his intentions far and wide, only three men showed up to the organizational meeting. To boost the Presidential campaign of Horatio Seymour, they put up a tall pole on Market Square, 9th and O streets. The trees they lashed together reached 55 feet into the air.

Not to be outdone, the Republicans somehow got a 100-foot pine pole at a cost of $300 and had it erected near the Democrats' pole.

During the night someone cut the Republican pole down and whittled it into pieces. A warrant was sworn for a stage driver who was accused of the horrible crime. A gallows was built using, yes, the remains of the Republicans' pole. A judge found the defendant not guilty due to lack of evidence. The stage driver left town shortly thereafter never to be seen in these parts again.

It may not be a coincidence that, in addition to such political fights, as late as 1890 the city had to pass an ordinance to remove the hogpens betwen O and P on 14th.

In 1878 the town needed a post office and and courthouse so $200,000 was spent to build the best and newest of facilities. The block on which it was built, between 9th and 10th on O street, had been the farmers' market. It had an artesian well for years. The building was used for a number of years, then when a new post office was built in 1905, the building was used for city offices. The city remained in the building until the new city complex was built in the late 1960s.

Since that time the building and the block have been sources of much debate and struggle. The fight has surrounded the preservationists, who want to save the building, as well as the old jail to the west and the second post office just to the north, and the downtown businessmen, who claim the city would be better served by using the block to increase retail sales downtown. The issue, and the fate of the buildings, has been tossed from city councils, to courts, to the voters and back again. Currently, the city leases space to non-profit organizations, and the old building still stands.

The hand-hewn limestone of the building is from Nebraska and is typical of early Nebraska limestone construction. The original roof was slate, and the arched windows on either side of the front entrance were once doors. The building was heated by wood, and chimneys once dotted the roofline.

Inside, to the right of the stairs is the old elevator with its ornate ironwork cage. There are Romanesque designs on Corinthian columns in the lobby. The meeting room on the second floor was the original courtroom. The ceiling once extended two floors, but was lowered when the city took over the building. The wood finish throughout the building is oak and ash.

The building is also the location for the tourist information center.

Near the old post office in the area around 9th and N were several houses of ill-repute, saloons and two carefully camouflaged opium dens. The former City Mission, which still stands on the east side of 9th between N and O, was once one of the houses of pleasure known as Lyndia's. The madam of the house left it to the city in 1907 so that "it could still be used by the clients who had used it so well." Those who heard another kind of call claimed that if the men who frequented Lyndia's wouldn't come to them, they would go to the men. A mission was started in the building to serve the German-Russian immigrants in the area. In 1987 a new mission was built at First and Q streets, and the old building was auctioned off.

The building at 13th and Q streets, which now houses a variety of shops, was the home of Nebraska Buick, which distributed cars to 501 dealers in several states.

The Burlington Northern passenger station at 7th and P was built during the climax days of railroad travel, in 1925. At that same time, the state built a mile of track from the railroad yards to the new Capitol building to carry building supplies. The former industrial area surrounding the train station was rescued from oblivion by artists who rented the old buildings to use as studio space in the 1970s. Since then shops, cafes and bars have flocked to the area known as Haymarket. Anne Burkholder, perhaps one of the finest of Nebraska's many artists, has a gallery among the shops.

A 78-ton steam locomotive, known as Old 710, is displayed at the train station. It stood for 35 years at the city's Pioneers Park before it was restored and moved here. The 1901 Burlington and Missouri River Railroad locomotive was used to pull passenger and freight trains for 52 years before it became a display at the park. To restore the engine it had to be transported to Mount Pleasant, Iowa, via semi-trailer truck. Several delays were caused because of legal issues involved in transporting such a massive object.

The locomotive is near the Water Tank Park on the north side of the old railroad station at 7th and P streets. On the north wall of that building is an unusual sculpture. Jay Tschetter of Yankee Hill Brick created "Iron Horse Legacy" onto the brick facade of the building. It is a quite stunning work, complete with bison skull and a train that jumps right out of the wall.

The old Rock Island station near 20th and O was saved from the wrecker a number of times and is a fine example of the old-style stations.

The National Bank of Commerce building at 13th and O streets was designed by I. M. Pei.

Pershing Municipal Auditorium at 15th and M features a mosaic made from 763,000 tiles, the largest such mosaic in the United States. McKinley High School, the city's first, was built in 1873 where Pershing stands.

Lincoln's first skyscraper, the Burr Block, was built in 1888. It still stands on the northeast corner of 12 and O streets.

263

The Miller and Paine building, in the southwest corner of 13th and O, housed a department store for decades until the blight of shopping malls killed it in 1988. Miller's took an active interest in the arts, combining retail marketing with support of the literary and visual arts. Their bookstore constantly featured autograph parties by Nebraska writers such as Mari Sandoz, Wright Morris and John Neihardt. Likewise, the store purchased paintings by Nebraska artist Terence Duren and others and placed them throughout the store. (For more information on Duren see entry for State Highway 92.) The legacy of Miller's, and another defunct downtown competitor, Gold's, is one of cultural as well as economic enrichment.

The State Historical Society operates a fine new museum at Centennial Mall at 15th and P streets. This is the museum to see for a comprehensive overview of the state's history. Beautiful displays and engaging exhibits are open year-round. The museum shop offers the finest Nebraska products, including Indian beadwork, folk art and books. The state archives are housed in the Historical Society Building at 15th and R streets.

Lincoln has a Children's Museum at 13th and O streets. The museum allows children to have hands-on experience with science, history and culture. It is closed Wednesdays.

The Plains Indian Cultural Center at 1100 Military Road presents a view of the significant contribution the native peoples of the area have made to the culture. Displays, special events and crafts exhibits, as well as a gift shop, are at the Center. It is open weekdays.

Lincoln is home to the University of Nebraska, and the location of the main campus just north of downtown keeps the city's downtown area alive and well.

The University was created by a bill passed in 1869 on the same day that the State Asylum was formed. Locals claimed that was a good thing, since the Asylum would provide teachers for the University, and the University would be needed to provide inmates for the Asylum. Others said that the University was needed to instruct those who thought the state needed an Asylum, and the Asylum was needed for those who believed Nebraska needed a University.

The Asylum became the State Hospital, on west Van Dorn, and the University had its first day of classes with 90 students and five faculty. Today, the state's University serves five hundred times that number of students. The original $100,000 budget for the school would not support the recruitment of a single quarterback for Big Red in this day and age.

The football team was called the Rattlesnake Boys, the Antelopes and, best yet, the Bugeaters before a sports editor christened the team the Cornhuskers in 1900.

Memorial Stadium, at 10th and U streets, was finished in 1928, just a couple of years after the Nebraska team defeated Notre Dame, one of the best-remembered games from the old days.

Nebraska's football team was next to the bottom for years before the Bob Devaney/Tom Osborne era, but there was another time of high national ranking. From 1929 until 1936 a man by the name of Dana Bible led the Cornhuskers to six Big Six championships in eight seasons. The Huskers even went to the Rose Bowl in 1943, where they were defeated by Stanford 21-13.

The Bob Devaney Sports Complex near the Fairgrounds on north 17th is a 5-acre indoor sports arena that seats 15,000. A special bill had to be passed in the Unicameral to bypass a state law that said no building could be named after a living person. For the uninformed, Bob Devaney led the University football team to national importance in the late 1960s and '70s.

The State Museum, Morrill Hall, at 14th and Vine Streets on the University campus, is perhaps the finest museum in the state. It includes Elephant Hall, where the remains of the giants that once roamed the state have been reconstructed. A large collection of dinosaurs and other prehistoric creatures are here, as is a very good children's encounter center, where kids of all ages can interact with artifacts from the natural world. The museum also contains the Ralph Mueller Planetarium, which gives sky shows throughout the day. The space capsule Apollo 9 spent more than two decades outside in front of the museum before a Kansas agency offered to give the museum other space objects in exchange for it. The University refused, although it could not afford the estimated half million dollars it would take to restore the item. In spite of this example, the museum continues to improve and to provide a special place of wonder for old and young alike. The museum includes a series of chronologically sequenced galleries to showcase life on earth, while concentrating on past environments found in Nebraska.

Morrill Hall, while named after the wealthy regent and vast landowner Charles Morrill, was started by Dr. Erwin Barbour in 1891.

Sheldon Art Gallery on the campus near 12th and R features

many collections in a stunning white building.

The Temple Building at 12th and R streets houses the University's fine drama department. The building was built in 1906 with funds donated by John D. Rockfeller. There was quite an uproar that his money was "tainted money," and to settle the dispute the regents accepted the money but built the building "off campus."

In the 1890s, the University had a kind of heyday with several soon-to-be notables attending or working on campus. Roscoe Pound, who would become Dean of the Harvard Law School and well-known as a football player, was a student. Literary giant Willa Cather and writer Dorothy Canfield, who would later come to fame in New England, were friends and students. Pound's sister Louise was already a world-class athlete and would win tennis championships in both the men's and women's divisions.

Architectural Hall on the University campus near 10th and R streets is the oldest and one of the most unique buildings on campus. It was the fifth building built for the campus and was constructed in 1895. A vocal fight by architecture students in the early 1970s ensured its survival and placement on the National Register of Historic Places.

The University of Nebraska Press has placed over 2,000 books in print since its beginnings in 1941. This has included its prestigious paperback line, Bison Books, noted worldwide for quality books on the American West.

The Agricultural School of the University is located several blocks east of the downtown campus at 37th and Holdrege. In 1914, a state referendum was held to decide whether the downtown campus should be moved to the Ag Campus site. The act lost in the statewide election.

The University still attracts many fine writers and artists, and the town of Lincoln is home to many poets, writers and artists. Among the best is artist Shelley Thorton, whose illustrations have graced dozens of the best magazines in America. Although she is best known for her work as an illustrator for *Scholastic Magazine,* Thorton's art has appeared in many books as well.

Wesleyan University was built as a Methodist College in 1888 in what was then fields 3 miles out of town.

The campus, at 50th and Huntington, is the site of one of the most famous ghost stories in America. In 1963, a secretary for Dean Sam Dahl walked into an office in the C.C. White Building. Suddenly all sounds ceased. There was a musty smell in the air. She walked into an adjoining room. A woman with a long, black dress stood at a cabinet. She turned and smiled at the secretary. Outside the window, where there should have been dorms and busy streets, was nothing but open prairie. The secretary had walked back in time. She ran from the room.

The secretary was interviewed by several people about her experience and soon left the city and never returned to the building again.

The Nebraska United Methodists operate a historical center at Wesleyan at 50th and St. Paul streets as a depository for documents and articles from the church's history in the state.

Union College, at 48th and Stockwell, is operated by the Seventh Day Adventists. It was started in 1891.

The now defunct Normal University and its community was at about 56th and South. The town of Normal was there, and that is where William Jennings Bryan lived. The nursing home Madonna at 56th and South streets was an asylum before it was a nursing home.

William Jennings Bryan came to Lincoln in 1887. He joined the Round Table Discussion Club, where political debates between men of honor were held as entertainment and education. Bryan and two partners started a law firm. In 1890, 20,000 Populists attended a picnic in Cushman Park, west of town. Their growing numbers sent Bryan to Congress in 1890.

Eventually Bryan became the only man from a major political party in United States history to lose the race for President three times. He ran twice against McKinley (1896 and 1900) and once against Taft (1908).

Just in case you think this might have been just coincidence, Bryan's brother and advisor, Charles Bryan, was the Vice Presidential candidate on the Democratic ticket in 1924. He too, lost. (But believe it or not, another Lincolnite, Charles Dawes, was the vice president for the winning ticket with Calvin Coolidge in the same year.)

Brother Charles Bryan did have some fine ideas. He persuaded the city of Lincoln to own and operate a gasoline station. Private gas stations took the city to court, but the Supreme Court said it was all right for a city to operate such a business. Bryan wanted the city to have a city-operated, lower-priced grocery store, but alas, that was never to be.

William Jennings Bryan spoke to an overflow crowd in 1922 at the First Baptist Church at 14th and K, where the silver-tongued orator told the crowd that the theory of evolution was the greatest menace of the age. Three years later in Tennessee, he defended his ideas in a courtroom against Clarence Darrow over whether anything but a biblical view of creation should be taught in schools. Just a few days after the final verdict in the Scopes' trial, he died.

Bryan Memorial Hospital, which now nearly surrounds the Bryan home, was started in 1922 after the Bryans gave their home, "Fairview," and ten acres to the Methodist Church.

Bryan's home, Fairview, is located at 4900 Sumner and is open weekend afternoons and by appointment. The home, which served as a stopover for a wide assortment of notable friends of Bryan's including President Woodrow Wilson, was built in 1901 using a combination of Neo-Classical Revival and Victorian architecture. In 1992, a major restoration of Fairview was done. The house serves as a museum and as the home of the Bryan Institute, which serves as a resource for hospital staff members and others throughout Nebraska by offering educational programs and seminars on health-care issues.

U.S. Senator and former Governor Robert Kerrey announced his bid to win the Democratic nomination for president on the steps of the state Capitol building on September 30, 1991, by saying he would fight for what America can be. Over 6,000 people cheered this first Nebraskan since Bryan to become a major presidential candidate. Despite high hopes and a bipartisan regard, Kerrey withdrew his candidacy within a few months after it became clear he would have neither the funding nor the votes to win a nomination.

The suburb of Bethany was formed as a result of the Cotner College, a Christian Church college that was there until the 1930s.

Havlock, another suburb, was a town that supported the Burlington shops that are located there. This is where boxcars and other trains are built or fixed. Plant tours are available by making special arrangements with the management.

General John J. Pershing lived in Lincoln during the 1890s and taught ROTC at the University. He bought a home at 1748 B street in 1919 after all but one of his children were burned to death in a San Francisco fire. Pershing was America's first six star general. After he was given the honor it was decided that he shouldn't be the only one, so they gave George Washington (who'd been dead for some time) the honor as well.

Richard "Dick" Cheney, U.S. Secretary of Defense under President Bush; Clifford Hardin, Secretary of Agriculture under President Nixon; Sam Yorty, former mayor of Los Angeles; and Theodore Sorensen, adviser to President Kennedy, were Lincolnites.

Charles "Lucky Lindy" Lindbergh learned to fly in Lincoln. The young man from Minnesota, who would be the first man to cross the Atlantic solo in an airplane, came to Lincoln on April 1, 1922, and enrolled in a flying school at 24th and O streets. He first took to the air at a field seven miles south of the Penitentiary.

Lincoln is justified in being proud of its parks.

In 1928, a New York stockbroker asked if there could be land purchased and developed into a park as a memorial to his parents. Five hundred acres was purchased west of the city, and later 100 more were added. When the park was dedicated in 1930 the stock broker felt it should honor all pioneers and not just his parents and so the name Pioneers Park came to be.

The park was laid out to feature the skyline of the city in the distance to the east, and the open farmlands to the west. Trees were planted to form openings to feature the best view. An outdoor amphitheater was added, along with grounds for a small herd of buffalo, a golf course, a nature center and wildlife sanctuary and other features. It soon became the most popular park in the city, and it remains so today.

In the early 1990s, the city started a reforestation program because of the large number of original trees that had died. The new program was designed so that trees would be planted over a 20-year period to avoid the problem of all of the trees dying at once.

Family albums around the world have faded photographs of children standing next to the stout buffalo statue that graces the entranceway to the park.

When the U.S. Treasury Building in Washington, D.C., was being remodeled, four of the building's columns were presented to the city of Lincoln. These columns were where Abraham Lincoln stood to review the troops during the Civil War. The columns have since moved all around the city, from O Street to the grassy slope at Pioneers Park.

The park can be reached by driving west on either Van Dorn or South Street. It is a mile west of the State Hospital. Just ask anyone

269

for directions.

On the way to Pioneers Park, at 1st and Van Dorn, a small, run-down-looking food place called Runza Restaurant offers a unique eating opportunity. In 1950, a few family members started to sell their mother's recipe for a German-Russian sandwich made from ground beef, cabbage, spices and onions and baked inside bread. Although they sold the trademark to a franchise organization, the family retained this, the original, non-franchised location. To put it another way, it is like you came across the McDonalds' brothers original drive-in.

Yankee Hill Brick, just south of Pioneers Park, was founded in 1870 and provided much of the brick for the brick streets that once dominated the city. A few brick streets still remain scattered throughout the city.

The beautiful Sunken Gardens at 27th and D were converted from a city dump in the 1920s. The design of this and other Lincoln parks was done by a man named Chet Ager. Ager is commemorated today by the Chet Ager Nature Center at Pioneers Park.

Antelope Park, which is near the Sunken Gardens, houses the Folsom Children's Zoo. The city has no other zoos, so this is a fine attraction for youngsters of all ages. The Herb Garden is a special treat for plant-lovers and the core of the town's extensive bike path routes pass by the zoo.

One of the city's most extensive parks is Holmes Lake, in the southeastern corner of the city. It includes a marina, an observatory and golf course.

The city also has a wilderness park, which stretches from 1st and Van Dorn south to Saltillo Road.

Near Wilderness Park, the State Prison, at the junction of US Highway 77 and State Highway 2, has been at that site since 1870, and a few of the buildings date to that time.

On February 11, 1912, the warden of the Penitentiary was stabbed to death after Sunday chapel. A month later, his successor and two other men were killed in a gun battle with some convicts. The convicts escaped, and for the next four days they were chased around the county while a vicious blizzard pounded the prairies. When they were at last cornered near Gretna, one convict was killed, another shot himself and the third was returned to the Pen to face a life sentence.

In 1955, prison rioters burned several buildings, and the city's citizens spent hours indoors waiting to hear if the streets would be filled with escaping prisoners.

Charles Starkweather was a 19-year-old, red-headed punk from Lincoln, his 14-year-old girlfriend, Caril Ann Fugate, a bored young girl. Together they roamed the city and Lancaster County for five days killing nearly anyone they met. They killed a young man who tried to help them when their car wouldn't start. They killed a housewife and her dog. By the time they were captured they had killed 11 people and had made national news as the first mass murderers of the post WWII era. Several of the murders were in Lincoln, and for those five days in 1958 Lincolnites seldom left their homes, and many refused to answer a knock on their doors.

Starkweather was tried and convicted and sent to the electric chair at the State Penitentiary. Fugate served 18 years in prison. In 1990, police said that Fugate mailed copies of her court testimony to various people in the city to convince them of her innocence in the spree. She claimed that Starkweather forced her to accompany him. Since then novels and movies and songs have retold the horrifying tale of those few days. There is something about the story of a lonely demented kid and the open stretches of prairie that must ring a kind of universal dark truth.

Years later, rock 'n' roll giant Bruce Springsteen would record a dark, somber album, call it "Nebraska" and have Starkweather as the central character of its lead song.

During the early 1970s, two Lincolnites named Zager and Evans had a number one hit worldwide with a song about what the future might hold. "In the Year 2525" was the group's only hit, but it was a gigantic one, and became one of the all-time largest-selling 45 records.

In the early 1990s, another Lincolnite, Matthew Sweet, earned a justly deserved place on the pop charts for his musical talents.

Lincoln has always prided itself on its fine, extensive and unique music scene. In addition to a symphony orchestra and the new performing arts theater, Lincoln has always been the home of num-

271

bers of fine musicians. Lawrence Welk, who was from North Dakota, got his start playing with his band in Lincoln. Now bluegrass instrumentalists and rock 'n' rollers have continued to refine Lincoln's exciting music scene. Lincoln's sometimes seedy Zoo Bar has a national reputation as one of the hottest places to see new music in the country.

You owe your hours of brain-numbing music, those happy grocery store tunes of Muzak, to a man from Lincoln. Royal Brewster started the elevator music business in 1930.

The *Back to the Bible* radio program originates in Lincoln. It was started in 1939 and at its peak was heard in dozens of countries.

Radio station KFAB, which started in Lincoln, was one of the first radio stations in the world to broadcast news over the air. This fact survives by being mentioned in dozens of broadcast journalism textbooks, and appearing on hundreds of final exams all across the country.

Communication issues of another sort hit the big-time on Easter Sunday 1992 as the local cable TV access chanel, which was controlled by city government, aired a show called (WARNING: The following sentence contains material some readers may find objectionable...parental consent advised) "The Piss Show," which showed a stream of water hitting a toilet bowl. Although the station managers thought the show should be pulled, the town objected, saying only they had the right to censor programming. The show was aired before an advisory board was formed to deal with such problems in the future.

Some of that hot air and water might have helped the largest tire fire in the state's history, which burned for three days starting October 25, 1990, in West Lincoln. Over 35,000 tires burned at the T.O. Haas Tire Company tire yard. For days, Lincolnites were treated to a thick plume of toxic smoke. The plume could be seen as far away as Omaha and Fremont. Over a million gallons of water was poured on the blaze at first, and then firefighters let the tires burn in hopes that the poisoned air would rise higher above the city and be blown away. Although they set up a dike to hold back the runoff water, the dike broke and the water emptied into neighboring Salt Creek. The fire at 640 W. P Street was eventually killed by dumping dozens of truckloads of dirt on the burning pile.

272

A man named Clinton Cushman tinkered around with a four-cycle water-cooled engine and soon Cushman motors flourished in Lincoln. They built "putt-putt" scooters, golf carts, parking meter police vehicles and lawnmowers. In 1957, they were purchased by Outboard Marine of Illinois.

Smith-Dorsey Pharmaceuticals was founded in Lincoln. Their first lab was at 15th & O. Millions of cold sufferers have learned the wonders of products that were invented by hard-working and fine people right here. Now a part of Sandoz Pharmaceuticals, the plant is located east of town on US Highway 6.

Both United Rent-Alls and the salvation of countless struggling English students, *Cliff Notes,* (which summarize the plot and themes of major books not read for English classes) were started here.

Sherman Field, two blocks west of 1st and South streets, was home to many big leaguers, including Ed Cicotte, a pitcher who was ruined with the Chicago Black Sox scandal.

Lincoln is home base for a number of insurance companies and at one time was known as the "Hartford of the West" because of this distinction.

The Nebraska State Fair, always held the first week in September, is in Lincoln. The Fairgrounds are located at 17th and Holdrege.

Lincoln is where you can find the American Historical Society of Germans from Russia, which includes a small museum at 631 D Street.

Lincoln is the home of the National Museum of Roller Skating. Now, don't laugh, for a large number of people went to a lot of trouble to see that the museum, and the Roller Skating Hall of Fame, would be located in Lincoln. In 1992, Roller Skating became an Olympic sport, so the Hall of Fame may well grow. The museum is the definitive source for the history of roller skating. It includes such items as an original Plimpton Skate, the first skate that enabled the user to steer by using a rocking set of front wheels — the modern skate. In case there was any doubt, the museum houses the largest collection of roller skates in the world. It is located at 7700 A Street and is open during the week.

The Nebraska Statewide Arboretum is located on the University of Nebraska East Campus near 40th and Holdrege.

In late 1957, jets from the Nebraska National Guard scrambled over the city to intercept a UFO that was sighted by the crew of a B-47.

Several of the pilots saw the object and described it as being as large as a hangar. It was a large, silvery globe.

On October 1, 1952, two men saw two white-silvery objects fly over downtown Lincoln. They said the objects were 100 feet wide.

Others all around the city saw something that same day. From Waverly on the east to Pioneers Park on the west reports came of a white object with orange lights.

A Lincoln boy, Eric Salem, recently made the magazine we all really dream of making: *People* magazine. When the 15-year-old ran for and won a seat on the Noxious Weed Control Authority, he became, according to the magazine, "possibly the youngest person ever elected to public office in the U.S."

Salem was also on Johnny Carson's Tonight Show and ran a serious campaign.

It is not true, as the locals here might suggest, that no one who remains in Lincoln will become famous. What more fame than *People* magazine is there?

In 1939, five college students from Middlebury College in Vermont were in Lincoln for a covention of their fraternity. The legend has it that two of them found a tin pie plate in a cornfield and began tossing it around. Soon the others joined in. They took their new game back to the college, where it spread like wildfire.

The pie tin was from a popular brand of the day, "Frisbie's." When Wham-O Manufacturing Co. got the trademark for the now famous toy, they changed the spelling to Frisbee.

Although there are sculptures and monuments in the East that claim the game was invented at Middlebury, its true origins are here.

Lincoln was the birthplace or home of many gifted folks.

Lincoln native Tom McCown, a gentleman in the finest sense, spends his time crafting the best of Hollywood movie scripts. Artist Shelley Thorton, who was mentioned above. Guitarist Bill Dye is a legend among studio musicians. He was born in Lincoln.

A recruiter for the Ku Klux Klan spent a good part of the 1970s and '80s writing hate letters from his Lincoln home until a Jewish couple, who were the brunt of some of those letters, turned the heart of the man. Through his friendship with the couple he learned that love was stronger and more important than hate and gave up his past. The remarkable story of this friendship made national news and became the subject of numerous articles.

The Center for Great Plains Study, at the University of Nebraska, is a clearinghouse for scholarship, teaching and information about the plains. It was founded in 1976 and is the most comprehensive and best-financed of any such center. Among its most noteworthy contributions to the culture of the plains is the sponsorship of an 11-volume edition of Lewis and Clark's journals of 1803-1806. In addition, the Center has a permanent art collection that includes 75 bronzes by Frederic Remington.

Lincoln was the boyhood home of writer Loren Eiseley. Eiseley was an anthropologist and a paleontologist, but gained his fame by writing insightful and thoughtful essays about the nature of humankind. His brooding, beautifully crafted works have been read for 50 years all over the world, and Eiseley has become the subject of scholarly biography and study.

Eiseley often wrote about his boyhood in Lincoln, and from those memories he expanded to thoughts about the world. His books are still widely available in most bookstores and libraries. He speaks most eloquently about Lincoln in the opening pages of *The Night Journey*, and throughout his autobiography, *All the Strange Hours— Excavations of a Life*.

Lincoln has a number of fine old mansions offering views of a wide range of architectural styles. Here are a few of them:

—The Lewis-Syford house, 700 N. 16th. One of the few remaining houses built in the French Second Empire style. Built in 1878.

—The Clark House, or F Street Castle, 1937 F. One of the better examples of Queen Ann style, this castle has a mishmash of

275

window shapes and sizes, chimneys and turrets.

    —Phillip's, or D Street Castle, 1845 D. This Romanesque castle contains 40 rooms and 16 fireplaces and cost $60,000 when it was built in 1889.

    —Tyler House, 808 D. This Queen Ann-style house was built as a kind of advertisement by the owner of a stone company in 1891.

    —Ziemer House, 2030 Euclid. This Romanesque and Shingle-style house was built in 1909 from stones transported from Colorado and cut on the site. The shingles, which are made from cedar, were applied wet and then bent to fit the contours of the roof. Rainwater is carried by copper gutters to an underground cistern. The porch was designed to be enclosed in the winter and has a hidden water closet.

Eight miles (2 miles.)

    At the intersection of NW 48th street turn south for one half mile, then go west one mile on W. Fletcher Ave. to Nine Mile Prairie, an area of preserved native grassland. This rare eastern Nebraska patch of native prairie grasses is owned by the University of Nebraska Foundation. It is open to the public but, aside from the parking area, has no roads.

Two miles (3 miles.)

    Turn off to Malcolm.

    North of Malcolm four miles to Branched Oak Lake, the largest and one of the finer of the many Salt Valley Lakes. South here to Pawnee Lake, another public access lake in the system.

Three miles (3 miles.)

    South to Twin Lakes State Wildlife Area, 270 acres of water on two lakes, northwest of Pleasant Dale.

Three miles (6 miles.)

    North 3 miles to Garland. The Garland Bank, built in 1904, still stands, although it ceased operations during the bank failures of the 1930s. The Folly Movie Theater, which was later used as a community hall, now houses grain at the Seward County Co-op.

Six miles (7 miles.)

    Seward.

    There is something about this town that remains unchanged and unspoiled from an earlier time. Perhaps it's County Courthouse

Square, with its large ornate courthouse built in 1905; or the shops clustered around the square and bearing names like the Corner Cafe, Jones' Bank and Books and Brushes. Perhaps it is the Blue River, which wraps lazily around three sides of the town. If this were Minnesota, there would have been an award-winning radio show based on a place like Seward.

Goehner's Grocery, on Seward St., just west of the courthouse, is one of the oldest surviving business buildings in the town. It is next door to the Seward Creamery, which dates from an earlier time as well.

At the corner of 8th and South, a local bandit named Orlando Cassler was hanged in the 1880s. According to local stories, this spot is haunted by the man's ghost, which has most often been seen just at sunset on cool evenings.

Those with metal detectors might prowl around the east block of 7th St. south of South St., since this was the city dump until 1914.

The Cottage Hotel at Highway 15 and Ash, just across the bridge, still stands from an earlier booming time.

A block and a half east on Ash to one of the town's early Burlington Depots.

Seward grew up around the Homesteading Act and the expansion of the railroads. The town boasted quite a boom in business and included bottling plants, mills, egg companies, a pipe organ company and a corn cob pipe factory in its day.

At the north end of 11th St., just at the railroad tracks, are the remnants of the old beer vaults, from when a fine local beer was produced in Seward.

The Armory, at 10th and Jackson, is built on the site of the Chautauqua ground.

One of Seward's largest employers, Hughes Brothers, who make electrical transmission poles and materials, got its start in 1921 after a freak storm destroyed power lines in the area and the electrical company needed replacements.

Columbia Avenue at College Avenue. Concordia Teachers' College dates to 1894 when the Lutheran Teachers' Seminary was begun in a single building in Seward with 12 male students. It is a four-year co-educational college affiliated with the Lutheran Church. The school includes The Center for Indian Ministries and Studies, which attracts many Indian students from all across the nation to gain the education needed to follow the Lutheran ministries.

East of the college at Locust Ave and Moffit is what some believe to be an Indian burial ground. Relics have been found in this area for years.

At the corner of Hillcrest Drive and 10th St. is the beautiful old Hughes home, which many claim to be the most beautiful house in this town of many fine old houses.

Follow 3rd St. north to Hillcrest to Seward's most unusual business, museum, farm supply, former mill and home of its most notable citizen. The House of Davisson is the location of numerous enterprises of one Harold Davisson, who, among other accomplishments, has created what he claims is the world's largest time capsule (it was built in 1975, to be opened in 2025) containing an entire car, a motorcycle and thousands of other items; the first modern pyramid in the United States (to cover the time capsule); who has written a half dozen books on local history, cooking, the building of the world's largest time capsule, pyramid, etc., and a book of unabashed self-promotion and congratulations; who promoted "the world's longest trip for a high school basketball game" (to Seward, Alaska, in 1953 — no one seems to remember who won); who built skating rinks, apartment complexes and sculpture for satire, "Utter Futility," to jab at the state's sculpture project along Interstate 80; who saved Seward's old hospital (at 6th and Bradford Streets); and who, it seems, is about as unusual a character as you'll meet in the entire state.

Seven miles (7 miles.)
Tamora, so named because the earliest settlers could not decide on a name, and always talked about coming up with one "tamora'." Now this tiny town is the location of the large, main office of the Tamora-Stapleton Farmers' Co-op. These co-ops are a way for farmers to share the costs of larger, expensive equipment, and to have a business that they own and run. The idea started in the 1920s,

278

although cooperative ventures such as this date back to the earliest pioneer days on the Great Plains.

Seven miles (6 miles.)
Utica.

Utica's Opera House (1883), City Hall (1912) auditorium (1936, WPA) and many older homes survive from its boomtown days.

Six miles (7 miles.)
One mile west and a half mile north of Waco is the Waco Basin State Wildlife Area. The 15-acre lake has been stocked with pike since 1988.

Seven miles (8 miles.)
York. Junction of US Highway 81. Please see that entry for information about sites in this area.

Eight miles (7 miles.)
Bradshaw.

The area around here was seriously affected by the great grasshopper plague of 1874, as entire farms were wiped out by the infestation. Grasshoppers literally swarmed in great dark clouds that blocked out the sun. They would descend on a field, their humming filling the air, devour every green plant to the ground and then move on. It was impossible to walk outside without crunching 10 or 20 bugs with each and every step.

Seven miles (4 1/2 miles.)
Hampton. This town was originally named Plano, but there was another Plano on the Burlington Railroad line, so it was changed to Murray. There was another town on the Burlington line named Murray so it was changed to...well, eventually they decided on Hampton.

One mile south and one and a half miles east on county roads to the site of Millspaugh Ranch. The ranch was established in 1861 to service the pioneers, freighters and others moving west on the Oregon Trail. Daniel Millspaugh was the first white to settle in Hamilton County and his grandchild the first white child born here (1863).

Four and a half miles (1 1/2 miles.)
One mile north to Pioneer Trails Lake.

One and a half miles (1 mile.)
Aurora.
Junction of State Highway 14. Please see that entry for more information about sites along that route.

Aurora was founded in 1871 when a bunch of men moved from Iowa (a good idea) and founded the town to make money. They didn't make it, but others did. One of the original men named the town in honor of his wife, who had moved from Aurora, Illinois (a good idea, too). The vote to name the town Aurora was 2 to 0, although only one man voted in the election. The politics of the county have improved somewhat since then.

The Hamilton County Fair is the oldest continuous annual county fair in the state. It was started in the fall of 1872 in the then county seat of Orrville, some distance from here. The first fair was centered on the original courthouse, and that area was also used as the race track. Long tables were spread for the communal picnic. It was held at the start of the great grasshopper plague, which lasted several years, but still people came to celebrate from all over the area.

An early resident was William Townsley. Townsley 'twas trying the trade of the tiny town's taxidermist. His very peculiar records of early Hamilton County, one might say his "stuff," can be seen at the Plainsman Museum described below.

The Nebraska Youth Leadership Development Center, a 27-acre facility for youth and adult groups, is located on the east edge of the city.

Camp Hamilton, a camp for Company H during training for World War I, was located in Streeter Park on the eastern edge of the city

Downtown Aurora still has the feel of an older Nebraska town, not yet inundated with the trappings of a modern, fast-food world. Many of the storefronts are buildings that have stood serving the community for decades.

The General Delevan Bates home at 9th and J Streets was the home of the Civil War veteran and hero. Bates was the commander of the 4th Division of the Union Army's "Immortal Three Hundred" at the battle of Waterloo. Bates, then a colonel, was shot in the head at the battle, but escaped death. He also fought at Gettysburg. He became a prominent citizen of Aurora. His home has been restored and is in private ownership.

The Hamilton County Courthouse, located in the center of town, is one of the most beautiful and unique courthouses in the entire state, and, some would say, the nation. The building was constructed in 1895, and still contains the original tile floors and other architectural wonders. Hard to believe that this stately building, with corner spires and built with red limestone, was built for under $60,000 — less than the cost of two legislators' salaries. The grounds are pristine and maintained in a similar fashion to the way they first were groomed. Take time to walk around inside.

The Plainsman Museum, at 210 16th Street, is one of the more interesting and exciting museums in the area. The Plainsman contains the consolidated collections of several museums, and has under its roof several complete historic buildings, early farm equipment and a vast doll collection. The new museum, dedicated during the nation's bicentennial, contains murals, exhibits and artifacts tracing the area's history from the Indians, the early Spanish explorers, and through the modern day. In addition, there is a courteous staff to assist the visitor. Among special treats in the Plainsman Museum is an exhibit on Dr. Harold Edgerton, the inventor of the strobe light, inductee into the National Inventors' Hall of Fame and member of the National Academy of Arts and Sciences. In addition to Dr. Edgerton's many other accomplishments, he helped to develop the underwater photography techniques used by oceanographer Jacques Cousteau.

One mile (14 miles.)
Turn north and go for one mile. Turn west and go for another one and a half miles to the Spafford grave, located in a grove of trees. The inscription once read:
"Rev. S.W. Spafford Died Nov. 9, 1876 Aged 47 years 8 months 11 days.
Farewell my wife my children all
From you a father, Christ doth call,
Mourn not for me, it is in vain,
To call me to your sight again.
—Lincoln Marble Works."

281

US Highway 34

It is not known if the Lincoln Marble Works wrote any other poetry as well.

Fourteen miles (5 miles.)
Just before the highway crosses the Platte River it crosses the route of the Nebraska City Cutoff of the Oregon Trail. This road went from Nebraska City west to the Oregon Trail 20 miles west of here.

Five miles (163 miles.)
Grand Island. Junction of US Highways 30, 34, 281 and State Highway 2.
For information about Grand Island, please see entry for US Highway 30.

US Highway 34 joins US 281 for 17 miles south, and then for another 145 west it joins US 6. For information about sites along 34 until west of McCook, please consult the entry for US Highway 281 and US Highway 6.

For information about State Highway 2, US Highway 30, US Highway 281 or Interstate 80, please see entries for those routes.

US Highway 34 joins US Highway 6 for the next 163 miles. For information about sites for this distance, please see the entry for US Highway 6

One hundred sixty-three miles (4 1/2 miles.)
Junction with US Highway 6. From here east to Hastings, US 34 and US 6 are joined. From Hastings to Grand Island, US 34 and US 281 are joined. For information about this route, please see entry for US Highway 6 and US Highway 281.

Four and a half miles (3 miles.)
Massacre Canyon. In 1873, the Sioux and the Pawnee, longtime rivals and enemies, had one of the worst and last of their many battles. The government had designated particular hunting grounds for each tribe, but the designation favored the Pawnee, who were more friendly toward the whites. In 1873, the Pawnee were coming up the Republican River on a massive buffalo hunt. Three hundred warriors and 400 women and children were moving into

Sioux territory. The warriors noticed spots on a far hillside up the Frenchman River and, at first thinking it was a large herd of buffalo, rode toward the hill.

As they approached, Sioux and Brule warriors, all wrapped in buffalo robes, threw off their disguises and attacked the Pawnee. The Pawnee were taken completely by surprise. The women and children hid in a ravine and the Pawnee warriors counterattacked. But then additional Sioux appeared and attacked the Pawnee from behind. The lone white witness, a man named Williamson who had helped to guide the Pawnee on the hunt, raised a white flag and rode toward the Sioux. His horse was shot out from under him.

The Pawnee women, in the ravine, began their death chants. The Pawnee fled back down various streambeds toward the Republican and it is here, in this narrow canyon, that the bloodiest of the fighting took place.

Soldiers from Fort McPherson arrived too late to save most of the Pawnee. The Pawnee returned to their government lands north along the Loup and never returned to their traditional lands along the Republican again.

In the cleanup, 65 bodies were buried in one grave alone. This battle ended hostilities and opened the land to cattlemen. The first ranches in Nebraska were in this area. They were started shortly after the graves had been dug.

One half mile east is a commemorative marker.

Near here in 1991 the remains of about 142 individuals were reburied after having spent a number of years in wooden boxes in the State Historical Society's offices in Lincoln. The remains were Itskaris, a part of the Central Plains Tradition group that lived in Nebraska from about A.D. 800 to A.D. 1400. These people were related to the Pawnee who once roamed this area. Representatives from the Pawnee Tribe of Oklahoma had fought for the remains for several years.

Three miles (3 miles.)
Trenton. Location of various reunions of survivors of the the battle at Massacre Canyon. In 1923, the 50th anniversary of the battle, many Sioux and Pawnee gathered here for a week of festivities.

Junction with State Highway 25. For more information on this area, please see entry for State Highway 25.

US Highway 34

Three miles (12 miles.)

In 1881, trouble was brewing between the cattlemen and the homesteaders. The cattlemen, encouraged by the release of a cowboy in Custer County who had killed a homesteader, began to pressure the homesteaders. For their part, the homesteaders, used to considering the cattle they found stranded from the cattle drives as their property, were unwilling to give up their habits. A couple of cowboys approached a homesteader near here and demanded the return of a cow. The homesteader refused, but added that he would give it up if the cowboys would go to the justice of the peace nearby and get an order from him. The cowboys said "there ain't no law in these parts" and said they would be back with a hanging rope. A mob was formed near the mouth of the Stinking Water to teach the homesteaders a lesson. Although the cowboys gave up the idea for a lynching, the hostilities between the two factions grew.

Turn off for Swanton Lake State Recreation Area on the Republican River.

Twelve miles (4 miles.)

Stratton.

This area once served as a rest stop for the Leavenworth and Pike's Peak Express, a stage line that carried folks to the Colorado gold rush. The wood along the river was thick and plenty here, which accounts for the stage stop.

One passenger on the stage line was Horace Greeley, who in spite of telling young men to go west, said of this place, "I would match this station and its surroundings against any other scene on our continent for desolation."

The town park at the west end of the village offers a nice modern rest stop for those who are not in too big of a hurry and want to sit a spell in Greeley's desolate spot.

Four miles (3 miles.)

Here, three miles east of Max was the town of Sandwich, which once was going to be the metropolis of Dundy County, but died when a local rancher would not sell land needed to expand the town. Most every building was moved to a new location, many to Max, and others to local ranches. The town lasted from 1881 until the last building was moved in 1955.

South of here in 1899, a 19-year-old transient, seeing himself as a latter-day Billy the Kid, killed a local rancher for $20, threw the body in the river and then drove a herd of cattle across everything in order to hide the evidence. The victim's false teeth and broken eye glasses were found, however, and the murderer arrested. He was convicted and sent to prison, where he died while attempting to make a break.

Three miles (3 miles.)

Max. The Max Public Park is only a faint reminder of its once grand canopy of trees, most of which have fallen in the years since it was first designated as a park in the 1920s.

When the dust storms rolled through here in the 1930s it was considered a good day if you could eat an entire meal before you were able to write your name in the dust that collected on your plate. Folks cleaned up their houses just enough to make them livable before the next storm came through a few days later.

In 1933, on May 26, a freak storm turned day into night. A thick tornado cloud, combined with a dust storm, passed over this area. However, most people had no phones or radios and were not aware what was causing so strange a phenomenon. It is generally believed that the good Lord hadn't heard from as many Dundy County residents before or since that strange day.

North of here are the deep canyon lands of Nebraska. Inquire locally as to the road conditions in the area.

Three miles (6 miles.)

At this spot, over one hundred years ago, something fell from the sky. On the afternoon of June 6, 1884, a cowboy by the name of John Ellis and his boys were working some cattle near here when a strange object came out of the sky and roared over their heads. It hit the ground and skimmed over the prairie for a mile before disappearing into a wash.

The cowboys rode to the wash. There they found metal machinery all over the ground. The metal was hot. The prairie grass was on fire.

A kind of vehicle was burning. It had a long, cylindrical shape. As the cowboys watched its bright light, their faces were scorched red.

The next day people came to the site and the area was combed. The vehicle was gone, but pieces of metal were found and collected. The story was carried in the weekly newspaper in Holdrege and in the Lincoln *Journal* on June 8.

There are, of course, many people who do not believe the story, and others who claim it is yet another UFO story neglected and laughed at by skeptics.

Six miles (11 miles.)
Benkelman.
Junction with State Highway 61. Please see that entry for sites along its route.

Benkelman was originally known as Collinsville and came into being as a railroad town and shipping point for the early cattle business.
Benkelman is the county seat, and at under 1,500 souls, the largest population center between here and McCook. However, Dundy County has seen better days and in 1925 reached its peak in population.
While Hiawatha, Ough and Allston were bickering and fighting over which town was to get the county seat, the citizens of Benkelman quietly built a county courthouse and the commissioners simply moved in. The current courthouse was built in 1918.

Benkelman is home to the active Dundy County Historical Society and the fine Dundy County Museum located in the old Moorehouse Hospital. It includes 13 rooms of exhibits and many area historical items from the pioneer and war years.

North of the business district, near the American Legion building, is a house that once was a fine Hotel known as Scotts. It was built in 1879. The Scotts was known for its lavish parties, which included dances often lasting a week.

The Ough Hotel was the first brick hotel, and the first building in Benkelman to have steam heat. It was built in 1908.

A terrible fire of undetermined origin burned half of Benkelman to the ground in 1911.

Benkelman was the birthplace of an actor by the name of Ward Bond who got to know John Wayne before The Duke made it big. When Wayne got to Hollywood, he remembered his friend Bond and got Bond parts in movies. Bond's most famous roles were in *Gone With the Wind,* and as the Wagon Master on the 1960 TV series

Wagon Train.

Just east of town is the Benkelman Fish Hatchery.

North of town a small lake provides a pleasing atmosphere for locals.

Just south of the town is the confluence of the north and south forks of the Republican River. This place, known for years simply as the Forks, has been an important gathering spot for centuries.

For a long while, the Forks was a logical meeting place for tribes of the northern lands to meet and trade with tribes from the south.

In June of 1867, George Armstrong Custer camped at the Forks when he was attacked by Pawnee Killer's band of Sioux. Later, 40 of Custer's troops under the command of a captain named Hamilton pursued the war party northwest for seven miles when they were led into an ambush. Most of the men escaped. Later still, Lt. Kidder was overwhelmed by Pawnee Killer's band near Beaver Creek, ten miles west of here and was killed. The trail through here, which roughly followed the same route as State 61 now follows, was for years known as Custer's Trail, or Buffalo Hunters' Trail.

The Leavenworth and Pike's Peak Stage route came through the Forks and then traveled on the south fork of the Republican to Denver.

One of the last Indian raids in this part of the country took place just south of here when the Cheyenne Dull Knife and his followers raided several ranches. Dull Knife was fleeing the Army that was ordered to send him and his band to Oklahoma. Dull Knife camped at the Forks as well.

Eleven miles (7 miles.)
Parks. Parks has been a settlement for a long while, starting off in the 1880s as a community and store for local ranchers. It was named after a local cowboy. It grew until the late 1920s when drought, grasshoppers, bad winters and a bad economy stunted and reversed its growth.

North of here on Rock Creek, Dundy County's first sheep ranch was started in the summer of 1880. When nearly all of the sheep died in the cold of the first winter, the owner left the county on foot,

US Highway 34

never to return again.

Parks, like so many other towns along the Republican, suffered greatly in the flood of 1935 when a wall of water rushed down the Republican Valley. Children were torn from their parents' arms, houses were swept away and entire towns were destroyed. In Parks, the rush of the water could be heard miles away. Some hog barns that were caught up by the flood were found in Cambridge, 70 miles downriver.

Near here is "Tater Hill" a tall hill where cowboys would go to spot stray cattle during the cattle drive days. They roasted potatoes on the hill, hence the name.

Ask locally for directions to the site of the Pike's Peak Stage Coach route and the stations along its way.

Twelve miles north and three miles west of Parks was the town of Lux, not much more than a post office and local stopping place. The post office closed in 1920. In 1934, a couple of local young men stole a car in Colorado and had hidden it in a valley just west of the post office. A neighbor called the sheriff, Chester Crosby, when he noticed that everyone on the ranch was armed. Sheriff Crosby got together a posse, drove out to the ranch and a gun battle erupted. The sheriff was shot in the arm, and in return shot and killed one of the men. The others surrendered and a slice of the Bonnie and Clyde days ended.

Five miles north of the Lux site is the site of the town of Rollwitz, which was named after a pioneer from Germany. This small town was built around a church and a school. It was born of the Kinkaid era of homesteaders around 1904. In 1943, a hailstorm and tornado destroyed a 25-mile area. The storm added to the troubled times of the 1930s and just about ended the community. An unmarked cemetery and old buildings, now moved and used as tool sheds, houses and barns on neighboring ranches, are the chief remnants of the town.

Many ranches in this area still have the original sod buildings, and many of them are used as sheds yet today.

Ten miles northwest of Parks is a state fish hatchery, which provides trout for many Nebraska streams. Located here is the Rock

288

Creek State Recreation Area, which is a fine and comfortable place to give one the feel of this beautiful and seldom-visited part of the state.

Several miles south of Parks *are the remains of a dugout hole in a cliff known as Horse Thief Cave, because the gentlemen who lived there in 1890 were suspected of being horse and cattle thieves. Finally, when it got too hot for them, these gentlemen moved on to the Dakotas.*

Seven miles (4 miles.)

The Texas Cattle Trail, a meandering route at best, crossed near here. Some cowboys followed the Beaver River up from the south until it joined with the Republican for one route north.

The first large cattle ranches in Dundy County started in the early 1870s with cattle brought up from Texas on this trail.

Many early day cattlemen, fearing the end of their way of life when the rash of homesteaders began in the 1880s, and later with the Kinkaiders in the early 1910s, had their cowboys stake out homesteads so that their ranch lands would remain open and fenceless. Ranches up to 20,000 acres were secured by these means.

In 1902, while helping to build the road that would one day become US 34, Frank Tecker's plow uncovered two caskets on the downslope of Trail Canyon. One was an adult and the other was a child with "the most beautiful red hair covering his skull. There was a silk string tie with a metal cross, and two China vases about three inches high, one at each shoulder." There was no marker, and to this day those graves remained unmarked and unknown on this hillside.

One mile south in the Trail Canyon was the site of a large Sioux village in 1859.

Near this area were a trading post and the cabin of a herd checker. The herd checker helped to sort out the cattle belonging to other trail drives that had strayed. Later drives would pick up the strays as a courtesy and take them to this point for sorting.

At the historical marker on the south side of the road is a notebook that serves as a register of names of all who have visited this site. Enter your name and linger a moment with the thought of those who have passed here over the centuries and whose names are now mixed with the dust blowing in this prairie wind.

Four miles (4 miles.)
Haigler.

McKay's Garage in Haigler was once a livery stable when such conveniences were needed in every town.

The school was built in 1914.

At the junction of Porter Ave. and US 34 the town well once stood for decades, serving the locals with cool and non-alkaline water.

The first Democratic candidate for governor of Nebraska was from Haigler. (He lost.)

Haigler was the town that grew up around Jack Haigler's Three Bar Ranch (see below).

One and a half miles (1 1/2 miles.)
Cross the Arikaree River, just west of Haigler.

This is the approximate site of the dugout and headquarters of Jake Haigler's Three Bar Ranch. He stocked his ranch, opened a post office, organized Dundy County, got a town named after him and eventually moved to Arizona taking 5,000 head of cattle with him to the south, surprising untold numbers of cowboys who were driving their cattle north. When Jake operated the post office, he simply flipped letters into wooden boxes marked with the general directions of the compass. Jake would give the entire box to any rider who happened to stop by and was headed in the right direction.

At this spot a battle took place between the Arapahoe and Sioux. A few hundred yards west is the site of a mass Indian burial, probably dating from that battle.

Before that this was the camping grounds of the prehistoric Yuma Tribe, which existed about 10,000 years ago.

West of Haigler, the green croplands attest to the early pioneers' ability to build and maintain a canal irrigation system. In 1917, Colorado sued the founders, claiming that water could not be diverted from one state to serve the needs of another. The Supreme Court ruled in favor of the Nebraska pioneers and established an important water rights precedence.

One and a half miles (4 miles.)
Site of ghost town of Sanborn. An ancient town, now a skeleton of its former glory days. A few old brick buildings in the area

date back to the town's founding days.

South of Sanborn on backroads is a marker where Colorado, Kansas and Nebraska come together. You can stand there and then tell people you were in three states at one time, but since you are so close no one will be the wiser if you want to just stay here and claim you were in three at once.

Four miles (0 miles.)
Colorado border.

Although the Interstate is possibly the state's busiest highway, the information that follows in this description sketches only about 10 percent of the sights and sounds available within a few miles of its course. The reason for this is that most travelers who chose to go via the Interstate do so for speed. They wish simply to get from here to there. Consequently, the traveler wishing to see the most interesting and beautiful places in the state should get off the Interstate and take some time.

You may locate sites near the Interstate by checking in the entry for the various roads that intersect I-80.

Exit 454A.

Rosenblatt Stadium, home of the College World Series, and Omaha's Triple A team, the Royals.

Henry Doorly Zoo. A natural environment zoo with the largest collection of species for many miles.

292

A mile beyond this exit is the home of Falstaff Beer north of the Interstate. This is Omaha's local beer, brewed here for a century.

Exit 452.

Omaha.

Nebraska's largest city with many activities for both the small-town lover and the urbanite. For more information on Omaha please see entry for US Highway 75.

Junction with US Highways 75, 275 and 6. Please see entries for those highways for further information about sites along their routes.

At the Travel Information Center is one of the unique features of Interstate 80 in Nebraska. The steel-plate sculpture, "Praxis," by Dan Peragine is one of several sculptures commissioned for the state's celebration of the national Bicentennial.

The idea was proposed in 1973 and the Nebraska Bicentennial Commission made a $100,000 grant to start the program off. Further funding came from the Nebraska Arts Council and the Nebraska Art Association, as well as from the National Endowment for the Arts. Although these grants were generous, a full $350,000 of the eventual $500,000 cost was raised by Nebraska businesses. The sculptures, which number nine but growing, are all abstract, which still causes quite an uproar by some locals who insist that art should look like something. On the other side there are those who maintain these sculptures do look like something: they look like Art.

Other sculptures are located at:

Eastbound at the Platte River crossing between Lincoln and Omaha; Eastbound at the Blue River Crossing near Milford; Eastbound at the Grand Island rest area. This one had the added trouble of being considered too erotic for public display.

Westbound at the rest area near the York exchange; Westbound at the Kearney rest area; Westbound at the Brady rest area; Westbound at the Ogallala rest area; Westbound at the Sidney rest area.

Exit 451.

The stockyards. Omaha was made what it is today by the stockyards, where cattle from all over the West are brought for transport to other places. In the old days the cattle were bought and sold here as well. While the stockyards are not as vast as they were in bygone days (some people thank their noses this is so) they are still quite impressive.

Interstate 80

Exit 450.

University of Nebraska at Omaha.

The train tracks south of the Interstate carry the numberless coal trains through the state of Nebraska. These trains, usually 60 to 80 cars long, rumble eastward carry coal to the factories in Ohio and Pennsylvania, and westward, and empty, to the coal fields of Wyoming and Montana.

Exit 445.

Junction with Interstate 680, which circles the outside of Omaha. Take this to Boys Town. See description for Omaha in the entry for US Highway 75 for more information.

Exit 440.

Papillion is five miles east.

Don't for a moment confuse this town as a suburb of nearby Omaha. Papillion not only has its own unique and interesting history but is proud not to even be in the same county as Omaha.

Named for the Papio Creek and the high hill nearby, which was first described by an early pioneer. He looked off to the north, where today the look-alike houses of the city of Omaha march ever closer: "As far as the eye could see was a wide expanse of rolling prairie, unmolested by the hand of Man. It lay in silent slumber just as it was left at Creation. No sign of human life was visible. It was still. The same death-like stillness as at the beginning of time."

The present town is a grandchild of the older Papillion City, a site about 2 1/2 miles northeast of here.

The house at 4th and Monroe was the location of the home of the grandson of Papillion's founders, the Beadles.

The building at the southeast corner of 3rd and Jefferson was the Wilcox Hotel, an early landmark dating back to the 1880s.

The railroad station is still standing with little change from the way it looked in its prime, except that the insides have been torn out and it is mainly used for storage today.

The Stautter home is one of the few buildings left from an earlier era with a German influence. The Sarpy County Historical Society has restored the house to its original beauty and it is open to the public. The City Hall building is the original courthouse and many of the old furnishings such as desks, cabinets and counters are still in use.

Papillion was visited by gypsies as well as Indians around the turn of the century. The gypsies would camp outside of town and children were warned not to go near them, for they were known for stealing children.

Papillion had a large mill, which for a time was water-powered by the Papio Creek. The creek had power too; it often flooded, causing the dirt streets of the town to turn to quagmires.

A flood in 1903 nearly ruined the town's newspaper, which had offices in the basement of the bank. In 1959, a devastating flood put the entire town under water and wiped out the Washington Street bridge.

In 1964 more than 5 inches of rain fell one afternoon on already soaked ground. A wave of water swept through the business district on June 16th. Trees, homes, cars and buildings were swept away and tossed about. Over $5 million of damage was done in the Papio Basin, and several lives were lost. Hailstones fell so thick that they could still be found 24 hours later.

*Offut and SAC are **seven miles to the east** of Papillion. Please see the entry for US Highway 75 for more information about other sites in this area. The unusual coffeepot water tower near this exit excites comments from everyone.*

Exit 439.

Exit for Bellevue and Papillion. Please see entry for US Highway 75 for information about this historic Nebraska town.

Exit 432.

Westbound exit here for Schram Hatchery, Aquarium and Platte River State Park.

Westbound Rest Area.

This rest area affords a panoramic view of the Platte Valley from bluffs along its banks. A stop here will give the traveler a feel for the beauty of Nebraska's spectacular Platte River.

In 1991, the carcass of the first bald eagle known to have hatched in the state in the 20th Century was found dead near its nest along the banks of the Platte near here. The most likely cause of death was that it fell or was blown from its nest. Traditionally eagles nest in the same location year after year.

Crossing the Platte River. Between Exits 432 and 420.

The Platte is the true Nebraska River. It was the path that humankind took westward for centuries. It started with the Indians who used the river as a road west, and then the French fur trappers. The pioneers used the Platte as a constant landmark for the Pony Express, the Oregon and Mormon Trails, all of which follow its banks. The designers of Interstate 80 knew a good thing when they saw it. The Interstate follows the Platte through all of Nebraska. Even many commercial airliners pass across the state in sight of the blue ribbon of the Platte.

The Platte was always referred to as being a mile wide and an inch deep, and at this crossing that is pretty true, but across most of the state the Platte is struggling to survive. Water wars between power companies, irrigation concerns, and the states of Colorado, Wyoming and Nebraska have left the health of the river in decline to such a great extent that only a concerted effort by all parties can hope to prevent its death.

Three miles north of here is where one of the most famous UFO sightings ever took place. A police officer claimed he saw a spacecraft. Under hypnosis, he revealed that he had been taken inside the craft and asked a number of questions. For the complete story see entry for US Highway 6.

Eastbound, two miles west of the Platte River.

Platte River Crossing Rest Area.

This rest area contains the sculpture "Memorial to the American Bandshell" by Richard Field, and is one of several sculptures at rest areas along the Interstate.

For more information about the creation of these works of art see above at Exit 452.

There was a plan at one time to build a gigantic arch over the Interstate between two rest stops between Omaha and Lincoln. The arch would symbolize the gateway to the West and would contain information about Nebraska and the West. It was going to be the biggest arch ever. Cars would pass under it with their riders in awe. Well, not only the Interstate, but the air above the Interstate, is under Federal jurisdiction and they vetoed the idea.

Exit 426

Eugene T. Mahoney State Park. This state park has been ranked as one of the top five state parks in the country since it opened in early 1990s. Located on 487 acres on the wooded bluffs above the Platte, the park services many local folks from Lincoln and Omaha, as well as long-distance travelers.

The park includes everything one might expect at a more commercially oriented park: minature golf, a large swimming pool with a long waterslide, a park lodge, marina, souvenir shop, grocery store, theater, and tennis courts, as well as the more traditional "outdoor" park activities such as camping and hiking.

Not for the "back-to-the-wilds" set, Mahoney is Nebraska's most popular park.

Exit 420.

Take this exit to get to the Platte River State Park. In this area, along Camp Creek and other small streams, the earliest inhabitants of the state, known usually as the Nebraska Culture, camped and built their earth houses.

The Culture probably flourished about 1,000 years ago. The Nebraska Historical Society has done much research on the Culture. Their museum is located in Lincoln.

Exit 405.

Junction with US Highway 77. Please see that entry for sites along this road. Many towns in this area were named by the Union Pacific Railroad as it moved west in the 1870s and '80s. Near here was the town of Arbor, now a ghost town.

The green signs you see all along the Interstate that advertise local attractions were a part of the original plans for the Interstate through Nebraska. The signs are made to look similar to the official roadside signs of the Interstate system. They advertise only a tiny part of the vast attractions available to the traveler along Interstate 80.

Exit 401.

Lincoln. The state capital and home of the University of Nebraska. Junction with State Highway 2, and US Highways 77, 34 and 6. Please see those entries for more information about sites along their routes.

Exit 388.

Pleasant Dale exit.

This exit is at the top of a hill created by a glacier during the ice age. The sand and boulders along the glacier's edge were deposited behind as it melted, leaving this hill.

Plans were made by an organization called World Peace Center to buy land and build a "Prairie Peace Park and Maze" at the site of a former truck stop at this exit.

Exit 382.

The church at the Milford exit is the First Lutheran Church first built in Stapleton in 1882 and later moved to this spot. For more information about sites in this area, please see the entry for State Highway 15.

Eastbound. Rest area between exits 379 and 382.

The Eastbound Rest Area at the Blue River contains one of several sculptures located at rest areas along the Interstate in Nebraska. This sculpture is called "Arrival" and was created by artist Paul Von Ringelheim.

For more information about the creation of these works of art see above at Exit 452.

Exit 379.

Seward County's earliest residents were the prehistoric Indians who predated the Sioux, Otoe, Pawnee and Omaha who lived in the area when the white man finally arrived. Although there is no evidence that the Spanish explorer Coronado ever made it as far north as Nebraska, Seward residents feel they have as much claim to the distinction as anyone. In 1500, Coronado reported a storm that dropped 8 to 10 inches of rain and dropped hailstones "as large as porringers."

Originally the county was named Greene, after a well-known Senator from Missouri, but after the start of the Civil War the name changed to honor the Yankee Secretary of State, William Seward.

Among many other things, Seward is the home of the state's "official" July Fourth celebration.

Junction with State Highway 15. Please see that entry for more information about sites in this area.

Exit 369.

South to Beaver Crossing. Beaver Crossing is located on the Nebraska City Cutoff Trail, which led from Nebraska City to join up with the Oregon Trail west of Hastings. This location was a popular camping spot for pioneers moving west along the Trail. The town's name came from the fact that this spot was considered one of the finer places to cross the Blue River. The fishing here is good — ask locally for the best holes.

An early-day farmer persuaded many others to plant lilies and iris and many of those beautiful flowers are still growing wild in the area.

Westbound rest stop between exits 360 and 353.

At the rest area near York is one of several roadside sculptures along Interstate 80.

This impressive stone sculpture, "Crossing the Plains" by Bradford Graves, is arranged along the four points of the compass.

For more information about the creation of these works of art see above at Exit 452.

Also located at this rest area is a time capsule, which was buried on October 5, 1977. It is to be opened on the Fourth of July, 2076, and contains local, state and national bicentennial publications and newspapers, and books about York County.

Exit 353.

One mile north the Nebraska City Cutoff of the Oregon Trail crosses US Highway 81. The Trail was an alternate route west, and serviced pioneers headed west from Missouri. The Cutoff joined the Oregon Trail in central Nebraska. Junction with US Highway 81. See that entry for information about sites in this area.

Anna Bemis Palmer Museum, with exhibits on pioneer life, is in York. Take exit 353 to 211 E. 7th.

Exit 348.

One mile east of here, on the north side of the Interstate, is Kirkpatrick Wildlife Management Area, which protects a fine series of wetlands. The area is visible from the Interstate and provides a nice scene of wild Nebraska for those in too big a hurry to stop and visit.

Exit 342.

An alternative route to the Oregon Trail, known by many names including the Nebraska City Cutoff, ran through this part of the state. Along its route were many stations that operated like the motels and filling stations of today. The first of these stations to be established in this area was located one and a half miles north of the Henderson exit. Known as Porcupine Ranch, it was started in 1863 by a man named Benjamin Lushbaugh, who was an Indian agent for the Pawnee.

Later the ranch served as a relay station for the Overland Stage route. The buildings were built into sides of hills and made from sod. The ranch provided food for travelers, had some items for sale, and usually could make basic repairs to equipment.

A historical marker designates the location of the Porcupine Ranch.

Exit 332.

Aurora is home of the fine Plainsman Museum, three miles north on State Highway 14. For more information about sites in this area please see the entry for State Highway 14.

Eastbound rest stop between exits 312 and 318.

"Erma's Desire," one of several sculptures along the Interstate through the state, is at this cozy rest area.

The project was controversial, but Erma seemed to spark the greatest debate in the state when it was unveiled. Some saw the spires of rusting steel as overly erotic and suggestive. Others saw them simply as rusty steel spires. Still others saw them as a work of art by John Raimondi.

For more information about these works see above at Exit 452.

Exit 312.

North: Grand Island. Among the many fine items in this area is the Stuhr Museum, one of the finest in the Midwest.

Easy access off this exit takes the traveler to Mormon Island State Wayside Area and Crane Habitat area.

The state recreation area was named for a winter stopover on the Mormon Trail, which was located four miles upstream of here. Some of the last Mormons to use the trail started too late to reach Salt Lake City and stopped here to spend the winter of 1884-85. A mother and two children died during the long winter and were buried here.

This state recreation area provides camping, fishing, and boating and provides an ideal place to watch the migration of the Sandhill Cranes each March. When Interstate 80 was being developed in the early 1960s, the idea came about to leave the pits created by construction to fill with water. These pits would create a chain of lakes along the interstate. Many of these have since been developed, but Mormon Island, and its companion area, Windmill Recreation Area near Exit 285, were the first and most extensively developed.

Please see entries for US Highway 34, 30, and 281 and State Highway 2 for more information about the sites in this area.

South: Hastings. The museum at US Highway 281 and 14th

Street is a fine one. Please see the entries for US Highways 34, 6 and 281 for more information about Hastings and the other sites in this area.

Just two miles to the south of the exit, across the Platte River, is Doniphan.

Go west on county road at Doniphan, 1.8 miles, then take a right and go 2.4 miles to the site of the Campbell Graves. Five graves are located within the enclosure, most of them of Campbell family members who died during an Indian raid in July of 1867. The Sioux entered the Campbell home while the father was away. They killed one woman and her son and kidnapped four children.

Some time later the government exchanged these hostages for $4,000 and a Sioux woman and her child who had been captured at Elm Creek. No one recorded the Sioux grievance that precipitated the attack. Near here was the site of another Indian raid.

An English farmer, George Martin, displeased with the beetles of Liverpool, came to Nebraska and started a farm. Martin and his two sons were hauling hay one day when the Sioux appeared. They wounded Martin and chased the two boys who were riding on one horse. An Indian fired an arrow that passed through the boy in back and entered the shoulder of his brother in front. The two boys were pinned together by the arrow. The boys fell from their horse and the horse tumbled over them. The Indians left them for dead, but they were later found and nursed to health by their parents.

Exit 300.

To Wood River. Please see entry for State Highway 11 for sites along that route.

Exit 285.

North to Windmill State Wayside Area, with an exhibit of antique wind machines. Cool and shady.

Exit 279.

Minden exit.

You can't have traveled on the Interstate and not seen the signs for the Harold Warp Museum. There's a lot more to see as well. For a description of this and other fine locations in the area, please see the entry for US Highway 6 and State Highway 10.

Every surviving member of the Whooping Crane family passes through about a 30-mile bottleneck on their way north and south. The highest concentration along that stretch is between this exit and exit 272. One of the best places to view the estimated 112 remaining whoopers and their grey sandhill cousins is one mile south of this exit, across the Platte River.

Exit 272.

You are entering the bottleneck passageway for the Sandhill and Whooping Crane migration. See above at exit 279 for details.

The Frank House Mansion, built in 1889, and other attractions are in Kearney.

Exit here for Kearney and Fort Kearny Historical Park. Please see State Highway 10 and US Highway 30 for more information.

Westbound rest stop between exits 272 and 263.

Westbound at the Kearney Rest Area is another of the several sculptures exhibited at various rest areas on Interstate 80 through Nebraska. "The Nebraska Wind Sculpture," by George Baker, gently swirls and turns in the wind. The stainless steel sculpture is the only kinetic one of the many that grace the road's rest areas.

For more information, see entry for Exit 452, above.

Exit 257.

US Highway 183. Please see that entry for more information. North at this exit and then take the gravel road one mile east to Chevyland USA, an auto museum.

Exit 248.

The area around here was seriously affected by the great grasshopper plague of 1874, as entire farms were wiped out by the infestation. Grasshoppers literally swarmed in great dark clouds that blocked out the sun. They would descend on a field, their humming filling the air, devour every green plant to the ground and then move on. It was impossible to walk outside without crunching 10 or 20 bugs with each and every step.

The Oregon Trail and the Pony Express route are on the south bank of the Platte River, just south of the Interstate, and the Mormon Trail runs right alongside of the Interstate on the north from here, seven miles to the east.

Exit 237.

Lexington and junction with US Highway 283. One of the state's largest and finest recreation areas, Johnson Lake, is ten miles south. There is much to see in this area. Please see the entries for US Highway 283 and 30 for more information.

Exit 222.

Cozad. One of the state's most interesting places is the Robert Henri Museum and Historical Walkway. Henri was the son of the founder of Cozad, John Cozad. John Cozad was a bit of a gambler and roustabout. His son changed his name to avoid the negative publicity generated by his father, and, as Robert Henri, became a well-known artist in the early years of this century. He even founded a movement in modern art for his non-traditional realism called "the Ashcan School."

Exit 199.

Brady. One mile south, turn west and follow the exact route of the Oregon Trail by following the country roads as they zigzag westward. Watch for historical markers along the way and signs of the rut marks from the wagons on hillsides. This route will lead you to North Platte and back to the Interstate.

The Platte River valley was to be the location for the nation's first east-west recreation trail. Legislation initiating the American Discovery Trail was passed in 1992 but the plans were for the trail to pass through Kansas and not Nebraska. Some senators urged both a northern and southern route for the 5,500-mile-long hiking path. In any event, this area is ideal for a beautiful hike, path or no path.

Westbound rest stop between exits 190 and 199.

Westbound at the Rest Area near Brady is "Nebraska Gateway," a stone sculpture by Anthony Padovano. One hundred thousand pounds of granite sit perched in the middle of shade trees. It is one of several sculptures along the Interstate.

See entry for Exit 452, above, for more information.

Exit 190.

Maxwell. You are entering the real West now.

To the north are the rugged and isolated Sandhills, Nebraska's natural wonder. They cover nearly a third of the state.

Two miles south of the Interstate and then south one and a half miles to Fort McPherson National Cemetery. There seems there could be no more remote or beautiful site for a cemetery of this vast size. This is one of the most comfortable and interesting places to get off the busy Interstate. Rest in the cool of the big shade trees.

Continue south from the cemetery for 1/2 mile to the site of Cottonwood Springs stage stop and Oregon Trail station. This was one of the most widely used stations on the Oregon Trail. A Fort McPherson once stood here as well.

West of here seven miles to a tall hill known as Sioux Lookout, which affords the best view of a wide area. The top of the hill and the trail up are public property. Ask locally for directions.

Exit 177.

North Platte.

North Platte has a rodeo every night of every summer. See Buffalo Bill Cody Museum for information.

Scouts' Rest Ranch, which was built in 1878 by Buffalo Bill Cody, is now a 65-acre state historical park. Items are on display from Cody's long life on the frontier as a scout, buffalo hunter and showman. His mansion has been preserved and you can get a glimpse of the hero himself by watching the film of Cody made by Thomas Edison in 1898.

There is a buffalo stew cookout going on most summer evenings, so for a taste of the Old West, the Rest Ranch is the place to be. Also in the summer is the Rough Riders Rodeo near the Ranch. The rodeo is run seven nights a week during summer.

North Platte is home to the gigantic Bailey Yards, the largest rail complex in the United States. The yard was named after the famed Union Pacific President, Edd Bailey, who grew up on a dry-farm homestead in eastern Colorado, got his first railroad job in his early teens and rose to become the president of one of the largest transportation companies in the world. Bailey Yard includes three locomotive repair shops and puts together trains bound for both coasts of America. There is a tour and an observation area.

North Platte is home to several museums, including the Railroad Museum and the Western Heritage Museum.

The Lincoln County Historical Museum is located on the way to the Buffalo Bill Ranch off Buffalo Bill Ave. It contains many fine displays and a small library of local books. On the grounds are several buildings including a school, a barn and the first two-story log house built in the county South on US Highway 83, one and one half miles.

Just west of here was the Cold Springs Pony Express Station. Continue south three miles to the turnoff for Mahoney Reservoir. Turn east and go five miles, and then north for three to the 3,200-foot hill known as Sioux Lookout (see above). For more information about locations in this area please see the entries for US Highways 83 and

30.

Between Exits 177 and 158

Although the surrounding hills may seem pretty dry, this area is within feet of one of the largest freshwater lakes in the world. Trouble is, it is underground.

The Ogallala Aquifer stretches from the Dakotas to New Mexico, although Nebraska sits on top of two-thirds of its volume. That volume is estimated to be enough to flood all 50 states with a foot and a half of water. It has as much water as Lake Huron and a quarter of Lake Ontario.

The water's source is the Rockies to the west, where centuries of snowmelt have seeped under rocks and moved slowly eastward into the huge underground lake.

Although early-day farmers didn't have the tools to reach and extract the water, today $30,000 pumps flood large areas of crop and rangeland in the area. The region produces up to 40 percent of the nation's beef and a quarter of its food. Without irrigation, however, these numbers would fall dramatically.

In the past 40 years, so many farmers and ranches have tapped the aquifer that concern has been raised about the longevity of the supply. Some estimate that over 10 percent of the water has been pumped out since 1940.

There is an ongoing debate about how long the water in the aquifer will last. Some predict that we will have used up one fourth of its vast supply in the early years of the 21st Century. Others note how years of heavy fertilization has poisoned much of the water.

Slowly, state legislatures have begun to pass laws that limit the number and flow of wells. Most people agree that conservation is critical to the health of the aquifer. Others claim that the laws are too weak and more drastic steps need to be taken to save the oasis of the Great American Desert.

Exit 158.

Sutherland.

The rest areas at Sutherland between North Platte and Ogallala are located near O'Fallon's Bluff, an important site along the Oregon Trail. The Trail had to pass along the side of the bluff because of the small distance between it and the South Platte River.

A stage station was located here, as well as a military post. O'Fallon's Bluff was also an important landmark for the fur trappers headed through this area in the decades before the mass migration of the California Gold Rush, the Mormon migration and the Oregon Trail.

At the eastbound rest area, the ruts from the wagon trains can be seen about 500 feet behind the area. Wagon wheels mark the area of indentation. It is estimated that between 1843 and 1863, 250,000 people moved west along the Oregon Trail. Today Interstate 80, as well as the jet planes from California to New York, follow their route.

Please see entry for US Highway 30 for further information about sites in this area.

Exit 145.

Paxton.

Among the many sites in this area is Ole's Big Time Game Lounge in downtown Paxton. A lot of animals that used to be alive are hung up here. See entry for US Highway 30 for more information about sites in this area.

Exit 126.

Ogallala.

One half mile south of the exit are the remnants of the Oregon Trail. Gills Station, a Pony Express station and stage stop, stood just west of State Highway 61. For more information about sites in this area, please see the entry for State Highway 61.

Ogallala served as the terminus for many Texas cattle drives in the 1870s and '80s. Here the railroad would ship the cattle east, and the cowboys who had been on the trail for weeks would unwind. Once called the "Gomorrah of the Plains," its present-day role as a convenience stop for tourists makes it a showplace for travelers through the state.

It is the gateway to Nebraska's largest lake, the gigantic Lake McConaughy, a few miles north of town. The lake has over 100 miles of white sand beaches and plenty of good fishing and boating.

At Lewellen, north of Ogallala, Ash Hollow State Historical Park gives a portrait of the human inhabitants of the area for the last 10,000 years. The Ash Hollow Cave, which is here, is a site used by nomadic tribes thousands of years ago. In addition, the ruts of the Oregon Trail are still visible here, preserving the traces of a much later band of nomadic travelers.

Eastbound rest stop between exits 117 and 126.

This is one of the finest rest stops in the country for the tourist. It is here where the tourist can still see the ruts of the early-day tourists, the pioneers who headed west over the Oregon Trail. The ruts are clearly marked and interpretive signs help explain the sights.

Westbound rest stop between exits 133 and 126.

At the rest area for the **westbound** traveler near Ogallala is one of the several sculptures that grace many of the rest areas along the Interstate in Nebraska.

"Over/Under" by Linda Howard is a nostalgic and graceful arch of suspended I-beams. Its beauty and simple design add delight to a stop here.

The sculptures were controversial, but little of the controversy centered on the fact that, of all the sculptures in the project, this is the only one by a woman. For more information about these sculptures, please see entry for Exit 452 above.

Exit 102

Interstate 76 to the dry, unattractive hills of eastern Colorado and smog-filled Denver.

Exit 85

Chappell. Adjacent to the exit ruts from the Oregon Trail and Pony Express route are visible. The routes passed through this area, and the active Deuel County Historical Society has marked the route and noted where the ruts can still be seen. Pull off and visit their fine museum located at 5th and Vincent and ask for directions to the Trail sites.

Chappell also has a fine art collection in its library. For information about this and other sites in and around Chappell, please see entry for US Highway 30

Exit 76.

Lodgepole. Just north of the interchange, the access road crosses the Pony Express route. Another half mile north and it crosses the Oregon Trail. Lodgepole has a nice museum.

Lodgepole Wayside area commemorates the contribution of the Union Pacific Railroad. Near here is one of the state's "highest points" this one is south and register's 5,426 feet. At least two other "highest points" exist in the state considered flat by many people. One is near the point where Colorado, Wyoming and Nebraska join, and another is north of Kimball in Banner County.

Westbound rest stop between exits 69 and 59.

Interstate 80

For Westbound travelers, the rest area near Sidney features the sculpture "Roadway Confluence" by Hans Van de Bovenkamp. The aluminum structure rises up from the grasslands of western Nebraska and is one of a series of sculptures along the Intererstate.

For more information about this unique series of displays, please see above entry for Exit 452.

Exit 59.

Sidney.

For more information about the sites and sights in this area, please see entries for US Highway 30 and 385.

Legion Park is the perfect place for a walk or a nap under shady trees. It includes a public swimming pool, tennis courts and playground equipment. Fort Sidney was established to protect workers building the Union Pacific railroad westward. With the discovery of gold in the Black Hills the fort expanded and became the starting point of the infamous Deadwood-Sidney Trail.

Fort Sidney, which many claim is haunted by the spirit of a woman who killed herself, is preserved and offers many exhibits for inspection.

Exit 38.

Potter, at Exit 38, features Buffalo Bend, a musical stage show of renown. It is performed every weekend from June through August.

Exit 20.

Kimball.

Those oil wells spotting the horizon help keep this area going, although ranching is still important to the citizens. If you can't see an oil well, you are probably looking at a site of an Intercontinental Ballistic Missile. This area has the highest concentration of ICBMs anywhere in the world. The Kimball Recreation Area includes a golf course, shuffleboard and tennis.

Stop off here instead of one of those cold rest stops. Oliver Reservoir offers swimming and boating and a cool place to pull off the road before leaving the state for hot and dry Wyoming. Every once in a while folks who live in Nebraska's Panhandle start to talk about how the government way the heck over in Lincoln doesn't pay them much mind. When this kind of talk gets especially loud it leads to the next subject: secession from the state. The Panhandlers often believe they would get better attention from Cheyenne if they were a part of

Wyoming, or, the most radical of the talkers will add, their own brand new state.

Exit 1.
      Welcome to Nebraska, if you are headed east. Your last chance to get off the Interstate and still be in the fine state of Nebraska, if you are headed west.
      Pine Bluffs southwest of here is the point where Colorado, Wyoming and Nebraska join and near there is the highest point in the state at 5,424 feet.

Zero miles (2 miles.)

Junction with US Highway 275 at the western edge of Omaha. From here through the southern part of Omaha, 92 is swallowed by the busy US Highway 275.

Two miles (4 miles.)

Venice. A small burg on the banks of the Platte, which here still looks much like it did for hundreds of years. Serious depletion of its waters due to greed and mismanagement farther west, however, have turned this once mighty river into a series of braided streams trickling through a tangle of oak and willow on what used to be its streambed.

Four miles (5 miles.)

Yutan.

State Highway 92

A large Otoe village of at least 100 lodges stood two miles southeast of Yutan during early pioneer times. The village had 70 lodges and was inhabited from the early Eighteenth Century through the 1830s. Lewis and Clark visited the village on one of their trips inland from the Missouri as they explored the route west in 1804.

The main leader of this large band was named Letan. After a treaty in 1833, the Otoe moved 15 miles southwest on the other side of the Platte. The pioneer village that replaced the Otoe one is a phonetic spelling of the chief's name. Traces of the Otoe village can still be found in the area. The first church and Sunday school exclusively for Indians was located at this village.

North via county roads for seven miles to Leshara.
Leshara was the site of a Pawnee village is one half mile northwest of the town. It was inhabited by the Grand and Republican bands of the Pawnee and may have served as an overflow village from other nearby Skidi Pawnee villages as well. The village was occupied into the 1850s.

Five miles (8 miles.)
Intersection with US Highway 77. For sites along the route of 77, please see that entry.

Eight miles (6 miles.)
Wahoo! You too can be hollering "wahoo" and it doesn't require being a yahoo.

For more serious information about this tidy town please see the entry for US Highway 77.

Six miles (4 miles.)
The tiny town of Weston, just to the south, is a good example of how small Nebraska towns can create a sense of place and belonging. Never a gigantic burg, folks from around here nevertheless have a history, a culture and a long tradition of making a living from what the land has offered them.

Four miles (1 mile.)
Turnoff for State Highway 79, north.
Seven miles north to Prague.
Near Prague is the ghost town of Rescue.
Rescue is an abandoned Saunders County town located three miles west and two and a half miles north of Prague.

Originally platted in 1875, it was once a stop on the Chicago, Burlington & Quincy's Ashland to Schuyler route completed in 1887. The railroad spur is now abandoned.

The last active business — an automotive garage — closed in 1948, but in its finest days the town had a store, post office, homes, saloons, a stockyard, grain elevator and a boxcar depot for the railroad. A few surviving buildings can be seen. The town is now owned by an individual and is on private property.

Continue north *on State Highway 79* **10 miles** *to Morse Bluff and the Platte River (see entry for US Highway 30 for further information about that area).*

One mile (4 miles.)

Intersection with State Highway 79, south.

Follow State Highway 79 **south 25 miles** *for a pleasant, backroad route to Lincoln.*

Five miles south *to where the Oxbow Trail crosses Highway 79. See below for a description of the Oxbow Trail.*

Nine miles south *to Valparaiso.*

Debate still rages on whether to pronounce this town Valpar-EYE-zo, or Valpar-A-zo. Either way, the name is better than the original name for the place: Raccoon Forks.

Four miles (4 miles.)

The Oxbow Trail crosses the highway near here. On the south side of the highway it heads almost directly south, while on the north side of the road it swings west and parallels State Highway 92 for about 2 miles. It then crosses to the south side of the road, continuing to parallel the highway for yet another two miles. At that point it heads northwesterly toward David City.

The Oxbow Trail was used as a route from Nebraska City to Fort Kearny to the west. The trail crosses the southern part of the county in a northwesterly direction.

Four miles (6 miles.)

The Oxbow Trail crosses the highway near here. To the north side of the road it heads toward David City and the Platte, while to the south the trail follows State Highway 92 for four miles (see above.)

Six miles (9 miles.)

Intersection with State 15:

North *on State Highway 15* **nine miles** *and then just to the*

313

west on State 64: Marker commemorating the site of Savannah, one-time county seat and the location of an important ferry crossing over the Platte from 1859-1873. Nothing remains of either site today, and the river has wandered a couple miles away to the north.

Across from the historical marker is the Presentation Catholic Church, rectory and school. The church was built in 1891, but was even then a few miles from the nearest town. Pioneer determination and faith has kept this a holy spot of worship. The site includes a grotto and the building of St. Mary's school (1916) no longer in use. Dark wooden pews and dramatic stained glass offer the traveler a quiet moment of contemplation.

For other sites along State Highway 15, please see that entry.

Nine miles (4 miles.)
Rising City.

Although probably risen about as much as it ever will, Rising City is a busy burg in the flat expanse of some of the richest growing soil on the planet.

In the 1930s, a local campaign was initiated to plant additional trees for windbreaks to help keep in place the precious soil. Tens of thousands of trees were planted as a result of the effort. Some of those tree lines are still visible in the area.

North of here on the banks of the Platte River at its confluence with the Loup was one of the fiercest and bloodiest battles in Nebraska history. The event is unusual, too, for its relative antiquity. In 1720 — 150 years before the Sioux Wars — a Spanish Conquistador, Pedro deVillasur, led an expedition to explore the French territory in the Missouri Valley.

At this place on August 14 his party was attacked by the Pawnee. DeVillarsur retreated to Santa Fe, but not before 43 of his men were killed in the battle.

The battle marks the earliest known conflict between Nebraska's native population and those from the outside.

Four miles (3 miles.)
Intersection with US Highway 81, north. Please see the entry for US Highway 81 for more information about sites in this area.

Three miles (10 miles.)
Shelby.

Shelby was the birthplace of one of the best artists of the Social Comment style of regionalism. Terence Duren was born here in 1907. When he got polio at the age of six, his father gave him a box of crayons and some paper. Although the disease left him partially paralyzed, Duren continued to paint and draw. Others began to recognize his talent.

By the time he was in his twenties he was teaching at the Chicago Art Institute, the Cleveland Institute of Art and at other schools.

After gaining a growing reputation in the East, Duren returned, not only to Nebraska, but to his hometown of Shelby. He continued to sell and exhibit his work worldwide, while he expanded his home on Main Street and added a painting cottage. His illustrations graced the cover of Omaha's *Magazine of the Midlands* and other magazines. His paintings were purchased to grace the walls of offices, stores and museums.

In Shelby Duren painted full time, incorporating Nebraska landscapes and portraits into his work and organizing a local theater group in the former Shelby movie house. He was visited by people from all over the world who came to admire and to purchase his work. He died in Shelby in 1968.

Today his work is housed in many Midwestern museums, including the Museum of Nebraska Art and Lincoln's Center for Great Plains Studies.

Ten miles (12 miles.)

Intersection with US Highway 81, south. Please see that entry for further information.

Twelve miles (2 miles.)

The Platte River.

The Oxbow Trail, an alternate route from Nebraska City to the Oregon Trail at Kearney, crosses the highway on the south side of the river. This road less traveled provides good access to some of the finer fishing spots along Nebraska's once great river.

On the west side of the river is the intersection with US Highway 30. For more information about sites in this area, please see the entry for that highway.

Two miles (4 miles.)

Site of Pawnee hunting grounds and burial site. This used to be the banks of the Platte, 130 years ago, and once two Pawnee villages stood here. The dreaded and thoughtless enemy of all this American and Nebraskan history, the Pot Hunter, has been here

315

many times and snuck away with arrowheads, pots and remnants of the once noble villages. It is a crime to remove any archeological artifacts from sites.

Four miles (13 miles.)

Intersection with State 14

This is the heart of the country made famous by Nebraska author Wright Morris. His novels, stories and photographs captured the turning of an era as the farmers in middle Nebraska pulled up roots during the hard years of the 1930s and '40s and moved on to what they hoped would be a better life, full of riches other than the gold of corn stalks and the silver of wheat.

Thirteen miles (10 miles.)

Along the western edge of the county, and roughly paralleling the county line north and south, is a portion of the original Mormon Trail. The Trail wound through here on its way to the Platte River, and, eventually, Salt Lake City. Between 1846 and 1861, tens of thousands of persecuted emigrants passed this way. Until the last few years of the exodus most of them carried their belongings in bulky carts pulled by hand.

Ten miles (9 miles.)

Intersection of US Highway 281. Please see that entry for information about sites in this area.

Nine miles (17 miles.)

Farwell. This was the location of the famed Folk School, started by the early pioneers. The Folk School was established in order to lay a foundation for a richer life. The buildings for the school still stand and are a major part of the structures of this small village.

Seventeen miles (5 miles.)

Loup City and the intersection of State Highway 10.

Sherman Reservoir is located at Loup City.

Built on Oak Creek in 1962, this lake has 65 miles of shoreline and provides a marina, camping, fishing and hiking. The purpose of the dam however, was not recreation, but to provide irrigation. The lake stores water for the irrigation season. Water is diverted from the Middle Loup River by the Arcadia Diversion Dam and then flows 18 miles through the Sherman Feeder Canal to this reservoir. Approximately 50,000 acres of farmland are irrigated by the water held here.

Best fishing is for walleye and crappie along some of the rugged shoreline of the lake. Bass and catfish fishing is also good here.

A series of hiking trails lead away from the lake. The Games and Parks Commission, which runs this recreation areas, also calls the gravel and asphalt roads leading to camping sites in this area "trails" as well. One such trail leads to Dead Horse Creek (see below.)

For more information about sites in and around Loup City, please see the entry for State Highway 10.

Five miles (8 miles.)

North of the road is Dead Horse Canyon. The mouth of this pretty little canyon is near the road. In 1873, a herd of 28 horses died in this canyon during a blizzard. The horses belonged to scouts for the U.S. Army. The name still has stuck with the canyon. Do not confuse this with a canyon by the same name near Fort Robinson in Sioux and Dawes counties.

Eight miles (7 miles.)

This area grows a good part of the world's supply of popcorn. Average annual sales have been 100 million pounds. Yields for an acre of popcorn are between 50 and 100 bushels.

On the average, Americans eat 45 quarts of popcorn per person annually. What most of them do not realize is that each type of popcorn has its own flavor.

Popcorn looks very similar to field corn, although at maturity the stalks are slightly shorter.

Seven miles (17 miles.)

Junction with State Highway 2. This is the center of what many consider to be Nebraska's best highway: Route 2. For further information about sites along this fine road, please see the entry for State Highway 2.

Seventeen miles (9 miles.)

Broken Bow. For more information about this town with a name right out of the Old West, please see entry for State Highway 2.

Nine miles (2 miles.)

Intersection with State Highway 2. State Highway 92 splits away and heads into the isolated Sandhills to the west. For more

317

information about sites north and south of here, see the entry for State
Highway 2.

Two miles (10 miles.)

Cedar Canyons. This maze of small canyons is home to a
wide variety of wildlife. Many birds frequent the area as well.

Ten miles (9 miles.)

The irrigated rich lands of the eastern part of the state give
way to the grasslands of the west along this stretch of 92. Fewer and
fewer corn and soybean fields grace the roadside, and are replaced
by such crops as dry beans, sorghum, sugarbeets, potatoes and hay.
In early summer, large fields of ripe wheat bow down in gentle
breezes. Nebraska grows over 2 million acres of wheat and produces
about 80 million bushels of Hard Red wheat.

Wheat has become such a refined plant that scientists
estimate it would not survive more than three years if humankind were
not around to care for it.

Nine miles (16 miles.)

Arnold.

In the late 1960s, Arnold was known all over the region for its
unfriendliness. Horror stories about people whose cars broke down in
the town, and the universally rude and threatening treatment they
received, spread like wildfire.

In 1968, a group of cross-country bicyclists paused at Arnold
Lake Park and had two of their members beaten to a pulp by local
cowboys.

Two weeks later, a lone bicyclist from Lincoln, unaware of the
town's reputation, had the misfortune to break down on the outskirts
of town. Without the intervention of a less bloodthirsty citizen, he too
would have suffered physical damage at the hands of the community.

Soon articles began to appear in publications giving Arnold
the title as the most redneck and unfriendly town in the state. Surely
this isn't still true. . .

Sixteen miles (4 miles.)

Junction with US Highway 83, south. Please see that entry
for further information about sites in this area.

Four miles (5 miles.)

Junction with US Highway 83, north at Stapleton. Please see

318

the entry for US Highway 83 for further information.

Five miles (9 miles.)

The highway follows the upper reaches of the South Loup River. This river, which joins the Loup 25 miles north of Hastings as a sluggish brown stream, seems wilder here as it comes down out of the surrounding hills before its 120-mile journey east to the Loup.

Nine miles (11 miles.)

The near ghost town of Ringgold, which was moved here from Dawson County and kept its name.

Tryon.

Some say the town is named after a local citizen. For other theories on how this unusual name came about, see the entry for State Highway 97.

McPherson County used to be larger, but in 1913 a section of the county seceded and became known as Arthur County. Today, McPherson county commissioner meetings often include a birthday cake and party, or a retirement celebration as a regular part of the day's business.

Total crime statistics for the last 100 years in McPherson County:

19 cattle stealing
1 corn stealing
1 livestock abuse
1 goat stealing
1 dog stealing
2 wife stealing
1 incest
2 murders
5 robberies
various "hootch" factories

biggest recent robbery: August 29, 1981 Gary's Conoco's safe was pried opened and $50 was taken in receipts.

State Highway 92 had its own booster club as the "Highway #92 Association" met in Tryon in 1927 to promote the road in order to "open the gate to the east." Wonder if the citizens wouldn't rather just as well have it closed nowadays, what with tourbook-totin' tourists everywhere. . .

Eighteen miles (4 miles.)

319

State Highway 92

Turnoff north to the White and Brown Lake vicinity and the south fork of the Dismal River where Buffalo Bill once had a ranch. This washboardy road is best avoided in dry, wet, snowy or dusty conditions. For more information about this ranch see entry for State Highway 97.

Four miles (6 miles.)

Turnoff to the south for Diamond Bar Lake vicinity. Good fishing and hunting. Inquire locally.

Ten miles southeast of here, accessible on back roads only, is the site of the small town of Forks, located at the forks of the East and West Birdwood Creeks. It had a post office until the early 1920s.

Six miles (11 miles.)

Flats, another town nearer to ghost status than not. Because of an early pioneer named Lombard, the area was called Lombard Flats. The U.S. Post Office, in its infinite wisdom, cut off the Lombard part because it was too long and simply left it Flats.

Eleven miles (24 miles.)

Junction with State Highway 61 at Arthur. For the next 24 miles State Highway 92 joins State Highway 61. Please see the entry for State Highway 61 for information about sites along this section of the road.

Twenty four miles (7 miles.)

Junction with State Highway 61. State Highway 61 continues south toward Ogallala, while State Highway 92 goes west from this junction. For the next 24 miles northward the two highways are joined. For more information about sites in this area see the entry for State Highway 61.

Seven miles (5 miles.)

LeMoyne, a tiny ranching community given a second life with the construction of Lake McConaughy.

Five miles (7 miles.)

The highway caresses the north shore of Nebraska's largest body of water — Lake McConaughy. Big Mac, as the lake is known locally, is an artifical lake created when the North Platte River was dammed. Although one of the state's most popular lakes, the size of the reservoir is large enough that even on the busiest days the traveler can still feel the isolation and beauty of the surrounding Sandhills.

The Mormon Trail is between the highway and the lake, although the backwaters of the lake have destroyed part of the route. Traces of the trail can still be seen in this area.

To the north was the traditional hunting grounds of the Sioux and Cheyenne. An important battle known as Bluewater Battle took place north and west of here near Lewellen. See entry for US Highway 26 for details.

Seven miles (42 miles.)

Just before Lewellen, State Highway 92 joins US Highway 26. For information about this section of the road, please see the entry for US Highway 26.

Forty two miles (1 mile.)

Junction with US Highway 26 at Broadwater. State Highway 92 crosses the North Platte River, while US Highway 26 continues west.

One mile (8 miles.)

Three miles east on a back road is the location of a frontier post station on the Oregon Trail. This back road east roughly follows the route of the Oregon Trail for about 45 miles to Ash Hollow. (See entry for US Highway 26 for a description of Ash Hollow.)

Continue west on State Highway 92. You are now roughly following the route of the Oregon Trail. The trail runs to your south for the first 5 1/2 miles, then it crosses the road and is on the north side of Highway 92.

Eight miles (8 miles.)

Junction with US Highway 385. See entry for US Highway 385 for more information on sites along this road.

About one quarter mile past this junction, and an eighth of a mile to the north is the grave of Amanda Lamin, who died here of cholera crossing the continent in 1840. Her husband left his wagon train and returned alone to St. Louis where he purchased a granite marker for his wife, and came back with it with the next party headed west. You might say such an added journey was stupid, but his action did give his wife a kind of immortality. Most history buffs, as well as local residents, would not otherwise have known the name of this poor woman who died so far from any home had it not been for her devoted husband. The site is on private land; inquire locally for viewing.

State Highway 92

A few ruts from the trail are still visible in this area, although recent farming has destroyed many of them. The Mormon Trail is on the northern bank of the river, and ruts from it are visible in places. Inquire locally at the Bridgeport Museum for directions to ruts.

Eight miles (13 miles.)

Bridgeport and the junctions of State Highway 92, 88, US Highway 385 and 26.

For the next 13 miles, State Highway 92 and US Highway 26 are on the same route. One of the most frequently mentioned sites on the Oregon Trail, Chimney Rock is clearly visible on the western horizon.

Please see the entry for US Highway 26 for more information about sites along this section of the road.

Thirteen miles (5 miles.)

Junction with US Highway 26. Chimney Rock. Please see the entry for US Highway 26 for information about this famous landmark.

Continue west on State Highway 92 at Chimney Rock for an interesting alternative route to Scottsbluff.

Five miles (1 1/2 miles.)

McGrew. The Oregon Trail followed the route of present-day Highway 92. To the southwest of McGrew can be seen several landmarks of the Trail including Castle Rock, Table Rock, Steamboat Rock and Roundtop. These bluffs appear in William Jackson's famous panoramic painting of the Chimney Rock area, which he originally sketched in 1866. The painting is on display at the Scott's Bluff National Historic Monument (see below.)

One and a half miles (4 1/2 miles.)

*Take the county road on the south side of the road **west for one and a quarter miles**. On the south side of the road, ruts from the Oregon Trail are still visible. Continue on this county road west another **three miles** when it rejoins Highway 92, or return to Highway 92 the way you came.*

Four and a half miles (1 mile.)

The tiny town of Melbeta, just south of Minatare on US Highway 26.

One mile (7 miles.)

322

One mile west of Melbeta is a marker commemorating the site of the Ficklin's Springs Pony Express Station. Both the Pony Express route and the Oregon Trail route criss-cross Highway 92 several times between Chimney Rock and Scottsbluff.

Seven miles (3 miles.)

Gering and Scottsbluff. Despite the closeness of big sister Scottsbluff, Gering holds its own with a fine museum, good places to eat and a kind of old-time charm in its wide streets and grain elevators. For more information about Gering and Scottsbluff, please see entry for US Highway 26.

Three miles (12 miles.)

Scott's Bluff, the must-see Scott's Bluff National Historic Monument.

At the southeast corner of the intersection of Highways 92 and 29 was the approximate location of Camp Mitchell, an early military camp location for protecting the mail route.

Scott's Bluff is an imposing bluff that pioneers moved under as they made their way through Mitchell Pass. It is estimated that a quarter of a million pioneers passed by this spot during a 20-year period beginning in 1843. They moved at an average of eight miles a day. The ruts left by their passing are clearly visible here as they move up through the pass at the base of the bluff.

The museum at the monument headquarters is a wonderful addition to the living history one can feel by walking through the pass itself. William Jackson's famous panoramic view of the area, painted from his sketch done in 1866, is on display here as well as many other exhibits.

Visitors can reach the top of the bluff by driving up a paved road or hiking the mile and half to the top. A self-guided trail at the summit passes overlooks where the view of the Platte Valley below is spectacular. Both the trail and road start at the Visitors' Center.

Walk west from the Visitors' Center along the clearly marked trail to follow the route of the pioneers. Once over the crest of the hill the modern world seems to vanish. A glance at the landscape will reveal the old route as it winds downhill. The flowers, wildlife and rocks seem just as they might always have been here, and the air is pure and sweet.

In 1828, a man by the name of Hiram Scott, a lone fur trapper, died at the base of the bluff after he was abandoned by his companions. Since that time the bluff has been referred to as Scott's Bluff.

A trip to the monument is not complete without a side trip to the alternate route of the Oregon Trail through this area.

Go west on State 92 two miles to junction with State Highway 71. Go south on 71 two miles.

This county road that intersects the highway follows the exact route of one branch of the Oregon Trail.

Turn west here and go six miles. *Stop the car.*

Two miles in front of you *is the route through Robidoux Pass and the site of the Robidoux Trading Post built in 1849 to take advantage of the flood of pioneers moving west.*

A later trading post was built two miles south of here a year later in 1850. Robidoux operated both posts for a while. That site may be reached by turning **south** *here and following the county road southwesterly for* **three miles.** *It is at the mouth of Carter Canyon. If you continue* **west** *here for another* **two miles,** *ruts from the Trail are visible on the southern side of the highway as the county road and the old trail climb toward Robidoux Pass. Several marked and unmarked graves of pioneers are in this area.*

In 1991 in Carter Canyon, the Gering Tourism Committee began to build a replica of the second Robidoux Trading Post at the precise location of the original. The land for the site was donated by Rupert and Goldie Ewing Bigsby. Mrs. Bigsby's father homesteaded the land in 1910 and she recalled growing up and finding teepee rings and other artifacts all over the property.

Joseph Robidoux was the founder of St. Joseph, Missouri, before he moved west to set up trading posts.

The site can be recognized by the hat-shaped bluff in the background, which appears in an 1851 sketch of the trading post.

Twelve miles (8 miles.)

The highway comes close to the headwaters of Horse and Sand Creeks, and the site of the largest gathering of Native Americans ever held. They came together for the signing of the Fort Laramie Treaty. See entry for US Highway 26 at Morrill for a description of this site.

Eight miles (0 miles.)

The small town of Lyman and the Wyoming border.

Zero miles (1 mile.)

US Highway 30 bridge on the Iowa/Nebraska border.

East of Blair on US Highway 30 to the DeSoto National Wildlife Refuge and the steamboat *Bertrand* museum and site. The museum is actually in Iowa, but since the location of the boat itself is in Nebraska, we will allow an entry here from someplace nice, but not quite as nice as Nebraska. The steamboat sank on April 1, 1865, loaded with cargo, and was discovered in the river mud in 1969 and excavated. The museum contains items taken from the boat in nearly perfect condition.

One mile (18 miles.)

Blair. Blair is the center for a large area of historic and natural beauty. For more information about sites in this area, please see the entry for US Highway 73.

325

US Highway 30

Eighteen miles (1 1/2 miles.)
Fremont.
Junction with US Highway 77.
There is plenty to see and do in the Fremont area. For more information about Fremont and the surroundings, please see entry for US Highway 77.

One and a half miles (2 miles.)
South here on Military Avenue to Beebe-McNeal Monument. This monument commemorates the Mormon Trail, which passed near here, as well as two pioneer families.

Two miles (4 miles.)
South one mile to Fremont Lakes State Park.
You are not a citizen of Eastern Nebraska until you have spent a July afternoon spread-eagle on the beach at Fremont Lakes. The lazy sun beats down on you as you gaze about the scenery, both natural and humankind. When that lazy sun beats a bit too much, you simply plunge into the water for a moment's relief from the heat. Don't bother moving farther than the campgrounds, where you can continue to laze away the hours until nightfall. After dark the park becomes a quiet and restful kind of place, a place for dreaming grand dreams of the future, and of an ideal life. At dawn a quiet float out on the water to catch breakfast. There are many thousands of people across the world who do not pass a hot summer without remembering just such days of idle and innocent youth experienced at this very same wonderful spot.

Four miles (1/2 mile.)
One half mile east of Ames.
You are now entering the original Lincoln, Nebraska. First named Albion after the ranch and hotel once located here, the name changed to honor Abraham Lincoln. It was called Lincoln when the first post office was located here, around 1862, and later the name changed again to Timberville, after Timberville Lake which was near by. The town died in 1868 after Ames began. Through here passed the Mormon Trail, the Overland Trail and the military road to Fort Kearny.

One half mile (8 miles.)
Ames.
Ames is the home of Research Unlimited, a fine establish-

ment founded by one of the best treasure-hunting guides and historians in the area.

*Take county road and go **five miles north** out of Ames to the Jamestown site.*

Here was once the town of Jamestown, founded by two men named Jim. The town thrived from 1870 to 1880. Through here was the Indian trail that Major Stephen Long followed on his exploration voyage of the West. Near here the expedition camped for several nights in the early spring of 1820.

Eight miles (1 mile.)
North Bend.
Junction with State Highway 79.
Settled in the 1850s by Scottish.

Go south here one half mile to the banks of the Platte on State Highway 79. To the west, Indian Peak is visible. Now, for most people that hill is not a peak, but for some local folks, and especially pioneers longing for the mountains of Oregon, that hill and its neighbors became a "peak" and a "range of peaks."

Indian Peak got its name from an incident that happened there long ago. In the early days, a group of Indians came up the Platte to hunt for beaver. While at this place, the chief's son became sick and died. They buried him on top of Indian Peak. In the spring they returned to take his body back to their homeland near Council Bluffs. For many years thereafter, Indians passing this point would pile stones and bring food and water to feed the spirit of the dead boy.

This small area, known as Morse Bluff, was settled by Czechs. The majority of the Czechs who settled the Great Plains were "freethinkers," those with no ties to organized religion. The growth of the freethinkers was fostered through a variety of associations. Among these organizations disputes broke out and other organizations were formed. In this area the Western Bohemian Fraternal Association was founded in 1897. The lodge at Morse Bluff was created in 1880 and reorganized under the new association in 1897. The present hall was built in 1911. Although there were disagreements, most of the associations had the goals of providing mutual life and health insurance, fellowship, community service and education.

For sites north out of North Bend on State Highway 79, see also the entry for sites north out of Fremont on US Highway 77.

US Highway 30

One mile (5 miles.)

In 1856, the first pioneers in the area settled near here. From this point to Schuyler (14 miles) the highway parallels both the Mormon and Overland Trails, which were just south of the highway.

Five miles (9 miles.)

Go north, five and a half miles.

On this creekbed Major Stephen Long and his expedition camped on their way to the Rockies. Also, a post office with the enticing name of Purple Cane stood here in the 1870s. This was also the route of a well-traveled east-west Indian trail.

Nine miles (17 miles.)

Schuyler.

Schuyler and Colfax County were named for Schuyler Colfax who was the Vice President of the United States when both the town and the county were formed in 1869.

Schuyler, the county seat, was at one time a ripsnorting cowboy town. This town was the first town on the Union Pacific Railroad, from which Texas cattle were shipped east.

The town still carries the predominantly Irish and Bohemian makeup it has held since it was founded.

In the 1860s, a wagon train moving west over the Mormon Trail through here reported that three or four Indians came riding over a hill, waving their arms and shouting.

The emigrants slowed their teams, but kept moving, their hands tightening on their guns "in case this meant war." It was the first time these travelers had ever seen Indians on their home land, and they were a bit frightened.

The Indians came closer and the whites began to understand what they were shouting was "tobacco." The Indians saw the pioneers and were running low on tobacco, so decided to ask for some.

The travelers told the Indians they didn't have any tobacco, and the Indians rode off. Now why this story survived over 120 years is unknown, but it seemed like an important thing to pass on.

The Old Oak Ballroom, a building some consider to rival the State Capitol for beauty, is located in Schuyler. It was built in 1937 by the WPA program. The gigantic roof-beams were cut from local oak, and native rock was used for the walls. The Ballroom is at the entrance to Community Park, on the Mormon Trail.

The Schuyler Historical Society is here, as well as many fine small parks.

Seventeen miles (7 miles.)

Columbus. Junction with US Highway 81.

Columbus is the county seat of Platte County and was first settled by the whites in 1856, folks from Columbus, Ohio.

The location near the confluence of the Loup and Platte rivers made the town a natural stopping place for settlers moving West. Ezra Meeker and many Mormons paused here on their way West.

Two prominent Indian fighters from the 1870s were from Columbus — Major Frank North and Captain Luther North. Frontiersman Frank North, when not working ranches with his pal William F. Cody, organized crack units of Pawnee Indians to serve as guides to the Army as well as bodyguards for men working on the railroads. From 1864 until 1876, Columbus was the center for these units under North's command.

Luther North lived in Columbus until his death in 1935 and could be counted on to tell tales of the Indians and his brother's exploits with Buffalo Bill Cody.

Columbus is the headquarters of the vast Loup River Public Power District. The dams, canals and electrical plants that cover a 200-mile area were a project of the 1930s. Today, these projects provide some of the water recreation in the area.

In Columbus is Glurs Tavern, a National Historic Site. Glurs is believed to be the oldest tavern west of the Missouri River. The tavern has been in existence since 1879, and except for prohibition days, when it still served as an entertainment and social establishment, has been serving the thirsty of Platte County continuously. In 1887, Buffalo Bill strolled into the bar, whipped out a thousand dollar bill, and bought rounds for the house. The place boasts of its small playground for children, who are not required to show I.D. cards in order to have a root beer.

The Platte County Historical Society is centered in Columbus and their museum is at 29th Ave. and 16th Street.

One little-known fact of the area is that Buffalo Bill's Wild West Show held rehearsals for its first show at Columbus. The show was to open after a dress rehearsal near Grand Island, in May of 1883.

At the rehearsals Buffalo Bill insisted on authenticity, which, according to him, meant that the stage had to have a half-wild and unbroken team of mules to power it. The hired Pawnees swooped into the arena on cue to "attack" the stagecoach. Onboard was the Mayor of Columbus, Pap Clothier, and other dignitaries. The mules bolted at the rifle shots and began to stampede. The Indians, sensing they had some good actors to deal with, intensified their war whoops. Buffalo Bill joined in trying to stop the stage. The mayor, when he finally came out of the shredded stage, had to be restrained from beating Cody to a pulp.

The Mormon Trail followed the Loup River west of Columbus, and the Platte River eastward.

Just to the south of Columbus, on US Highway 81 is the site of one of the oldest historical events in Nebraska history. On August 14, 1720, a Spanish Conquistador from Santa Fe, Pedro deVillasur, and his men were attacked by over 2,000 Pawnee. Over 40 of his men were killed and the party retreated to the Southwest.

For more information about deVillasur and the surrounding area, see entries for US Highway 81 and State Highway 92.

Seven miles (10 miles.)

Duncan. Small village between here and there.

For the next 22 miles the road closely parallels the Platte River, and offers fine views. Across the river was the Oxbow Trail, and its route is still followed by an occasional county road.

Ten miles (14 miles.)

Junction with State Highway 39.

For information to the south, please see entry for US Highway 81.

North on State Highway 39 to the Mormon Trail and Genoa, site of the last great concentration of Pawnee ever held. For more information about this area, please see the entry for State Highway 14.

Fourteen miles (10 miles.)

Junction of State Highway 92.

Take 92 east, two miles to the site of a Pawnee Village. See entry for State Highway 92 for further information.

Ten miles (9 miles.)

Central City.

Central City was first named Lone Tree after the large cottonwood tree that grew, solitary and brave, on the bank of the Platte. This tree was on the Oxbow Trail and the Overland Stage Route, which connected people who crossed at Council Bluffs with the Oregon Trail. The tree died, mainly due to tourists carrying away bits and pieces of the trunk, and the town moved a few miles away to the

330

present location of Central City. A concrete monument of the tree...supposedly designed to look a lot like the original trunk of the tree (all that stood for the last several years of its life) now marks the spot, **three miles** straight south out of Central City.

One of the earliest settlers of this area was the Hord family, who originally settled in Virginia in 1654, moved to Wyoming, and finally settled in Merrick County after buying up a good part of the area. Hord's eleven ranches held as many as 50,000 cattle and 90,000 head of sheep. He got a lot of his livestock by sending men down to Mexico where they would procure (we mean "steal") cattle for his ranches. He also owned lumber mills, coal plants and feed outlets in as many as 25 Nebraska towns.

According to a member of the the local Merrick County Historical Museum, "the Hord family made a great many contributions to this town and area" besides providing cattle from Mexico.

After the eldest Hord died, his family donated his 19-room house to the city of Central City for a hospital. The Merrick Manor Retirement Home is now on this site.

Central City was once called the irrigation capital of the world back in the days when people knew what an artesian well was and before they had heard of $30,000 Briggs and Stratton pumps.

The Merrick Museum is in Central City and is located in a fine old Victorian home. Some of the displays in the house are fixed to remind one of a home 100 years ago.

Central City is an important literary town for it is here, and in the area around the town, that America's foremost novelist of the last 30 years, Wright Morris, has set many of his finest novels.

When people who have read his works are talking about him, you are likely to hear things like "why this guy hasn't won a Nobel Prize, I'll never know..." Or, "this guy is the best writer in America, it is a shame he isn't known by everyone.."

One of this master's best novels is a work called, appropriately enough, *Ceremony at Lone Tree.* If you are a tourist and haven't read this wonderful work, or any work by Morris, rush to your nearest library or bookstore and get something, anything he has written. If you are a Nebraskan and haven't read Wright Morris, shame on you!!!

Nine miles (14 miles.)

Near here the Mormon Trail rejoined the Platte River for its westward journey. It swung north here to take the easier route down the Loup River, eastward, until it rejoined the Platte near present-day Columbus.

US Highway 30

Fourteen miles (2 miles.)

On the county line between Merrick and Hall Counties is a marker commemorating the California Overland Trail. This was also the Mormon Trail. The road was used by the migrating Mormons, gold seekers and Oregon pioneers.

Three quarters of a mile south of here, and a mile east is the site of a sad battle. In 1868 two men had left their sons on the banks of the Platte in order to proceed to the Loup River to hunt elk. When the men returned a few days later they found that the boys had been killed, and all their supplies had been taken. This was during the Sioux hostilities, when the Sioux were making a last great stand to save their traditional homeland.

Two miles (5 miles.)

Grand Island.

Junction of US Highways 281 and 34 and State Highway 2.

This location was known for a long while for the large island that was formed when the nearby Platte River broke into a couple of channels around a large mass of land.

The fur trappers who wandered this way in the 1700s from Canada used the island as a well-known site for navigation through the wilds. Members of John Jacob Astor's party reached "an island about seventy miles in length which they presumed to be Grand Isle." This was in 1812. Stephen Long, who explored the western states in 1820, passed this way as well.

Soon after these early explorers, the American fur trappers followed their trails to the fur streams of western Nebraska and Colorado. The famous explorer John Fremont wrote these words on September 19, 1842, while camped about where Grand Island is today: "I can not write because of the mosquitoes..."

Grand Island was formed when a "town company" set out from Iowa to find a spot to build a town that would make them some money. They wanted land to the west of the Missouri, and land that might eventually sit in a good spot for a rail line — the lifeblood of pioneer communities.

A group of settlers came out this way in 1857 and staked homesteading claims and then assigned a part of their claim to the company for a share of the hoped-for profits.

There was a financial panic in 1857 and that, combined with a few other factors, made the original plan fall apart. Still, there were now settlers in the area that would one day become known as one of Nebraska's finest cities.

Many of the earliest non-native settlers in this area were Germans who settled on prosperous farms on the good earth of the Platte Valley.

Grand Island, capital of the United States of America. Impossible? Well, that's what a great many people had planned on for a long while. By 1866, the railroad did make it near where the land company had scattered its settlers. By then, the idea of a city located near the center of the United States, which would make travel from each coast an equal burden and would make protection from outsiders an ease, was growing in the minds of a number of enthusiastic settlers. Grand Island, the nation's capital! There was a concentrated effort to lobby the powers in Washington to make just such a change.

The idea may seem absurd to us, but such a move is common even today in countries like Brazil and others. Think of it, think of the possibilities: instead of standing, as you are now, in a pleasant town full of friendly children and reasonable men and women, you could be in the nation's capital! Instead of smelling the faint, earthy odor of the stockyards on the edge of town, you could be watching Congress pass laws! Instead of spending your hard-earned money on a vacation through Nebraska, you could be watching the Pentagon spend it for you! Why, instead of touring the sugar plant where that white, sticky sweet stuff without any nutritional value is manufactured, you could be touring the President's mansion where...well, never mind — their plan fell on the usually deaf ears of the policy makers anyway.

There is much to see in this overllooked city of Nebraska. Grand Island even has a growing artists' community just to the north of the railroad tracks near downtown. Yes, there are those writers and artists who would prefer the quiet streets and friendly faces of the Midwest to the hustle and bustle of a New York, or to the satin and silk of an L.A.

Stolley State Park is at the southern edge of town, on Stolley Park Road. The trees that originally defined this park were planted by William Stolley, who built a farm and made a fort here on the banks of the Platte River in 1857. Remnants of Stolley's efforts at bringing his kind of civilization to the plains is still evident here. Stolley had worked for a naturalist before coming west and believed in foresting the plains. He single-handedly planted 6,000 trees in 1860 alone.

US Highway 30

In 1864, the Sioux increased their attacks on pioneers traveling the California trails. Stolley built his own fort, called Fort Independence, here. It was made of wood, but surrounded by sod to ward off flaming arrows. It had a 90-foot-long underground stable and was quite large. The reconstruction was built in 1940.

Grand Island is also the site of one of the state's finest museums. The Stuhr Museum of the Prairie Pioneer is just south of town at the junction of US Highways 281 and 34.

The Stuhr Museum is dedicated to the memory of the pioneer and strives to keep that memory alive in its exhibits and rides. The main building introduces the visitor to the culture and times of the pioneers. The unusual and beautiful buidling was designed by architect Edward Durrell Stone and includes an art gallery, gift shop and displays.

On the vast grounds is "Railroad Town" a re-created pioneer settlement. Over 60 buildings were moved to the site and restored, including the cottage where actor Henry Fonda was born in 1905.

A replica of a Pawnee earth lodge, complete with furnishings, is also at Stuhr.

The antique farm and auto exhibit features 200 pieces, including an 1880 threshing machine and many horse-drawn machines.

If all of this weren't enough, the museum also has an operating turn-of-the-century steam train, which provides rides through the complex and past the buffalo preserve.

The Stuhr, which charges an entrance fee, is one of the state's finest museums.

According to historian and author John Sorensen's book, *Our Show Houses: The history of movie theaters in Grand Island, Nebraska,* the town was home to a number of fine art deco theaters. One, the Capitol, was an "atmospheric" theater, which meant that such things as mood-creating incense, cloud machines, stuffed birds suspended above the audience, a pond in the foyer and electric-powered stars in the ceiling created an atmosphere appropriate for the movie about to be shown. Of the town's classic theaters' only the Grand remains.

The great movie actor Henry Fonda was born in Grand Island in 1905. His home is preserved at the Stuhr Museum (see above.)

334

During one night in August of 1965, a rash of UFO sightings was made. Reports came from Air Force bases and weather stations and individuals from Oklahoma to South Dakota and from several places in Nebraska. Several people in Grand Island were among those who saw the strange lights in the sky.

Turn on Blaine Road to the site of Blunk's Mill. This was one of the larger water-powered grist mills in a good distance. It was a mile-long mill race that created a 10-foot drop in the water to create power to turn the waterwheel. It started operation in 1877 and soon gained a reputation as one of the best, and cheapest, mills around.

For more information about Grand Island and the sites in this area, please see the entries for US Highways 281 and 34, Interstate 80, and State Highway 2.

Five miles (8 miles.)

Alda.

In 1883, a school teacher was brought to trial here for assault and battery because, it was claimed, he whipped one of his pupils a bit too much. The courtroom was so crowded with the curious that a new room had to be found. During the trial the defendant was out on bail and continued to teach. The case ended in a hung jury. The case gained considerable statewide publicity.

Just south of this village is an historical marker placed to mark the California Overland Road. This road was used by gold seekers and pioneers and connected with the Oregon Trail at Fort Kearny. A hundred yards or so of the ruts can still be seen stretching southwest of the marker.

From here to Grand Island to the east and Gibbon, 22 miles to the west, the Mormon Trail followed the north bank of the Wood River.

Eight miles (8 miles.)

Wood River.

The town was formed with the coming of the railroad. When the railroad decided to move, the town moved too. The older town site is at the Catholic cemetery.

This was an important town on the road to California gold fields, now generally known as the California Overland Trail. All along the general route of US 30 were also road houses and farmers who enjoyed a brief boom by supplying travelers with fresh eggs and butter.

335

US Highway 30

For more information about this area please see entry for State Highway 11.

Eight miles (6 miles.)

Shelton, on the Hall/Buffalo County line.

Near here passed the Mormon Trail. During the early settlement of Salt Lake City, the Mormons were seldom able to afford oxen to pull their belongings to the promised land. Instead, and at the insistence of the church's leader, Brigham Young, the faithful pulled handcarts across the west. These carts were usually pulled by four adults, men and women, while the children and old walked.

The town of Shelton began when some English converts to Mormonism broke an axle on their handcart. They camped here and soon decided the axle could not be fixed. They built a hut on the banks of Wood River in order to sit out the winter. Instead of returning east or going on to Salt Lake, they opened a store and settled here.

Except for those stranded in the high passes of the Rockies in winter, few perished as a result of the journey. Part of the reason was that other Mormons operated farms and supply points along the Trail to help those who came along. The first and most important of these was at Winter Quarters, now Florence (see entry for Omaha). Near here was the site of one such resupply point. The acres of corn and wheat were home to another family that didn't make it to Salt Lake City.

One of the first newspapers printed west of the Missouri, the *Huntsman Echo,* was started here in 1858.

Six miles (2 miles.)

Gibbon.

Free home sites and reduced railroad ticket fares brought a colony of 61 settlers to this area in 1871. An instant community was born, although many of these colonists lived in railroad cars for a long while. Gibbon Heritage Center, located in the old Baptist Church, is a museum containing artifacts of local history.

One item of local historical interest is that the television host and writer Dick Cavett was born here in 1936. Cavett's subtle humor and wit and his intelligent insights make him a rare talent in modern entertainment.

Two miles (4 miles.)

Near here was the home of James E. Boyd, who was the governor of the state from 1891-92. Also near here was a brewery,

336

which sold its kegs of beer to Fort Kearny for $6 each.

Four miles (7 miles.)

Junction with State Highway 10. South of here are many interesting historical sites. For information on these and other sites along this road, please see the entry for State Highway 10.

Seven miles (1 mile.)

Kearney.

Believe it or not, in the late 1880s a convention was held in St. Louis in order to make Kearney the capital of the United States. Folks must have decided that there was enough fertilizer around these parts without bringing in the politicians. In case you went to sleep during second-grade geography and have been asleep ever since, the effort, thankfully, failed. A similar effort was undertaken to make Grand Island the capital. (It also failed.)

Kearney and Kearny, for Nebraskans is the same thing. Both were meant to honor Gen. Stephen Watts Kearny, but someone, somewhere, began to misspell his name, so now, both spellings appear in various places. Kearney, the town, prefers Kearney.

Kearney is the home of several interesting museums and attractions. The Trails and Rails Museum is at 710 West 11th Street in Kearney. This fine museum is operated by the Buffalo County Historical Society and is located in the 1898 Union Pacific depot. It contains a fine collection of rare photos, diaries, letters and archives of the area's history. In addition, the first frame schoolhouse, built by the early Mormons, as well as the Freighters Hotel are on the museum's grounds. The museum, which is free to the public, is open during the summer months, and in winter by appointment.

The Old Baptist Church, corner of 22nd and 4th Ave. President Harry S. Truman attended services here during the 1948 Presidential campaign.

The Frank House is an example of Midwestern elegance at its best. It was built in 1889 to impress out-of-towners, and it still does.

West on 25th Street (Highway 30) to College Drive. North on College Drive, one block. The Kearney Canal and Power Plant was built in 1886 and is still producing electricity.

Downtown Kearney has many buildings constructed during the boom years from 1885 to 1925. Many of these have the date imprinted somewhere above the first floor.

The Kenwood area, from the west side of 8th Ave. south to 13th, contains many fine examples of Kearney's Victorian houses.

US Highway 30

The University of Nebraska at Kearney is at 25th Street and 9th Ave. Many of the buildings on the west campus once housed the State Tuberculosis Hospital.

Fort Kearny Museum is one block north and one block east of the Interstate 80 exchange. This museum contains items from Fort Kearny and the surrounding area.

Museum of Nebraska Art, 24th and Central Ave. This is an official collection of art about Nebraska or by Nebraskan artists, a fine and unique collection. It is located in the old Kearney Post Office, which is on the National Register of Historic Places. In 1991, the museum started an expansion and renovation project that added significant space to the facility.

The mission statement of the museum says they provide "a kaleidoscope of treasures reflecting times past and futures projected. A visual feast of continuously changing color, theme and texture enriching life with art."

The museum includes work by over 250 Nebraskan artists. Some of the works of William Henry Jackson, George Catlin, Robert Henri, George Lundeen, Aaron Pyle and Grant Reynard are on display. The museum is open Tuesday through Sunday afternoons and is closed for major holidays.

The museum of Nebraska Aviation is also located in Kearney, as is the Kearney Area Children's Museum at 2013 Avenue A.

Kearney is near the heart of the Crane migration area. Near here, thousands of Sandhill Cranes and many of the world's estimated 112 Whooping Cranes pass on their way south for the summer. On one April weekend in 1992, 45 Whooping Cranes were sighted.

There are many interesting historical and natural sites just outside of Kearney:

Two miles south of Kearney, on State Highway 44 and across the Platte River.

Location of 'Doby Town, which existed during Fort Kearny's heyday. Named because it was built of adobe bricks. Here was located a well-known house of ill repute.

Three and a half miles west of here was Platte Station, a Pony Express station. Near here also may have been another station known to early travelers as "17 Mile Station."

Two miles east on State Road L-50 East to Fort Kearny. This

338

fort serviced the area from 1848 until 1871.

It served as headquarters for the military in western Nebraska for a good part of that time, and also as a reassuring sight to travelers along the Oregon Trail.

An "old" Fort Kearny had been built near Nebraska City, but it was soon clear that such a location had little value in protecting citizens on their way west along the Oregon Trail. So, in 1848 the new fort was being built.

In addition to those heading for Oregon, the California Gold Rush of 1849 brought at least 30,000 travelers through the Fort's parade grounds.

The Pony Express had a "home" station here, and later a telegraph office. The fort grew larger, and its significance and importance along with its size. Finally, however, the bloom of the westward expansion was off, the Indian wars settled, and the railroad built. There was less and less of a reason for the soldiers to be stationed at this once critical point in America's great land. By 1871, the usefulness of Fort Kearny had largely been replaced by other forts, and this place was abandoned.

In 1928, most of the land was purchased from local farmers by the Fort Kearny Memorial Association, and eventually the area was made into a state park.

Along the banks of the Platte is the Kearney County Recreational Area and the Hike/Bike Nature Trail. Come on, get out of the car and see some of nature's beauty.

Continue **east on this road for seven miles,** When the road turns north to cross the Platte is Hook's Ranch, or Dogtown, a stage station and trading post at the junction of the Oregon Trail and the Fort Kearny Trail from Nebraska City. An early pioneer wrote "Dogtown is the first settlement west of Marysville and an ugly one at that." This is also the location of Valley Station, a later-day stage stop, and Lowell Cemetery, an early-day cemetery.

Along this stretch of county roads is the best place to view the early spring migration of the Sandhill Crane. This bird winters in South Texas and Mexico, and summers in northern Canada, but each year the entire flock of birds traverses a very narrow strip of land along the Platte River. You are now at the spot where the greatest concentrations of birds can be found. Bear in mind that the birds are very easily frightened, and contrary to what most people think, your car makes a *much better blind than approaching them on foot. The birds are less likely to scatter when seeing a car than when seeing a person on foot.*

The sandhill's deep honking, rattling call is distinctive, and is often how one first knows the birds are near. Some of the estimated 112 Whooping Cranes left in the world travel with the sandhills. The whoopers are easily distinguished from the sandhills, even at a great distance, because of their bright, all white feathers. For more information about sites in this area, please see entry for State Highway 10.

One mile (1 mile.)

This location was once the site of a cotton mill, a sight not particularly common in Nebraska. Legend has it that a group of investors planned to harvest the "cotton" from cottonwood trees and mill it here. Truth of the matter is cotton was shipped here from Texas where it was processed into denim for the China trade. Cottonmill Park provides a little recreation for the weary traveler.

One mile (5 miles.)

Stop. Look east. Look west. This was known as the 1733 spot to early travelers because it was purported to be 1,733 miles to San Francisco and 1,733 miles to Boston.

Five miles (7 miles.)

Near here the first Mormons heading west sighted their first buffalo. This is the start of the area that held the massive herds of buffalo.

Seven miles (8 miles.)

Elm Creek.

Home of Chevyland USA. Yes, folks. Just what you think. A vast collection of Chevrolet cars.

Eight miles (11 miles.)

Overton.

South five miles to a "T" intersection across the Platte River. A half mile to the east of this intersection was the campsite of the ill-fated Fletcher Cotton wagon train.

On the night of August 7, 1864, the wagon train pioneers stopped to camp on the banks of a small stream. This was near the popular camping ground for pioneers known as Plum Creek.

The next morning the group moved out and started west over the Oregon Trail. They were never to make it to the next evening alive.

You can follow their movements.

*Drive **west from this "T" intersection exactly two miles.** It was at this spot where the party was attacked by Indians, probably Republican Sioux. All 11 men were killed and a woman was captured by the Indians. Nearly a year later she was found by a trapper up on the Powder River who traded for her. She was finally returned to her home in Iowa.*

The remains of those killed were buried near here, one and a half miles to the east of the monument. Plum Creek Cemetery, one and a half miles west and a quarter mile north, includes many pioneer graves as well.

***One half mile northeast** of the cemetery, on the banks of Plum Creek, was the Plum Creek Station, which was the only station between Julesburg Colorado and Fort Kearny that was not destroyed during the Sioux uprising of 1864. All 14 people at the station were scalped, however. They were buried at the Plum Creek Cemetery as well.*

For other sites in this area, please see the entry for US Highway 183.

Eleven miles (4 miles.)
Lexington.

Lexington was founded after a Pony Express station and trading post known as Plum Creek (see above for Overton) started to grow.

The railroad came by on the other side of the river and the people moved north across the Platte and renamed their location after the battle of Lexington. (O.K., smarty pants, in what war was the battle of Lexington fought? Answer at the end of the paragraph.) Lexington had a reputation for being a pretty rough and tumble town as many gamblers and thieves held out here preying on pioneers headed west, and rich miners heading back east. After a long while, the citizens took the law into their own hands and drove the banditos out.

The Battle of Lexington was in the American Revolutionary War.

Lexington is home to the Dawson County Historical Museum. The museum folks like to think that they offer travelers much more than other sites in the state. One measure of this is that they have full-time and part-time employees and have been here since 1970.

Junction with US Highway 283. Please see entry for that road for sites along its route.

***Two miles south** on County Roads to Power Plant Number*

341

2. During the winter months this has become the residence of migrating bald eagles. They roost in the neighboring woods and hunt the open waters in the surrounding areas. The Central Nebraska Public Power and Irrigation District has opened the area to allow for public viewing of the eagles. Inquire locally for details.

In the spring the migration of Sandhill Cranes can be seen in the area as well. Best time is from early March through mid-April.

Four miles (1 mile.)

At this point in 1867 on the adjacent railroad tracks, the Cheyenne Indians, led by Turkey Leg, derailed a train by destroying a small bridge. They were upset by the presence of the train in their territory. They attacked the train crew, scalped them and raided the contents of the train. After finding boxes of cloth, the Indians tied one end to their ponies and galloped for miles, stringing the colorful material behind them.

One mile (4 miles.)

Junction with State Road L 24-A.

South on L 24-A two miles. Just as the road turns west, and just before the second bridge across the Platte, on the southeast side of the road is the site of the Willow Island Station stage stop, a place to get a wet drink and a change of horses before moving on.

Four miles (6 miles.)

Near here in 1847 a group of Mormons led by Brigham Young came across a gigantic herd of buffalo. The herd stretched from the river to the distant bluffs and beyond.

The entire countryside in every direction was black with the beasts, and one member estimated that at least 10,000 were in the immediate vicinity.

Herds 50 miles long and 25 wide, which took days to pass a given point, were not uncommon before 1860.

Six miles (10 miles.)

Cozad.

Cozad is located smack dab on the 100th meridian. This is the line many consider to mark the start of the true American West. (Or, for you Easterners, the start of the true American East!) It seems like a good candidate. From here to the west things seems to open up — crop lands are traded in for sage lands; crowded and bustling cities for open and endless skies. The land itself just appears to change around this point, and there seems to be a change, too, in the very air.

Cozad had at one time been the spot where the Union Pacific continental railroad tracks were to have joined. It didn't work out that way, so don't go looking for golden spikes anywhere.

Aside from naming a town after himself, the town's founder, John Cozad, bought 40,000 acres of land and started planting hay and selling lots for a new town in 1873. He believed the fine air around these parts would cure any ill. Cozad soon built a brickyard and a hotel. The hotel held new settlers while their houses were being built from Cozad's bricks.

Cozad was a good example of a frontier town's smooth man. He was a gambler and quite a cut-up with the ladies. Cozad shot a man in town one gloomy day. Those who were there said he did it in self-defense, and a later investigation bore this out.

However, those were touchy days, and it never took much for a town to find an excuse to get a mob together for a lynching. Cozad, afraid for his life, gathered up his family and left his hotel and his brickyard and his town. Seems he headed east of the 100th meridian, changed his name and dropped into obscurity.

That seemed to be that until one of Nebraska's greatest writers, Mari Sandoz, started to investigate Cozad's history and wrote a book, *Son of the Gamblin' Man,* which tells the story of this fascinating character's life. Other local historians, including Harry Allen, did much of the background work to discover the true story of what happened to the Cozads after they left town.

Cozad's son, Robert Henry, became quite well known as an artist, going by the name of Robert Henri, and an entire movement in American art, "The Ashcan School," was based on his non-traditional realism.

Just west on 8th Street off Highway 21, exit 222 from I 80.

The town's most beautiful and interesting attraction is the Robert Henri Museum and Historic Walkway. This was originally the hotel Robert Henry's father had built, and was Robert Henry's boyhood home. The museum is connected to several other of Cozad's famous landmarks by a walkway.

Many a child, traveling cross-country, has stood in front of the original Pony Express station and had their picture snapped by doting parents. A century-old school house as well as the old country church are a part of this tour.

A local author, Betty Menke, has written an enjoyable and entertaining account of the Cozads and Cozad's history, which is available at the museum and in local stores. The book's dollar and a half price is a steal.

Ten miles (5 miles.)
    Gothenburg.
    Gothenburg Pony Express Station is in Ehman Park along State Highway 47. Used as a Pony Express station from 1860 to 1861 and later as a stop for the Overland Stage. Small museum, free, open most days.
    The reconstructed station in Gothenberg is for tourists...to see where the Pony Express route was you must travel **south three miles** (see below) and then go **east one mile** to the Midway Pony Express station. The station building there, now a ranch building, is the real thing.
    Old Brown House Doll Museum, 1421 Avenue F, Gothenburg (1/2 block from Pony Express station). Museum of dolls and toys, small admission, open most days in all seasons but winter.
    Lake Helen is on the north edge of Gothenburg on State Highway 47. It was originally built in the 1890s as a reservoir for factories the town hoped would be built nearby. The economic panic of 1893 put an end to those great plans, but the lake remained. It is now a park.

*   Hiles Canyon is **5 miles south** of Gothenburg on State Highway 47. Named after early-day ranchers who had their Kokomo Horse ranch here. Kokomo was a famous racing horse. The owner of this ranch and beautiful canyon was the first Gothenburgian (if that is what they are called) to own and fly an airplane.*

*   Midway Station is **two miles south** of the Platte River on State 47. At this juncture there is a county road leading east. Take this road **one mile east** to the Midway Stage Station, which still stands.*
*   The cedar log house was used as a home station for the Pony Express as well as an Overland Trail Stage stop and a trading post. The building has two distinct types of log construction: the western half is a post and sill type construction, and the eastern part, a later addition, is a saddle and rider design.*
*   This little building has quite a literary history as it is mentioned in Mark Twain's* Roughing It, *as well as Charles Dawson's classic* Tales of the Oregon Trail.
*   The Midway station was so named because it is midway between Kearney, Nebraska, and Laramie, Wyoming.*
*   Ruts from the Oregon Trail are visible in the area.*

Five miles (8 miles.)

To Interstate 80.

Three miles southwest of here was the Gilman's Ranch, which served as a stage station for travelers on the Oregon Trail. The ranch had an iron pump, which was a novelty. Ask at Gothenburg locally for directions.

Eight miles (9 miles.)

Brady.

This is beautiful country, with the cottonwood-lined banks of the Platte and the wild hills to the north and south. This land seems unspoiled since the earliest times.

*One can follow the route of the Oregon Trail by going **south, one mile** past the Interstate, and then turning west. Follow the county roads as they zigzag westward and watch for historical markers, signs of the ruts from the trail and other sites all the way to North Platte.*

Nine miles (14 miles.)

Maxwell.

*South of **Maxwell, two miles to Interstate 80 and then south one and a half miles** to Fort McPherson National Cemetery. This is the most peaceful rest stop along the Interstate, no pun intended. Stop here and sit in the cool shade of the trees of this lovely, although isolated, final resting place for so many dearly loved fathers and sons.*

*Continue **south 1/2 mile** to the site of Cottonwood Springs stage stop and Oregon Trail station. This was one of the most widely used stops on the way west due largely to the springs just south of here. The state maintains a Special Use Area one mile south in the canyon.*

This was also the site of Fort McPherson.

*Go **west of here seven miles** to a tall hill known as Sioux Lookout. The view from the monument there is breathtaking. You can't get lost, the county roads to the northwest all head there.*

*Return to the south bank of the Platte River and take the county road **west eight miles** to the Fremont Slough State Special Use Area. One half mile west of here was a well-used ford across the river.*

Fourteen miles (13 miles.)

North Platte.

US Highway 30

Junction with US Highway 83, Interstate 80 and State Highways 70 and 97. For more information, and for information about sites along that highway, please see entry for US Highway 83 and Interstate 80.

North Platte is a fine larger city with a lot going for it. The tidy and interesting downtown area has a variety of shops and stores for the curious. Those seeking a less unique experience might find the shopping malls that ring the city more appropriate.

Museums here include the Railroad Museum and a western heritage museum.

This is the home of the Lincoln County Historical Museum (2403 N. Buffalo). The museum has several interesting buildings, including the old Brady depot, a Lutheran church from Hershey, a one-room schoolhouse and a log home. In addition, a few of the markers that once marked both the Mormon and Oregon Trails have been brought to the museum for safekeeping.

The museum is located on the way to the Buffalo Bill Ranch known as Scout's Rest, a State Historical Park. The ranch home that was once owned by Buffalo Bill is preserved here. He built the home during the peak of his popularity with the Wild West Show in 1886. An addition was built onto the rear of the house in 1909. The Cody family lived here until 1913 when the need for cash forced him to sell his ranch lands.

Sixteen acres of the original land he owned here is encompassed in the park. Follow US Highway 30 on Rodeo Road just west of town and then follow signs.

The expansive Bailey yards, the largest railroad complex in the United States, is located in North Platte. There is an observation area and tours of the area are available.

The North and South Platte Rivers join just east of North Platte.

On November 7, 1958, during a worldwide rash of UFO sitings, a TWA pilot reported seeing a bright, lighted object flying at incredible speeds over North Platte.

One of the inviting aspects of North Platte is that this town, which offers so many cultural and commercial opportunities, is located in the middle of one of the state's most isolated regions. A short drive in any direction from town will put the traveler in the open lands of prairie hills that look much the same as when the Sioux and Cheyenne roamed this area centuries ago.

South of town, on US 83, one and a half miles south of the

346

Interstate exchange, and just to the west was the Cold Springs Pony Express station.

Continue south on 83 three miles *to turn off for Mahoney Reservoir.*

Turn **east and go five miles, then north three miles** *to the 3,200-foot hill known as Sioux Lookout. This hill served as a lookout for the local Indians as they watched for buffalo, and for the whites moving along the Great Platte River Road. From this vantage point the Indians could signal hunters or warriors to attack. A statue of a proud Sioux in a double war bonnet was erected on the top of the hill in 1931, but vandals have destroyed much of the structure. Although the statue stands on public land, most of the routes up the hill are on private land. A move is under way to have the entire hill made into a state historical park.*

For other sites near here see entry for Maxwell, above. The county roads that zig-zag along the river to the southeast roughly follow the route of the Oregon Trail. For a refreshing break from the US Highway habit, take the **30 miles to the Brady turnoff.**

Thirteen miles (6 miles.)
Hershey.
Two miles south, *just south of the Interstate is Hershey Special Use Area and the site of the Fremont Springs Pony Express station.*

Six miles (12 miles.)
Sutherland.
Junction with State Highway 25 south. Please see entry for State Highway 25 for sites along this road.

Twelve miles (9 miles.)
Paxton.
North of here the large siphon tube that diverts water from the North Platte watershed to the South Platte is worth seeing. Paxton is also the location of a small museum in a reconstructed sod house. The bridge here across the South Platte is at the location of Ford Number 2, or Middle Ford, a popular crossing on the Oregon Trail.

Nine miles (3 miles.)
Along Highway 30 is a Pony Express Station marker. Alkali Lake Station was important to the Pony Express and to the military as a supply point. The station was located about one and a half miles

southwest of the marker, on the south bank of the river.

Three miles (8 miles.)
Roscoe. This was a crossing of the South Platte during the Oregon Trail days. This crossing was used by very early travelers in the 1830s, and by later travelers along the trail. It was not a common crossing.

Eight miles (9 miles.)
Ogallala.
Sure, the Big Mac is here in Keith County. Supporters of Lake McConaughy spout facts and figures like waterfalls. For a number of those facts, please see the entry for the lake in the entry for US Highway 26. But many people miss the true beauty of Keith County because they simply come for the lake and nothing else. The real beauty of the county lies away from the marinas and beaches.
Start in Ogallala, a place for most people to stock up on gas, cold drinks, junk food and bait. Instead of the convenience store tour of the city, take some time here.
The city park, on the northern edge of the city, is the finest place to get away from the roar of the Interstate for miles. Let the kids play on the swings here while you put together a large lunch. Lean against the trunk of one of the old cottonwoods and elms and fall asleep in the shade, serenaded by locusts.
On the way to the park (and yes, on the way to Big Mac, too) is the "Mansion on the Hill." This late Victorian house of brick was built in 1887 and is the oldest brick building in the area. It houses artifacts and displays of the town's exciting past. It is operated by the Keith County Historical Society.
The building cost $10,000 to build in 1887, although the brick was 16 inches thick and the stone trim had to be hauled from Lincoln. There are two fireplaces in the house and tile floors are from New Jersey. The stone near the front door was a carriage-step, which allowed folks to step out of carriages with a bit more grace.
Three blocks west of the park on 10th Street is Boot Hill. This was the original cemetery for the town, and in addition to some fine, upstanding citizens, many of the town's less desirable elements were buried here "with their boots still on." Usually the accommodations included a couple of canvas sheets between two plank boards. This is the place where the name "Boot Hill" for a cemetery originated.
The most curious story of this cemetery is that of Mrs. Lillie Miller whose perfectly preserved body was dug up 25 years after it

was buried here. Miller died in childbirth in the 1860s. Years later her body, and that of her child, were being exhumed for reburial at the new Ogallala Cemetery. Three of the workers passed out and a fourth ran from the site when their digging revealed Mrs. Miller's perfectly preserved body. Even the skin of her face appeared as soft and pure as the day she had given her life trying to give birth to her child. One of the great mysteries of this phenomenon was that the baby's body, which lay with Mrs. Miller, had not petrified. Mrs. Miller's remains were so heavy that a crane and a derrick had to be brought in to remove them from the site.

At the top of the hill is the gravesite of Rattlesnake Worley, a cowboy who was killed by an outlaw of the cowboy days over a nine-dollar bet in a game of poker.

By the turn of the century, most of Boot Hill had returned to sod and even the wooden markers that had located the graves had withered to dust. No marble or granite markers were placed in the original cemetery.

After the Civil War, Texas cattlemen sought new markets for their cattle, and started heading them north on newly plotted trials. The Texas Cattle Road wound up through the Texas Panhandle, across western Kansas via Dodge City, and ended — as much as such a haphazard route ended anywhere — in Ogallala. Cattle ranchers from Wyoming, Colorado and Nebraska met the cowboys from Texas to buy their cattle. Later, cattle were shipped east via the railroad. During the cowboy heyday (roughly the 15-year span, 1870-1885, although the trail was used until 1895) Ogallala was as typical a Wild West town as could be found on any Hollywood set. Its few permanent residents waited peacefully through the winter and spring until the first of the cattle drives arrived in May or June. Then more and more drives arrived until the streets were full of hundreds of trail-weary cowboys looking for a way to spend their hard-earned wages and to let off a bit of steam. Saloons, brothels, gambling parlors and flop houses lined the streets. On the river bottoms south of town, 15 herds of 3,000-5,000 head each milled about.

The "old" downtown was a strip of businesses that lined Railroad Street and serviced the three to four month boom season of cowboys and cattlemen. Ogallala's celebration of its wild past surely pales in comparison to what it must have been like in those wild days.

Front Street is a recreation of what the old town looked like. It is a block-long area of shops and stores and comes complete with a genuine re-created shootout every night during the summer in the parking lot behind the saloon.

In the current downtown, at the intersection of US 26 and 2nd Street, is one of those unusual places you can find every so often in places like Ogallala.

The city's Fantasyland is a gigantic display of animated creatures. There is nothing quite like this place anywhere else in the state. The displays were originally built for a department store in Minneapolis, then later purchased by the Brandeis store in Omaha. Finally the city of Ogallala bought the entire collection and housed it to resemble the Walt Disney book *Fantasyland*. Many of the displays were created locally. Now it cost a couple of bucks to get in here, but kids under 6 are free, which goes to show you the philosophy the city fathers had behind this place. It'll be a place to remember.

Also downtown is the Petrified Wood Gallery. Needless to say, the gallery is unique as are the music boxes made from the rock and crafted by local twin brothers.

Ogallala's Regional Arts Council is an active and strong arts organization, which has brought fine cultural programs and events to the area. The council sponsors an artist-in-residence program and ballet. Symphony and drama are regularly featured in Ogallala.

One mile due south of Ogallala, and just west of the road was Gill's Station, a Pony Express and military supply station. Both the Oregon Trail and the Pony Express Trail crossed the road approximately one half mile south of the Interstate exchange.

Nine miles (1 mile.)

Brule. Named after a branch of the Teton Sioux from the French word for the tribe.

One mile (3 miles.)

South of here, on the south banks of the Platte River, was a Pony Express station known as Diamond Springs Station. The building was made of cedar.

Three miles (6 miles.)

Oregon Trail marker. Just south of this marker on the South Platte was the Lower California Crossing, used by most of the pioneers headed west on the Oregon Trail. In those days the crossing was a dangerous one. The Platte sometimes could be a raging stream, and even in the best of times was 3/4 of a mile wide, swift and with quicksand that could bog down a wagon. Often several teams of oxen were used to pull a single wagon across the river at this spot. The Upper Crossing, used largely by freighters, was at Julesburg, Colorado.

On the south bank of the river was a small trading post known as Beauvais Station.

Just northwest of the highway is California Hill. This was one of the first large hills that the pioneers had to climb on their journey west, although it pales in comparison to hills they would later meet in Wyoming. The trail climbs 240 feet in a little over a mile and a half. Ruts are still visible on the hill.

Six miles (14 miles)
Big Springs.

The town of Big Springs may stick in the minds of some since it was the scene of a senseless and bloody bank robbery in the late 1960s. A lone gunman entered the bank and killed several people. A twisted and sad reminder of the violence that was once commonplace in the West.

The cowboy trails that passed through this area were active well into the 1910s, when most of the land still had no fences. That era is still an active part of the living memories of many local ranchers and citizens.

Fourteen miles (7 miles.)
Junction with State Highway 27 north. Please see entry for that highway for information about sites along its route.

Seven miles (10 miles.)
Chappell.

This is the county seat of Deuel County. The town was named for an early founder, the county for an Omaha businessman.

Chappell is also the location of the Deuel County Historical Society. The society operates a museum and the Sudman-Neumann Heritage House at the corner of 5th and Vincent. The home of German pioneers, it features elaborate historic furnishing, a room dedicated to local artist Aaron Pyle and items from the career of Congresswoman Virginia Smith.

The town is located on both the Oregon Trail and the Pony Express route and celebrates the fact with the Pony Express city park, which provides the modern immigrant a place for a quiet lunch.

Local sources say that Chappell Lake, near the Interstate

exchange, has great fishing.

This is the most productive wheat-raising area of the state, and shortly after the turn of the century the area was swarming with homesteaders who were claiming land under the new Kinkaid Act.

Chappell is located on Lodgepole Creek, and from here west both the Interstate and US Highway 30 follow the creek. It was so named because the Indians gathered their lodge poles from its banks.

Chappell is also proud of the Charles Chappell Library's art collection, which is one of the finest collections of art between Omaha and Denver. It was donated by Mrs. Henry Chappell in memory of her husband, who was a Union Pacific Railroad executive. The collection includes many Orientals and paintings by Aaron Pyle, a local artist who was a student of Thomas Hart Benton.

There are many stories of buried treasure along the Lodgepole. In bygone days, Cheyenne and Sioux raiders often attacked settlers in this area, and desperados robbed banks and trains. Such legends have led to persistent rumors of treasure buried along the creek. Although nothing has been found, neither have many been willing to seek out this isolated creek to search for riches.

Traces of the Oregon Trail ruts are numerous in the area. The Historical Society has marked the route through Deuel County and will direct the visitor to these sites. Trail ruts are visible adjacent to Interstate 80 exchange, a half mile south of town.

Ten miles (17 miles.)

Lodgepole.

Here is the location of Lodgepole Museum one block north of the highway. One mile south of town, the access road to I-80 crosses over the Oregon Trail. A bit closer to the Interstate, it crosses the Pony Express route. (By the way, the state's highest point is near here, at least according to the folks who live here, but don't mention this to anyone in either Kimball or Banner county.)

The area between Lodgepole and Sidney was well known for the numbers of train wrecks that happened here. The reason seemed to be the tendency of the engineers to open the throttle and let her go, and the poor quality of the early bridges. This was also the site of several armed robberies of trains by bandits, possibly including some by "Doc" Middleton.

Seventeen miles (3 miles.)

Sidney.

Junction with US Highway 385. Please see entry for US Highway 385 for information about sites along this highway.

Sidney was as close as you could get to the Black Hills by rail, and when gold was discovered there in 1876, Sidney became a boom town, serving as a jumping-off place for many of the strange characters the lure of gold brought out West. At one point, Sidney had 23 saloons in a one-block area. Nearly two thousand people passed through Sidney each day.

Train conductors usually announced the stop by saying, "Sidney...don't get off here if you want to live." A well-documented story has it that at one saloon where a dance was in progress a man was shot and killed. Rather than stop the dance, the party people simply propped the corpse up in a corner. Before midnight another man had been killed. His body was placed in the same corner. Before dawn a third man was killed and the dancers decided enough was enough. The party ended.

In the 1880s a man was lynched from a telegraph pole near the city's center in a grand case of misunderstanding. He was offered the choice of either jumping off the ladder, or having the ladder pulled out from under him. He chose to jump, saying, "I'll jump off gentlemen, and show you how a true man dies. Goodbye, one and all."

Doc Holliday, Luke Short, Bat Masterson, Wyatt Earp and Dr. Walter Reed all spent time in Sidney. Calamity Jane gave birth to an illegitimate child here.

Don't let this history scare you off, though. Sidney is a clean and proud town and boasts several churches, good restaurants and friendly people.

Legion Park and Memorial Gardens, 10 blocks south of Highway 30 on 10th Avenue. Three railroad cars are here, as well as a pond stocked with fish for the young anglers. It has sunken gardens, tennis courts and a swimming pool. At the intersection of the highway and 13th Avenue is Cabela's Wildlife Exhibit. The display contains over 200 specimens of wildlife.

Fort Sidney is located on Sixth Ave., just south of Highway 30. This is one of the most attractive and best run local museum sites. The staff has prepared brochures to explain the history of the fort, and are waiting to answer your questions. The museum is free and open all year round. Troops stationed here took part in the massacre at Wounded Knee when, as many claim, the Indian ceased to have an effect on the American West. The site includes the ammunition storehouse, barracks, and officer's quarters. The fort was established in 1867 and abandoned in 1874.

US Highway 30

This is the location of one of the best-known and most frequently retold ghost stories in middle America. One day in 1868, a young woman, the wife of one of the officers at the fort, was carrying a load of clean clothes up the back stairs in one of the dwellings in the officers' quarters. She looked up at a strange sound, lost her balance, and fell down the steep stairs. When her husband found her, her neck was broken, and her face was frozen in a ghastly look of fear.

The husband, overcome by grief, ordered that the service stairs be sealed off. A pantry was built over the new wall, and at the top of the stairs, a closet was built in a bedroom to seal off the staircase.

Nothing more was heard about the incident until the 1930s when, suddenly, visitors and residents in the quarters claimed they could hear footsteps, and the sound of something falling, coming from inside the walls.

An old citizen of Sidney, Melchoir Herbert, who had been a soldier at the fort, began to tell people that the explanation was easy: the place was haunted. No one believed his story about the hidden staircase. He died in 1958 at the age of 91.

The sounds continued, however, and in 1975, when the quarters were being renovated, a workman stuck his head inside some drawers in the pantry and discovered the staircase, which had been sealed for over a hundred years. Suddenly, old Melchoir Herbert's story seems to make more and more sense.

The sounds have continued to this day, and they most frequently occur during the month of October, which some believe is the month in which the poor young woman died.

The Upper California Crossing branch of the Oregon Trail enters Nebraska from Colorado along the same route as the present-day US Highway 385. It follows 385 to its juncture with Highway 30 and then the trail is along the south side of 30 and parallels it all the way to Sidney.

A later branch of the Pony Express route also followed this path.

At the western edge of the city a marker designates the Deadwood/Sidney Trail. After gold was discovered in the Black Hills this trail became a very busy stage route, moving passengers and freight from the railroad in Sidney to the gold fields in Deadwood, South Dakota.

During one night in August of 1965, a rash of UFO sightings was made all over the Midwest. Reports came from Air Force bases and weather stations and individuals from Oklahoma to South Dakota and from several places in Nebraska. During that night, Captain Lee Beekin and four other men of the Sioux Army Depot in Sidney saw several objects in the sky.

Listen to Captain Beekin's report: "They looked like a naval ship going through the sky. There was a large one and four smaller ones flying in a triangle. They were all white."

Three miles (3 miles.)

Iris Gardens. If you like iris, you'll love it here. Over 800 varieties are displayed.

Three miles (3 miles.)

Two miles north on spur S17A: Sioux Army Depot and a fine museum on the college campus.

This place was established in the 1940s to produce ammunition for the war effort. Many of the buildings can be seen from the highway.

The tri-state area here (Nebraska, Wyoming and Colorado) contains the largest concentration of Intercontinental Ballistic Missiles of any place in the world, including Russia. Scattered across this area are missile silos containing 200 Minutemen III missiles.

The combined firepower of the missiles in this area is enough to wipe out the northern half of the world six times over. The combined firepower of the missiles in this area is equal to 45 times all the bombs dropped in the entire World War II.

One hundred years ago, the Sioux fought the coming of the white man to their last breath. The Sioux believed in a vast power that would one day wipe out the earth. Let us all pray that they were wrong.

Three miles (6 miles.)

A rare glimpse of sod and rock houses, which were once, not so long ago, the main type of dwelling in the greater part of the state.

Six miles (2 miles.)

Gunderson Mill. On the south side of the highway is the site of a mill established in 1878. It was a 36-foot-square building and stood nearly 50 feet tall — quite a skyscraper in those days. It was the home of Snow Water Patent Flour...many would say a product far better than Powdermilk Biscuits.

Two miles (3 miles.)

Lodgepole Creek. They say that this creek is the longest creek in the world. That is if you define "creek" by saying it is smaller than a stream, larger than a slough and wetter than a wash.

The Point of Rocks to the north was a major landmark for travelers in the old days, and still is by those who travel this stretch of road regularly. The Sioux rolled rocks off of this mound to try to derail the trains that passed along here.

The point was used as a lookout for scouts keeping a watchful eye for those same Sioux as the railroad crews repaired track.

Just beyond here is a bend in the creek and the Hank Redington Ranch. The ranch is located on the Texas Trail — the trail up from the Lone Star State that was used for cattle drives to the railheads, the Black Hills and Montana. This ranch may have been the first ranch in the Panhandle.

Three miles (9 miles.)

Potter.

In downtown Potter (yes, there is a downtown) the Buffalo Bend Stageshow is an act you will not want to miss. This theater proves that artistic souls producing quality entertainment need not live in places like Lincoln or Hollywood. Shows are every weekend during the summer.

Potter is also the home of the Potter Museum.

The largest hailstone observed in the United States fell here on July 6, 1928. It was 17 inches in circumference and weighed nearly 2 pounds. Never mind it wiping out the corn crop, the watermelons were goners.

Nine miles (8 miles.)

Dix, in Kimball County. Kimball County is in wheat country, and chances are that's what you see growing all around the countryside. Alongside many fields are oil wells; more than 1,400 of them are in the county, drilled to depths of over one mile.

Nine miles (8 miles)

Kimball.

Junction of State Highway 71. Please see that entry for sites along its route.

Originally named Antelopeville, many people in Kimball are glad the name was changed to honor a vice-president and general manager of the Union Pacific Railroad.

The Plains Historical Society Museum is located at the corner

356

of Second and Chestnut in the old Knights of Pythias Woodmen Degree of Honor Royal Neighbors Hall (don't ask how such a name came to be). It was built in 1905 and was used for lectures, meetings and the first movies ever shown in Kimball.

This is also the location of the oldest building on Main Street, the Old Stone Store, built in 1894 at the then high wages of $1.00 per day for the construction workers. It has served as a store, a rooming house, a ballroom and a saloon.

Kimball has two parks to rest at, as well as a public swimming pool three blocks south of the stop light and then east of Sixth Street nine blocks. One block north and five blocks east of the stop light is a marker commemorating the Lincoln Highway. This road, built in the 1920s, was the first paved, coast-to-coast road. It followed the general route of the Oregon Trail and was used by daredevil drivers who for years had driven across the continent for sport.

Eight miles (13 miles.)

Oliver Lake, a state park for visitors of all ages.

Southwest of here on a rise in the distance is a spot 5,426 feet above sea level, the highest in the state (never mind folks in Banner County to the north who claim a spot in the outreaches of their county for the same honor. No one from the East Coast is going to imagine the state as anything but flat anyway, no matter what you tell them.)

Thirteen miles (0 miles.)

Wyoming border.

Zero miles (2 miles.)
Ogallala. Please see entry for US Highway 30 for information about Ogallala.

Two miles (25 miles.)
Junction with State Highway 61 north. Please see entry for State Highway 61 for information about sites along this road.

Ten miles to Lake C.W. McConaughy. Big Mac. The facts: It is 35,000 acres. It is Nebraska's largest reservoir, and therefore the state's largest body of water. Its dam is the longest dam of this type of construction in the world. The largest walleye caught in Nebraska, a 16 pounder, came from its cool deep waters. Many other record fish have been caught here. It has 105 miles of white sand beaches. It is the location of one of the largest open class inland sailing regattas in the U.S. Its shorelines offer crowded people-watching beaches, or remote campsites. Yes. It is all true. But one fact Big Mac fans often miss is that because of the lake more people pass through Keith County and see less than any other county in the state.

First of all, to really appreciate Keith County, to really fall in love with the place, go immediately to your local bookstore and buy a copy of one of the best books written in the state in the past 20 years, Keith County Journal by John Janovy Jr.

Next, drive away from the lake and see a number of the interesting sites around the place.

Twenty five miles (3 miles.)

Ash Hollow State Historical Park.

Over the surrounding hills and through this deep canyon passed the Oregon Trail. By the waters of these streams and springs, many thousands of pioneers camped. Although the stream is now no longer in its original stream bed, thanks to the construction of the highway, Ash Hollow is one of those places in the west where one can get a real sense of what it must have been like in the pioneer days.

But centuries before the Oregon and California settlers passed this way, the area was home to many Indian peoples, including the Dismal River People, ancestors to the Plains Apache. Traces of their life can be found here as well.

And even before that this land was home to prehistoric rhinoceros and mastodons. Their remains, too, have been found near here.

The park preserves a small rock shelter where evidence of human occupation has been found that dates back 3,000 years. The rock shelter is important because it helped scientists establish a time sequence for the occupation of the plains. Other sites in the park indicate that the area was used as much as 8,000 years ago.

The first whites to come this way were probably members of John Jacob Astor's overland party, which came by here in March of 1813.

In 1835, a daylong battle between the Pawnee and Sioux, traditional enemies on the plains of Nebraska, was won by the Sioux, and the Pawnee were forced to move down river to a place near present-day Grand Island.

As more and more people moved west, various routes over and around hills and other obstacles were tried. A bad crossing on the Platte at O'Fallons Bluff led pioneers to use a better spot known as Lower California Crossing, but that crossing sent the loaded wagons into Ash Hollow where they met with the steep Windlass Hill.

Two miles south of the Visitors' Center is Windlass Hill, one of the first main hills the pioneers faced moving west. To get down the hill some pioneers tied ropes to the wagons and then eased them down the hill by having several people pull against the rope. Others simply locked the brakes and skidded all the way down. Although the hill is steep, few serious accidents were recorded here.

The arroyo, or wash, that runs down the side of the hill started as wagon ruts over a hundred and thirty years ago. There are many pristine ruts still visible in this area.

A visitor's center in this fine state park will orient the traveler to the many interesting sites here. A path leads from the Center to the Rock Shelter, where there are exhibits as well. Be sure you ask for directions to the site of the trading post as well as the pioneer cemetery and other places of interest. Ask directions to the old Fort Grattan, where the Indians attacked an encampment of pioneers and suffered terribly for this action some months later.

Perhaps hundreds of people were buried in the area. According to Oregon Trail scholar and author Gregory Franzwa, who has written many fine books on the Oregon Trail, it is estimated that one out of every 17 people who started on the Trail died before reaching the coast. That would mean a gravesite on the average of every 193 yards.

Just at the north end of the park, and before crossing the river, a county road leads off to the west. Take this road **one and a half miles** to the grave of A. Kelly, who died on July 14, 1852.

Three miles (2 miles.)

Lewellen. Junction with State Highway 92 on the north side of Lake McConaughy. Please see the entry for State Highway 92 for more information about sites in this area.

Two miles (10 miles.)

Two miles west of Lewellen, Highway 26 crosses Blue Water Creek. See below for description of the Battle of Blue Water.

Twelve miles (16 miles.)

Oshkosh, and b'gosh Wisconsin ain't got nothing on us! Location of the Garden County Historical Society and the county seat of Garden County.

*Take the county road **east out of Oshkosh 7 miles** to the Blue Water Battlefield Overlook. At this creek in 1855, Little Thunder's band of Sioux was eliminated in retaliation for the Grattan massacre.*

The Brule Sioux Indians had been accused of killing Lt. John Grattan and 28 men. A few weeks earlier Grattan and his men had probably been killed when they approached some of Conquering Bear's band of Sioux. Grattan had been sent to find and arrest an unknown Indian who had been accused of killing a single stray cow.

As a result of the death of the cow, the government ordered all Brule to move to the south side of the North Platte River. Little Thunder's band did not move and so a force of nearly 1,000 soldiers set out to force them to move. They met about a mile upstream from here on September 3rd when the soldiers surrounded the village in the night. Some soldiers climbed the surrounding hills, while others worked their way up ravines from the Platte River.

With the daylight, the Brules, who had seen the soldiers coming but were cut off from a retreat, raised a white flag in order to talk. While the Brule leaders talked, soldiers deployed in a skirmish line and prepared for battle. With the white flags still raised, the line of soldiers opened fire, wounding the Brule leader Little Thunder and killing several women and children instantly. Since the village was virtually surrounded the death count for the Brules was very high. Many children died when they were trampled by the charging horses of the soldiers. Some of the Brule escaped, but many were killed or captured.

A few hours later the great Sioux holy man Crazy Horse, then about 13 years old, stumbled upon the ruined village and helped a surviving Cheyenne woman back to safety. Some believe that Crazy Horse's shock at seeing the mutilation of the Brule helped shape his life and create the great warrior and spiritual leader he eventually became.

Sixteen miles (14 miles.)

Lisco. Named after a rancher who owned over 30,000 acres in this area. South, across the North Platte River, was the Oregon Trail.

Fourteen miles (14 miles.)

Broadwater in Morrill County.

Morrill County was a critical one in the development of the American West as the Oregon Trail, the Mormon Trail, the Sidney to Deadwood Trail, the Black Hills Trail and one route for the Pony

US Highway 26

Express all passed through here, most of them along the banks of the North Platte.

In addition, several important landmarks of those trails are still visible today.

*Just **three miles east** of here are Ancient Bluff Ruins, an eroded sandstone bluff that was a well-known landmark for travelers on the Mormon Trail, since this was the first point where one could see Chimney Rock (don't strain, Chimney Rock was much taller, and the air less carbon-monoxided back then).*

***North** on the road out of Broadwater, about **5 miles** to the Cavalry Remount Station, used during the Indian Wars when Fort Robinson was in its prime. This was the location of a battle between soldiers and Indians. Inquire locally for exact location.*

***North two more miles.** Covalt Buffalo Herd. Ask for directions locally to view this fine herd ranging the grasslands much as they always have. Also on this road is the Nebraska Boys Ranch.*

*Cross the North Platte River at Broadwater and **continue west on State Highway 92** for one of the most delightful trips in the state. The road follows the Oregon Trail, and ruts and gravesites line this route. Please see the entry for State Highway 92 for more information about sites along this area.*

Fourteen miles (1 1/2 miles.)

Bridgeport, the county seat of Morrill County.

Bridgeport is near the spot where the early Pacific Fur Trading Company employees, on their way to Astoria on the Oregon coast, camped during the winter of 1812-1813.

In Nebraska, no accomplishment is too small, and Bridgeport boasts one of the largest, if not the largest International Harvester dealers in the world. If you have never been inside of a farm implement dealership, this is the one to see.

Bridgeport's State Recreation Area is a fine spot, and draws bird hunters from all over the Midwest because of its location on the flyway and the North Platte River.

The Bridgeport Museum is a must-see spot for travelers.

***Five miles south** of Bridgeport on State Highway 88: Jailhouse and Courthouse Rocks. These are two of the more significant natural markers on the Oregon Trail.*

There are two stories of how Courthouse Rock got its name.

362

One is that its shape suggested its name for the early travelers through the area. The other is that 12 outlaws were tried here, found guilty and shot to death on the butte's summit. Cowboys gave the name to nearby Jailhouse Rock, because, after all, what else is near a courthouse but a jail? The rocks actually looked different in pioneer days, as the Brule clay and Gering sandstone that forms the buttes weathers easily in the harsh Nebraska storms.

Many, many seasons ago a Pawnee warrior challenged the wisdom of his entire tribe. His grandmother, whom he dearly loved, had been left behind on the prairie as the tribe moved to their winter quarters. The tribe left these old ones to die when they felt such people slowed the movement of the rest. Storms, raging Sioux and the displeasure of his own people would not stop this warrior.

He rescued his grandmother from her lonely death-spot, and brought her back to the tribe. Soon after, the warrior was walking along the North Platte river when he found a great white horse, with fiery, pink eyes. It was said in the tribe that this great horse had been given to the warrior by the Great Spirits as a reward for saving his grandmother. From that time on the Pawnee began to change their custom.

With this great horse the warrior became famous in battles with the Sioux. With this great horse the warrior managed to run down three antelopes and kill them all with a single arrow. For this, he won the love of a chief's daughter. Before long the warrior gained the status as a wise and powerful man in the tribe. It was here, atop Courthouse rock, that this Pawnee wise man came to meditate and to receive the wisdom from the spirits of the other world. At this magic place then, the power of the Pawnee came to earth. Eagles and other dramatic birds roost on the rocks, perhaps carrying some of the Pawnee warrior's secrets.

The Pony Express route passed to the west of Courthouse Rock and joined the Oregon Trail just west of Bridgeport. Also to the west, along the creek bed, is a cliff that served as a post office for the travelers along the Oregon Trail. Here, under the words "Post Office" scratched into the sandstone, people left letters for those who were following behind them to find.

For a continuation of sites to the west along State Highway 88, see the entries for State Highway 92, US Highway 385 and State Highway 71.

Return to Bridgeport.

Two and one half miles (8 miles.)

Pioneer Cemetery. The ruts of the Oregon Trail are visible on either side of this cemetery. Paul Henderson, whom many consider to have been the greatest Oregon Trail scholar, is buried here within sight of the trail he loved. The first bridge across the North Platte River, the Camp Clarke Bridge, was built in 1876. This bridge was about three miles west of the present town, and Bridgeport was formed when the Burlington Railroad passed through the present site. The site is just north of here.

For the next several miles the Oregon Trail is to the north of the highway. Several trails important to the settlement of America's West come together here. The Oregon Trail, the Mormon Trail, the Pony Express Trail, the Sidney-Deadwood Stage Route and the continuation of the Texas Cattle Trail to Montana all pass near here.

Eight miles (1 1/2 miles.)

Eight miles past the cemetery, stop the car. Here is a spot commonly known as the Jackson Panorama.

William Jackson stood here and sketched the scene before him in 1866. In front of him were hundreds of wagons, and several separate wagon trains, stretched out along the clearly visible trail passing Chimney Rock. In 1931, Jackson used the sketch to paint a large watercolor of the scene. The sketch and the oil painting are on display in the Oregon Trail Museum at Scott's Bluff National Monument.

One and one half miles (3 miles.)

Just to the south of the highway is Facus Springs, a watering spot along the trail, and the place where an early settler, Facus by name, was shot and killed.

Three miles (3 miles.)

Junction with State Highway 92, west. Just to the west near State Highway 92 is Chimney Rock.

This tall and unusual-looking formation was the most often noted landmark on the Oregon Trail.

People who enjoy this kind of thing have located 97 individual references to the rock in pioneer diaries. Chimney Rock was probably first sighted by a white man in 1813 who was with a group of traders returning from Astoria on the Oregon Coast.

Pioneers scratched their names in the surface and camped near here, as this was such a noted point of the trail and such a geological curiosity. In addition, a dependable springs was located near the rock, which made for an ideal camping spot.

The sight of the monument meant that the easy part of the pioneers' journey was over and the long climb and hard struggle over the mountains of the west was about to begin.

In 1832, Captain Benjamin Bonneville wrote, "At this place was a singular phenomenon, which is among the curiousities of the country. It is called the Chimney. The lower part is a conical mound rising out of the naked plain; from the summit shoots up a shaft or column, about one hundred and twenty feet in height, from which it derives its name. The height of the whole is 175 yards and may be seen at the distance of upwards of thirty miles."

The tower is considerably shorter today than it was during the pioneer migrations. Wind, rain and even target practice have shortened it since the pioneer days.

Although Chimney Rock is a National Historic Site, the State Historical Society operates a small museum and visitor's center on State Highway 92 at its closest approach. In addition, county roads lead to its base.

In 1992, as a part of the state's 125th birthday celebration, donors could purchase a square foot of Nebraska on what what known as the Quasquicentennial Acre, or Q Acre, near here along the Oregon Trail. The money was used to support various Quasquicentennial events and toward funding for the visitor's center at Chimney Rock.

Use caution while hiking here since the area is famous for its rattlesnakes.

Just southeast of the base is an old cemetery with many unmarked graves believed to be from the migration time period.

Please see the entry for State Highway 92 for more information about the many interesting geological and pioneer sites in this area.

Three miles (13 miles.)

Bayard. Bayard's Cemetery holds several unmarked graves, which are believed to date to the days of the Oregon Trail. The Bayard area is known for its good trout fishing. Inquire locally.

Two miles south of Bayard and one and a half miles west on Oregon Trail Road to a commercial operation, the Oregon Trail Wagon Train, which offers cookouts, camping and covered wagon rides.

US Highway 26

Thirteen miles (8 miles.)

Minatare. Eleven miles north of here is the attractive Lake Minatare. See Scottsbluff, below, for further information.

Eight miles (2 miles.)

Just to the south of the highway is the site of Rebecca Winters' grave. This is a very well-maintained grave dating to the Oregon pioneer days along the Oregon Trail.

Rebecca Winters was a Mormon who died of cholera in 1852. Her final resting place is 15 feet north of the railroad tracks, just as the highway swings to the north and away from them. It is about a quarter mile from the parking area, picnic table and bronze marker erected by the state.

The Chicago Burlington and Quincy Railroad changed the route of its tracks to avoid disturbing the remains of Rebecca. As the crews were building the line they came across a small mound, and across the top was a wagon wheel with a plank. The plank had an inscription that read, "Rebecca Winters, age, 50 years." The engineer of the survey crew moved the tracks to leave the grave alone.

Little did they know that the words had been scratched there by a friend who had stayed up most of the night to see that her companion's last remains were marked.

For years the workers on the railroad would stop the train and place flowers on the grave.

In 1991, the great-granddaughter visited the site.

Two miles (8 miles.)

Scottsbluff.

This is the oasis of the Panhandle, many would agree. Friendly people, a cultured society, art, entertainment and history all await the traveler or resident at the Scottsbluff and Gering area.

As the highway enters Scottsbluff, Nebraska Western College is located on the eastern edge of the city. This is one of the largest colleges in the western part of the state. Its round buildings, resembling the pattern of green made by a pivot irrigation system, are unique.

The old Burlington depot is located at 14th and Broadway Streets. The Union Pacific depot is located on State Highway 71 in Gering (see below). At Scottsbluff's Riverside Park is the largest zoo in western Nebraska. It is **one mile south** of 26 on State Highway 71. It also offers camping. Scottsbluff is the location of the West Nebraska

Arts Center which offers exhibits of the art of the area.

The Scottsbluff/Gering area is hell-bent for promotion and has done a fine job in attracting businesses and conventions to the area. The towns boast several motels and quality restaurants and are proud of the area's interesting sites.

Ten miles NE of Scottsbluff is Lake Minatare State Recreation Area. Good fishing for walleye, perch and northerns. Public boat ramps and fishing. One unusual attraction is a lighthouse at the lake. Another are the windmills at Watson Ranch off State Highway 71. Near here are Nine Mile Creek and Sheep Creek, which offer good trout fishing.

Junction of State Highway 71. Please see that entry for sites north and south along this route.

Gering. Gering celebrates Oregon Trail Days during the third week in July to commemorate the first wagon train to reach the area. It is two days of fairs, food and horseshoe pitching contests.

The North Platte Valley Museum is at 10th and J Streets in Gering and is open seven days a week.

The museum has many well-designed displays that provide a glimpse of the area's life before television. There is a re-created ranch house, sod house, cattleman's shack, pioneer home and blacksmith shop, as well as many other displays. The museum is known for its excellent chronology of the human habitation of the area.

The WyoBraska Museum of Natural History is located in the old Union Pacific depot. Among the many creatures on display is a reproduction of the giant Baluchithere rhinoceros, which stood 18 feet tall when it roamed Asia 25 million years ago. The reproduction is based on a reproduction that was made for the State Museum at Morril Hall in Lincoln. That model had to be destroyed because of its health hazard when it was discovered that asbestos had been used for its covering.

The museum's core collection came from the founder's collection of wild-game trophies. Since 1989, others have added their collections of trophies to the expanding holdings of the museum.

Three miles to the west of Gering on State Highway 92, or west of Scottsbluff on Highway 29 and then south on 92 is Scott's Bluff, the must-see Scott's Bluff National Historic Monument.

The sites in this area are so spectacular and so numerous that any traveler in the area owes it to the gods of wonder to see as many sites as possible. For an extensive description of these sites, please see the entry for State Highway 92.

Eight miles (6 miles.)
Mitchell.

To follow the approximate route of the Oregon Trail turn south at Mitchell and take the first west turn south of the North Platte River. Following these county roads as near to the river as possible will keep you along the same route so many hundreds of thousands of pioneers used.

A fine rock 'n' roller was born in Mitchell. Randy Meisner, originally a member of the band *Poco* and later of the *Eagles*, was born in Mitchell.

Six miles (7 miles.)
Morrill.

Named for Charles Morrill, who owned a large chunk of Nebraska in the early days. After he contributed so much of his time and energy in helping the University, he was honored by having the state's finest museum, Morrill Hall on the University campus in Lincoln, named after him.

Take county road L-79D south out of Morrill and then take the first road west, south of the North Platte River Bridge.

Take the first right turn (north) in three miles. In one half mile you will cross a small bridge. Stop the car.

This is the valley of Horse Creek. In 1851, the United States Government invited Indian tribes from all over the West to meet at Fort Laramie, 50 miles west of here in Wyoming, to try to settle centuries of Indian wars. To the surprise of everyone, thousands of Indians appeared at the fort for the talks. Since there was no good grazing land for horses, or enough water for those assembled, the Indians camped here, along Sand Creek and Horse Creek, so named for the good grass it provided their horses.

The treaty negotiations brought together tribes that had never met, from the Crow and Black Feet of Montana, to the Sioux and Iowa of the Great Plains. It is believed that here, along the banks of this sandy creek, was the single largest gathering of American Indians ever.

Try to imagine these hills covered for miles with thousands of tepees and campfires. An astounding mixture of costumes, music and language now largely forgotten, was everywhere. There have been few people who have visited this site in the many years since that gathering.

The treaty was negotiated in part because the government realized that this route would soon become a popular one for the whites, and they did not want the Indians fighting while "citizens" were passing through. The treaty lasted three years until a white by the name of Grattan fired on some Indians accused of stealing a cow.

The Oregon Trail followed this same county road route. Just to the southwest of here was the Horse Creek station, a station on the Pony Express and Oregon Trails.

Seven miles (0 miles.)

Henry, and the western end of US Highway 26 in Nebraska. Henry is located just on the better side of the Wyoming border. Just southwest of the town is the site of Red Cloud Indian Agency at the end of a dead-end road as it reaches the river.

South of Henry 3 miles *to where the Oregon Trail crosses State Road L-79C.*

Both CBS News and *National Geographic* magazine have called this highway one of the ten most beautiful in the country. It has been a route for travelers since there have been travelers in the state. Indians used part of the route, and later the pioneers crossed the state along routes then known as the Old Freighters Trail, the Steam Wagon Road and the Nebraska City Cutoff.

Zero miles (9 miles.)

Nebraska City.

The state's most exciting and interesting state highway begins in this old river town. There is much to see in Nebraska City; for information please see entry for US Highways 73 and 75.

West of Nebraska City on State 2. This is the so-called Steam Wagon Road, so named for the steam wagon that was supposed to make it to Denver and back twice a month. (See entry for US Highways 73 and 75 for details.)

Nine miles (4 miles.)

Dunbar. Dunbar was a stage station on Ben Holladay's Overland stage route, and much later, when the railroad replaced the stage route, the town continued to hold on. The population of the town has not changed much in over 100 years.

Four miles (4 miles.)

At about this point, the Nebraska City Cutoff of the Oregon Trail crosses the highway diagonally from the northeast to the southwest. For the next five miles it parallels State 2 on the south side of the road, about a half mile from the highway.

Four miles (5 miles.)

Syracuse. Did the highway curve to miss Syracuse on purpose? A question more than a few Nebraskans have asked while driving from Nebraska City to Lincoln. Is this the highway? A question

State Highway 2

more than a few Nebraskans have asked after missing the curve and heading up one of the town's residential streets.

Syracuse grew from a stage station on the Overland Stage route from the Missouri to Denver. This place had originally been known as Nursery Hill, after a spot just south of here on the stage route that had been the location of a trading post and stage station.

Junction of State Highway 50; please see that entry for more information about sites in this area.

Five miles (7 miles.)

Unadilla. The name means "meeting place" in Iroquois. There were no Iroquois Indians here — the town was named after a town in Illinois.

At the south end of the village is the Little Nemaha River and a state campground. Along the south banks of the Little Nemaha was the Overland Stage Route as well as the Nebraska City Cutoff of the Oregon Trail. Some traces of ruts are still visible in Otoe County. Inquire locally.

Seven miles (1 mile.)

Palmyra. Near here, Richard Pugsley, a schoolteacher, turned farmer, turned gunmaker, owns and operates the Thunder Valley Gatling Gun Company. The company is the only place in the world that makes exact reproductions of the Nineteeth Century 10-barrel revolving gun that can spray 600 rounds per minute.

The gun, named after its inventor, Richard Gatling, was used by the British to stop a charge of 10,000 Zulu warriors and by Teddy Roosevelt in his charge up San Juan Hill, Cuba, in 1898, as well as in many battles in the American West.

Each Thunder Valley Gatling is hand made. They start at around $15,000.

One mile (3 miles.)

To the south here is "Second night stop," a camping place on the Nebraska City Cutoff. Oakley's Store once stood here to serve the pioneers, and stones from its foundation are still visible.

Three miles (4 miles.)

Turn off for Bennet.

On January 27, 1958, the mass murderer Charlie Starkweather killed two people who had stopped to help Starkweather and his girlfriend, Caril Ann Fugate, after their vehicle had gotten stuck in the snow. They forced the victims into a concrete cave two miles east of Bennet and killed them. In all, ten people were to be killed in the five-day spree.

The Nebraska City Cutoff of the Oregon Trail crosses two miles south of Bennet.

Four miles (8 miles.)
Cheney. An old community now nearly invisible compared to the spreading giant of Lincoln.

The Nebraska City Cutoff of the Oregon Trail crosses one half mile south of here. The road was also known as the Steam Wagon Road because it was supposed to carry steam-powered wagons that everyone thought would be invented and would replace the horse.

There is a rare round barn south of Cheney. Ask locally for directions.

Eight miles (92 miles.)
Lincoln.

For information about the state's capital city, please see the entry for US Highway 34.

At Lincoln, State Highway 2 is swept up by Interstate 80, and US Highway 34 does not resurface again until Grand Island. For sites between Lincoln and Grand Island along this route please see entries for US Highway 34 and Interstate 80.

Ninety-two miles (7 miles.)
Grand Island.

See entry for US Highways 34, 281, 30 and Interstate 80 for information about Grand Island and other sites in this area.

Seven miles (6 miles.)
Abbott, a scattering of houses on a bend in the road. Near here was the Robert Taylor sheep ranch, which was one of the largest sheep ranches in a five-state area. The ranch in Hall County alone took up nearly all of Prairie Creek Township, about 10,000 acres. At the turn of the century, before modernized haying equipment, 1,400 acres alone was in alfalfa.

The railroad siding that was here was originally named Taylor's siding, but the railroad company didn't think it was enough of a neutral name to the place so it was renamed Ovina, from the Latin ovis, meaning sheep. *Taloris ovis*.

For the next few miles you pass through the prairie creek area. All of this land was once under the control of Robert Taylor. During the great grasshopper plague of 1873 and 1875, this area was one of the hardest hit in the state. The insects destroyed virtually all of the green and living plants. Sulphur was used to try to smoke the grasshopper out of the corn.

A prairie fire swept through here in 1878, and later two men were found shot to death with cards attached to their shirts. The cards read: "Shot for setting the prairie fire."

In order to settle in this area, one early pioneer drove his team of ten horses through 700 miles of winter snow to reach the area before others. The snow in some places was 12 inches deep.

In 1887, a 240-acre farm along Prairie Creek sold for $5,200 with house, granary, running stream water and stock.

Two miles north of Abbott and three and a half miles west (on county roads) to Runnelsburg. These are the ruins of the town of Runnelsburg, which was more or less owned and operated by a man named R.S. Runnel. A stage route to connect Grand Island with the Black Hills was supposed to run through here, which gave Mr. Runnel much of his enthusiasm. The railroad replaced the trail, and the railroad passed south of here so Runnelsburg soon drifted into ghosthood. Mr. Runnel sold his farm for $14 an acre in 1884 and moved permanently to California.

Six miles (16 miles.)
Cairo. A railroad boom town that boomed in 1887 as a result of the Grand Island and Wyoming railroad, which passed through here. Cairo went from a cornfield to a town of 250 in a few months. Folks here have no intention of letting it slip back the other way.

Since you are in Cairo, you might wonder where the Suez is. Well, it is a street here on the west edge of town.

For more information about sites in this area please see entry for US Highway 30.

Sixteen miles (11 miles.)
Ravenna, named after the town in Italy. Near here, in 1874, a pioneer brought the first shorthorn cattle into the area.

Location of Ravenna State Lakes, on the banks of the South
Loup River.

Eleven miles (6 miles.)

Junction with State Highway 10 at Hazard.

One wonders why someone might select to live in a place
named Hazard. However, somewhere over 50 people have overcome
their hesitation and call Hazard their home. The name is supposed to
have been selected when the citizens could not find a name not
already in use. "Well," one pioneer said, "we'll just hazard another
name." The rest, as they say, was history.

Those early-day residents would never have imagined that in
1992 an internationally popular pop singer named Richard Marx
would write a song called "Hazard" about the fictional disappearance
and mysterious death of a woman named Mary. Marx chose the town
of Hazard for the setting of his song after studying a list of names of
Nebraskan towns. The song reached the Top 10 and brought brief and
unusual recognition to this tiny burg.

Hazard Days, which feature a tactor pull, street dance and
barbecue, are held in August.

The Beaver Creek Wayside Area, just west of the village, is
a nice out-of-the-way facility that allows non-motorized boats only.
There is additional camping at Litchfield Recreation Area, six miles to
the northwest on State 2.

For more information about sites along State Highway 10,
please see that entry.

Six miles (9 miles.)

Litchfield and Litchfield Recreation Area.

Nine miles (6 miles.)

Mason City. The stunning feature of Mason City is the work
of its major artist, Richard Martin, on the southern edge of the city.
Martin creates sculptures of cats, dogs, roosters and other items from
old tools and pieces of farm equipment. His entire yard and house are
decorated with his work — the roof, the lawn, the porch and inside —
so it won't be hard to locate the home of the master. In addition, Martin
creates wind sculptures that are balanced so that the slightest breeze
sets them in motion. Martin doesn't sell his sculptures, by the way,
although he has been known to give a few away.

State Highway 2

Six miles (9 miles.)

Junction with US Highway 183. Please see the entry for that highway for information about sites along that route.

Nine miles (8 miles.)

Berwyn in the vast Custer County.

Custer County was home to one of the West's little-known photographic genius. Solomon Devore Butcher, who lived from 1856 until 1927, settled in Custer County in the pioneer days. He was not like his neighbors, for he was restless and eccentric. Others said he was afraid of farming. "Not at all," Butcher would answer them, "I could lie down and go to sleep along side of it anytime."

Butcher tried a variety of things to make his life full: he joined the military, went to medical school, tried teaching school, owned a gallery, sold land in Texas and was a traveling salesman. He invented an "oil detector" and created a patented alcoholic medicine, "Butcher's Wonder of the Age."

He spent 15 years taking photographs and collecting personal accounts of the pioneers in Custer County, and finally produced his masterwork, *Pioneer History of Custer County Nebraska,* in 1901. The book sold a few copies during his lifetime.

Now Butcher's photographs, many of which are stored at the State Historical Society collection in Lincoln, are considered artistic views of the rugged life of the pioneer.

In 1991, novelist and children's book author Pam Conrad published *Prairie Visions, The Life and Times of Solomon Butcher,* which tells the story of the photographer. Her fine, well-written book is the result of years of research and interviews about this unusual Nebraskan.

Eight miles (8 miles.)

Broken Bow.

Yes, this county was named for THAT Custer. The hills of this county are good for raising alfalfa and cattle. Broken Bow, the county seat, was named when an early settler found a broken bow and some other Indian artifacts in a nearby burial ground about the same time the rest of the community was trying to think up a name for the town that was unique. For a long while pieces of this bow, like pieces of Christ's cross, showed up at various places around town.

There is a tour of the historic homes of Broken Bow. Ask at the library for information.

Custer County Historical Library and Museum is free and

open to the public.

During one night in August of 1965, a rash of UFO sightings was made around Broken Bow and the entire Midwest. Reports came from Air Force bases and weather stations and individuals from Oklahoma to South Dakota and from several places in Nebraska.

A rancher near Broken Bow saw the objects, as did several other people in the area.

Just west of town is a marker that celebrates the rebirth of the Grange movement in Nebraska, when the Custer Grange met in 1911.

Broken Bow is at the junction of State Highways 2 and 92. For information about sites along State Highway 92, please see that entry.

Callaway is 20 miles southwest of town and offers the Seven Valleys Museum, with a large collection of Indian and pioneer artifacts. It also has preserved the first Custer County courthouse — a long building. Near Callaway is the site of the Mitchell and Ketchum lynching, a part of a larger conflict between ranchers and pioneers during the 1870s. See entry for US Highway 183 north of Westerville for details.

Southwest of town, 15 miles on State Highway 21 to the South Loup River and the Pressey Wildlife Management Area, which offers fishing, camping, bird watching and hunting.

Five miles north take the right fork in the road and go one more mile to Dead Man's Canyon. This beautiful canyon was named after a battle that took place here in July of 1887 between two posses and other assorted lawmen and two men who were believed to have robbed several farm families in the area. One suspect was killed and the other fled on horseback.

Eight miles (11 miles.)
Merna.
Junction with State Highway 92, west. Please see that entry for information about sites along its route.

Ten Miles north of Merna on county road to Victoria Springs State Recreation Area.

State Highway 2

A series of springs once bubbled out of the sandstone here, creating different colored waters, depending on the chemical makeup of the rocks through which they flowed. Early pioneers capitalized on the beauty of this area and set up trading posts to serve the tourists who sought out the springs. The waters were often used for their alleged curative powers. Today, a pretty pond and a single clear springs are the center attraction for this out-of-the-way and quiet spot.

West of Merna 2 miles is Cedar Canyons, a waterless maze of canyonlands, which are home to a wide variety of wildlife. In addition to coyotes, deer and other animals, this is a good birding spot, with occasional sightings of eagles, chickadees, cedar waxwings, owls and other fine feathered friends.

West of Merna on State 70 and 92, 25 miles to Arnold. See entry for State Highway 92 for more information about this small town.

Eleven miles (21 miles.)

Anselmo. This small burg got its start thanks to the railroad. From here on, the Sandhills dominate the geography. These sandhills are wet enough to support a rich texture of native grasses. The pioneers learned that plowing this land caused wind erosion. Now, a hundred years or better later, the same lesson is being learned again by those who insist on breaking through the grass in order to plant irrigated croplands.

The large church on the west side of town is the Catholic Church and is known as the Cathedral of the Plains.

*To the **east six miles** to Silver Springs Recreation Area. The springs are there along with a log cabin built in the early days.*

Twenty-one miles (10 miles.)

Dunning and junction with State Highway 91.

Fifteen miles northeast on State Highway 91 to Brewster.
When you take out the road map of Nebraska and fold it in half the crease will split Blaine County in two. That might be the only reason why Blaine County might attract your attention. Take a look at that crease. Well, you might say, there seems to be a fairly good-sized town there, Brewster, at the junction of State Highways 91 and 7.
The Dismal River flows through the area, and that river,

378

despite its name, offers some good fishing and boating. So does the Loup. But outside of that, you might ask, what else could possibly be in Blaine County?

You are right about the river, it is a heck of a name for a pretty little river. Trouble is, Brewster, the county's seat and main town, has all but dried up and blown away. All except for one place that not only has refused to give up the ghost but is actually bringing folks off the main highways to Colorado, the Black Hills and Yellowstone. Off those roads and out into the center of the Sandhills.

A trio of enterprising young men have taken over an old store in the town and turned it into "Doc Middleton's" an old-fashioned saloon, restaurant, community center and news exchange. The place is named for a famous Nebraska outlaw who once owned a saloon in Brewster during one of his attempts to go straight. (For a more complete discussion of Doc Middleton, see entry for US Highway 20.)

The actual existence of the place owes a lot to the town spirit and sense of community. The population of Brewster has dwindled to somewhere between 20 and 40 from a peak of not many more.

When the men decided to open a place in Brewster, no one in the town was telling them to go away. Instead, everyone pitched in and helped to build the saloon. In the first few months of operation, when the owners couldn't get to town because of other jobs or work on their ranches, somebody nearby, oftentimes whoever was handy, would unlock the place and put on a fresh pot or two of coffee for the local folks who gather there in the morning. Fresh flowers appear on the tables due to the thoughtfulness of someone else.

Sounds a little unusual, even for the friendly Sandhills. Thing of it is, Brewster was just about dead and buried before Doc Middleton's opened. The town's population had dropped 50 percent in a few years, and the only thing in town besides a couple of houses were the courthouse and the post office. Now, with the restaurant, there's a place local folks can go and talk about the poor cattle-ranching economy, the way the remaining empty buildings on the four-block main street seem to be just blowing away, and county business, such as it is. But at least there's a place, and that helps explain the unusual community atmosphere you'll find at Doc Middleton's.

Expect to stand out like a sore thumb from all the locals who will most likely be gathered around a single spot in the center of the room. The place will grow quiet as you come in and everyone there gives you the once-over. After that, though, things return to the way they always are at Doc's. Incidentally, they don't serve breakfast, although they are open early in the morning for coffee and conversation.

Hows the food? How else do you think the food would be at a place like this?

Brewster is probably the smallest county seat in the country.

The area's most notable claim to fame was having the number one high school football champions a few years back.

After filling up at Doc Middleton's, a drive southeast toward Taylor on Highway 91 is a must. The beauty of the Loup River Valley is unequaled.

Ten miles (14 miles.)

Halsey. This is the gateway to the Nebraska National Forest, a man-made forest of beauty.

It is something of a matter of pride that the Nebraska National Forest — the Halsey Forest — is entirely artificially planted. Outsiders raise their noses when told this information.

Established in 1902 by Teddy Roosevelt, the area contains 93,000 acres. The forest was the idea of Charles E. Bessey, a famous University of Nebraska botanist who knew that the Sandhills could support a large forest.

Between 1903 and 1921, 13,500,000 seedlings were set out. In the last year alone 2,200,000 jack and yellow pines were planted. They first tried planting the seedlings directly into the soil, but the plants did not survive.

Eventually it was discovered that if a trench was built, the trees had a much higher rate of survival. The planting crews would follow a trench made by a horse-drawn plow, which turned up the soil of the grasses of the hills. Trees from here are now transplanted to Niobrara division in Cherry County.

Don't come here expecting the close-in forests of other areas. The sparse hills and coolies hold enough trees to qualify as a forest in Nebraska.

Fourteen miles (15 miles.)

Thedford, the county seat of Thomas County. Please see the entry for US Highway 83 for more information on this town rich with history and life.

Fifteen miles (11 miles.)

Seneca. An interesting and previously unknown method of keeping track of time was developed by Senecans who kept shades up and doors open so that the sun would shine onto their floorboards. People called around to check and compare when their shadow claimed it was high noon. In this manner, little by little a Seneca Standard Time was agreed upon, and you could be reasonably certain that when your shadow said it was noon, everyone else saw their shadows as noon too.

Horse races were often held on Railroad Street to determine the fastest local horse.

Seneca, in the extreme western edge of Thomas County, was founded in 1888 and was named for the Seneca Indians. In the old days at its peak, during the 1920s, Seneca had three grocery stores, a telephone office, dress shops, a theater, post office, two auto dealers, a livery stable, two large hotels and two banks, and it was a division point for the railroad.

When the courthouse in Thedford was destroyed by fire in 1920 Seneca residents pounced on the opportunity and demanded an election to move the county seat to their town. They lost by a vote of 362 to 514.

In 1948, during the presidential campaign, President Truman stopped by for a barbecue in Seneca. The town had gas lights, a movie theater, electric lights, and an ice-making factory before any town for miles around had these services.

Slowly the railroad began to lose interest and money in Seneca. In 1968, the last railroad train came through town. Despite the slowly shrinking size, Seneca has survived. Today the town has a population of, well, somewhere under a hundred.

The Seneca Church was built in 1909, and since the town's population has been declining it has been difficult to keep a vital church membership. Still, there are those who believe wherever there are two or more...

The Seneca Cemetery dates from 1899.

Seneca was home of a farmers' union that was half social organization, half cooperative farm effort. The union movement, which was big in the 1920s, has largely died out in the Sandhills.

During the blizzard of January 1949, a southbound passenger train stalled in Seneca and the passengers spent several days in the depot and Ruby's Cafe until the tracks could be cleared. The cafe had people sleeping on tables and chairs and did more business in those couple of days than it had ever done.

Four miles north on county roads to the site of Buffalo Flats. The post office in this area was a cracker box in the home of one of *the residents. People came by to pick up mail there.*

The church at Purdum was built in 1908. The cemetery predates the church by about 25 years.

Near here is the Lone Star Cemetery, a small cemetery dating from the turn of the century.

Eleven miles (25 miles.)
Mullen.

Mullen is the county seat of Hooker County. Mullen was named after a local agent of the railroad when the town was founded. It is the county seat of the sparsely populated Hooker county. So sparsely populated, in fact, that Hooker County is the least populated county in the state. Note that the license plates here begin with the rare number 93, indicating that out of the 93 counties in the state, Hooker is last in population. This is not a shameful thing. On the contrary, Hooker residents feel a kind of pride and honor at having what no other county has as much of: empty space.

No, the county was not named for the businesswomen who worked in Mullen a century ago, but rather after a noted Civil War general.

Mullen is at the very heart of the Nebraska Sandhills, a unique geological and ecological formation unlike any other place in the world. The Sandhills were laid down thousands of years ago after the great ice sheets rolled back to the north. At first settlers believed the sandy and rolling hills would be good for nothing better than scattered cattle grazing. However, in time they learned that areas of the land supported some crops. When the gigantic Ogallala aquifer, an enormous underground sea of water stretching over the entire state of Nebraska and going as far south as Texas, was utilized, farmers began to reap the harvest of crops grown on the hills.

Today, a developing controversy centers on land use in the Sandhills. Some claim that the pivot irrigation systems that have turned the land into large circular gardens of green crops are depleting the nutrients from the soil, as well as adding to the erosion of the hills and the depletion of the aquifer. Others claim that everyone should leave the care and husbandry of the land to those who know the land the best, namely the ranchers and farmers who have spent their lives here. In any event, the Sandhills region of Nebraska is a special and

382

remote gift for all people to visit and to marvel over.

*South of Mullen, **four miles** to a narrow paved road leading off to the west. Down this road **15 miles** to the banks of the North Fork of the Dismal River, cross the river and continue another eight miles to the banks of the South Fork and the site of the North and Cody Ranch. This grassy expanse of hills was once the range of thousands of buffalo, antelope and deer. In 1877, William F. Cody, who would later become world renowned as Buffalo Bill, along with Major Frank North, purchased a herd of cattle at Ogallala and spent a good part of the summer driving them to this range land. Here the men started a ranch that would become known as the North and Cody Ranch. Not much is known about the success of this ranch, or Buffalo Bill's part in it, but for years the ranch was made welcome to any traveler who happened this way. In later years, many dignitaries were entertained here. Today, the quiet and peaceful river flows through beautiful country of grasslands and thickets along the banks.*

Twenty five miles (1 mile.)

Whitman, in the heart of the Sandhills.

"It's a great country for cattle and men," said pioneer Ellen Moran, "but hell on horses and women."

The earliest settlers around these parts were people with names that hinted at pioneer spirit. People like Old Gus Buchfinck, Fetus Carrothers and Bryant Greathouse, who homesteaded in the late 1880s near Whitman. These men came to the area in covered wagons looking for good, cheap land for cattle and families. Some, like George Moran, husband of Ellen, were lucky. They had 13 children, and nearly single-handedly populated early Whitman.

Others, like Effie Brown, weren't so lucky. She was shot to death in the Whitman Hotel by her husband in 1900 after he had gotten drunk in the local saloon.

Here was the Whitman Barn, which served as a supply point for wagon trains heading for places as far away as the Snake River country of Idaho and the Arkansas River to the south.

The Whitman post office, which is the oldest in Grant County, was established in 1887.

Whitman once served as a major cattle shipping point for railroads. Special Saturday evening runs made shipping easy for the local cattleman. Sixty or more cars of beef was not an unusual train length in Whitman's shipping heyday. Also, of lesser importance, were the four passenger trains a day that once stopped here.

As the highway passes near the railroad tracks: this was once all cattle yards and stock pens for cattle awaiting shipping.

Whitman's hotel cost 35 cents in its heyday during the early years of this century.

Whitman at its peak during homesteading years, and when the Kinkaid Act opened the Sandhills in 1900, had two hotels, two livery stables, two doctors, two general stores, pool hall, lumberyard, photo shop, drugstore, icehouse, cattle yard, coal chutes for trains, a barbershop, and a blacksmith (who had a shop across the south side of the railroad tracks). Fred Troop's saloon was the busiest of the seven saloons.

The brick bank, which still stands, dates back to the town's big days around the turn of the century.

The Whitman firehouse was the post office in 1928.

In its 100 years of history, there have been only five robberies in Whitman. All of them have taken place at the post office. The total stolen during these five break-ins has been $72.38.

Just north of the school is the old parsonage of the Methodist Church, built in 1898.

The IOOF Hall was once a pool hall. In 1976, the pay phone on the main street of Whitman was purchased by the Whitman Women's Club extension group "Out Our Way." The phone is a useful item for stranded tourists.

On a nice hill overlooking the village one quarter mile south of town is the cemetery. The oldest grave is from 1888. Included here are the graves of the Weaver family's five children, who all died within a 7-month time span in 1889. The Weavers were the owners of Whitman's first big store.

While the homesteaders, who were called Kinkaiders because of the act of Congress that allowed them to settle this land, helped the economy of the area, they were usually the butt of jokes.

"You know what an S.O.B. is, don't you?" a rancher, even recently, said. "Well, a Kinkaider is 10 times worse than that."

North of Whitman: *This road was once the main wagon road north to the Black Hills. In 12 miles the road crosses the Middle Loup River. Here was a common resting place for wagon trains heading north. Teams were watered in the sluggish waters of the river, and teamsters could decide if they really wanted to continue on this madness, or return to Whitman.*

North of Whitman 18 miles. *This area was once the common first night camping ground for wagon teams leaving Whitman.*

Southwest of Whitman: *Here the last free land in the state of Nebraska was opened for homesteading and settled. Most of the land had once been deemed a "forest preserve" by the state, but when the attempt to grow trees failed, it became homesteading land. Many homesteaders, hearing that the land was a "forest preserve," came expecting to see lots of green. They were disappointed.*

The Kincaid Act allowed settlers who had already filed on 160 acres in the drier parts of western states to file on three more quarter sections, giving them a square mile of land. Tracts were given out during a weeklong drawing, done in Hyannis. One hundred numbers were drawn each day, and the winners could then file claims on their choice of a section of land. This became Whitman's largest "boom" time, the streets lined with the tents of those hoping to win at the drawing.

One mile (4 miles.)

The airport is to the north of the highway. Here in 1938 a mail bag containing 374 letters and two packages gained a page in history by being the first, and last, airmail delivered to the town.

Four miles (7 miles.)

North of here, at the old Monahan Ranch during the gigantic prairie fire of 1892, Sidney Manning had just started back for Whitman when he noticed the fire sweep over a ridge and race toward him. Manning survived the fire by jumping down an open water well. "I didn't know if I would drown or burn," Manning said. The wind of the fire swept a large pile of cattle chips into the well and on top of Mr. Manning. Nothing Manning said about the chips has survived.

This fire covered hundreds of square miles and is possibly the worst natural disaster in Nebraska's history.

Seven miles (8 miles.)

Hyannis.

The Hyannis County Courthouse is the home of the Grant County Historical Society Museum. Many fine displays of the local area's history can be seen here. It has limited hours, but can be opened by appointment. The courthouse was the central location of many famous Grant County sheriffs.

This town, as well as Whitman and Ashby, were named after towns in Massachusetts by early settlers from that area.

Oldest building in town is the house lived in by Ada Coons. This was the first building in town and still stands. It was built in 1887.

The Bank of Hyannis was built in 1915. When first built as a bank, the south half of the main floor was used as a saloon.

Bud Moran, who still is talked about in these parts, was the first sheriff of the territory that now includes Grant County. While in Whitman, Bud Moran held a madman in the jail for safekeeping. Three men had brought him in and left him in Bud's office.

Listen to Bud tell it: "He was so violent the cowboys which brought him in had roped him. When they left, he informed me that he was the devil and made a leap at me. He tried to bite me. I was sure scared then. I didn't have time to run, so I just throws him over my shoulder out of sheer terror of him. When he hit the floor that took some devil out of him, and I was on him before he could get up and put the handcuffs on him. He looped his arms around a dog I had in the office and bit its ear off. When I tried to pry his mouth open he swallowed the dang thing, eyeing me resentful-like all the time."

Main Street on east side: Dredla's building, built in 1914, was the site of the Ashley Store, which also served as post office from 1906 until 1918.

Near this building was the first drugstore in town, and although the owner was not a pharmacist, he did quite well by selling medicines that contained a fair amount of alcohol, and also, we might assume, headache remedies.

The barber shop has been in existence since 1938.

386

West side: The hotel was built in 1898 by Sherman Sears and has always looked pretty much the same as it does today. The door on the north was for men, and the one on the south for women only. This was so that the women would not have to pass by the men who gathered in the lobby and talked about the things that interested them, namely women. The third floor was not as nice as the other floors and the manager would rent these rooms to cowboys, ranch hands and other individuals he might consider less than refined. The rooms here were cheaper, however.

The building next to the hotel was built in the late 1880s as well, and has served as a tack shop for a great part of that time.

Next to the Masonic Temple and Post Office stands a building that was once completely remodeled after a cowboy came into the building on his horse. Seems that he had just gotten off a long week of branding and was wanting a bit of excitement. His horse ended up having the most excitement — it fell through the floor, which was the initial reason for the extensive remodeling.

The last building on Main Street was the site of the first Bank of Hyannis, which was built in 1893.

The Baptist Church uses a part of the original Hyannis Opera House, which was built in 1896 at a cost of $745. Both the Opera House and an older Beems gas station were destroyed by a propane gas fire.

Near the lumberyard is an old house that was built in the late 1890s and later moved into town. In its basement a local inventor built and rebuilt a perpetual motion machine. The machine was often being repaired and there are not many who saw the thing run; however, it was a contraption of spokes and a wheel, filled with water. For a while the machine was displayed in the store.

At Hyannis Park was the site of the first schoolhouse: 1888.

Train depot on the tracks was built in 1901. Here Teddy Roosevelt spoke in 1904. He came to town on a special train, made his address from a specially built bandstand near the tracks. There was a very large crowd for the only President to visit in the history of the town.

State Highway 2

In 1896, a party of people broke into Whitman County Courthouse and took all of the county's records. The records were then hidden in a blowout south of town. As a result, Hyannis became the county seat in 1897.

The town library was the recipient of an unusual gift in 1942. The *Omaha World Herald* sponsored a scrap metal drive for the war effort, called the "Scrap Harvest." Grant County was the winner of the competition, raising nearly 650 pounds of scrap per capita. The old wagon wheels, guns and tools today might have brought a much higher price than the $1,000 the county won, but for Vernon Moran, who collected 96,953 pounds of scrap by himself, the honor far outweighed the prize. The money was used for the library.

The rodeo grounds, near the football field, hosts the most popular event in these parts. "The Old Timers Rodeo" includes a parade, and the celebration draws thousands to Hyannis. The tradition of a rodeo here dates back to the late 1880s.

Frye Lake, north of town, is a good fishing spot.

The Hyannis Cemetery is on the hillside to the north and affords a view of the beautiful Sandhills of the surrounding country side. The oldest gravesite is from 1890. A local eccentric, Major Guelliner, demanded he not be buried "like everyone else." He is buried with his head to the east.

West of Hyannis. Here was once St. Mary's Cemetery. Here was the grave of Mart Managan. Managan dug his own grave, built a fence around the site, purchased a coffin and placed it in the open grave covered with a piece of tin. He lived for 12 years after this, but was confident of his burial arrangements. Little did he know that the small cemetery, including his remains, would be moved to the cemetery in Hyannis to make way for the Grant County airport.

Eight miles (5 miles.)
Ashby
This rustic western town has had it all: shoot 'em ups, a blacksmith shop, a church that was once a store, and even a cowboy's ghost.

388

At a dance hall in Ashby a man who had been a Lieutenant in the Army always made everyone stand and salute him when he walked in. Once, when someone new to town didn't, the Lieutenant shot him. The man had a wad of bills rolled up and placed in his pocket, which stopped the bullet. Nothing is known about the eventual outcome of this story.

Charlie's Store is the location of the town's store since 1914. Once there were two stores in Ashby, within yards of each other. The store's former owner, Edward Montgomery, was not happy that another store had started in town. In 1921 the new store burned to the ground. The cause of the fire was never determined.

In 1920, a common sight was John Halloren and store owner Edward Montgomery riding up and down Main Street on their horses, whooping and hollering and carrying on. The two men would be stark naked. Most town folk knew they had probably been snipping a bit of alcohol. Charlie's is a good place to stop off for a cool bottle of pop and friendly conversation.

The present school was built in 1915 after a series of one-roomers. All 12 grades were not taught in Ashby until 1930.

Ashby started as a railroad town in the late 1800s. The oldest thing in town is the lumberyard, which has been in existence since Ashby's earliest days. The flush bathrooms were added in 1976. The cement structure on the north side of the railroad tracks was the base for the water tower, which once was Ashby's source of water for train, town and business.

The Ashby church, on Main Street, was once a building for one of the town's three lumber yards. In 1920 it was purchased and a steeple was later added to the storefront structure. The addition was built in 1977.

An old shack on Main Street was once known as King's Place and was where old bones were brought duing WWII to be made into calcium.

The Ashby Town Hall, now the location of the Veterans Club, was famous across the Sandhills for having the best dance floor in the area.

The cemetery is east of town and the oldest grave is that of an infant who died in 1915.

There was an old cowboy named Dubs who lived in Ashby. He built himself a shack on some land just west of town and kept pretty much to himself, remembering the old days of cattle drives and camping under the stars.

Dubs would walk into town every once in a while to check his mail and get groceries. It was a pretty uncommon thing to see a cowboy walking, but he seemed to like the exercise.

Then he stopped showing up. After a few weeks some folks decided to go out and check on the old timer.

What they found was Dubs, sitting in a chair in his shack, stone-cold dead, his face frozen in a silent scream of fright.

Since that time residents of the area report seeing an old cowboy walking alongside of Highway 2, just on the western edge of town. There are those who swear that when they see this man he looks as if he is from another age.

The road southwest of Ashby was formed when a man drove his car to Denver, and marked his route by painting the fence gates blue.

This road, in 30 miles, leads to the southeastern edge of the vast and beautiful Crescent Lake National Wildlife Refuge, and eventually to State Highway 27. Please see the entry for State Highway 27 for more information.

North, 14 miles to Old Mason, or Stansbie/Perrett Cemetery. About 20 graves including Roberta Wilson's who was found by settlers and buried after a blizzard on Feb. 9, 1891.

Five miles (4 miles.)

Five miles to the south are located Big and Little Buckboard Valley, where various skeletons of horses and the ruins of old buckboards have been found. No one knows more details about the lonely pioneers who may have perished here.

The highway east and west of here is a particularly straight east/west line. This is indirectly thanks to the United States Army. The

Army had this idea that its soldiers could meet the 20th Century on bicycles. In an attempt to prove so they had three companies of men bicycle from Montana to St. Louis in 1897. At this point they were having so much trouble that they followed the railroad tracks in order to make their way. Their path later served as a road, and now it is this stretch of Highway 2.

For more information about these bicyclists, please see entry for State Highway 27.

Part of the original pioneer wagon road is visible on either side of the highway east and west of here.

The Sheridan/Grant County line here is the location of a sand cut on the railroad line that made it almost impossible to complete the route west due to sand spilling over the tracks.

Four miles (10 miles.)
Bingham, a town slowly blowing the way of many other ghost communities in the Old West. Once a community that boasted a bank, hotel, stores, cafe and filling station, it now barely holds on to the sand under its feet.

Ten miles (8 miles.)
Ellsworth. Once the headquarters for the gigantic Spade Ranch. Junction of State Highway 27 north. Please see entry for that road for information about sites along its route.

Morgan's Cowpoke Haven Museum and Tack Shop is here. You are not a true traveler of the wilds if you pass up a place with a name like this.

Eight miles (8 miles.)
Lakeside: World War I potash was processed here, making this a temporary boom town. The only real winners in the short-lived boom were ranchers who sold lakes with the potash dissolved in their waters, and the railroads, which brought in coal to fire the plants and hauled away the potash.

Junction for State Highway 27. You are near the heart of Mari Sandoz country. Please see entry for State Highway 27 for more information about sites in this area.

State Highway 2

Eight miles (16 miles.)

Antioch. Originally named Reno, the wise Post Office thought it might be good to change the name so as not to confuse the place with another Reno a bit farther west, a bit larger and in a bit drier country.

This was the location of the largest of the World War I era potash-processing communities. At its peak, the town had a population of 5,000 and contained five potash reduction plants.

Water was pumped from local lakes and stored in large holding tanks near the town. From there the water was pumped to the reduction plants, where it was heated by coal-fired furnaces while it turned in revolving reduction drums. All that remains of this industry are a few brick and concrete foundations scattered about the area. Homes that once held the workers at these plants have mostly been destroyed or hauled away to Alliance during the 1920s.

Today, the town looks more like a ghost town than anything else.

Sixteen miles (18 miles.)

Alliance. Junction with US Highway 385. Please see that entry for more information about sites along its route, and for information about Alliance.

Eighteen miles (12 miles.)

Hemingford.

An old song of the Sandhills is sometimes still sung around these parts. It is commonly called "The Kincaider's Tune" after Sen. Moses Kinkaid, who helped to open this area to the last batch of homesteaders in 1904:

> The corn we raise is our delight
> The melons too, are out of sight.
> Potatoes grown are extra fine
> And can't be beat in any clime.
>
> The peaceful cows in pastures dream
> And furnish us with golden cream.
> So I shall keep my Kinkaid home
> And never far away shall roam.

If the homesteader had a different view of the country, there are other appropriate verses:

I've reached the land of drouth and heat,
Where nothing grows for man to eat.
For wind that blows with burning heat,
Nebraska land is hard to beat.

Al Reneau was a ranchman's name,
Skinning Kinkaiders was his game,
First mortgages only, at a high percent,
Work you down on your cattle to the last red cent.

The Nebraska Sandhills are a unique geological area unlike any other in the world. The name is misleading, for the Sandhills contain thousands of lakes and marshes as well as meadows and even some forests. They were created by the wind and by erosion after a great inland sea dried up, some 100 million years ago. The great ice sheets further transformed the area so that today these hills constitute one of the most productive cattle range lands in the world. Just like the thousands of buffalo that once roamed this area, the cattle now feast on the rich grasses of the delicate hills.

The area is ideal for birdwatches and nature lovers. Secluded lakes and meadows provide homes for shore birds, cormorants and phalaropes as well as hawks, larks and golden eagles. Deer and pronghorn antelope populate the area as well. Elk have been reintroduced to the Sandhills and range in Box Butte County.

Twelve miles (9 miles.)

Junction of State Highways 2 and 71. They follow the same route from here north to the South Dakota border.

For further information about sites along State Highway 71, please see that entry.

Nine miles (8 miles.)

On the Dawes/Box Butte County line: Marsland.

Marsland is located on the Niobrara River. This was a major stage and Deadwood Trail stop. Horses were changed here, and travelers could get a bite to eat, a sip of whiskey and other pleasures. In the back of one saloon the owner stacked all of the empty whiskey bottles. It was said the stack was as high as a haystack. The unusual name came from a man who was from Lincoln, and there are more than a few locals who will tell you Mars is exactly where many Lincolnites seem to come from.

State Highway 2

Marsland reached its peak when the railroad came its way. It became a major shipping point for the ranches in the area. This town once had a hotel, livery stable, creamery and a water mill. Now a few buildings remain, but most of the glory of this town is left to the ghosts who inhabit it.

Seven miles east of here via the county road is Box Butte Reservoir, good fishing and boating.

West of Marsland for the 20 miles to Agate. The road follows the Niobrara River on the south, and, on the north, the road follows the Fur Trader's Trail, which was used by the earliest white travelers in this area.
Agate: Agate National Mounument. See Sioux County, State Highway 29. It is 22 miles north of here on State Highway 29 to Harrison.

Nine miles (8 miles.)
One mile east of State Highways 71 and 2:
Belmont. A ghost town founded in 1886 by a dairy farmer. The dairy used a treadmill with dogs to power it in order to separate the cream. Two dogs worked while the third rested. Each dog worked for 10 minutes, and rested for five. Not bad hours for a dog. The town once had nearly 50 buildings. Most of these are gone, although the brick school building and a few others still stand.

A short walk north of Belmont will take you to an unusual sight in Nebraska. Here is the only railroad tunnel in the entire state. It was built in 1888. Nebraskans are so sensitive about being considered the flatlands that a special marker has been placed here to let the tourists from Oklahoma know there are tunnels in this state. Don't tell any Oklahoman that the tunnel has not been used since 1983, when a bypass was built.

From here to Crawford, State Highways 71 and 2 roughly follow the old Sidney to Deadwood Trail. The Trail was used by huge wagon trains to supply the Red Cloud Agency, where as many as 13,000 Indians were camped, as well as to service Deadwood once gold was discovered in the Black Hills. Many clear ruts can be seen still on this route. Keep your eyes open for the easiest route up and through the hills, and you'll spot them.

Eight miles (17 miles.)

394

Crawford. See US Highway 20 entry.

Seventeen miles (0 miles.)

North of Crawford are two spectacular sites.

Follow the small brown signs off of Highway 2 across ten miles of gravel and dirt roads farther and farther into the back country to the Hudson-Meng Bison Kill site.

Discovered in the late 1970s, this site has great archeological significance. Here, 10,000 years ago, the hunting-gathering people who lived then probably drove a herd of buffalo off a cliff in order to provide meat for themselves. Trouble was, the herd they drove, or that had been driven by other means, was enormous. It is estimated that the site contains the bones of at least 600 bison. The number may possibly be quite a bit higher. This is the largest bison kill site ever discovered.

So many bison were killed here that researchers aren't certain how much of the meat might have been wasted. Another mystery is that very few skulls have been found. The skulls are fragile, and one theory is that the skulls did not survive 10,000 years in the ground.

The site is frequently being excavated by archeologists. Be polite and friendly and considerate of their work and they may take some time out of the trenches to answer questions.

Future plans call for the creation of a $5 million Lost Skull Learning Center, which would be a major stop on the 350-mile natural history corridor between Nebraska's Interstate 80 and Interstate 90 in South Dakota.

Follow the signs 17 miles to Toadstool Geological Park. Camping and picnicking and water is available here.

This extensive park is a geologist's dream. The land seems to have been twisted into a nightmare of strange beastly shapes, whittled and carved by the wind and the rain. Although somewhat isolated, and in the heart of the lifeless Nebraska badlands, Toadstool Park is one of the state's most interesting sites. The ash from a distant and ancient volcano helped paint and shape these balancing rocks and serpent-like boulders.

Cottonwood Creek flows through the park. It was somewhere along this creek where Crazy Horse took his 1,500 people to camp after he surrendered at Fort Robinson in May of 1877.

You are in the vast Oglala National Grasslands. For more information on this area see the entry for US Highway 20.

Highways 2 and 71 end at the South Dakota border.

Zero miles (24 miles.)

Highway 275 enters Nebraska in southeast Omaha as it crosses over the Missouri River from Iowa. For information about Omaha please see entry for US Highway 75.

Twenty four miles (4 miles.)

Junction with US Highway 6, Dodge Street, Omaha. Please see entry for US Highway 6 for information about sites west on this highway, and US Highway 75 for information about Omaha.

Four miles (4 miles.)

Junction with State Highway 92. This beautiful and seldom traveled road stretches from here, where it breaks away from US 275, west 400 miles through the heart of the state's magnificant Sandhills, past Chimney Rock and through the saddle of Scott's Bluff to the Wyoming border. For information about State Highway 92, please see

396

that entry.

Four miles (4 miles.)
Waterloo.

Two Rivers State Recreation Area near Waterloo has a trout lake, camping and cabins.

Turn off to Elkhorn, which was a Union Pacific station in 1865. It was first named Chicago, then Douglas, then Elk City and finally Elkhorn. Elkhorn is the home of the German Farmers Mutual Fire Insurance Company, which was the first non-native company of its kind.

Four miles (10 miles.)
Valley.

The Valley Community Historical Museum is preserving items of local heritage, including prehistoric bones of the giant mammoths to items from the pioneer life of the Valley area. The museum is in the 1873 school house, which also served as a Baptist and Catholic church before becoming the museum. The museum is free and open on Sunday afternoons or by appointment. This pretty little town was founded in 1864 and is still home for over 2,000.

Ten miles (11 miles.)
Fremont. For information about Fremont, please see entry for US Highway 77.

Junction with US 77 and US 30. Please see entry for those highways for information about sites along their routes.

For eleven miles north of Fremont US Highway 275 and US Highway 77 follow the same route. For information about sites along this stretch, please see entry for US Highway 77.

Eleven miles (3 miles.)
Junction US 275 and US 77. US 275 leaves 77 and branches off to the west.

Three miles (7 miles.)
Hooper. The main street of Hooper is considered by many to be one of the best preserved nineteenth-century main streets in the state. The construction is of native brick and cast iron and all but two of the contiguous buildings were constructed in the 1890s.

US Highway 275

Main Street is listed as a National Preservation Site because of its unique architecture.

The Wickwire Hotel was built in 1885 when a local farmer decided to branch out from growing hogs and corn. The building is made from locally produced brick, and at one time the main floor had a lobby and a "sample room" for traveling salesmen.

Hooper was once known for its hog cholera serum plant. We just thought you might like to know.

Seven miles (3 miles.)

Scribner. Yes, folks, this town was named after Charles Scribner of the famous New York publishing house, which did not publish this book. Scribner was the son-in-law of one of the founders.

The museum is located in the old Milligan Building, built in 1884. The town hall was built in 1906 of local brick. The Soll Opera House was built in 1898. Patrons hoisted themselves to the second floor theater with a hand-pulled elevator.

The Harder Hotel. Built in 1901.

The Musbach Museum. This was a dry goods store, and was donated to the city to use as a museum.

East of Scribner on Bridge Street, **then** turn **north** on the first county road east of the Elkhorn River Bridge. The Scribner Brickyards were built in the 1890s. One of the "bee hive" kilns can still be seen as well as the brick horse barn. This is one of the few remaining nineteenth century brickyards in the state. Near here was the Black Hills Wagon Trail.

Just **west** of Scribner **on 275** is the Mr. Cottonwood Historical Marker. To quote: "It grew from a trackwalker's probing staff thrust into the ground in 1871 by the late Herman Wegner. Protected through the years by the C & NW Railroad and after by a city ordinance. A living symbol planted unwittingly, made by God, protected by Man."

One half mile west, and one half mile south of Scribner is the location of the old Peeble Mills, built in 1868.

Eight and one half miles west of Scribner on county roads is the site of Glencoe, post office established in 1871.

Three miles (1 mile.)

Junction for Snyder.

Four miles west of junction: Snyder.

Snyder town hall was built in 1903 and has recently been renovated.

The Snyder Opera House was built in 1900 and had a main floor restaurant and saloon, and a second floor entertainment hall.

Five miles west *of Snyder: Dodge. You are in Dodge City, Dodge County, and oddly enough the names are not related. The county was named after an Iowa Senator, and the city after an early pioneer. The town hall was built in 1895 and the bell tower once held a large fire bell.*

One mile (1 mile.)

One mile east to Dead Timber State Recreation Area.

One mile (3 miles.)

Crowell. Crowell was founded in 1883.

Cuming County was settled first by whites in 1856 when a man by the name of Benjamin Moore, having made it through the roughest winter of his life, decided to stay. The bones from the many animals that died that winter could be found in the area for years to come.

Three miles (4 miles.)

Near here in 1859 was a battle with the Pawnee. While on their traditional summer hunt the Pawnee reached the Elkhorn River and attacked some settlers near this place. Other Pawnee attacked farms at West Point and other locales.

There were many encounters with the Pawnee during these weeks in June, and while most of them did not result in loss of life, the event at this spot was tragic for the Pawnee.

One party of 30 volunteers was in a barn when they saw 11 Pawnee approaching. As the Indians entered the house, lured by an offer of food, the whites surrounded the cabin. Gunfire broke out and the trapped Pawnee rushed out of the house. Only two Pawnee survived. Two others who were injured in the battle were thrown on a wagon headed toward West Point. Neither was to make it. According to *History of Cuming County,* "one died on the way, and the other was supposed to be dead and thrown into the river at the Dupray place. He proved, however, to have been playing 'possum,' and struck out for shore, but never reached it. An ounce or two of lead caused him to sink and rise no more."

Volunteer troops under the command of John M. Thayer, a major-general in the Nebraska Territorial Militia, and other locals, set out to find the offending Pawnee under orders from the Governor.

399

US Highway 275

After a variety of smaller, largely non-violent encounters, the 300 volunteers met the nearly 3,000 Pawnee near Battle Creek, some 50 miles northwest of here. Instead of fighting, the whites talked treaty and the differences were settled without further bloodshed, but with a treaty claiming the Pawnee had given up their traditional land.

For further information see below west of Norfolk when the highway crosses the Elkhorn River.

Four miles (7 miles.)

West Point. This town, located on the lovely Elkhorn River, is one of the state's oldest settlements. It was founded in 1857 by a man who set up a brickyard and a sawmill. A small war broke out between the founder of these businesses and two other competing ones. We are talking real bullets and real hangings here. The opposition set fire to the mills, shot at the owner and hanged one of his workers.

West Point was so named because the settlers thought of this place as the furthest west the white settlement of America would get for a while. Try explaining this to the folks in Newport, Oregon.

One group of early settelers was called the Nebraska Settlement Association and settled near present-day West Point.

The vote to make West Point the county seat was held in 1858. The vote was 12 for and seven against.

West Point is the location of the Cuming County Museum, located in the old train depot. The museum itself is quite old and its exhibits are in fine condition.

On the east edge of West Point is Wilderness Park, 120 acres set aside for the enjoyment of human and animal alike.

Northwest of West Point Highway 275 parallels the lovely Elkhorn River. Just off the highway between West Point and Beemer is the De Witt Cemetery, designated as an official Nebraska Historical site. It is at the oldest settlement in Cuming County.

Northeast of West Point 10 miles on State Highway 9 and then east for eight miles on State Highway 51 is the John G. Neihardt Center to honor one of Nebraska's greatest writers. See the entry on US Highway 77 for more information.

Seven miles (7 miles.)

Beemer. Beemer also has a wilderness park. This one is 230 acres and provides access to the Elkhorn.

South of Beemer, two miles on county roads: Immanuel Lutheran Church. This is the oldest Missouri Synod Lutheran Church in the state. It was established at this location in 1868.

Seven miles (5 miles.)

Wisner. For as long as there has been a Wisner (since 1871) this town has served as a feeding and shipping point for livestock. Thousands of cattle are fed along the lots that cover the sloping bluffs along the highway. Anyone from Nebraska knows what the smell really is. The smell is the smell of money.

By the way, Cuming County is known as the livestock capital of Nebraska.

Twenty miles east *of Wisner on State Highway 51 to the John G. Neihardt Center to honor one of the state's finest writers. See the entry for US Highway 77 for details.*

Five miles (1 mile.)

Junction with State Highway 15, north. For information about sites along this route, please see entry for State Highway 15.

One mile (8 miles.)

Just south of the highway: Pilger.

One of Nebraska's least recognized yet most famous Hollywood actors came from a farm just south of this small rural community. Blue Boy, a prize-winning Hampshire Hog, had a nearly starring role in the movie "State Fair." And you thought it was just Marlon Brando who was from Nebraska!

Junction of State Highway 15, south. For information about sites along this route, please see the entry for State Highway 15.

Two miles north *of Pilger is a recreation area with an inviting 40-acre lake.*

Eight miles (8 miles.)

Junction with State Highway 57, five miles south to Stanton. Please see the entry for State Highway 15 for information about Stanton.

Eight miles (5 miles.)

Norfolk.

Junction with US Highway 81. Please see the entry for US Highway 81 for information about Norfolk (yes, the hometown of Johnny Carson) and for sites along the route of Highway 81.

Five miles (5 miles.)

US Highway 275

The Shell Creek Cattle Trail crossed near here on its way north. Likewise, a trail to the Black Hills followed this route. Supply trains of 30 wagons — each drawn by from eight to 12 oxen — left Norfolk for the Black Hills during the gold rush days of the 1870s. The trip often took as long as two months.

Five miles (7 miles.)

The Elkhorn River. This river is one of the more popular rivers in the state for recreational purposes.

Two tenths of a mile past the river on the right is the site of the Pawnee Battleground.

In the summer of 1859 a series of difficulties with the Pawnee was escalating. Recently the Pawnee had "agreed" to give up their land on the Platte River and move farther north.

However, just as they were about to start their migration, a group of settlers near present-day Fremont had an altercation with the Pawnee. The whites say the Indians robbed a man. The Indians, although no one listened, say a white man raped an Indian. As the Indians moved up the Elkhorn Valley it is said they raided local farms, stealing cattle and pigs. Bands of nervous volunteers were organized, which resulted in several minor skirmishes. In the one of the bloodiest, 10 Pawnee were killed. In the entire series of events only a single white was killed, a man who was accidentally shot when a group of volunteers panicked during a false alarm.

In any event, the Pawnee fled up the Elkhorn River. Under orders of the territorial governor, General John Thayer was dispatched to follow them. He encountered the Pawnee camp at this spot on the morning of July 12, 1859.

Nearly 3,000 Pawnee, Omaha and Ponca were camped on the plateau. The whites had some difficulty crossing Battle Creek, so the advantage of a surprise attack was wasted. The Indians dropped back, probably to regroup and counterattack since they outnumbered the whites 10 to one. The whites, however, captured an old Pawnee chief who then talked his people into a non-violent settlement. Apparently the old man understood that if they wiped out these 300 troops the whites would only send greater and greater numbers of soldiers to fight the Pawnee. Eventually the Pawnee surrendered six men and paid for damages demanded by the whites at Fremont and other locations along the Elkhorn.

This spot marks the place where the troubles with the Pawnee ended.

Seven miles (5 miles.)

Millstone State Camping Area.

Five miles (7 miles.)

Tilden. This town lies in the counties of Antelope and Madison. It was named after Samuel Tilden, who lost the Presidential race in 1876 to Rutherford Hayes.

An unknown hack writer by the name of Ron Hubbard was born in Tilden. He later fooled around with an electrical machine much like a lie detector and decided to create a religion based on this and his idea of perfect science fiction. From his efforts a group known as the Scientologists was formed, and L. Ron Hubbard became famous.

Since then, no one in Tilden believed Hubbard's thinking was ever quite clear.

Seven miles (6 miles.)

Oakdale.

Tintern Monastery. This is a special and an unusual place. This monastery was founded by the Monks of Tintern, an order based on the teachings and visions of Father Clifford Stevens. Stevens started the monastery in a barn in 1984. This is the first order to be established since the 13th Century, and the first order ever to originate in the United States.

The monks take a vow of poverty and study the ancient languages of Hebrew, Greek and Latin. They live a cloistered existence and support themselves by making crafts and growing much of their own food.

A new chapel was dedicated in 1990. It is a 200-seat, hexagon-shaped building by Bill Yoor. Yoor, who was an engineer in Baltimore, gave up his job and possessions to become a Tintern monk. When his local diocese didn't recommend him to the order, Yoor designed the chapel while he waited. A nun from New Mexico designed the sanctuary, and the adobe walls and small spaces for statues of saints are typical of many New Mexican churches. For visits to the monastery, ask directions in Oakdale.

Six miles (17 miles.)

Neligh, county seat of Antelope County, and home of the Neligh Mills. The Antelope County Historical Society is located on the highway and is open Friday and Sunday afternoons.

Neligh Mills is a branch museum run by the Nebraska State Historical Society. It was built in 1873 and was the most important flour mill in northeast Nebraska. It continued to produce flour until the 1950s. The mill was powered by water from the Elkhorn River.

In this area are the Antelope Historical Museum and various historical markers. This is a must-see point of interest if you are traveling in this section of the state.

Just west of Neligh is the junction with State Highway 14. For information about sites along its route, please see the entry for State Highway 14.

Seventeen miles (11 miles.)

Six miles north, just on the county line, is the highest point in Antelope County at around 2,100 feet.

Eleven miles (0 miles.)

Junction with US Highway 20. It is 13 miles to O'Neill. Entry for US Highway 275 ends. For more information about sites along this route, please see the entry for US Highway 20.

Zero miles (5 miles.)

Missouri River and the Iowa border.

US Highway 20 enters Nebraska at South Sioux City in Dakota County. Dakota County was named for the tribe of Indians known as the Lacotah, or Sioux who lived in this area for a long while.

South Sioux City is a part of a community that spans three states.

Sioux City proper is in Iowa, and North Sioux City is in South Dakota. It is pretty plain, however, that South Sioux City, Nebraska, is the finest looking of all three.

South Sioux City itself had at one time been the location of four different towns that eventually merged to form a single entity.

Down along the shore of the Big Muddy Missouri River you will see the largest marina anywhere along its banks.

While watching the boats, reach down and take a handful of the soil here. You can only find this particular soil — a wind-blown remnant from the Ice Age known as loess — one other place in the world, and that is in China.

When Prohibition was adopted in Iowa, South Sioux City got quite a reputation as a center of vice. Saloons that featured women of the night, fist and gunfights, and gambling and dancing were the highlights of those days.

This was the location of the Pacific Shoreline Bridge, an example of engineering skills. Built in 1890, and finally demolished in 1981, the bridge had swinging center spans to allow for boat traffic. The spans could be powered by four men and roatated at a moment's notice to let a boat pass by.

Five miles (4 miles.)

Jackson — a sleepy community in the shadow of the three big sisters to the east.

Just north of here was the original site of the quiet town of St. John's, founded just before the Civil War by a Catholic priest who wanted to set up a missionary for the Omaha Indians. The settlers who followed him became known as the Father Tracy Colony. The priest went away to serve in the war, and the town moved to this location in order to avoid the threat of flooding by the Missouri. Later the town's name was changed to Jackson.

Four miles (5 miles.)

By 1882, these areas had a long enough history to be able to form a Dakota County Old Settlers' Association. The association held reunions, and at one, in 1893, an old-timer by the name of Ed Karney read a poem he had written to commemorate the event. It seemed to be a hit with the crowd, and in the hope that it still might serve some entertainment value, it is reproduced here:

Hail Pioneers!
Hail Pioneer — through the woodland — glad resounding
Come the shouts of joy and glee;
Banners waving, mirth abounding,
Causing sorrow — grim to flee
Once a year — the scene's repeated
While autumn still is young.
And thou — oh Pioneer who in these sylvan shades
Didst first Dame Nature battle give, first rudely mar
The forests' grim repose — carving from out her rugged
trunks
A lowly, happy home — aya, upon her bosom, wildly fair

Made there thy haven and thy rest.
Hail, Pioneer — nor deem it wrong
When autumn with the ripened stores comes tripping o'er the
    hills
With its garnered fruits and grains;
Hail then, oh sturdy Pioneer — who when thy years were
        young
Thy strength and vigor, zeal and nerve, against Dame
        Nature flung
Unfair seemed then the conflict as a gnat against lion strong
But God was with the Pioneer; to Him the thanks belong,
Full long thy ardous labor — full sore thy grievous pain,
But now the victory's won — thy toil hath beautified the plains
For ages thy praises will be sung, thy name held ever dear.
Long mayyest thou live, and dying find sweet peace —
        oh PIONEER!

Junction with State Highway 12. For information about sites along this route, please see entry for State Highway 12.

Five miles (5 miles.)
Turn off to Waterbury, one mile south. Once this town had 40 buildings and 200 people. It is much smaller than that now. The name comes from a local springs that never froze in winter.

Five miles (1 mile.)
To the **north three miles** is the small farming community of Martinsburg on State Highway 9, north.
Martinsburg was founded in 1872 by Jonathan Martin, who built a grist mill and store. Many of the buildings here have been burned over the years, including a large dance shell where Lawrence Welk often played.

One mile (12 miles.)
Turn off for Allen, **three miles south** on State Highway 9.
Allen is the home of the Dixon County Museum, which includes four buildings and a wide assortment of exhibits tracing the history of this area.
The town started in 1891 on land donated by a man named Henry Allen, who set the condition that the town that was built here remain dry. . .dry, anyway, of alcoholic liquids.
The Friends' Church predates the settlement of the town.

US Highway 20

Lop-alop Farm, just north of town, has a variety of small exotic animals and birds and holds an annual exotic animal swap.

Twelve miles (2 miles.)

Intersection of US 20 and State Highway 15.

Two miles north of this intersection is the location of the old town of Norris, abandoned after it was bypassed by the railroad. One mile farther east and a quarter mile north is the location of the old Norris Cemetery. For information about other sites north and south on 15, please see the entry for State Highway 15.

Two miles (1 mile.)

One mile east of the intersection of US 20 and this county road is the location of the former town of Claremont Junction. The town eventually died, which is what happens when you are known as a former town.

One mile (14 miles.)

Laurel.

In the town cemetery, on the southwest corner of the village, is the grave of a Mrs. Gleason who was born in the 18th century and died in the 20th.

The junction with State Highway 15, south is here. For a continuation of sites along that route, please see entry for State Highway 15.

Fourteen miles (4 miles.)

Randolph.

Randolph is known as the honey capitol of the world. When you buy that Sioux Bee Honey, keep in mind that the honey may be packaged elsewhere, but Randolph's 16,000 colonies of bees (or roughly 160,000,000 bees), which produce more than a million pounds of honey each year, are where it really comes from.

Four miles (6 miles.)

Junction with US Highway 81. For sites north and south along this highway, please see the entry for US Highway 81.

Six miles (3 miles.)

Junction with State Highway 121, north. To the north are such sites as the Wild Horse Holding Facility and the best pastry this side of heaven. For information about these and other sites, please see the

408

entry for State Highway 14.

Three miles (10 miles.)

Osmond. In the Catholic cemetery near Osmond are the remains of John Kortena, a local eccentric who lived here in the early days. John lived in caves, but managed to pay a personal visit to every newborn baby in the area. He had a horse, but kept it inside a barn for its entire life. The horse's hooves curled up from lack of use. John is buried in the vest he always wore rain, snow or shine...the same vest where he always kept $2,000 in cash tucked away in a pocket.

Ten miles (12 miles.)

Plainview. Well, yes, but there are people in the Bronx who would trade this view for theirs any day.

In the cemetery is a marker commemorating students who died in the blizzard of 1888. The marker itself is historical, as it was placed here by the heroine teacher who saved many of her students during the worst blizzard ever to hit this area.

Junction with State Highway 13. For information about sites along State Highway 13, please see entry for US Highway 81.

Twelve miles (5 miles.)

Junction with State Highway 14. This highway runs from the Kansas border to the border with South Dakota. For information about sites in this area and along its route, please see entry for State Highway 14.

Five miles (2 miles.)

Royal. Marlow Jensen and his son Justin live here. The two men are skilled at a dying art. They are wheelwrights, men who wrought and repair wooden wagon wheels. People from all over the nation send wheels here to be repaired by these skilled craftsmen.

North of Royal three miles is the Grove Lake Wildlife Management area, where camping is allowed.

Two miles (4 miles.)

Turnoff for Ashfall State Historical Park.

North six miles on county road to Ashfall Fossil Beds. Ten million years ago a massive volcanic erruption, probably somewhere in present-day Idaho, sent a thick, choking cloud of volcanic dust eastward. The dust fell onto this land, which then resembled the savannahs of East Africa, and smothered every living thing.

409

US Highway 20

The fossilized remains of these creatures are preserved in their death poses in exquisite detail. Visitors can watch the ongoing excavations in the "Rhino Barn." Workers uncover mother rhinos and their babies, three-toed horses, camels and other creatures that once roamed this part of Nebraska.

The Visitors' Center includes interpretive displays and a laboratory where the fossils are prepared for display and research. Nature trails weave through the scenic rangeland of the Verdigre Creek Valley.

The site was discovered in 1971 after heavy spring rains eroded the edge of a cornfield and exposed the complete skull of a baby rhino. Since then over 100 skeletons have been unearthed. The site is unusual in that the skeletons are nearly all complete and in pristine condition. The unborn fetuses of rhinos have been discovered in some of the female skeletons as have footprints of the herd made moments before the darkness of the cloud fell upon them.

An additional 40 other animals have been collected along with various plants.

The site is a must-see of the area.

Four miles (11 miles.)

Orchard. This town was named for the miles of apple orchards planted here in pioneer times.

According to Lilian Fitzpatrick's fine book *Nebraska Place-Names,* Antelope County was named to remember an antelope one of the first settlers shot for dinner while guiding an early group of tourists through the area in 1867.

From Orchard to O'Neill, US 20 passes through or very near to a half-dozen or better small communities both dead and alive. The highway parallels the Elkhorn River and winds its way uphill. As the road slips past hills speckled with yucca, the entire sense of western America begins to unfold. Or, for those of you traveling east...the entire sensation of the peopled and cultivated eastern America begins to reveal itself.

Eleven miles (13 miles.)

Junction with US Highway 275, south. For information about this highway, please see entry for US Highway 275. US 275 joins US 20 at this point, northward.

Thirteen miles (8 miles.)

O'Neill.

410

At 4,000 proud and friendly folks, O'Neill is the largest town in any direction for close to 100 miles. Its location in the heart of the Elkhorn Valley makes it an ideal place for both the small garden farmer as well as the rancher. I wouldn't get the oxygen masks out just yet, but O'Neill is at nearly 2,000 feet in altitude, and from here westward the gradual climb to the continental divide is apparent.

O'Neill is the county seat of Holt County, and the Courthouse is the center of the town's activities. The peaceful and quiet streets around the Courthouse simply shadow a much wilder and reckless past.

During the early years of this century, O'Neill was known as one of the roughest towns around. To give you an idea just how rough things were around here, a man by the name of Barrett Scott, who was the Holt County Treasurer, took off for Mexico with his pockets apparently full of the county's money. He was found and brought back to O'Neill to face trial.

He was released on bail, but while free he was kidnapped. His body was found 30 miles north of here on the banks of the Niobrara River. Scott's body was wrapped in a horse blanket, and the hanging rope was still around his neck. A boot heel mark was in the middle of his forehead, and his body was mutilated.

Forty men were arrested and a dozen were brought to trial. None of those 12 ever served time for Scott's murder. By the way, no one has so much as stolen a dime from the coffee fund much less embezzled county funds since that day.

O'Neill was founded by, and named after, John J. O'Neill, who was quite a flamboyant character in his own right. He was an Irish-American and spearheaded a group to encourage Irish settlement of the American West. The first colony to settle under O'Neill's director-ship was right here in 1874. O'Neill had earlier fought for the Union in the Civil War and had commanded a Black infantry. Later he was a major figure in the so-called and short-lived Fenian invasion of Canada.

The town of O'Neill was one of the oldest towns in the state to traditionally have Sunday shopping hours for most stores. This was originally (and is still true) to help service those out-of-towners who could make it to town only on the weekends.

Eight miles (10 miles.)
Emmet, named after an Irish patriot.

North of here, all the way to the Niobrara River, some 30 miles distant, are numerous Indian burials, often located on small hilltops. These burials were encased in limestone rock slabs and were regarded by the ancient peoples who once lived here as sacred places. Don't disturb them — think how your would feel if someone dug up great-grandfather Herkimer.

Ten miles (19 miles.)

Junction with State Highway 11. For information about sites along this route, please see the entry for State Highway 11.

Atkinson. The second settlement founded by John O'Neill and his Irish. In case you wondered, no, the town did not look like this in the late 1870s when first settled. A small lake just outside of town provides camping and recreation facilities.

Nineteen miles (11 miles.)

Junction with State Highway 137.

Twenty miles north on Highway 137 to Mariaville Bridge, the eastern end of the Federally designated Scenic River segment of the Niobrara.

Eleven miles (9 miles.)

Bassett and the junction with US 183. For information about Bassett and points south, please see the entry for US Highway 183.

North of Bassett 15 miles to the Niobrara River, a Wild and Scenic river. Northwest of Bassett are the Pine Glen and Thomas Creek State Wildlife Management areas.

Nine miles (3 miles.)

Long Pine is a half mile south of the highway.

This tiny town with the attractive name would be called Mazi-sneede Wachishka if the white settlers had not translated the name of the local creek from its original Omaha. Just outside of the town is Long Pine Recreation Area, another fine and beautiful area for the camper, hiker, fisherperson and nature lover.

One half mile past the turnoff for Long Pine, the highway crosses the canyon that is formed by Long Pine Creek. Who says Nebraska isn't beautiful? Good fishing here.

Three miles (6 miles.)

Junction of US 183, north. Please see entry for US Highway 183 for information about this area.

As you come in sight of Ainsworth, you enter an area known as Bone Creek. This area was named because of the thousands of buffalo skeletons that once littered the floor of the valley.

Six miles (10 miles.)
Ainsworth.

Ainsworth was named for a railroad construction engineer and was founded in 1883.

The Civil War Memorial at the County Courthouse park was built in 1948 because of the donation of a Civil War veteran, L.K. Alder. Alder volunteered at the age of 17, and served nearly two years under General Sherman, accompanying Sherman on his famous "march to the sea." The Nannie Osborne homestead is the oldest structure in Ainsworth. The home was built in 1879. Nannie was divorced from her husband when she moved to Ainsworth from Fort Hartsuff, 70 miles to the southeast. It must not have been easy for a divorced, single woman in 1879, especially one who wanted to build such a fine home.

Sellors Memorial Museum. This small but interesting museum was not built by pioneers, but as a memorial to all Brown County pioneers. The logs were cut from trees along the banks of the Niobrara and hauled here in 1936. It was expanded in 1967.

North out of Ainsworth for 13 miles on county roads until you reach Plum Creek. Here are many fossil beds in the limestone of the deep canyon along the creek. Camels, rhinoceroses and prehistoric horses have been found in these fossil beds.

Discovered in 1925 by Morris Skinner and James Quinn, the find included the bones of mastodons, a large elephant-like creature. Although many of the fossils were sold to the American Museum in New York and Denver, the find inspired the University of Nebraska Museum Director E. H. Barbour to create two teams of fossil collectors to search the state for other fossil beds. Known as the South Party and the North Party, Barbour's teams would make several significant discoveries during the 1930s.

Ten miles (1 mile.)
Turnoff to Long Lake on Highway 20.

Some miles south of here, at the junction of Long Lake turnoff and Elsmere Road, was the site of the only sod high school ever built in the United States. This is no pioneer story. Lakeland High School, which once stood here and was built entirely of sod, was constructed in 1934. That's right, 1934.

Because of the Depression and the drought, many students

413

in the isolated western part of Brown County were going to have to drop out of Ainsworth High School. For eight years, a total of 33 students attended the small campus-like high school, which consisted of the school, a barn and a his and a hers two-seater.

All of the buildings, including the privies, were made from native sod. The school marm and her family lived in the sod school. The instructor, Mary Holm, cooked her family's meals on a Coleman stove.

All parents are required to stop here a moment, for this place is the original prototype of all those "when I was your age, we had to ride 20 miles on horseback to get to school" stories. Most students arrived by horseback, and many lived over five miles away. They arrived by traveling across country, stopping to dismount and open, then close, numerous gates.

Mrs. Holm was not the only teacher. Two others worked at the school in the seven years it existed.

South on Long Lake Road to Long Lake Recreation Area. Local folks will tell you that the best fishing to be found is in Long Lake. Don't believe them. There's good fishing there, all right, but to find the truly great spots you need to act like you are a local person and just listen. (Fishing hint: It rhymes with June and spoon.) A fine camping area is located here.

One mile (10 miles.)
Johnstown. Small community of windmills, horses and houses. Johnstown was once the home of John Berry, who drove the mail stage to Fort Niobrara.

Take county roads northeast of Johnstown 18 miles to the Nature Conservancy's Niobrara Valley Preserve Outreach Center. The center is a classroom laboratory for students and teachers as well as researchers who wish to explore the area. The center includes a kitchen and bunkhouse for up to 10 people.

This section of the Niobrara is under the protection of the Wild and Scenic Rivers Act.

This area would also be the location of the Buffalo Commons. The commons was the brainchild of two Princeton professors who offered a solution to the problem of declining populations in prairie counties on the American Great Plains. Their idea is to let the land revert to its pre-pioneer state and to reintroduce the buffalo to those places that have become all but ghost counties. Thousands of acres from Texas to the Canadian border would be the open range of buffalo and the home of native grasses. The professors claim that such a use is the only wise land-use left after a century of blown-away crops, struggle and poverty.

Needless to say, many residents of these areas think replacing pioneers with buffalo isn't such a good idea. Their claim to stewardship of the land is significant, as most residents in these Sandhills can trace their ancestors back to the days of covered wagons and the Homestead Act. Still, the residents might be the first to admit it has never been easy to make a living out here, and the first to nod when you point out the empty towns and abandoned ranch houses.

But. . .buffalo?

An excellent and unbiased look at the idea of the Buffalo Commons idea as well as its founders, is Anne Mathews' Where the Buffalo Roam — The Storm Over the Revolutionary Plan to Restore America's Great Plains.

Ten miles (19 miles.)

Wood Lake in Cherry County.

Cherry County was named for a soldier who was killed near Fort Niobrara. It is said that Cherry County is the largest county in the United States. If that turns out to be only local boosterism, bear in mind that this county is larger than Connecticut, Delaware and Rhode Island combined, and a lot more livable, many Cherry County citizens might add.

Wood Lake was a name given to this town by early settlers. They knew it meant that here, finally, were some trees around a small lake, but others not from around here might think it implied a lake in the woods.

Nineteen miles (2 miles.)

Junction with US Highway 83. For information about sites along this highway, please see the entry for US Highway 83.

Two miles (3 miles.)

The highways cross the Niobrara River, Nebraska's wildest river, at the Bryan Bridge, named for William Jennings Bryan, Nebraska's only presidential candidate (unless you consider Gerald Ford, who was born in Omaha). The man lost three times. Don't worry, the bridge is probably safe. The river here is extremely beautiful as it winds through a shallow canyon.

In 1991, President George Bush signed a law designating a

415

nearly 76-mile segment of the Niobrara starting here and going east as a Scenic River. Local landowners were among the few who fought the bill, preferring local control of the land rather than Federal control. Despite their opposition, the law was applauded nationwide for protecting the rich biological diversity along the pristine river.

See State Highway 12 for more information about sites east of here along the Niobrara.

Three miles (11 miles.)

Valentine.

The canoe and white-water capitol of Nebraska.

This is the county seat of the vast Cherry County. This is as close as you'll get to the way life was in the Old West. The town is proud of its ranching and farming history and the flavor of the west is everywhere here. Lake Minnechaduza on the northern edge of the town was formed in 1892 when a local flour mill dammed the Minnechaduza Creek for a mill run. The name is from the Indian name for the stream.

Valentine is the home of the Cherry County Historical Museum at South Main and Highway 20. It is open six days a week during the summer months, and three days a week during fall and spring. In winter it is open by appointment only. The museum contains pictures, articles and other materials that show the history of Cherry County, Fort Niobrara, Valentine and other local communities. Some of the unusual items include a baptismal font, the weapons and disguise used in a train holdup in 1890, one of the first typewriters, a vast collection of arrowheads and Indian artifacts, a button collection, a research facility containing many printed county documents, and a log cabin built by Valentine's first postmaster and moved to the museum grounds in 1982.

Valentine is also the canoe outfitter headquarters for trips on the Niobrara. Several outfitters and rental places abound in the community for the spectacular trip down Nebraska's beautiful Niobrara. The 76-mile stretch of the river east of Valentine is a designated wild and scenic river, which allows for protection and tourist regulation of the river. Studies have been done to determine whether the area should be made into a national park as well.

In 1991 a rancher near Cody, some 40 miles distant, decided the cheapest way to get 450 head of cattle to the Valentine market was the old-fashioned way. He and about 20 riders drove the cattle three days to Valentine, not as a publicity stunt or for a lark, but for business. The cattle were auctioned off.

Four miles east of Valentine on State Highway 12 is the Fort Niobrara National Wildlife Refuge. This area is home to many of the large animals that once roamed this area, including buffalo, elk, antelope and deer. A small herd of Longhorn cattle was introduced here not long ago. It is over 20,000 acres and was originally set aside by President Theodore Roosevelt. The Niobrara formed a 100-foot-deep canyon through part of the refuge, and streams enter the canyon in waterfalls.

Every year, the Refuge is the site of the Bison and Texas Longhorn Cattle Sale. Each year surplus animals are sold on the first Wednesday in October. Only a limited number of the animals can graze on the refuge and the others are sold. Before the sale some of the animals are given to zoos and nature preserves. The Longhorns here are one of the oldest breeds still around and are prized for their pure bloodline.

Many fossils have been collected in this area. Near the refuge headquarters is the site of the original Fort Niobrara, which includes a museum. The fort was built in 1880 to protect settlers from the Sioux.

The refuge is one of the finer areas in Cherry County. For more information about other locations along Route 12, please see entry for State Highway 12.

Follow State **Highway 97 southwest** out of Valentine **35 miles** to the Samuel McKelvie National Forest. After about **10 miles** the road crosses the Niobrara River. It was near here that Doc Middleton had a hideout.

At *32 miles* from Valentine on State 97 is the turnoff for Snake River Falls. Snake River Falls is the most dramatic waterfall in the state and is the highlight of the beautiful Snake River. The Snake River plunges over a 22-foot cliff in a deep canyon. Behind the falls is a natural cave, which was used for years by horse thieves and other banditos. Today it serves as a delightful place for local children to cool off in late July.

At *34 miles* the Merritt Reservoir provides fishing and boating and flood control, but destroyed some of the most beautiful river scenery in the state. Still, camping above the shore of this isolated lake can provide the visitor with morning views of unspoiled prairieland breaking out of darkness into the dawn like a box turtle from its shell.

There is camping in the national forest, with developed sites at Merritt Reservoir and at the National Forest Headquarters 19 miles

US Highway 20

south of Nenzel west of Valentine (see below). A passable road goes from here to the western section of the forest.

See the entry for State Highway 97 for more information about this area.

At Valentine are the junctions of State Highway 12 and US Highway 83. Please see those entries for more information about sites in this area.

Eleven miles (8 miles.)

Crookston, where a mill on the Minnechaduza Creek was an important early-day business.

Eight miles (12 miles.)

You have passed into (or from if you are headed east) Mountain Standard Time while traveling through the rolling Sandhills.

Twelve miles (7 miles.)

Nenzel at the junction of State Road 16F.

South on 16F for 20 miles to the campgrounds of the *Samuel McKelvie National Forest. Along the way you will pass a few scattered and old homestead ranches, including that of the historian and early politician A.E. Sheldon, whose* History of Nebraska *is still a viable history of the state.*

Seven miles (15 miles.)

Cody. If you missed the western flavor of the area so far, Cody, named after a local pioneer and not Buffalo Bill, should give you an idea.

Ten miles south of here, on private land, are the Boiling Springs, one of the great natural wonders of the county. Ask locally for directions and permission to visit the place.

Also south of town is one of the state's ostrich ranches. That's right, one of several ostrich ranches in the state. This one started in the late 1980s when the birds could be bought for a mere $2,500. By the early 1990s, they were selling for as high as $10,000. However, only those who are not chicken should get into the business, since by the mid-1990s the fad seems to have peaked. There seems to be just so much of a market for the big bird's feathers and meat.

Fifteen miles (9 miles.)

418

Eli, notable for its name, which was after Daniel Webster Hitchcock, whose nickname was "Get-There-Eli." For a long while this town was known by the full Get-There-Eli.

Nine miles (30 miles.)

Cottonwood Lake Recreation Area. An 80-acre lake stocked with fine fishing fish.

*Merriman. Just to the west of the recreation area is the junction of State Highway 61 at Merriman. This highway travels through some of the most isolated territory in the state. It is **70 miles** to Hyannis down this road. This road is meant only for the traveler seeking complete isolation and beauty.*

North on Highway 61 to the most unusual state park in the system: Arthur Bowring Sandhills Ranch. The ranch was willed to the state by the late U.S. Senator Eve Bowring as a tribute to her husband, who spent his life ranching. A visitor's center provides a fine introduction to ranching in the Sandhills and the ranch house includes many artifacts from the Senator's career. It's a working ranch and state historical park, and a visit to the ranch is a visit back in time.

For those of you interested in Highway 61 revisited, please see entry for State Highway 61.

Thirty miles (15 miles.)

Gordon.

Gordon was the part-time home of Nebraska's most famous outlaw, "Doc" Middleton. He was born in Texas under a different name and arrived in the Sandhills region in the late 1870s, having already killed a number of men in Texas and Kansas, as well as being on the Texas Rangers' "Most Wanted" list for stealing horses. (A crime considered by many to be worse than murder.)

After being held in long chains in a log jail in Sidney for stealing 34 horses, Middleton escaped during the night by shoveling a tunnel to the outside.

On another occasion, Middleton was chased by a posse from Ogallala to Sidney, during which he crossed the Camp Clarke Bridge near Bridgeport in Morrill County with his reins in his teeth and his .45s blazing the night sky, traded his horse for another and escaped the pursuit of the posse.

He later spent much time around Bassett, Neligh, O'Neill and Atkinson, as many of those area ranchers were on friendly terms with the outlaw. So friendly in fact that at one point Middleton was also named the first deputy sheriff in Sheridan County.

US Highway 20

In 1885, Doc Middleton wrote a short article about his life in the Gordon paper. "It is utterly false that I stole horses from either stockmen or citizens. On these occasions I resorted to a game of bluff to protect myself and made it work. I do not deny that I drove off horses from the Indians. I did do that, but it was not from choice that I did so. I have sowed my wild oats and reaped the harvest and now, having settled down in the determination to be a man among men, I can afford to tell the truth, I claim that among those who know me best, my word is as good as that of any man and will not be doubted."

It was generally agreed, however, by those who knew him best, that the Badlands Badman was "an outlaw and a killer who was also gracious and refined, a gentleman of the road who would steal your horse but pay for his dinner."

Doc Middleton had a wife and children. One of his sons, Ponca Bill, once said that his father always buried the men he shot, which was more than some could say...and he always came home at least twice a year. An excellent book on the life of Doc Middleton was written by Harold Hutton of Bassett. Some copies of the book are still available at bookstores throughout the state.

Mari Sandoz wrote many of her books about this area. Many folks will know a good deal about this fine writer. The Mari Sandoz Room is located at the Tourist Information center on Main Street. A museum dedicated to her is located 26 miles south on State Highway 27 at the Double R Ranch.

Winship Park is the location of the Tri-State Old Time Cowboys' Museum. It is free and open summers or by appointment.

Gordon is also the location of the Scamahorn Museum and the Store of Yesterday operated by the fine Sheridan County Historical Society.

Junction with State Highway 27. South of here are many sites that the author Mari Sandoz wrote about in her famous book, *Old Jules*. For information on these and other locations, please see the entry for State Highway 27.

Fifteen miles (9 miles.)
Rushville.

Don't laugh at this small Nebraska town. More famous people have visited it than will ever visit you or I. These have included Buffalo Bill, Presidents Teddy Roosevelt and Calvin Coolidge, John J. Pershing, Frederic Remington and many others.

Home of Sheridan County Museum, a small but interesting

420

county museum worth the hour spent inside. Near here is Smith Lake, noted for a long while for its good fishing.

Junction with State Highway 87. This road has many interesting sites along its route, including many places the author Mari Sandoz wrote about. For more information please see entry for State Highway 87.

An interesting circle tour, which will allow you to view many sites of interest in the history of the relations with the Sioux Indians, can begin at Rushville. For a description of this tour, please see entry for Hay Springs, below.

Nine miles (2 miles.)

Turn off to Walgren Lake. *The lake is **five miles south.***

Walgren Lake is an alkali lake, and home of Nebraska's only known sea monster. This monster was well known in pioneer days, and many a modern sighting has reinforced its existence.

In 1921, a rancher was passing near when his horses reared up. He looked out across the lake and saw an animal spouting water about 150 yards from shore. He estimated that the animal was 10 feet long, a yard wide and was dark in color.

Later that same year it was seen again, with the same description, Once again, late in 1921, two state workers heard a very loud splash near the shore, although they did not see anything.

Then in August 1922, several witnesses saw a 20-foot-long creature in the shape of a fish.

In 1923, an association was formed to drag the lake and catch the monster. Everything was set until the landowners of the lake learned that the association was going to charge admission and asked for a cut. The plan fell through.

As it is said in these parts, any devil who can scatter fossilized bones over the Sandhills to confuse those of little faith, can put a sea monster in an alkali lake.

For further information about sites in this area, please see the entry for State Highway 87.

Two miles (10 miles.)

Hay Springs and location of the Heritage Center Museum operated by the active Sheridan County Historical Society.

***North** of Hay Springs on county graveled roads are many interesting historical sites.*

***Seven miles north of town** is the "chosen land" of Crazy Horse.*

US Highway 20

Eleven and a half miles north of Hay Springs brings the brave traveler to one site of Camp Sheridan, established to keep the Sioux in tow and to protect the early settlers from 1874-1881.

About 1/2 mile further north is the location of the Spotted Tail Indian Agency, 1874-1877.

One mile north of the Agency site is a second site of Camp Sheridan.

It was near here that the Sioux often held their Sundance. The Sundance was a purification ceremony that tested the strength of members of the band. Those who could endure the sometimes brutal pain that the ceremony involved were given great respect by others, for they were considered holy and to have paid for the wrongdoings of others by their suffering.

Five miles to the east is Beaver Wall, an escarpment with breath-taking views that increase in grandeur with every mile. From the top, one can see from the Black Hills to the buttes at Crawford, a distance of nearly 150 miles. If you cross the wall, a left turn will take you back to Highway 87. A right turn will take you through Metcalf Reserve, and on the marked gravel road toward Rushville pass through Metcalf Game Reserve. A great place to hike, since the county road is the only road through the preserve. Wild turkey, deer and antelope are common here.

Twenty miles south to return to Rushville, or go back the way you came to Hay Springs.

Ten miles (2 miles.)

Dawes and Sioux counties were once a part of a single large county known as Sioux County, which encompassed an area from the North Platte River to the state line. In the late 1800s, they were divided into approximately their present sizes.

Here, where the Little Bordeaux Creek crosses the highway, was the location of a village named for the trader, James Bordeaux. A farmstead and a railroad siding are all that remain of the community.

The long ridge you see in front of you is Pine Ridge, a series of bluffs, hills and escarpments that cut across this corner of the state.

It was near here that one of the most incredible stories of the Old West took place. In 1823, a man named Hugh Glass set out for the Yellowstone with a party of prospectors and explorers. Near what would one day be either Nebraska or South Dakota, he was attacked by a grizzly bear.

The bear tore at Glass' flesh, leaving gaping holes in his sides, arms and legs. The rest of his party, certain that he would die,

422

left two men to watch over him and bury him when he died. After five days the men grew restless and stole all of his belongings — his gun, knife, and supplies — and left him to die alone with the coyotes and wolves.

Instead, Glass survived and slowly crawled 100 miles to a fort on the Missouri in what is now western South Dakota. He rested a few days until he found a party heading for the Yellowstone. He set out with them, still very weak, but in search of the men who had left him.

A few days later this party was attacked by a party of Arikara Indians who killed everyone in the party except for Glass. Glass continued on alone and nearly two months later he reached the Yellowstone.

However, the men who had abandoned him, he soon learned, had returned downriver to Fort Atkinson near the present-day town of Fort Calhoun, north of Omaha. Glass immediately turned around and, rigging a canoe out of buffalo hides, began to float the river.

He hooked up with a party of couriers delivering supplies to various Army outposts. Along the way these men were attacked by more Arikara, and — you guessed it — Glass escaped.

He strayed across this part of Nebraska and, walking and floating various rivers, he eventually made it to Fort Atkinson about a year to the day after he had been attacked by the bear.

The men he sought were at the fort, but by then Glass had cooled some, and in time the men ironed out their dispute and became friends. Glass' story is told in verse by Nebraska's poet laureate, John Neihardt (see entry for Bancroft).

Two miles (5 miles.)

Near here was the site of the Sweat Colony, a religious utopia movement of the late 1880s founded by Levi G. Sweat from Missouri. The colony made up a good portion of the area's earliest white inhabitants. A few of their descendants still populate the area.

Five miles (1 mile.)

Museum of the Fur Trade has exhibits on the fur trade in North America. The trading house of James Bordeaux (1837-1876) is located on the grounds. The exhibits include weapons, furs, trade goods and an Indian garden with many of the plants used by local Indians. It is open every day during the summer, and during the winter by appointment. Don't be put off, the superintendent will open the museum for you. It is a good idea to call ahead of time, however.

*Within a **quarter mile** of here are a handful of historic loca-*

423

tions. About a quarter mile to the east turn north on the road that curves north across the railroad tracks.

Just to the west, and visible from the road, is the site of the Joseph Bissonette's log trading post, which was in operation from 1872-1877. The Nelson saloon, post office and stage station are also located here.

In about a half a mile this road crosses Bordeaux Creek, three miles downstream, and on the west bank was the location of a commonly frequented Sioux campsite.

Six miles to the northeast you might catch a glimpse of Sheridan's Gates, two buttes through which the military road led to Camp Sheridan.

One half mile east of the museum the scenic Bordeaux Road runs south through table lands and canyons until it connects with US 385, 15 miles away.

About four miles south on this road, along the west bank of the creek was Spotted Tail's camp from 1870-1872. The road intersects with King's Canyon Road about six miles south at a place known to locals as "the Cliffs."

One mile (2 miles.)

One mile west of the Museum of the Fur Trade: Take Slim Buttes Road north. That farmstead on your right also served as an old dance hall many moons ago.

Two miles (3 miles.)

Chadron.

If there ever was a town that once had saloons with swinging doors, cowboys who used their .45s to finish any and all heated discussions, and other wild types, Chadron was it. Some might say that there is still a bit of this Old West flavor to the place.

Some of Chadron's early citizens, such as ranchers Charles Coffee (not from Colombian mountains) and Bartlett Richards, are members of the Hall of Great Westerners at the National Cowboy Hall of Fame in Oklahoma City. During the Massacre at Wounded Knee in 1890, many of the surrounding area families gathered in Chadron for protection. They needed none; the Indians were wiped out fairly thoroughly.

Chadron's most famous citizen might well be Milford (Dub) Miller who was a tackle for the Chicago Bears from 1934 until 1937. Miller wasn't quite a refrigerator, but the Bears were considered the best team in the nation. At the time of Miller's seasons with the Bears,

424

a good professional football player made about $125 per game. That figures out to something like $2,500 per year, including bonuses. Miller, who is remembered locally as a good, kind-hearted man, died in 1981.

Another unusual Chadron resident was Clyde Beedle, an eccentric strongman who entertained people from everywhere with his amazing feats of strength. Beedle was well-known for being able to drive a spike through a one-inch-thick board with his bare hands. He often could be seen pulling the 4-ton fire engine across Chadron's First Street by his teeth. He also amused himself by bending a 3/8ths-inch bolt into a circle, by tearing a deck of cards into quarters, and diving over straight-back chairs while carrying 35-pound weights in each hand. Perhaps one of his most inspiring activities was to tie a rope around his neck and then get four strong men to pull with all their strength. Beedle did not choke. He died in 1975 at age 81, but before his death he was still able to squat press 250 pounds, and bench press 325.

First off, put this book on the seat of the car and drive directly to the Chadron Chamber of Commerce and pick up a copy of their excellent *People and Places From the Sidewalks of Yesteryear—A Walking Tour of Chadron*. This little book, also available at some bookstores, will provide an enjoyable afternoon in the town on an easy and rewarding one-mile tour.

You could drive, but better yet, get out of that gas-hog for a moment and walk south on Main Street from downtown. Chadron has many Victorian houses, as well as other classic styles such as bungalow (usually a low-slung, comfortable-looking sort of house with a wide porch on several sides), and Georgian Revival. Many of these styles, as well as some other eccentric ones, can be seen in the blocks immediately adjacent to downtown on Main Street.

Also stroll around the streets that run parallel to Main. Among the other things you will see are the old houses that once belonged to one of Chadron's founding families, the Coffees. (No, they didn't go to pot, nor were they half-perked.)

Chadron's downtown contains some unusual and historic buildings. Perhaps one of the most unusual is the Blaine Hotel at 2nd and Bordeaux streets.

The hotel opened in 1892, and a year later this building served as the starting place for an event known as "The Great Cowboy Race," where hundreds of cowboys raced from Chadron, Nebraska, to Chicago, Illinois. Some dignitary stood on the balcony just above the main entrance and fired a gun into the air and all that was seen then was a cloud of dust fading off in the direction of Chicago.

The World's Fair was going on in Chicago, and hell, that seemed as good a reason as any to have a race. Among the competitors was the outlaw "Doc" Middleton (see entry for Gordon, Nebraska, above). The Humane Society was dead set against the race and they kept a careful eye on the entire affair, following the horses' conditions through the 1,000-mile race. Although lots of cowboys started the race, only 9 or so were serious about it. The prize was $1,000. The first man to reach the finish line (which was the entrance to Buffalo Bill's Wild West Show) took 13 days and 16 hours.

Across Bordeaux Street is the Niles Hotel, once used by the railroad to house work crews.

Don't sell Chadron short. Near here were the law offices of Fannie O'Linn, the first woman postmistress in the state as well as the first woman in Nebraska to be admitted to the bar. The story goes that she owned land west of here, hoping to sell it to the land company, which would then form a town named after her. The price was too high and instead the land company bought some land farther east.

For a long while people believed that the town was named after Pierre Chadron, an old-time French fur trapper and squaw man who trapped in these parts. That's a pretty nice bit of romantic stuff fit for a Michener novel, but in the late 1970s researchers determined the town was more likely named after Louis Chartran, a trader and trapper.

Either way, the ghosts of these old pioneers haunt the coolies and hills of the area to this day. At 2nd and Main the white brick building was the home of a bank when it was built in 1885, and catty-corner is the First National Bank building, which was built in 1917 by C. F. Coffee (no drip, this guy).

It was at this location on July 4, 1900, that Teddy Roosevelt stood in the noonday heat and spoke to the thousand or better gathered there. His speech was more than likely the same one he had given across the Panhandle, but the crowd cheered all the same.

Roosevelt liked this neck of the great American woods, and it is easy to see why.

At the corner of 2nd and Chadron Streets you can see two curbs, as the older one, when the streets were wider, is still visible. On the east side of Chadron Street, hitching rings are still visible. There are those from the eastern part of the state who might want to believe these are still used by wild cowboys. I'm not going to tell you any differently.

City Hall (234 Main) was built in 1917, and the Pace Theater, next door, was built in 1925. The first movie to be shown in the Pace was "Sea Hawk," not a talkie, so a local band provided the music. Across the street is the old Opera House, built in 1888. Many of the buildings on that side of the street are brick, and date from the late 1880s. This is because most of the rest of the town was destroyed by a fire in 1887.

The Federal Building, now the Post Office, at 278 Main was a pork barrel project of Moses P. Kinkaid. Yes, the same Moses P. who revised the homesteading act and invited thousands of farmers to try their hand at making the Sandhills bloom. These homesteaders were known by the then derogatory name "Kinkaiders."

Unlike many other counties in Nebraska, Dawes County had a reasonable way of determining which city should be the county seat. Instead of fisticuffs, or gunplay, or outright skullduggery, the citizens of Dawes voted for their county seat. The county Courthouse at 4th and Main reminds some of the Nebraska statehouse in Lincoln.

Some blocks from here, $26,000 was found stashed in the basement of a house at the corner of Fifth and Maple. The money was mostly in silver dollars and was found shortly after the owner, John Sweeney, died in 1959. The money was hidden in the cellar, behind two locked doors. There were 105 glass jars filled with silver dollars wrapped in $20 rolls. Fifty-two more jars were found in an old trunk and a cream can. Fifty-three other jars were later found stashed in the basement. Some bills were in jars or paper bags with the amount written neatly on the lid. Sweeney was a bachelor and worked for the railroad all of his life. The house was appraised at $1,430.

Chadron State College is at the southern edge of the town. The Military Road, which ran from Fort Robinson to Camp Sheridan, cuts across the campus.

South of town five miles is the wonderful Dawes County Museum. It is open every day during the summer months and on many weekdays during winter. For a description of this museum and the many historic sites within a few miles of it, please see entry for US Highway 385.

Go north one mile on the eastern edge of Chadron to the site of Chadron Cemetery, which is now abandoned. Several gravesites

*are still marked. Just west of town is the junction with US Highway 385,
south. For information about sites along this route, please see entry
for US Highway 385.*

Three miles (4 miles.)

Junction for US Highway 385 north. Please see the entry for
this highway for information about sites along its route.

Just to the north of the Chadron Airport, along the White
River, was the location of the great Sundance, which was held in 1877
by all the Sioux tribes in the area. This great dance was one of the last
great gatherings of the Sioux. The Sundance involved testing a man's
courage and spirituality by having him stand and stare at the sun.
Some participants were also hung by large bone hooks that had been
pierced through their breasts. The ones who endured this dance
gained great respect and honor in the tribe as shamans and because
they were believed to have atoned for the wrong deeds of the entire
tribe.

The butte, two miles to the southwest, is named Trunk Butte
for somewhat obvious reasons.

Four miles (7 miles.)

A road known as Deadhorse Run goes south off of US 20. It
follows Chadron Creek to US 385.

About 1 1/2 miles west of Deadhorse Run is an alternative
route to Whitney along the banks of the White River.

*A small but still kicking town founded in 1885, Whitney was
once considered as a possible county seat. The population is less
than 100 and many empty buildings attest to the fact that Whitney has
seen better days. Near here, a large Sioux lodge once stood on the
banks of the White River. Whitney Lake, two miles to the northwest,
is a good fishing and skiing spot. Whitney may also be reached by
following US 20 for another 7 miles and then taking the paved road two
miles north (see below).*

Seven miles (3 miles.)

Turnoff to Whitney. Straight **west** of here, **two miles,** along
the banks of the White River, Crazy Horse set up his camp after
moving away from Fort Robinson. See also entry directly above.

Near here the highway crosses the White River. To the east,
on the east bank of the river, was the site of the Whetstone Indian
Agency, which existed from 1872 until 1874.

Just south of this site is the location of an old military campsite used often during the Indian "troubles." Please observe no-trespassing signs, and respect private property. Also please observe the rather large rattlesnake crawling around your Reeboks.

Just to the west, on the north side of the river was the location of a longtime Sioux camp.

Ask locally for directions.

Three miles (6 miles.)

Historical marker. **Two miles north** of here is the location of Crazy Horse's camp of 1877. To the south can be seen Crow Butte. See entry for Crawford, below, for a description.

Six miles (4 miles.)

Crawford.

The town has a nice feel of the Old West about it. Friendly folks sit around in the cafes and saloons in friendly conversation while their children play nearby. People generally don't see a need to lock up at night like they do in the big cities.

The cultural center in downtown Crawford displays the finest in regional arts and crafts. The White River Park has been stocked with trout for children under 16 years of age. Crawford also boasts a fine city park, and a swimming pool on First Street near Highway 20. This park was heavily damaged in the Flood of May 1991.

Calamity Jane lived here for a while.

Crawford is home to the fine Old West Trail Rodeo held each summer during the Fourth of July weekend.

For tours along State Highway 71 and 2 north and south out of Crawford, including nearby Toadstool Park and the Hudson-Meng Bison kill site, see entry for State Highway 2.

For a dramatic look at a piece or two of the Old West, follow this side trip out of Crawford:

*Go **east** out of Crawford on the County road. You will pass Crow Butte to the south of this road.*

Crow Butte was the location of a major battle between warring Indians. It seems the entire thing started when Crow Indians raided James Bordeaux's Trading Post, some 25 miles to the east in 1849. They were alleged to have taken 47 horses and 35 mules. The leader of the raiding party was a Crow named White Bear. Bordeaux gathered together a band of Brule Sioux fighters including Red Leaf, Cloud Man and Two Strikes and followed the Crow.

429

A major skirmish happened a few miles to the north of here on the banks of the White River. Some of the Crow escaped, but the remainder fled south, the Sioux in hot pursuit. The Crow were backed up against the north face of this butte. They abandoned their horses and then climbed up the single trail to the top of the butte. The Sioux camped below and waited for the Crow to come down for want of water.

For the next three days and nights the Sioux could hear the Crow singing and caught glimpses of them dancing at the top of the butte. Fires lit up the sky from the top of the butte at night. Finally a Sioux scout found a long rope made of rawhide, hair and horse ropes. The Crow, some time before, had slipped down the butte using the hastily made rope. The body of a Crow was found at the bottom of the cliff, a victim of a long fall off the rope. Other Crow had stayed behind to keep the fires burning at night to distract the Sioux. Their fate can only be imagined.

For years this Butte was called "Place Where the Crows Danced" or "Dancers' Butte."

In another 2 miles turn south and follow White Clay Creek for a Nebraska wilderness experience. This rugged and yet beautiful area is open to camping and picnicking.

About 5 miles along White Clay Creek the road rises to the top of Pine Ridge. Swing west here for another mile or so to Squaw Mound, the highest point on the Pine Ridge escarpment. Continue past the Ponderosa Special Use Area to State Highway 2. North here to return to Crawford, or, if you are still seeking backroad adventures continue:

West of here four miles to Deadman Creek, reached by county roads. The creek was named by the Indians who feared its powers of evil after the cholera epidemic killed so many. They would not go near the place.

Deadman Road, which follows the creek, is roughly the same road used by fur traders in the very earliest years of white occupation of this area. Down Deadman to the Fort Pierre-Fort Laramie Trail. From about 1837 until 1850 more than a quarter of a million buffalo robes bought from the Indians and tons of fur company trade goods were hauled over this 300-mile-long road. It followed the White River through this area. It is said by some to have followed an earlier Spanish road that went from Santa Fe to the Missouri River, north of here in present-day South Dakota. During its use in the mid-Nineteenth Century, it was the shortest overland connection between trading posts on the Platte and the steamboats of the Missouri River.

The trail continued to get heavy use through the 1880s. Ruts can be seen along this route between Fort Robinson and Fort Laramie today.

__Three miles west of__ Deadman Creek is the ghost town of Glen. Although local folks may resent being called ghosts, this town has seen its heyday as a cattle shipping point.

If you made it to Glen, you are now following the White River upstream toward its source. To the north is the Peterson Deer Refuge, and __ten miles west,__ just south of the T intersection, is the ghost town of Andrews. Andrews was a major railroad shipping center.

Much of this area was damaged by one of the largest forest fires in the state's — history the July fire of 1989.

This route is known locally as "Corkscrew Road." Turn north, __three miles__ to US Highway 20 return to Crawford or continue southwest to Agate Springs National Monument. For directions, please see entry for Corkscrew Road, below, west of Fort Robinson.

Four miles (1/2 mile.)
Fort Robinson.
This is one of the finest in the Nebraska State Park system. Not only is this spot critical to the history of the state, but also to the history of the Native American in the west. It is a park with complete tourist facilities, and yet has enough wide open spaces and wilderness for the individual who wants a bit of alone time.

South of the Lodge and then east one mile on a gravel road to the site of a German P.O.W. camp from World War II. Foundations, blockhouses, flagpole, sewer openings and the outline of the boundary of the camp are still visible through the sunflowers and weeds in a large field. The camp was built to hold 3,000 prisoners, who were forced to work as farm laborers on area farms, or worked at the post for a wage set by the Geneva Convention.

Fifty yards past the P.O.W. camp is the site of the Red Cloud Agency, established in 1873 The agency served as a place for "friendly" treaty Indians to get their treaty goods. As the Sioux were pushed into smaller and smaller areas the so-called Red Cloud Agency moved as well. Other Red Cloud Agencies were on the North Platte River near the Wyoming/Nebraska border and farther north on the Missouri River in South Dakota and still later to its present location on the Pine Ridge. It was at Red Cloud Agency that the Sioux Red Cloud and his band of Sioux signed the treaty that the government used for its claim to the Black Hills. The state has marked the location of buildings that once stood here.

431

In 1874, acting agent Frank Appleton was killed here by a Sioux warrior. Mules were stolen and Lt. Levi Robinson was killed while on a wood train escort from Fort Laramie. When the 1,000-man Sioux Expedition set up camp here a month later to protect the agency it was named in memory of Robinson. Later a more permanent location was built to the west: the present Fort Robinson.

From the small hilltop at the Agency site one can see a panorama of war memorials:

—Four miles due east is "the place where the Crows danced" — Crow Butte, where a Sioux and Crow battle was fought.

— To the northwest is Warbonnet Creek, where troops from Fort Robinson fought hostiles trying to rejoin Crazy Horse after the Battle of Little Bighorn.

— Within sight are the lands where Dull Knife and the last of his band of Northern Cheyennes were captured after fleeing the harsh land of Oklahoma. Later, when they escaped imprisonment, nearly all were killed or captured within a short distance of here (see below, west of Fort Robinson on US Highway 20). Many died on the area that is now the campground while trying to run to the White River.

— California Joe, General Custer's favorite south, was shot and killed on a hill visible to the southwest.

— From here, too, the ruins of the World War II P.O.W. camp rise ghostlike from the prairies.

— Finally Fort Robinson itself, just beyond the woods to the west, was the location of the Cheyenne outbreak as well as the killing of Crazy Horse.

Damage from the May 1991 flood is visible just past the railroad tracks on the gravel road. It was here that an 18-foot wall of water rushed down the creek, wiping out the Fort's dump, supply yard, a half-mile section of the road and a bridge. Two men were stranded in a tree in the middle of the rampage for several hours after they had been taken by surprise by the water while checking on the condition of the bridge.

The 1989 fire came close as well and traces of it are visible in the area.

Perhaps the greatest Sioux leader of all time, Crazy Horse was killed at Fort Robinson.

Crazy Horse never traveled beyond the territory of his native people, never sat for a photograph and seldom camped with his band, but set up his lodge some distance away. He was said to have had many powerful dreams and visions, including a vision of his own

432

death: that it would come because of disloyal native peoples. He was the last holdout against white intervention and occupation of the area. A participant at the Battle of Little Bighorn, and other important conflicts, Crazy Horse was supposed to be able to deflect bullets.

After much hesitation and promises of food and blankets for his people, Crazy Horse finally surrendered with his band of 900 Sioux in the summer of 1877. Among those in his band was the young holy man Black Elk, subject of the book *Black Elk Speaks.*

Crazy Horse was acting on promises that he would be heard for grievances he claimed against his people. The Army, however, had issued orders that Crazy Horse be captured and taken to Military Division of the Missouri Headquarters.

As a result, Crazy Horse was taken prisoner on the night of September 5, 1877. Having believed that he was to be treated fairly and not harmed, Crazy Horse let himself be led away.

Once he realized the room where he was being taken was actually a prison, something happened.

The historical marker on the Fort grounds near the reconstructed site continues the military's justification for murder by claiming he was trying to escape. Most oral history from the Sioux, however, says his death was a premeditated assassination. In any event, the lone prisoner was being guarded by several armed soldiers and Indians when an Indian by the name of Little Big Man grabbed his arms from behind. Other Indians, including Red Cloud and American Horse, watched without joining in the struggle. More soldiers wielding bayonets moved forward and an instant later the great man was mortally wounded. By morning he was dead. His body was carried north by his parents where its final resting place still remains a mystery.

The greatest book on this great leader is Mari Sandoz's *Crazy Horse*.

The gigantic park has several back country trails, which allow for some fine hiking in the Pine Ridge country so well-known to Crazy Horse and Red Cloud.

Overnight facilities are available at the campground, the main lodge building and in the old officer's quarters. The Post Playhouse is on the grounds and operates a fine repertory theater during the summer months for nightly entertainment.

Equestrian facilities and a small weekly rodeo are also attractions of the park.

The Fort Robinson Museum, located on the Parade Grounds

433

at the former Post Headquarters, is an excellent place to get an overview of the history of the Fort. The museum's well-crafted displays and interesting artifacts are a branch of the State Historical Society.

The Trailside Museum, operated by the University of Nebraska, exhibits fossils of the Pine Ridge and Nebraska Badlands regions. Geological field trips visit regional fossil sites daily.

Through the cooperation of the State Games and Parks Department, the State Historical Society and the University of Nebraska this park offers a paradise for naturalists, photographers, historians, kids, adults and anyone else.

One-half mile (1 mile.)

Smiley Canyon Road. Take this road for a scenic backroad view of this unique area of the state.

This is the old Highway 20 route, which ceased to be used because of all the winter accidents here. This is a beautiful canyon in any season. The road reunites with Highway 20 in about five miles and is the more beautiful route.

Much of this area was burned during the massive fires in the summer of 1989.

On the afternoon of Saturday, July 8, the 110-degree heat was broken for a little while by a storm that passed over the area. At 3:18, a fire call came into the Crawford Fire Department: lightning had struck in Smiley Canyon, a witness shouted into the phone, and trees were bursting instantly into flame.

For four days, the fire jumped roads and firelines and roared through the isolated canyons of the Peterson Wildlife Management Area here in Smiley Canyon. National Guardsmen, Forest Service firefighters, volunteers and others worked around the clock to contain the blaze. Two converted bombers were called in to dump retardant on trees in the fire's path.

When the last embers were finally cooled, the Fort Robinson Fire had destroyed 48,000 acres and had become the largest fire in Nebraska's history. The still-visible damage from that fire has its own beauty in the reminders it carries of nature's destructive forces.

This road passes through the Fort Robinson buffalo preserve.

Near here in the autumn of 1991, the first mountain lion killed in the state in 107 years was shot by a deer hunter. Lyle VonSpreckelsen saw the lion at about 8 at night. "This cat just drifted out of the trees about 140 yards in front of me. The first thing I noticed was that 2 1/2-foot tail. I fired and missed. It froze and looked away from me. The second shot was in the shoulder and killed the lion," he said.

It had been 20 years since a lion had been sighted in the state. This one won't be back to bother ranchers or to roam the rocky cliffs of the once wild land again.

One mile (2 miles.)

Turn off to the south.

This road, known locally as "Corkscrew Road," provides an exciting, backroads adventure 38 miles to Agate Fossil Beds National Monument. Much of the first half of this road roughly follows the historic Fort Robinson/Fort Laramie Trail, which passed from the Wyoming border northward from the mid-Nineteenth Century on.

*Head **south** across railroad tracks up and over pine hills for **two and a half miles** until you come to small wooded cemetery on the east.*

*Turn **west** and go for **three and a half miles** to a "T" intersection marked by four mailboxes on the north side and an old house with green trim on the south.*

*Travel **south 20 and a half miles** up and down pine hills and tallgrass prairie to another "T" intersection, noted by the pink school-house in the northeast corner of the intersection.*

*Turn **west** on a somewhat improved road and go **seven and a half miles** to the entrance to Agate Fossil Beds. The trip will make for an unforgettable backcountry car journey through Nebraska.*

Other equally exciting and historic auto routes are in the area and a map is available from Fort Robinson Park Headquarters.

Two miles (3 miles.)

Historical Marker concerning the Cheyenne Outbreak.

In 1877, 300 Northern Cheyenne were told by the government to go to an Oklahoma reservation. The government promised them that if they did not like it there, they could come back north. After nearly a year of starvation on the reservation, and with repeated unanswered requests to return north, several hundred Northern Cheyenne decided to return. For weeks they were chased north by a growing number of soldiers and citizens.

One hundred and fifty men, women and children of Dull Knife's band were captured near Fort Robinson and held there in the winter of 1878. After a daring escape, the Cheyenne took to these surrounding hills and hid for two weeks while soldiers searched for

435

them. Despite the bitter cold, the Cheyenne would not surrender.

Captain Wessels, the commanding officer at Fort Robinson, and soldiers under the command of Randal MacKenzie discovered them and attacked. In the battle, 64 Cheyenne and 11 soldiers were killed. A very few of the remaining Cheyenne escaped.

For a more complete telling of the story, please see the entry for US Highway 385 south of Chadron. Nebraska's fine author Mari Sandoz told the story of the Cheyenne in her book *Cheyenne Autumn* The book was made into a movie by director John Ford.

Three miles (8 miles.)

The road toward Harrison passes the Fort Robinson timber reserve to the north, and the White River Valley and the Peterson Deer Refuge to the south. At the top of the ridge you are just shy of being 5,280 feet above the sea. That's one mile to you metric folks.

Eight miles (7 miles.)

Western turnoff for Smiley Canyon. See above just west of Fort Robinson for further information.

The winter of 1949 is considered by many in these parts to be the worst winter ever in the Pine Ridge country. During the month of January alone 61 inches — that's five-plus feet — fell near Chadron. For a good part of that month the temperature never got above zero. The worst single day of a two month long bad spell was on January 2. For three days the winds blew at hurricane force and the snow continued to fall. Drifts up to 40 feet tall were what the survivors saw when they finally climbed out of their houses. Some places reported that nearly 3 feet of snow fell in two and a half days.

Freight and passenger trains were non-existent. The first one finally reached the Sandhills on January 28th, after being dug out by the 5th Army. The Army brought in small tracked vehicles to provide relief, but they, too, were slowed by the storms. There were reports of people stranded in their ranch homes for 4 to 6 weeks before finally hearing the low roar of the Army's vehicles.

Thousands of bales of hay were airlifted to the livestock in the area. The losses weren't as great as in some blizzards, but still many cattle died as a result of the storms. Some estimates put the number at nearly 200,000 cattle and 150,000 sheep killed as a result of the storm in the west.

Still, other animals somehow survived. Pigs, buried in a snow drift for 32 days, were found alive. So were geese, horses and cattle.

Some people died trying to walk a few hundred yards from

stalled cars to ranch houses. Others survived, but remembered the winter of '49 as the all-time worst, even more of a disaster than the great blizzard of 1880-81.

Seven miles (3 1/2 miles.)

Turn **north** on Pants Butte Road for **five miles** to Sowbelly Canyon and Coffee Park. A lovely small park for day use only. It is run by the city of Harrison and often overlooked by the traveler. Swings, picnic facilities and the beautiful outdoors are its greatest features. You may wish to continue to Sowbelly Canyon Road and follow it for **five miles** into the town of Harrison rather than return to Highway 20.

Three and a half miles (9 miles.)

Harrison.

Please see entry for State Highway 29 for information on Harrison and for information about the remote and beautiful sites north and south of here.

Nine miles (1/2 mile.)

Just before the Wyoming border: Here from the late 1880s until the 1940s was a major railroad siding for shipping cattle out of the grasslands. Such sidings were an extremely important part of ranch life. Often thousands of cattle and a good many cowboys would be here on a Saturday afternoon waiting for the freight to pull up to the siding so that the cattle could be loaded on for shipment.

One half mile (0 miles.)

Wyoming border.

This tour begins at the junction with US Highway 20, eight miles west of South Sioux City. For more information about this area, see entry for US Highway 20.

Zero miles (8 miles.)

Junction with US Highway 20, eight miles west of South Sioux City, Nebraska.

Eight miles (5 miles.)

Ponca. Ponca is one of the oldest towns in the state, it was surveyed in 1856. The town's name is from the tribe of Indians that once lived here and who were banished to Oklahoma during the Civil War. (See entry for Santee Indian Reservation, below, for a more complete description of these people.)

The town has many fine old and historic buildings, including the opera house, hotel, print shop, blacksmith shop and many old

438

frame houses. A walking tour of Ponca's historic buildings is available. Ask locally for a copy, or be sure to stop by the museum at 3rd and Iowa Streets for the tour and a view of their displays.

Local brick kilns provided the bricks that can still be seen in many local buildings. Some pits — all that remain of the kilns — can still be found on Big Hill Road, and another on the other end of town. Ask locally for directions.

In 1944, the worst of several floods spilled into town. At 2:30 in the morning of July 6, 4 feet of water rushed down Main Street. Every house and business in town was flooded. High water mark at the Courthouse was 18 inches.

Be sure to try to catch the Ponca Rodeo, held each summer. One of the finest for miles around. . .and if jumping horses isn't your idea of fun, try out the frog jumping contest held each summer in early August.

Two miles north of Ponca: Ponca State Park. This park is nearly 1,000 acres of some of the finest woodlands in the state. These hills and valleys attract cross-country skiers in winter and backpackers and horse packers in summer. A fine example of the quality of Nebraska State Parks. The park sits on top of bluffs with fine long views of the Missouri River and its valley. It includes areas of woodland, and rolling hills as well as trails, cabins, camping and water sports for the tourist.

Five miles (6 miles.)
Take county road to north eight miles to Ionia Volcano. When Lewis and Clark passed this way in 1804, they recorded this bluff overlooking the Missouri in their journals.

The chemical makeup of this clay and shale cliff causes it to smoke when fresh rock is exposed to water, hence the name. The Ponca held this cliff to be a sacred place. Its purpose in their world was to serve as a place to purify and clarify the soul. No one was allowed near here unless they had prepared with many days of fasting and prayer. If one were properly prepared and had a pure heart of simple faith, the Great Spirit might still speak to those who listened.

Erosion has caused the bluff— which at Lewis and Clark's time was probably 160 feet high — to shrink to less that 50 feet tall.

Across the road is the cemetery for the town that once stood here.

Downstream of here, along the west bank of the river, Lewis and Clark reported large mounds that indicated an Indian village of great size had stood there not long before.

Six miles (6 miles.)
Newcastle. A town that was nearly dead when, in 1893, it persuaded the railroad to bring a spur this way. It then thrived until the mid-1930s, when the railroad stopped sending trains this way to collect local crops. It is still alive, although once again a shadow of its former self.

Six miles (2 miles.)
Maskell. The surrounding hills and valleys were inhabited by a greater population of prehistoric mammals and historic Indians than by the peaceful and gentle farm dwellers who dot the countryside today. Indian burials in this part of the world were on top of the hills, and because of this, the hills were believed to have a life of their own.

Two miles (3 miles.)
You have just entered Cedar County. This scenic county is rich in natural beauty, but you will have to leave the main highways to see the best part of it.

Three miles (1 mile.)
Turn off to Wiseman Monument. See below.

One mile (5 miles.)
Junction with State Highway 57. *Turn south on 57.*

In about seven miles on the west side of the road an iron fence marks an ancient private cemetery for the Morten family.
In another mile and a half the road swings to the east, then after a mile, to the south again. Just after this curve is the site of the Old Territorial Military Road, which ran from Plattsmouth to Niobrara. The trail began in 1857. On the south side of the lane that leads to the family home, the ruts of this road are still visible. This is private property — please ask to see the ruts.

Return a quarter mile north to the intersection with county road. Go east one mile. In the field to the south are buffalo wallows and a trail used by buffalo. Both the wallows and the game trail may still be visible in places. This land belongs to the Anderson family. Please ask their permission to view the trail.

Return to State Highway 57. Continue south. At the third intersection with county roads, turn east and go three miles. Turn south and go one half mile.

Just to the northwest of the bridge that crosses the creek is a long stretch of ruts from the Old Territorial Military Road of 1857. Also at this location, just to the east of the road, was the site of St. Peter's Trading Post and Stage House, which serviced travelers on the road.

Retrace route one mile north *to intersection with State Highway 84. Take 84 west nine miles to Hartington. See the entry for State Highway 15 for information about Hartington.*

Return north, six miles to Intersection of State Highway 57 and 12.

Five miles (11 miles.)
The town of Wynot, Nebraska, a question some people have answered with satisfaction. In the old days an elderly German woman answered every question posed to her with (you guessed it) "Why not?" Soon it became kind of a local joke to answer everything with "W'ynot." When it came time to name the town there really wasn't much of a choice.
You are entering one of the more interesting areas of Cedar County. Among many other tales, several ghost stories have circulated for years about this once very populated and important location in Nebraska.

North from Wynot past the Catholic cemetery, go **one mile.** *Take the right fork and go for another quarter mile. This old mill served the important function of providing flour and feed for local farmers. The mill building was built in 1868 and served as a flour and saw mill until the 1930s.*

Northwestern Cedar County

West from this T Intersection one eighth of a mile to a monument commemorating the first school district in the county.

One half mile further west to the "Y" in the road. In the crook of this "Y," on top of the hill was Fort Jackson, built in 1864 to protect local citizens from attacks by Indians.

West two miles to State Road S-14H, then north three miles on State Road S-14H. One mile west of here is the brick house of the Lammers. They are the only remaining early-day pioneer family in the county. The house is located on the original homesteading site and is 120 years old. The bricks were made on the property. One mile southeast of this intersection is the St. Helena Catholic Cemetery. It is the 4th oldest cemetery in the state and there are graves that date from the early 1860s.

One mile farther north on State Road S-14H to St. Helena and the site of the Felber Tavern. For over a century, this was the center for information, comfort, supplies, gossip, card games, booze, neighborly conversation and news.

West one quarter mile of St. Helena, then north on graveled road for one and a half miles, then west for two and a half miles. On the northwest corner of this intersection is the site of the Bentz Hill Massacre. Dr. Lorenzo Bentz was killed here by Indians in 1864 as a warning to other settlers who might be so silly as to try to settle in this area.

West five miles to US 81. See entry for US Highway 81, or, to continue with State Highway 12 tour, return to the mill site.

At the mill site, go one quarter mile east. Hill on the north side of the road was the site of a large Indian village that stood here nearly 900 years ago. Tradition has it that the Indians who lived here were unfriendly, and when the first settlers came this way the other local Indians called the long since abandoned site "Bad Village." However, many others believe that this name indicates not the character of the inhabitants of the village, but rather the evil spirits that existed and still exist there. In any event, the village was unusual since the Indians who lived there, or the ones who came after, built a wall around the entire place to keep others out, or to keep something in.

One half mile further east, just as the road turns south, is the location of the first courthouse in the county. The building was never completed and the structure was used instead for church services. This is also the location of "Old St. James." The town later moved to its present site, 1 1/2 miles south of here.

One and a half miles south: Unincorporated village of St. James. Location of the first church in the county, a Methodist-Episcopal Church.

East out of St. James 3 miles to the site of the Wiseman Massacre. On a Tuesday afternoon, July 23, 1863, Phoebe Wiseman was returning from Yankton with supplies. Her husband was in the Army and far away someplace in the Dakotas.

As she approached her cabin at this spot, she knew something was wrong. There was none of the usual noise and activity of her

443

children. The door was open and she saw the body of an Indian lying on the floor. There was blood on the floor, and smeared on the door. She ran frantically around the side of the house. Her eight-year-old son William was on the ground on his back. A half-dozen knife wounds told her that he was dead.

The stricken woman fled to the village of St. James where she spent a horrified and sleepless night. In the light of day a party from the village set out to her cabin. They found three children dead and two others near death. All had been mutilated.

Her husband swore revenge. In the coming years, Winnebagos on their way south would be shot at by a lone gunman well-hidden in the woods along the river. The skeletal remains of other Indians have been unearthed near the Wiseman property. For years, the place was shunned by Native Americans, who claimed the spot was cursed.

A monument stands as a memorial to the Wiseman children.

This incident set off a series of killings on both sides that ended only after the government set up Fort Jackson near St. Helena.

You are near the banks of the Missouri here, just a half mile north for a nice view.

Eleven miles (5 miles.)
Intersection with US Highway 81. Please see entry for US Highway 81 for information about sites along this route.

Five miles (7 miles.)
Crofton. A small village named after Crofton Court in England. North on 121 from here to Devil's Nest, a lookout over the vast Lewis and Clark Reservoir.

Devil's Nest, now in part a private recreation development, has been known for centuries in this neck of the world. It is a meadowy, teardrop hilled, chalk-cliffed, wooded wonderland of wilderness. It also can be reached by traveling west from US Highway 81 just south of the border.

Seven miles (5 miles.)
Turn off for Bloomfield. This is the location of the Wild Horse Holding Pens. For further information about this site and others in this area, please see entry for State Highway 14.

Five miles (11 miles.)
You have just entered the Santee Indian Reservation, loca-

tion of the Santee Sioux since 1868.

The Santee were moved here from their homelands in Minnesota and the Dakotas after they had fought against the whites in an "uprising." This was one of the most concentrated attacks the Indians ever made on the white intruders. Because of the Civil War, the Indians believed that the whites would be weakened and that the Army would have their attention on the War Between the States. In 1863, several attacks took place simultaneously all across the West. The Santee in Minnesota made the most serious of these attacks, destroying all the stage stations for hundreds of miles along trails, and attacking settlers and towns.

The government captured 500 Indians in Minnesota and sentenced most of them to die. That saintly President, Abraham Lincoln, commuted the sentences of all but 38 of them. As a result, the government decided to ban the Indians from Minnesota and brought them here, and formed this reservation as a kind of prison camp, really.

Trouble was, this was Ponca land. In order to solve this slight problem, the goverment forced the Ponca to leave their land, and they were forcibly removed to what we now call Oklahoma. Along the way to Oklahoma, a great Ponca chief, Standing Bear, lost his son to illness. The chief turned around and, carrying the body, attempted to return to his ancestral home along the Missouri to bury his son. He was stopped by troops in Nebraska. However, citizens and friends in Omaha, including General George Crook, fought for the chief's rights, and eventually the courts made a famous decision some 100 years after the Constitution was adopted. They decided that "an Indian is a person within the meaning of the law."

The decision had far-reaching consequences and has established a common law history for equal rights to Native Americans. A television movie of Standing Bear's story was made in the 1980s.

Eleven miles (1 1/2 miles.)

Junction with State Road S-54 D. *Nine miles down this road to Santee. This is the metropolitan center of the Reservation.*

The Santee Reservation is one of six reservations in Nebraska. The others are: the Omaha and Winnebago in Thurston County; the Fox and Iowa in the extreme southeastern corner of the state; and a small piece of the Pine Ridge Reservation in the Panhandle county of Sheridan.

One and a half miles (3 miles.)

State Highway 12

At the western boundary of the Santee Indian Reservation is the Bazile Creek Wildlife Area. Bring your binoculars for fine views of wildlife and their habitat.

Near here is a chalk cliff known as Maiden's Leap, with a profile resembling a woman's face. Legend has it that Jesse James jumped from the cliff to his horse to escape a posse that was closing in. A ferry crosses the Missouri just north of here, and although there is a toll, it is a wonderful ride for the kids and the adults with young hearts. There isn't much reason to leave Nebraska, so turn right around and ride the ferry back.

Three miles (1 mile.)

Near here is the once and sometime home of author Danny Liska. Born in 1929, Liska's writing career is best comprehended by inspecting one of his several self-published "Bigfoot" series of books.

The subjects of these books range widely, from *Two Wheels to Adventure* — an account of his trip via motorcycle from Alaska to Argentina — to *Ponca Curse,* which recounts events of 1863 when soldiers raided a Ponca village near Bazile Creek and killed four women.

In *Our Valleys-the Niobrara and Verdigris,* Liska provides the most far-reaching history of this area ever attempted. The book includes editorials regarding early political squabbles, sketches of early desperadoes and dances, and a long section on the unexplained or unexplainable.

Liska, who founded an organization to study UFOs and other phenomena, writes about Nebraska snakes as big around as a pail, sightings in Knox County of hairy manlike animals, monsters, ghosts, menhorses of the Missouri, a rash of UFO sightings and cattle mutilations, unsolved murders, phantom horses, little people the size of dogs, sea creatures in the Missouri, a half-deer, half-woman temptress, wooly mammoths, black panthers, hyenas, black wolves and essay upon essay signed every few pages, lest we forget, by Liska.

The book is not for a Ph.D. dissertation bibliography, but is certainly one of the most curious Knox County publications by the most curious of its citizens.

Liska's Bigfoot Ranch is near here, where he lives with his wife, the South American god-woman from Colombia.

One mile (1 mile.)

Niobrara.

446

Junction with State Highway 14. For further information about sites in this area, please see entry for State Highway 14.

Niobrara has one of the oddest histories of any town in the state. The town was once located on the site of a Ponca Indian village. After hearing of the beauty and productivity of this land, a small group of pioneers set off to settle the area in May 1856. They reached this spot, and while hundreds of Ponca Indians watched, the settlers marked off the land that is now considered "Old Town." They built cabins and a small fort. The Poncas, as might be expected, did not appreciate this occupation. In the winter of 1856 they tried to run the settlers off. The Indians burned all of the buildings except for the small fort, where the settlers held them off. The men spent the winter living in the tiny cabin, and soon the town became the first county seat of Knox County.

In 1881, the rising waters of the Missouri caused Niobrara to move for the first time. They moved buildings and homes a mile and a half to the southwest. That should have been enough movement for one town, but with the creation of Lewis and Clark Lake in the 1960s and '70s, the groundwater began to rise and Niobrara was forced to move again. It is hoped that between God and Man, Niobrara has seen its last of moves.

Niobrara was the home of a well-known 24-piece Indian band, that is, a musical band, which toured the Midwest in the early years of this century.

One mile (16 miles.)

Niobrara State Park. Camping and Picnicking.

This area was known as Devil's Nest because of the jungle of grass, ravines and trees along the rivers.

Sixteen miles (4 miles.)

Monowi. A small Boyd County town with a name that means "snow-on-the-mountain-flower."

Boyd County is one of the more remote and less frequented counties in the state, and as such can boast of some of the most beautiful and least viewed beauty around. But its remoteness also caused it to be selected as Nebraska's low-level radioactive waste site. See below for description.

Boyd County, like Keya Paha County to the west, is bordered on the south by the lovely Niobrara River, Nebraska's great treasure.

Four miles (3 miles.)

State Highway 12

A sign on Highway 12 directs the traveler to Sunshine Bottom. It is said that the robins stay here all winter long, for the valley is warmer than any of the surrounding area. The valley is being discovered, however, and homes are creeping up its sides. Glimpse it quick.

Three miles (10 miles.)

Lynch.

A 40-foot mural of a steam locomotive graces the wall of a downtown building. The work was done by local resident Lonnie Gordon, an artist and house painter. Gordon displays his work by frequently painting scenes of Nebraska landscape on his automobiles.

*Turn **north** here at school house and go **one and a half miles** to the site of an old Indian village. This rather large village covered nearly two square miles. Remember that taking items from a ruin is not only an assault on the rights of everyone, it is now a criminal offense.*

Wolf Island is in the Missouri River near Lynch. The island was named by local folks for...well, you figure it out.

*A trip **north** of Lynch to the Missouri would be well worth it, since much of the traffic touring the river bank on the more frequented highways will be avoided.*

Ten miles (3 miles.)

Intersection with US Highway 281, south. Please see entry for US Highway 281 for information about this area.

Three miles (5 miles.)

Spencer.

Junction with US Highway 281.

For information on Spencer please see the entry for US Highway 281.

On the hillside between Spencer and Butte the word "Angel" can be seen carved out of the trees. It is easier to see in winter. No, the Almighty hasn't spoken here, just a local farmer and an idle tractor. The farmer's name is...well, you get three guesses.

Five miles (4 miles.)

*South on this county road for **two miles**.*

One of the more unusual items in this area is the round barn located on private land southeast of Butte. The round barn was a popular style of barn building in the late 1800s. Some claimed that such a design was the ideal way to build for convenience, economy and ease of operation. The idea was that feed for the stock could be placed in the center, and the stalls would radiate around the location, so that the least bit of work had to be done to distribute the feed.

In addition, many cowboys used the round barn for horse stock, using the round yard outside for breaking and training the horses. Go through the southeast gate and follow the road to the bottom of the hill to inspect the barn. If you aren't from around here ask at the Reimans' Ranch for permission to inspect the round barn. And always remember to close gates behind you.

Four miles (2 miles.)

Butte.

Junction with State Highway 11. For more information about sites along this route, please see entry for State Highway 11.

For information on Butte, please see entry for State Highway 11.

Two miles (10 miles.)

Adjacent to the highway is the site of a proposed 320-acre low-level radioactive waste deposit facility. The $40 million facility could store radioactive wastes from Oklahoma, Nebraska, Kansas, Arkansas and Louisiana.

Although the Niobrara River is only three miles south of the plant, and the state of Nebraska officials said the site does not meet the minimum standards for wetland drainage for such a depository, engineers for the facility claim there is no chance of contaminating the river or groundwater.

The selection of the Boyd County site was made in 1991 after several years of heated debate. Opponents said the site was not safe and was selected simply because of the remoteness of the location. During the early 1990s, the debate continued while the facility owners sought proper permits.

Ten miles (5 miles.)

Twin Buttes. If you are not here at either Christmas or Easter you might appreciate knowing that the large cross at the top of these buttes is lit during those holidays. If you are here then, you have to wait until dark to appreciate it.

Five miles (12 miles.)

Location of White Horse Ranch. For years, Ruth Thompson

raised her albino horses at the ranch. From this stock, several generations of horses have populated ranches and horse barns all over the world. Thompson only comes to the ranch part of the year now, and she no longer breeds the horses, but every year around Father's Day, albino horse breeders congregate here to show off their pure white, albino stock.

Twelve miles (15 miles.)
Cross the Keya Paha River, which flows out of the Rosebud Indian Reservation in South Dakota to join with the Niobrara River 20 miles southeast of here.

The name is from the Dakota Sioux and means "river with the turtle hill."

The beautiful countryside you are now traveling through has been recognized by the Federal government. South of here 15 miles on State Highway 137 is Mariaville Bridge, across the Niobrara River and the eastern end of the Wild and Scenic designation of the Niobrara.

In 1991, after five years of debate and discussion, President George Bush signed a law creating the protected scenic designation for a 76-mile stretch of the Niobrara. Although some local residents believed they could protect the land and the river better, the government disagreed and the law passed and was hailed by Congress as "a great day for Nebraska." The law "created a legacy for our children and grandchildren."

Many local river guides offer canoe and raft tours on the river. Ask locally.

Fifteen miles (8 miles.)
Burton. A tiny town made up of a collection of small churches.

Eight miles (5 miles.)
Junction with US Highway 183. Please see that entry for more information about this area.

Five miles (3 miles.)
Springview.

For information on Springview please see entry for US Highway 183.

South of here is the Federally designated Scenic River, the Niobrara, as well as two wildlife management areas and Keller Park State Recreation Area. Please see the entry for US Highway 183 for more information about sites in this area.

Three miles (19 miles.)

South on county road five miles to the site of Meadville, on the banks of the Niobrara. This ghost town provides a fine view of the Niobrara. This town was founded by a gentleman named Mead, the post master, road builder, ferry boat operator and roadhouse owner. The story is that Mead studied for the ministry, but then lost the faith. He came to Keya Paha County and started his various businesses along this spot on the river. He was a wild and reckless man until a traveling minister by the name of Captain Charles Frady came to Meadville and preached. Mead was so inspired that he regained his faith to such an extent that one Sunday he shot at swimmers bathing in the river who were not keeping the Sabbath holy.

Nineteen miles (1 mile.)

Norden.

South of here six miles to the Niobrara River and the Nature Conservancy's Preserve Headquarters on the banks of the river. The Preserve is located on the south side of the river, about one mile east on dirt road.

West on the south side of the river four miles to Fairfield Creek Falls and a privately owned campground.

One mile (10 miles.)

Past the cemetery is a county road on south side of Highway 12.

South on county road five miles to the Niobrara River and Rocky Ford, Coleman Creek and Muleshoe Creek. At Rock Dam near Rocky Ford is a privately owned campground.

Continue on this county road, which follows the north bank of the beautiful Niobrara 12 miles to Sparks. Many natural wonders and beauties are here for the off-the-main-roads traveler. A few privately owned campgrounds offer tent spaces for boaters and others.

Of particular beauty are the falls of the Big and Little Cedar Creeks. Two lovely small falls on the south side of the river about at the mid-point of the distance to Sparks, and just south of the Middle Niobrara Public Use Area.

Ten miles (3 miles.)

Sparks.

For a lovely side trip along the north bank of the Niobrara take

451

county road south out of Sparks, which ends near Norden. (See entry immediately above this one.)

Three miles (2 miles)

The turnoff for Smith Falls. If you are this close, you must turn off to see the tallest waterfall in the state.

Four miles south on Smith Falls Road to the falls, which cascades from a creek 52 unbroken feet down to the Niobrara River.

For the lion-hearted:

At the "T" intersection in four miles turn left, and then an immediate right. One hundred yards down this road, park the car and follow the path over the covered barbed wire to a hand-powered cable car. You may stand in this car and turn the crank to wheel yourself over the middle of the swift, deep Niobrara River. Look upstream and on the far bank for the best view of the falls.

Those less fool-hardy:

At the "T" intersection in four miles turn right, and go 200 yards. Cross the Niobrara over wooden bridge and park the car. Walk back across the bridge and look downstream for a partial view of the falls.

But you'd better hurry if you want to view this place while it is undisturbed. The State is building a state park here. The park's picnic area, camping pads, electrical hookups, foot bridge and unsightly walkway to the base of the falls will replace the relatively undisturbed and isolated access to this place.

What may even make it more visible are the plans, viewed as a remote possibility, of creating a National Park in this area.

Two miles (3 miles.)

Take county road south four miles to Berry Bridge and Berry Falls. Parry Falls is two miles east on dirt road south of bridge. Respect private property and the rattlesnakes in the area.

County road continues west into Fort Niobrara National Wildlife Refuge (see below) and, in seven miles, to Valentine.

Three miles (6 miles.)

Just south of here is the Fort Niobrara Wilderness Area, which was designated in 1976 by Congress to protect the land as a refuge for flora and fauna. Hiking the area can be one of the most rewarding outdoor experiences in the American West, but check with rangers first about the dangers of buffalo and the condition of trails.

452

Six miles (4 miles.)

The Fort Niobrara National Wildlife Refuge. This area is home to many of the large animals that once roamed this area, including buffalo, elk, antelope and deer. A small herd of Longhorn cattle was introduced here not long ago. It is over 20,000 acres and was originally set aside by President Theodore Roosevelt. The Niobrara formed a 100-foot deep canyon through part of the refuge, and streams enter the canyon in waterfalls. Many fossils have been collected in this area.

Near the refuge headquarters is the site of the original Fort Niobrara, which includes a museum. The fort was built in 1880 to protect settlers from the Sioux.

The refuge is one of the finer areas in Cherry County. Check at headquarters for directions to Fort Falls, Short Creek and the more remote Stinard and Sears Falls in the Wilderness area.

The Scenic Rivers Act protects the Niobrara River; however many canoe and raft trips are available from commercial outfitters. The river is not overly dangerous and can be canoed by the novice, but careful, beginner. A fine Canoeing Guide was written by Duane Gudgel and is available at bookstores in the state.

Four miles (0 miles.)

Valentine.

Junction with US Highways 20 and 83. For information about Valentine, please see entry for US Highway 20.

For further information about other sites in this area, and along these highways, please see entry for US Highway 20 and US Highway 81.

Bibliography

Alleman, Roy V. *Blizzard, 1949,* Patrice, St. Louis, 1991.

An Architectural Album, Compiled by the Junior League of Lincoln, Nebraska, North Printing, Lincoln, 1979.

Andreas, A.T. *History of the State of Nebraska,* Unigraphic, Evansville, IN, 1975.

An Informal History of Nemaha County, 1854-1967, (np), (nd).

Arthur County Historical Society, *History of Arthur County,* (np), (nd).

Bailey, Edd H. *A Life With the Union Pacific,* Saltillo, St. Johnsbury, VT, 1989.

Bailey, Barbara. *Picture Book of Nebraska,* Whitman, NY, 1956.

Baltensperger, Bradley H. *Nebraska, A Geography,* Westview Press, Boulder,1985.

Banner County History, Bayard, NE (nd)

Bartlett and O'Sullivan. *History of Cumming County Nebraska with Complete Directory,* Fremont Tribune, West Point, NE, 1884.

Beaver City Centennial Committee, *The History of Beaver City, 1872-1972* (np), (nd).

Bleed, Ann and Flowerday, Charles, eds. *An Atlas of the Sand Hills,* Institute of Agriculture and Natural Resources, University of Nebraska, Lincoln, 1989.

Bonham, Barbara, ed. *Historical Hilites of Franklin County,* Franklin Co. Historical Society, Campbell, NE, 1967.

Boyd County Nebraska, 75th Anniversary, 1966.

Boye, Alan. *A Guide to the Ghosts of Lincoln, 2nd edition,* Saltillo, St. Johnsbury, VT 1987.

Brown, Elinor. *History of Lancaster County, Then and Now,* self-published, Lincoln, 1971.

___, *Nebraska Travel-Rama,* Midwest Publishers, Ceresco, NE, 1973.

Brubaker, Ethal. *Our Nebraska,* Johnson Publishing Co., Lincoln, 1963.

Bryson, Conrey. *Winter Quarters* Deseret Books, Salt Lake City,

Bibliography

1986.

Butcher, Solomon. *Pioneer History of Custer County*, [np] 1901.

Carpenter, Allan. *Nebraska*, Childrens Press, 1978.

Cather, Willa. *O, Pioneers!*, Riverside, Boston, 1913.

___. *My Antonia*, Knopf, NY, 1918.

___. *A Lost Lady*, Knopf, NY 1923.

Cedar County Historical Society, *Pioneer Families of Cedar County*, (np) 1967.

Centennial History of Hamilton County, Hamilton County Centennial Association Aurora, NE, 1967.

Centennial Year, Grand Island, Nebraska, Centennial Souvernir Book Committee, Grand Island, NE 1970.

Clark, Jerry E. *Nebraska Diamonds: A Brief History of Baseball Major Leaguers From the Cornhusker State*, Marking History, Omaha, 1991.

Colvin, Rod. *Evil Harvest*, Bantam, NY, 1992.

Compendium of Historical Reminiscence and Biography of Western Nebraska, Alden, Chicago, 1909.

Conrad, Pam. *Prairie Visions, the Life and Times of Solomon Butcher*, Harper Collins, New York, 1991.

Copple, Neale. *Tower on the Plains: Lincoln's Centennial History, 1859-1959*, Lincoln Centennial Commission, Lincoln, 1959.

Cornerstone-Historical Preservation in Nebraska V. 1-, Nebraska State Historical Society, Lincoln, 1979-.

Crabb, Alexander R. *Empire on the Platte*, World Publishing, 1967.

Creigh, Dorothy W. *Nebraska, A History*, W.W. Norton, New York, 1977.

___. *Nebraska, Where Dreams Grow*, Miller and Paine, Lincoln, 1980.

Curry, Margaret. *The History of Platte County, Nebraska*, Murray and Gee, Culver City, CA, 1950.

Dick, Everett. *Conquering the Great American Desert*, Nebraska State Historical Society, Lincoln, 1975.

___. *The Sod-House Frontier*, Johnson Publishing, Lincoln, 1954.

Deuel County Historical Society, *Deuel County, Nebraska*, (np) (nd).

Dustin, Dorothy D. *Omaha and Douglas County, A Panoramic History*, Windsor Publishing Co. Woodland Hills, CA, 1980.

Dundy County Heritage, Dundy County Extension Council, Pruett Press, Boulder, (nd)

Eiseley, Loren. *All the Strange Hours: The Excavation of a Life*, Scribner, NY, 1975.

456

___, *The Immense Journey*, Random House, NY, 1957.

___, *The Firmament of Time*, Atheneum, NY, 1960.

___, *The Night Country*, Scribner, NY, 1971.

Faulkner, Virginia, ed. *Roundup: A Nebraska Reader*, University of Nebraska, Lincoln, 1957.

Fitzpatrick, Lilian L. *Nebraska Place-Names, including selections from Link,J.T., Origin of the Place-Names of Nebraska*, Bison, Lincoln, 1960.

Federal Writers Project. *Nebraska, A Guide to the Cornhusker State*, Viking, New York, 1934.

Flodman, Mildred. *Early Days in Polk County*, Union College Press, Lincoln, (nd).

Fradin, Dennis, B. *Nebraska in Words and Pictures*, Childrens Press, 1980.

Franzwa, Gregory M. *Maps of the Oregon Trail*, Patrice Press, Gerald, MO, 1982.

From 'Hoppers to 'Copters: Stories of Nuckolls County for 100 Years, Nuckolls County Committee, 1967.

Gaffney, Wilbur, ed. *The Fillmore County Story*, Geneva Community Grange, Geneva, NE 1968

Garfield County Historical Society. *Garfield County Roundup; A History of the People*, Quiz Graphic Arts, Ord, NE, 1967.

Graff, Jane. *On a Bend in the River: The Story of Seward and Seward County, Nebraska*, Henderson, NE 1967.

Grant County, *Its Friends and Neighbors*, Grant County Historical Society, 1980

Greeley County Historical Society. *Greeley County History*, (np), (nd).

Gudgel, Duane, *Niobrara River Canoeing Guide*, Plains Trading Company Archives, Valentine, NE 1990.

Haines, Aubrey L. *Historical Sites Along the Oregon Trail*, Patrice Press, Gerald, MO, 1981.

Hansen, E.K. *Echoes From the Past*, Union College Press, Lincoln, NE, 1976.

Hansen, Ron. *The Assassination of Jesse James by the Coward Robert Ford*, Knopf New York, 1983.

____. *Desperadoes*, Knopf, New York, 1979.

____. *Mariette in Ecstasy*, HarperCollins, New York, 1991.

____. *Nebraska*, Atlantic, New York, 1989.

Hayes County Historical Society. *History of Hayes County*, (np), (nd).

Henri, Robert. *The Art Spirit*, J.B. Lippencott, NY, 1923.

Henry, Stuart. *Conquering Our Great American Plains*, E.P. Dutton, New York, (nd).

Bibliography

Historical Markers in Nebraska, compiled by National Society of DAR in Nebraska, Franklin Press, Beatrice, NE, 1951.

Historical Sites Around Fairbury (brochure), Jefferson County Historical Society, (np) (nd).

Historical Booklet Committee. *Honor Our Heritage:Portrait of Progress in Phelps County,* (np), 1973.

History of Colfax County, (np) 1967.

Homestead Centennial, Beatrice, NE 1962.

Horan James D. and Sann, Paul. *Pictorial History of the Wild West,* Crown, New York, 1954.

Horgan, Paul. *Great River: The Rio Grande in North American History* (2 Volumes) Rinehart, NY 1954.

Human Side of Railroading, Association of American Railroads, Washington, D.C. (nd).

Hutchinson, Duane. *Doc Graham, Sandhills Doctor,* Foundation Books, Lincoln, 1971.

Hytrek, Anthony J. *The History of Fort Robinson, Nebraska From 1900 to the Present,* Chadron State College, Chadron, NE 1971.

Important and Interesting Sites in Nebraska, Nebraska State Historical Society, Lincoln, 1961.

Janovy, John Jr. *Keith County Journal,* St. Martins, New York, 1978.

Johnsgard, Paul A. *Those of the Gray Wind: The Sandhill Cranes,* St. Martins, NY, 1981.

____. *Crane Music: A Natural History of American Cranes,* Smithsonian, Washington, 1991.

Johnson, Leonard, ed. *Nebraska. . .The Good Life Grows,* Quasquicentennial Project, Lincoln, 1991.

Johnson, Niel M. *Portal to the Plains: A History of Washington County, Nebraska,* Lincoln, (nd).

Jordon, Robert P., *Nebraska, The Good Life,* National Geographic Society, Washington, D.C., 1974.

Kloefkorn, Wiiliam. *A Life Like Mine,* Platte Valley Press, Lincoln, 1984.

Kooser, Ted. *Not Coming to Be Barked At: Poems,* Pentagram Press, Milwaukee, 1976.

Kuzma, Greg. *Adirondacks,* Bear Claw Press, Ann Arbor, 1978.

LaMere, Oliver, and Shinn, Harold B. *Winnebago Stories,* Rand McNally, New York, 1928.

Lass, William E. *From the Missouri to the Great Salt Lake: An Account of Overland Freighters,* Nebraska State Historical Society, Lincoln, 1972.

458

Bibliography

Lee, Wayne C. *Wild Towns of Nebraska*, Caxton, Caldwell, ID, 1988.

Lemon, T. H. "Early Days on the Little Blue" in *Proceedings and Collections of the Nebraska State Historical Society*, v. 15.

Liska, Danny. *Our Valleys The Niobrara and Verdigris*, Relikassa Ltd., Bogota, Colombia, 1986.

Manson, Mae. *Prairie Pioneers of Box Butte County*, Iron Man Industries, Alliance, NE 1970.

Mathews, Anne. *Where the Buffalo Roam —The Storm Over the Revolutionary Plan to Restore America's Great Plains*, Grove Weidenfeld, New York, 1992.

Mattes, Merrill J. *The Great Platte River Road*, Nebraska State Historical Society, Lincoln, 1979.

McCleery, David and Gale, Kira, eds. *Resource Guide to Six Nebraska Authors*, A Slow Tempo Press, Lincoln, 1991.

McDermott, Edith S. *The Pioneer History of Greeley County Nebraska*, Citizens, Greeley, NE, 1977.

McKee, James L., and Duerschner *Lincoln, A Photographic History*, Salt Valley Press, Lincoln, 1976.

___. *Lincoln, The Prairie Capital, An Illustrated History*, Windsor Publishing, Woodland Hills, CA, 1984.

Molstad, George. *History of Dakota County Nebraska*, Dakota County Historical Society, Dakota City, NE, 1982.

Morton, J. Sterling and Watkins, Albert. *Illustrated History of Nebraska (3 Volumes)*, Jacob North and Company, Lincoln, 1913.

Morris, Wright. *God's Country and My People*, Harper & Row, New York, 1968.

___. *Ceremony at Lone Tree*, Atheneum, NY, 1960.

___. *Field of Vision*, Harcourt, Brace, NY, 1956.

___. *Fork River Space Project*, University of Nebr., Lincoln, 1981.

Mufon Symposium Proceedings, Dayton, Ohio, 1978.

Murphy, Edward B. "The Massacre at Oak Grove Ranch," in *Nebraska State Historical Society Publications*, v. 19.

Nebraska History Magazine, Nebraska State Historical Society, Lincoln, various dates.

Nebraskaland Magazine, Lincoln, NE., various dates.

Nebraska Travel, Nebraska Department of Economic Development, Lincoln, 1972.

Neihardt, John. *Black Elk Speaks*, University of Nebr., Lincoln, 1961.

___, *The River and I*, University of Nebr., Lincoln, 1974.

___, *The Cycle of the West*, University of Nebr., Lincoln, 1972.

Bibliography

Newman, Peter C. *Caesars of the Wilderness,* Vol II, Penguin, Toronto, 1987.

Nicoll, Bruce N. *Nebraska: A Pictorial History,* Bicentennial Edition, University of Nebraska Press, Lincoln, 1975.

____, and Keller, Ken R. *Know Nebraska,* Johnson Publishing Co., Lincoln, 1951.

O'Connell, Frank. *Farewell to the Farm,* Caxton, Caldwell, ID, 1962.

O'Hara, W. H. *In All Its Fury—The Great Blizzard of 1888,* J & L Lee, Lincoln, 1988.

Olson, James C. *History of Nebraska,* University of Nebraska Press, Lincoln, 1966.

Parks, Clark K. *Traveling Interstate 80 with Otto,* Construction Publications, Cedar Rapids, Iowa, 1990.

Palmer, H. E. "History of the Powder River Indian Expedition of 1865," in *Transactions and Reports of the Nebraska State Historical Society,* v. 2, 197.

Perkey, Elton A. *Perkey's Nebraska Place Name,* Nebraska State Historical Society, Lincoln, 1982.

Perlman, Bernard. *Painters of the Ashcan School —The Immortal Eight,* Dover, NY, 1979.

Perry, Alice P. *History of Cass County,* (np) 1967.

Powers, Lester C. *Hitchcock County, 1873-1973,* Hitchcock County News, Trenton, NE 1973.

Rogo, Scott D. ed. *UFO Abductions: True Cases of Alien Kidnappings,* Signet, New York, 1978.

Rosicky, Rose. *A History of Czechs in Nebraska,* Eastern Nebraska Genealogical Society, Fremont, 1976.

Russell Ed. *The Lives and Legends of Buffalo Bill,* University of Oklahoma Press, Norman, 1960.

Sandoz, Mari. *Cheyenne Autumn.* McGraw Hill, NY, 1955.

____. *Crazy Horse, The Strange Man of the Oglalas,* Alfred A. Knopf, NY, 1942.

____. *Old Jules,* University of Nebr., Lincoln, 1969.

____. *Sandhill Sundays and Other Recollections,* University of Oklahoma Press, Norman, 1930.

____. *Son of a Gambling Man,* Potter, NY, 1960.

Scheele, Roy. *Pointing Out the Sky: Poems,* Sandhills Press, Ord, NE, 1985.

____. *The Voice We Call Human,* Juniper Press, 1991.

Sheldon, Addison, E. *History and Stories of Nebraska,* University Publishing, Lincoln, 1913.

____. *Nebraska, The Land and the People,* Lewis Publishing, Chicago, 1931.

Scott, Lynn. *The Covered Wagon and Other Adventures,* University of Nebr., Lincoln, 1987.

Sidney: *The Majestic High Plains,* Spelts-Bailey, Grand Island, 1987.

Sioux County: *Memoirs of its Pioneers,* Harrison Sun-News, Harrison, NE 1976.

Sorensen, John. Our Show Houses: *The History of Movie Theaters in Grand Island, Nebraska,* Hall Co. Historical Society, Grand Island, NE, 1990.

Stevens, Morgan. *Memories of Perkins County,* Stevens Co, Astoria IL, (nd).

Story, Ronald D. ed. *The Encyclopedia of UFOs,* Dolphin, New York, 1980.

Strait, Treva. *The Price of Free Land,* Lippencott, NY, 1979.

Thedford, Nebraska, (np), (nd).

Thompson, Glenn. *Faceless Fred the Phantom of Phelps County* (pamphlet), Holdrege Area Chamber of Commerce, Holdrege, NE, 1992.

Tobias, Nebraska (np), (nd).

The UFO Evidence, National Investigations Committee on Aerial Phenomena, Washington, D.C., 1964.

Valley County Historical Society, *A View of the Valley: Valley County, Nebraska,* (np) 1973.

Wayne County Historical Society, *Wayne County Anecdotes and Historical Notes,* (np), (nd).

Welch, Roger. *Shingling the Fog and Other Plains Lies,* Sage, Chicago, 1972.

_____. *Omaha Tribal Myths and Trickster Tales,* Swallow, Chicago, 1981.

Where the Buffalo Roamed: Stories of Early Days In Buffalo County, World Publishing Co, Shenandoah, Iowa, (nd).

White, John B. *Published Sources on Territorial Nebraska,* Nebraska State Historical Society, Lincoln, 1965.

Wilcox, V. R. *A History of Nuckolls County, Nebraska,* unpublished Master's thesis, 1935.

Wilson, D. Ray. *Nebraska Historical Tour Guide* Crossroads Communications, Carpentersville, Illinois, 1988.

Wilson, James C. *Itzatenango and Friends,* Moo Cow Press, Santa Fe, 1974.

_____. ed. *Saltillo Review,* Lincoln & Santa Fe, Vols. 1-5, 1971-1976.

Index

A

Index

Index

466

Index

468

Index

F

Index

G

Index

Index

Index

Index

Index

482

Index

484

Index

Index

488

T

Index

Index

X, Y, Z

Other titles by Alan Boye available from the University of Nebraska Press

Holding Stone Hands
On the Trail of the Cheyenne Exodus

Tales from the Journey of the Dead
Ten Thousand Years on an American Desert

CPSIA information can be obtained
at www.ICGtesting.com
Printed in the USA
FSOW02n1419200715
9001FS

9 780803 259683